About Pearson

Pearson is the world's learning company, with presence across 70 countries worldwide. Our unique insights and world-class expertise comes from a long history of working closely with renowned teachers, authors and thought leaders, as a result of which, we have emerged as the preferred choice for millions of teachers and learners across the world.

We believe learning opens up opportunities, creates fulfilling careers and hence better lives. We hence collaborate with the best of minds to deliver you class-leading products, spread across the Higher Education and K12 spectrum.

Superior learning experience and improved outcomes are at the heart of everything we do. This product is the result of one such effort.

Your feedback plays a critical role in the evolution of our products and you can contact us – reachus@pearson.com. We look forward to it.

STUDY GUIDE
for
MICROECONOMICS

STUDY GUIDE
for
MICROECONOMICS

EIGHTH EDITION

ROBERT S. PINDYCK
DANIEL L. RUBINFELD

Jonathan Hamilton
University of Florida

Valerie Suslow
University of Michigan

ISBN 978-93-528-6270-2

First Impression

Published by Pearson India Education Services Pvt. Ltd, CIN: U72200TN2005PTC057128, formerly known as TutorVista Global Pvt. Ltd, licensee of Pearson Education in South Asia.

Head Office: 15th Floor, Tower-B, World Trade Tower, Plot No. 1, Block-C, Sector 16, Noida 201 301, Uttar Pradesh, India.
Registered Office: 4th Floor, Software Block, Elnet Software City, TS 140, Block 2 & 9, Rajiv Gandhi Salai, Taramani, Chennai 600 113, Tamil Nadu, India.
Fax: 080-30461003, Phone: 080-30461060
Website: in.pearson.com; Email: companysecretary.india@pearson.com

Printed in India at HT Media Ltd, Noida

CONTENTS

PREFACE

This Study Guide accompanies the Eighth Edition of *Microeconomics* by Robert Pindyck and Daniel Rubinfeld and, when used in conjunction with the textbook, can be a useful learning tool to help reinforce the basic concepts presented in the text. This Study Guide presents numerous problems and provides detailed answers to help you gain practice in working through economics problems. You should not use this Study Guide as a substitute for the text, which provides complete coverage of the material.

CONTENTS OF THE STUDY GUIDE

Each chapter of the Study Guide corresponds to a chapter in the textbook. At the beginning of each Study Guide chapter is a checklist of the important concepts covered in the corresponding chapter of the textbook, followed by Chapter Highlights, which presents a brief definition of each concept. Short summaries of each key concept and associated exercises are presented in Concept Review and Exercises. At the end of each chapter is a Problem Set and Self-Test (with multiple-choice questions). Answers to all exercises are given at the end of each chapter.

Some sections and exercises within those sections are marked with an asterisk to correspond with starred (advanced) sections in the text. Other questions in the Study Guide are marked with an asterisk to indicate that the exercise requires calculus or is heavily mathematical.

ACKNOWLEDGMENTS

Our thanks go out to a number of people for their assistance with previous editions of the Study Guide, as well as this Eighth Edition. Special thanks to Professor Jürgen Blazejczak for helpful suggestions. We also thank the editorial staff at Pearson, who provided valuable input at each step of the way.

QUANTITATIVE SKILLS REFRESHER

If your basic algebra skills are rusty, you will find it difficult to work through quantitative economics problems and to manipulate the many lines and curves used to illustrate economic concepts. A good grounding in mathematics will allow you to concentrate on the economics rather than on the algebra. Your instructor can recommend a review book to you if you feel your math skills are particularly weak. If all you need is a quick refresher, the following notes may be of help.

FUNCTION NOTATION

If sales are related to advertising expenditure in a linear fashion, we could write:

$$\text{Sales} = 100 + 0.5*\text{Advertising}$$

Other times we may not have the explicit equation and can only write the general functional form: Sales = f (Advertising), where f ( ) denotes that there is a functional relationship. A *function* is denoted $y = f(x)$, and is read "y equals f of x." A function is a rule or method for assigning a unique value of y for each x. We say that y is the dependent variable, which is determined by the independent variable x.

LINEAR FUNCTIONS

The rate of change in the dependent variable as the independent variable changes is the *slope* of a function. Symbolically, the slope is expressed as $\Delta y/\Delta x$, which is read "the change in y caused by a change in x."

In Figure 1 (on the next page), as we move from point A to point B, sales increase from 110 to 140. Over the same interval, advertising increases from 20 to 80. Thus,

$$\frac{\Delta\text{Sales}}{\Delta\text{Adv.}} = \frac{110-140}{20-80} = \frac{-30}{-60} = +0.5$$

The rate of change from B to C is also +0.5. Thus, the slope of the line drawn in Figure 1 is constant and equal to 0.5 between any two points on the line. In general, any linear function can be expressed as $y = a + bx$, where a and b are fixed numbers (they are constants that are specified in the equation or given in the problem). The term a is defined as the y-intercept (where the line crosses the y-axis) and represents the value of y when x is equal to zero. In Figure 1 the y-intercept is 100, making the equation of the line Sales = 100 + 0.5Advertising. The term b is defined as the slope. In general, for any linear function, $y = a + bx$, the slope is equal to b and the y-intercept is equal to a. The x-intercept, which is equal to $-a/b$, can be found by setting y equal to zero and solving for x.

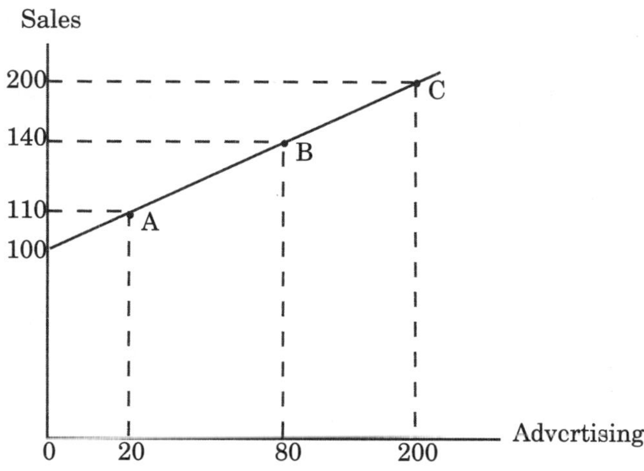

Figure 1

What if you were asked to find the equation of the line, given only points B and C? You can solve for the equation of a line given any two points on the line. After finding the slope, write the equation in general form as $y = a + .5x$. Now plug in any point on the line into your equation. Take point C in Figure 1, for example: then $200 = a + .5(200)$, or $a = 100$. Therefore (again) the equation of the line is $y = 100 + .5x$. The x-intercept of this line is found by setting $y = 0$ and solving for x: $0 = 100 + .5x$, or $x = -200$.

Suppose you are given two points on a different line and are asked to find that equation. The points are $(x_0, y_0) = (2,46)$ and $(x_1, y_1) = (15,20)$. The slope of the line is $\Delta y/\Delta x = (46 - 20)/(2 - 15) = 26/-13 = -2$. So far, we have $y = a - 2x$. Now plug one point into the equation to find a: $20 = a - 2(15)$, or $a = 50$. Therefore, the equation of the line is $y = 50 - 2x$. The slope is -2, the y-intercept is 50, and the x-intercept (setting $y = 0$) is 25. This negatively sloped line is drawn in Figure 2.

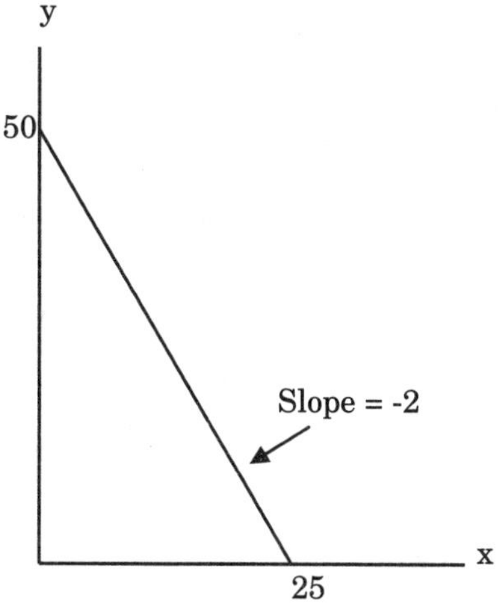

Figure 2

NONLINEAR FUNCTIONS

The slope for nonlinear functions is the same as before, $\Delta y/\Delta x$, but it takes on different values at different points along the curve. Focusing on the revenue function in Figure 3, we see that if sales increase from 0 to 100 units, revenue goes from 0 to 500, implying a slope of 5. But if we look at sales between 50 and 100, revenue increases from 375 to 500 and we get a slope of 125/50 or 2.5. Thus, the slope of a curve depends on where you measure it. It is therefore useful to have a measure of the rate of change at a point (i.e., the slope for infinitesimally small changes in x and y). Graphically, this is the slope of the line tangent to the point in question. At sales of 50, the line in Figure 3 labeled l is the line tangent to the curve at point E. This tangent line has a slope of 5, as inspection of Figure 3 shows.

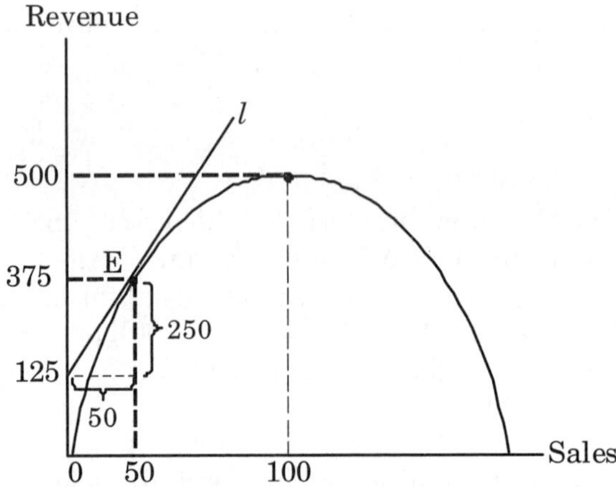

Figure 3

*CALCULUS

Here is a brief review of the basic rules for taking derivatives of functions:

Function	Derivative $y' = dy/dx$	Example
y = constant	$y' = 0$	$y=10 \Rightarrow y' = 0$
$y = x$	$y' = 1$	—
$y = kx$	$y' = k$	$y = 10x \Rightarrow y' = 10$
$y = kx^2$	$y' = 2kx$	$y = 3x^2 \Rightarrow y' = 6x$
$y = kx^n$	$y' = knx^{n-1}$	$y = x^{31} \Rightarrow y' = 31x^{30}$
$y = f(x) + g(x)$	$y' = (df/dx) + (dg/dx)$	$y = 10x - 0.4x^2 \Rightarrow y' = 10 - 0.8x$
$y = f(x)g(x)$	$y' = f(x)(dg/dx)$ $+ (df/dx)g(x)$	$y = (2x)(x^3) \Rightarrow$ $y' = 2x(3x^2) + 2(x^3) = 8x^3$
$y = g(z(x))$	$y' = (dg/dz)(dz/dx)$	$y = 10z$, where $z = 3 - 5x \Rightarrow$ $y' = (10)(-5) = -50$

APPROACHING ECONOMICS PROBLEMS

Most economics problems can be approached in three different ways: intuitively, graphically, and mathematically. The intuitive approach works well for simple problems. As you progress, your economic intuition will develop. For the more complex problems, however, you might find that you will miss some of the finer points (i.e., the right answer!) if you rely on intuition rather than putting pencil to paper. That said, it is worth emphasizing that even if the intuitive approach can't always provide you with the exact answer, you should never ignore your economic intuition. There may be times when the algebra or the graphs become confusing. Or, you may make a simple algebraic error and find that the answer you get "just doesn't make economic sense." In those cases, let your intuition guide you to the correct answer or at least the correct approach to the problem, even if you can't work the problem through to the end.

For both simple and complex problems you can always turn to graphs to capture the essence of the problem. The benefit to learning how to use graphs is that they focus your attention on the necessary elements of the problem. If you don't conceptualize problems well using equations, try drawing the graph first, and it will clarify the set up of the equations. Using graphs also forces you to prove to yourself that you understand the material. Don't take your instructor's word for it when he or she draws several curves and says that something must be true. Redraw the graph and convince yourself that it is true.

Whatever your preferred approach to solving economics problems, you must first concentrate on learning the basic definitions and building blocks. The way to do that is to actively work through each problem and graph in this Study Guide and the text.

CHAPTER 1
PRELIMINARIES

IMPORTANT CONCEPTS

- Positive Theories
- Normative Theories
- Microeconomics
- Macroeconomics
- Perfectly Competitive Market
- Noncompetitive Market
- Nominal Prices (Current Dollars)
- Real Prices (Constant Dollars)

CHAPTER HIGHLIGHTS

Economics concerns itself with the allocation of scarce resources across competing wants and desires. It is a social science that seeks to answer both positive and normative questions. *Positive theories* try to describe the world: for example, why do firms in different industries exhibit different pricing behavior? How will the savings rate change in response to a change in the tax law? *Normative theories* are used to prescribe policies for both governments and businesses: should the government regulate pharmaceutical prices? Should a business enter into an international joint venture? It is important to remember that normative economics must rest on a base of positive economics or to suggest a policy solution to an economic problem, one must first understand who will be affected by the policy and what the probable effects will be. Economics does not tell us what policies should be chosen, but helps guide those who must make the decisions.

Microeconomics is the branch of economics that studies the behavior of individuals, such as consumers, workers, and firms. *Macroeconomics*, the other principal branch of economics, concentrates on the study of economic aggregates, such as the gross national product, the unemployment rate, and the money supply.

A *market* is a collection of buyers and sellers who interact with the intention of trading a good or service. The extent of a market is defined by its geographical and product boundaries. Some products are traded in local markets, while others are worldwide in scope. Similarly, some markets deal in a single product, such as raw sugar, while others cover a variety of differentiated products, such as subcompact, compact, and mid-sized cars.

A *perfectly competitive market* is one with many buyers and sellers, in which no individual buyer or seller has a significant impact on the price. In competitive markets, a single price, known as the market price, will usually prevail. A *noncompetitive market* is one in which individual firms can affect the market price. In noncompetitive markets, sellers may sometimes charge different prices. The important point in this introductory chapter is to recognize that all markets do not look alike.

In order to compare prices of goods and services in a given market over time, it is crucial to take account of changes in the overall price level. *Nominal prices* are the "raw" or observed price data, with no adjustments for inflation. They are sometimes called "current dollar" prices. *Real prices* are prices that are adjusted according to an index of the overall level of prices. They are sometimes called "constant dollar" prices because the price index attempts to hold constant the value of a dollar over time. The most commonly used overall price index is the Consumer Price Index.

CONCEPT REVIEW AND EXERCISES

THE THEMES OF MICROECONOMICS (Section 1.1)

The authors discuss a variety of fundamental themes in this section, for example, the different economic actors (consumers, workers, firms) and the role of theories and models. We focus here on the distinction between positive versus normative analysis.

There is a difference between asking "what will happen?" and "what is best?" Business managers and public policy makers ask both kinds of questions. *Positive analysis* deals with explanation and prediction. What will happen to teenage unemployment if the federal government raises the minimum wage by 25 cents? *Normative analysis* deals with what ought to be. Realizing that some teenagers will be better off with a higher minimum wage while others will lose their jobs, is raising the minimum wage in the general public interest? Normative analysis often involves weighing improvements in economic efficiency against changes in the distribution of income (equity). Microeconomics can only point out the costs and benefits of the potential action or actions; it cannot tell us what the best policy is. That is up to each person or society to decide. It is important to realize, however, that positive analysis must come before normative.

Exercise: ◗ ◗ ◗ ◗ ◗ ◗ ◗

1. Identify the following statements as positive or normative:

a) Solar energy will be used increasingly over the next hundred years.

b) Taxes on wealthy citizens of the United States are too high.

c) If the U.S. government lifts the current sugar quotas, the price of sugar will fall and the corn syrup industry will suffer.

d) An increase in advertising by one major automobile company will affect the sales of the other automobile companies.

e) Mergers between two companies should always be allowed.

WHAT IS A MARKET? (Section 1.2)

A market is a collection of buyers and sellers that interact, resulting in the possibility for exchange. In this chapter, it is only necessary for you to have a basic understanding of the difference between a competitive and a noncompetitive market. We will be spending time discussing markets in detail in later chapters of the text.

A *perfectly competitive market* is characterized by the fact that there is a "going market price" which all buyers pay and all sellers receive, and no one player in the market can individually affect that price. Each buyer and each seller is much too small a part of the overall market to have their actions affect the market price. Even if an individual seller offers to sell double the amount they usually sell, it is just a drop in the bucket compared to the total sales in the market. In a *noncompetitive market*, a single firm is large enough (relative to the size of the market) to affect the price of the product. Also, there can be more than one price in a noncompetitive market, especially if there is brand loyalty on the part of the consumers towards certain products.

Note that when we speak of a "market," that market may be local, regional, national, or global. For example, you might think that the market for contact lenses is local—you must get them through your local optometrist. However, there are mail order companies that sell contact lenses nationwide. Knowing this might make you change your opinion of the extent of the market. In addition, the market may encompass one good or many related goods. Is it accurate to say that there is one market for automobiles? Or, is it more realistic to talk about a market for subcompacts, a market for compacts, a market for minivans, and so on?

Exercise: ◗ ◗ ◗ ◗ ◗ ◗ ◗

2. Decide whether you think the following markets are competitive or noncompetitive and why:
a) The market for wheat
b) The market for colas
c) The market for local residential electricity

3. Decide whether you think the following products should be defined as a market and why:
a) McDonald's hamburgers
b) Fast-food restaurants in Cambridge, Massachusetts
c) All restaurants across the United States

REAL VERSUS NOMINAL PRICES (Section 1.3)

When comparing prices over time, they should always be adjusted for inflation (the movement in prices overall). That is, prices should be measured in *real* terms (constant dollars), rather than in *nominal* terms (current dollars). For example, suppose overall prices have gone up by five percent over the last year and you received a five percent increase in your wages. Your nominal wages have increased, but in real terms you are no better off than you were last year.

In order to calculate the real price of a good, you need a measure of the movement in overall prices. The most commonly used measure is the Consumer Price Index. Table 1.2 of the text shows that the CPI went up from 82.4 in 1980 to 130.7 in 1990. This means that consumer prices rose 59 percent from 1980 to 1990. (The percentage increase is (130.7 – 82.4)/82.4, which is 0.59 or 59 percent.) Therefore, since we know from Table 1.2 that the nominal price of a college education went up from $3,502 in 1980 to $7,619 in 1990, we can calculate whether a college education grew more or less expensive in real terms between 1980 and 1990. The real price of college education in 1990, in terms of 1980 dollars, is:

$$(CPI_{1980}/CPI_{1990}) * \text{Nominal price in 1990} = (82.4/130.7)*\$7619 = \$4{,}803.41.$$

Therefore, the real price of a college education rose by 37 percent between 1980 and 1990 (comparing $3,502, which is already in 1980 dollars, with $4,803.41).

In general, the real price of a good in year Z in terms of base year B dollars is:

$$\text{Real price in year Z} = \frac{CPI_B}{CPI_Z} * \text{Nominal price of good in year Z.}$$

Exercise: ▶ ▶ ▶ ▶ ▶ ▶ ▶

4. The nominal price of a college education rose from $7,619 in 1990 to $21,550 in 2010. The CPI was 82.4 in 1980, 130.7 in 1990, and 218.1 in 2010. What was the real price of a college education in 1990 in terms of 1980 dollars? In real terms, was a college education more expensive in 1990 or 2010 (use the 1983 base year when the CPI equaled 100)?

PROBLEM SET

5. State whether each of the following questions is positive or normative. If it is normative, what positive questions would have to be answered before the normative question can be answered?

a) If a freeze wipes out 15 percent of this year's Florida orange crop, what will be the impact on orange juice prices at the supermarket?

b) How much oil conservation (from switching to smaller cars, carpooling, etc.) will a $0.50 per gallon tax on gasoline achieve?

c) To fund airport expansion, should the United States use a tax on airfares or a tax on jet fuel combined with airport landing fees?

d) If all small businesses are required by law to provide health insurance to their employees, will the number of small businesses decline?

e) Would higher gasoline prices (through taxes) or federal government standards on automobile fuel economy be a better way to reduce gasoline consumption?

6. You have been hired to take a historical look at whether consumption of gasoline has been affected by changes in the price of gasoline over time. To complete the analysis, you need to adjust nominal gasoline prices per gallon for changes in the overall price level. Use the data below to calculate the real price of gasoline for 1977 and 1989 using 1970 dollars.

Year	Gasoline price ($/gallon, including taxes)	Consumer Price Index (1982–84 = 100)
1970	0.28	38.8
1977	0.58	60.6
1989	1.10	124.0

7. Since 1985, the barriers between markets in European countries that are members of the European Union have been lowered considerably.

a) What is happening to the geographical extent of the market for many goods in Europe as a result?

b) Do you expect that lowering barriers would tend to make markets more competitive or less competitive?

8. Examine the data in the table below, showing sales of cars and light trucks in the United States for selected years over the period 1980–2010. Do you think it is reasonable to study the market for cars in isolation from the market for light trucks? In other words, is there a single market for cars and light trucks or two separate markets?

Year	Car sales	Light truck sales
1980	8,981,800	2,215,800
1987	10,170,900	4,704,200
1994	8,990,400	6,054,500
2000	8,852,100	8,491,600
2002	8,108,700	8,713,200
2006	7,820,700	8,683,400
2010	5,728,600	5,826,000

9. Asking whether a tax on carbon dioxide should be imposed to prevent ozone depletion is:

a) a question of positive economics.

b) a question of normative economics.

c) not an economic question; it involves chemistry and physics.

d) a) and b)

e) None of the above is correct.

10. Asking whether an increase in the minimum wage will increase unemployment is:

a) a question of positive economics.

b) a question of normative economics.

c) a political question, not an economic question.

d) a) and b)

e) None of the above is correct.

11. A perfectly competitive market has:
a) many buyers and sellers.
b) several large buyers.
c) a meeting place for buyers and sellers.
d) a) and b)
e) a) and c)

12. Which of the following markets do you think is perfectly competitive?
a) The market for local phone calls
b) The world soybean market
c) The world oil market
d) b) and c)
e) a), b), and c)

13. Which of the following markets do you think is noncompetitive?
a) The international television market
b) The U.S. grain market
c) The local newspaper market in your city
d) All of the above are correct
e) None of the above is correct

14. The constant dollar price of a good:
a) is the same as its real price.
b) is the same as its nominal price.
c) adjusts for inflation in the overall price level.
d) b) and c)
e) a) and c)

15. If the real price of a college education has risen during a period of inflation:
a) its nominal price has not changed.
b) its nominal price has risen slower than a general index of prices.
c) its nominal price has risen faster than a general index of prices.
d) its current dollar price has not changed.
e) None of the above is correct.

ANSWERS TO CHAPTER 1

EXERCISE ANSWERS

1. a) Positive.
b) Normative.
c) Positive.
d) Positive.
e) Normative.

2. a) Competitive: many small buyers and sellers.

b) Competitive (although debatable): There are two large firms, Coke and Pepsi, and a number of smaller firms. At times these firms behave very competitively.

c) Noncompetitive: There is usually just one regulated regional or state public utility which sells electricity to local residences.

3. a) Too narrow: McDonald's hamburgers compete with other McDonald's products (e.g., chicken sandwiches) and they compete with meals sold at other fast-food chains.

b) This may constitute a reasonable product market, although you might also want to include frozen dinners. Geographically, this market is too broad. Even though Cambridge is not a large city, fast-food restaurants tend to compete most intensely with other fast-food restaurants located within easy walking or driving distance.

c) Too broad, both in terms of the product and geographic definition: First, a fine four-star restaurant does not compete with fast-food restaurants. Second, restaurants compete in local markets, not in a nationwide market.

4. The real price of education in 1990 in terms of 1980 dollars is:

$(CPI_{1980}/CPI_{1990})\$7{,}619 = (82.4/130.7)\$7{,}619 = \$4{,}803$ (rounding).

The real price of education in 1990 in terms of 1983 dollars is:

$(CPI_{1983}/CPI_{1990})\$7{,}619 = (100/130.7)\$7{,}619 = \$5{,}829$ (rounding).

The real price of education in 2010 in terms of 1983 dollars is:

$(CPI_{1983}/CPI_{2010})\$21{,}550 = (100/218.1)\$21{,}550 = \$9{,}881$ (rounding).

Thus, the real price of college education rose almost 69% between 1990 and 2010.

PROBLEM SET ANSWERS

5. a), b), and d) are positive questions—what will happen in response to an event?; c) and e) are normative questions—which is the best way to achieve a particular goal? For airport expansion, you would need to know how demand will respond to each of the taxes. For gasoline consumption, you would need to understand the different responses to a gasoline tax and to tighter fuel economy standards.

6. The real price in 1977, expressed in terms of 1970 dollars, equals the 1977 nominal price times the ratio of the CPI in 1970 to the CPI in 1977. This is $0.58(38.8/60.6) = $0.37. The real price in 1989 is $1.10(38.8/124.0) = $0.34.

7. a) Before barriers were lowered, the geographical extent of many markets would stop at national borders. Now markets can overlap borders, so the geographical extent of the market for many products has increased (particularly the ones with low shipping costs).

b) If *different* firms produced goods in the various countries when trade barriers existed, then more firms are competing in the larger geographical markets after barriers are lowered. This should make markets behave more competitively. However, if the *same* firms sold a single good in several countries before barriers were lowered, then the lowering of barriers does not increase the number of firms competing on the market, and we might not expect such markets to become more competitive.

8. The data reveal that light trucks account for an increasing fraction of total car and light truck sales (from 20% in 1980 to 50% in 2010). It is possible that consumer tastes or supply conditions have changed over time in some way and that these two markets are distinct. However, minivans and sport utility vehicles are types of light trucks that compete very closely with certain cars (e.g., station wagons). It is therefore probably more appropriate to consider cars and light trucks as a single market now.

SELF-TEST ANSWERS

9. b) The question asks whether a given policy *should* be adopted.

10. a) This is a descriptive (positive) question about the response in the labor market to an increase in the wage rate.

11. a) There must be numerous small buyers and sellers for a market to be perfectly competitive. A meeting place is unnecessary.

12. b) The world soybean market is comprised of numerous buyers and sellers. The local phone market is traditionally served by one (regulated) company. The world oil market has a number of sellers, but some of these sellers have formed a cartel (called OPEC) to restrict competition.

13. e) Even though most cities have only a single daily newspaper, they face competition from local television, radio, and Internet sources for news. They also compete for advertising with these news sources. One should be careful not to define a market too narrowly.

14. e) By definition, the constant dollar price is equal to the real price, and both adjust the nominal price for the effects of inflation.

15. c) When the nominal price of a college education rises faster than the rate of inflation, the real price of a college education will rise.

CHAPTER 2
THE BASICS OF SUPPLY AND DEMAND

IMPORTANT CONCEPTS

- Supply Curve
- Demand Curve
- Market Equilibrium
- Equilibrium Price
- Elasticity
- Price Ceiling and Price Floor
- Excess Demand and Excess Supply

CHAPTER HIGHLIGHTS

Competitive markets (where no individual buyer or seller can control the price) can be analyzed by using the model of supply and demand. A *supply curve* shows the quantity that producers are willing to sell at each price they are offered. Since producers will offer to sell a greater quantity at a high price than at a low price, supply curves slope upward. A *demand curve* shows the quantity that consumers are willing to buy at each price they must pay. Since consumers wish to buy a smaller quantity at a high price than at a low price, demand curves slope downward. The two curves together determine the *market equilibrium*. At the *equilibrium price*, the quantity supplied equals the quantity demanded.

Elasticities provide a useful way of summarizing the response of one economic variable (e.g., quantity demanded, quantity supplied, level of advertising, or savings rate) to a change in another variable (e.g., price, income, or tax rate). The *price elasticity of demand* is defined as the percentage change in quantity demanded that results from a one-percent change in price. If the demand for a good is price *elastic*, a one-percent increase in its price causes the quantity demanded to fall by more than one percent. If the demand for a good is price *inelastic*, a one-percent increase in its price causes the quantity demanded to fall by less than one percent.

The response of quantity demanded or supplied to a price change will often depend on the time horizon. For most goods, demand is more price elastic in the long run, reflecting the ability of consumers to change to substitute goods over time if the price of the good they are using rises. Supply also tends to be more elastic in the long run, although for different reasons: in the short run, sellers face capacity constraints, while in the long run, sellers can expand production capacities.

Government intervention in the form of price controls can force a market out of equilibrium. A government *price ceiling* is designed to set a price below the market equilibrium price. This creates *excess demand*: consumers will demand more at the regulated price than producers are willing to supply. If the government sets a *price floor*, then the regulated price will be above the equilibrium price and *excess supply* will result.

CONCEPT REVIEW AND EXERCISES

SUPPLY AND DEMAND (Section 2.1)

Supply and demand analysis is a fundamental tool of microeconomics. It is, however, only appropriate for competitive markets where individual buyers and sellers lack the power to change the market price. In Chapter 10, you will learn how to analyze markets where a buyer or seller can control the price.

A *supply curve* tells us how much of a good will be offered for sale at each price. As the price of the good increases, firms will supply more. How much more they can supply will depend on how easy or difficult it is to have workers to put in overtime or hire extra workers in the short run. In the long run the firm might increase the size of their facility. Supply curves therefore slope upward.

A *demand curve* tells us what quantity consumers will wish to buy at each price. When the price of a good increases, a smaller quantity is demanded. This happens for two reasons: (1) each consumer buys less of the good, and (2) some consumers may stop buying the good completely. The demand curve is downward sloping.

THE MARKET MECHANISM (Section 2.2)

The *market equilibrium* is found at the price that equates quantity supplied and quantity demanded. At any other price, the market has either excess demand or excess supply. In the usual case of upward sloping supply and downward sloping demand, excess supply drives prices down, and excess demand drives prices up. When the price settles at the equilibrium price, there is no pressure for the price either to rise or to fall.

Exercise: ◗ ◗ ◗ ◗ ◗ ◗ ◗

1. Consider the market for compact cars. Figure 2.1 (on the next page) depicts the demand and supply for compacts. Explain the adjustment process towards market equilibrium if the price for compact cars is initially P_1 (perhaps this was the equilibrium prce before a shift in the supply or demand curve). Explain the adjustment process towards market equilibrium if the price is initially P_2.

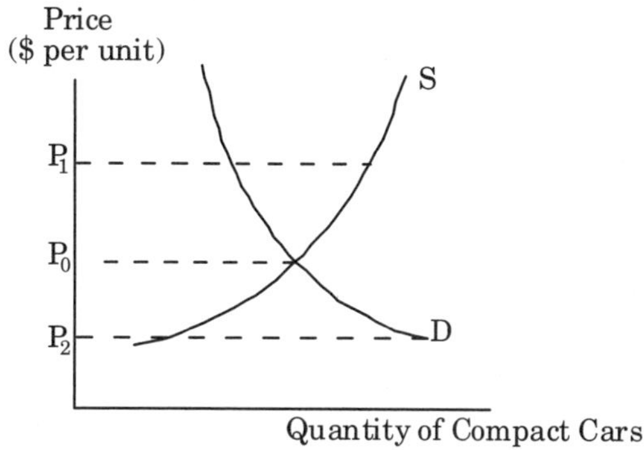

Figure 2.1

CHANGES IN MARKET EQUILIBRIUM (Section 2.3)

We *shift* a supply or demand curve when something *outside* the market for the good being analyzed changes. When the *price of the good itself changes*, that is depicted as a *movement along* one of the curves.

Shifts in demand occur primarily when the price of a related good changes (either a substitute or a complement) or when incomes or advertising changes. Demand can also shift for certain goods when the weather changes (suntan lotions, for example), and when laws change (lowering or raising the legal drinking age). Shifts in supply occur primarily when costs of production change (wages, raw materials prices) or when there is a technological advance.

For example, consider the market for soda. An increase in the price of tea, juice, or bottled water would cause an outward shift in the demand curve for soda. This is shown in Figure 2.2(a) (on the next page) by the shift in demand from D_0 to D_1. (Note that for simplicity we often draw a parallel shift. The demand curve could certainly shift and rotate at the same time, but without more information we use the simplest assumption, which is that there is a shift in the intercept, but the slope remains the same.) An increase in the price of pretzels or potato chips (complementary products that are consumed with soda) would cause an inward shift in the demand curve for soda, as shown by the shift from D_0 to D_2. An increase in the price of plastic or glass (an input into the production of bottled soda) would cause an upward shift of the supply curve for soda, as shows in panel (b) of Figure 2.2. However, an increase in the price of soda itself does not shift the demand or supply curve; it simply causes a movement along one of these curves.

This can be seen in panel (b), for example: the increase in input costs causes the supply curve to shift, which in turn causes a movement along the demand curve (price rises and equilibrium quantity falls). Demand will respond to the price increase as a movement along the curve, not as a shift.

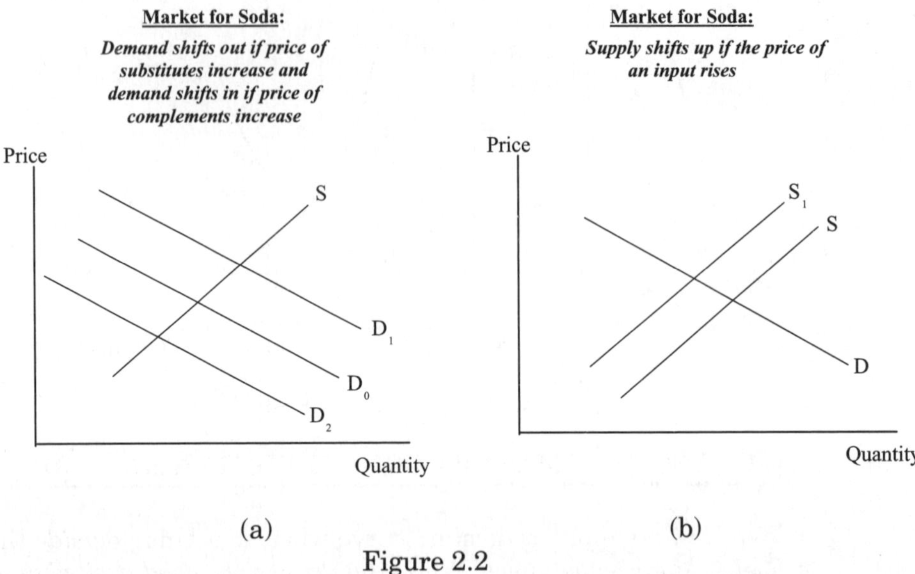

Figure 2.2

Exercise:

2. Consider the demand and supply curves for several markets—the market for mineral resources, the market for wheat, the market for gasoline, and the market for steel. Show how each of the following market changes would shift the demand curve, the supply curve, or both. How will the market equilibrium price and quantity change from the original equilibrium? (Note: Think only about the short-run effects of these changes and do not concern yourself with multiple shifts due to long-run effects.)

a) The costs of producing mineral resources rise as the resources are depleted and it becomes harder to extract the mineral deposits from the earth.

b) Due to floods in the Midwest, half of the wheat crop in the United States is destroyed. At the same time, the price of oats (a substitute for wheat) decreases due to a sharp rise in the number of farmers growing oats in response to consumer demand for health food.

c) The federal government fears that we will run out of oil and decides to ration gasoline sales in the United States to half of current sales.

d) All steel companies in the United States negotiate a new wage contract with the steelworkers' union. The union has accepted a wage decrease to help the steel companies through hard times.

TUTORIAL: WORKING WITH SUPPLY AND DEMAND CURVES

SUPPLY CURVES

The relationship between the quantity supplied (Q_S) and the market price (P), is written in the linear form

$$Q_S = c + dP \,.$$

In general, we can find the values for c (the intercept) and d (the slope) if we have two points on the line. Figure 2.3 shows a supply curve for coal from a single mine, where price is measured in dollars per ton and quantity in tons per week. With Q on the left-hand side of our equation the slope of the *equation* is $\Delta Q_S/\Delta P$ = d. However, because we typically put quantity on the horizontal axis, the slope of the line we *draw* is $\Delta P/\Delta Q_S$ = 1/d. For a straight line, $\Delta Q_S/\Delta P$ is the same between any two points. Thus, you can derive the slope by taking

$$(Q^2 - Q^1)/(P^2 - P^1) = (3{,}000 - 2{,}000)/(5 - 4) = 1{,}000,$$

or $(Q^3 - Q^1)/(P^3 - P^1) = (5{,}000 - 2{,}000)/(7 - 4) = 1{,}000$, and so on.

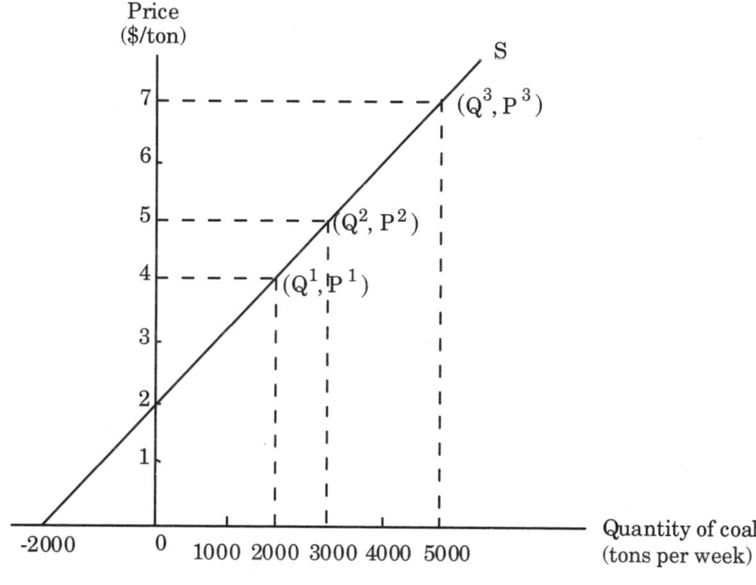

Figure 2.3

The value of c is the quantity on the line where $P = 0$ (which may often be a negative number). To find c, use the slope, along with any one of the points on the line, and plug this information back into the equation of the line. For instance, we could use the point $(Q^2, P^2) = (5{,}000, 7)$, and solve $5{,}000 = c + 1{,}000(7)$ to find $c = -2{,}000$. Try solving for c using one of the other points on the line and convince yourself that this method will always give you the same answer for c.

Exercise: ◗ ◗ ◗ ◗ ◗ ◗ ◗

3. Use the points in Table 2.1 to derive the equation of the supply curve for copper wire.

Price ($/pound)	Quantity (pounds)
P	Q
1.00	500
0.75	350
0.50	200

Table 2.1

DEMAND CURVES

Now let's do the same thing for the equation of the demand curve, using Figure 2.4. We can write the demand curve in the general form

$$Q_D = a - bP,$$

where Q_D is measured in pounds and P in dollars per pound. Since demand curves have a negative slope, for convenience we write the equation with a minus sign on the price coefficient. The slope of the equation, $\Delta Q_D/\Delta P$, equals $-b$. We find the slope by choosing two points (Q^1, P^1) and (Q^2, P^2) in Figure 2.4 and using the formula:

$$(Q^2 - Q^1)/(P^2 - P^1) = -b.$$

Therefore, the slope of the equation is $(5{,}750 - 5{,}250)/(0.60 - 0.70) = -5{,}000$.

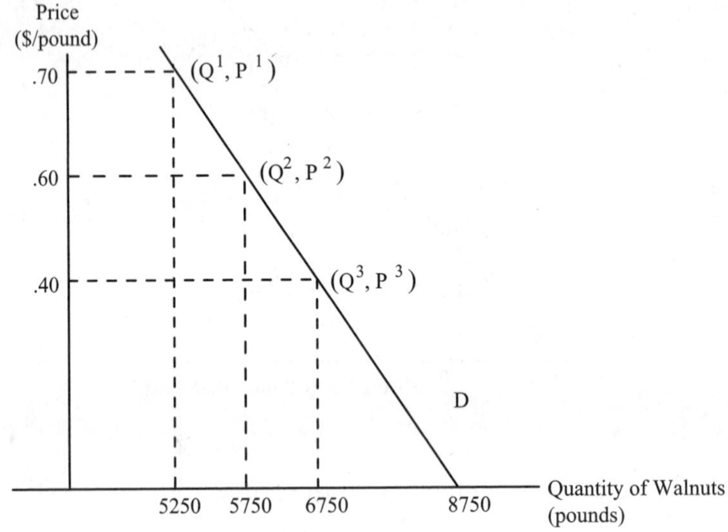

Figure 2.4

Exercise: ▶ ▶ ▶ ▶ ▶ ▶ ▶

4. Verify that if you calculate the slope of the equation describing the demand curve in Figure 2.4 using the points (Q^3, P^3) and (Q^1, P^1), you get the same answer as above.

The intercept of the demand curve, a, is the quantity demanded when the price equals zero. Since $Q^2 = a - bP^2$, we know $5{,}750 = a - 5{,}000(0.60)$, or $a = 8{,}750$. We can pick any point on the demand curve to find the intercept after finding the slope. The equation for the demand curve depicted in Figure 2.4 is, therefore, $Q_D = 8{,}750 - 5{,}000P$.

Exercise: ▶ ▶ ▶ ▶ ▶ ▶ ▶

5. This exercise uses the market data given in Table 2.2.

Price (P)	Quantity Demanded (Q_D)	Quantity Supplied (Q_S)
\$10	1000	100
\$20	800	500
\$30	600	900
\$40	400	1,300

Table 2.2

a) Plot the supply and demand curve with quantity on the horizontal axis and price on the vertical axis.

b) Derive the intercepts and slopes for the demand curve $Q_D = a - bP$ and the supply curve $Q_S = c + dP$.

c) Make sure that the equations you found are correct by plugging in P = \$10 and P = \$40 and verifying the quantities with Table 2.2.

d) Find the equilibrium price and quantity.

TUTORIAL: SHIFTING SUPPLY AND DEMAND CURVES USING EQUATIONS

The supply and demand curves that you derived and graphed in Exercise 5 are two-dimensional plots of price and quantity, holding all other variables constant. If any of these "other variables" change, supply and/or demand must shift. On the demand side, these other variables include consumer income, prices of substitutes, prices of complements, advertising, and weather. On the supply side, these other variables include the price of capital, price of raw materials, price of land, price of labor (wages), and technological change.

Exercise: ▶ ▶ ▶ ▶ ▶ ▶ ▶

6. Consider the demand for beer during the summer months. Let

$$Q_D = 30 - 5P + 0.01I - 2R,$$

where Q is measured in thousands of six-packs, P is the price per six-pack in dollars, I is income, and R is the number of rainy days during the summer. The supply curve is given by $Q_S = -100 + 20P$.

a) Plot the supply and demand curves if I = \$20,000 and R = 15. What is the equilibrium price and quantity?

b) If I = \$20,000 and R = 10, plot the new demand curve and find the new market equilibrium. Compare this to the original equilibrium. Does the movement in Q and P make sense with the decline in the number of rainy days from 15 to 10? Is it necessary to shift the supply curve in order to see the supply response?

ELASTICITIES OF SUPPLY AND DEMAND (Section 2.4)

An important property of supply and demand curves is the responsiveness or sensitivity of quantity to a change in price. If the annual demand curve for toy trucks is $Q_D = 100{,}000 - 2{,}500P$, where price is measured in dollars, we know that each \$1 increase in the price of trucks causes the quantity demanded to fall by 2,500 trucks per year. Why not use 2,500 as our measure of the responsiveness? The reason has to do with the arbitrariness of the units used for measurement. If price happened to be measured in cents, the demand curve would be $Q_D = 100{,}000 - 25P$. Now each 1-cent price increase causes the quantity demanded to fall by 25 units instead of 2,500. Elasticities avoid this confusion over the choice of units by using *percentage changes*, which are unit-free measures.

The *own-price elasticity of demand* is defined in general as:

$$E_P = \frac{\%\Delta Q}{\%\Delta P} = \frac{\Delta Q/Q}{\Delta P/P} = \frac{P}{Q}\frac{\Delta Q}{\Delta P}.$$

For linear curves, $\Delta Q/\Delta P$ is constant. If we write the equation for a linear demand curve as $Q_D = a - bP$, then $\Delta Q/\Delta P = -b$. We can then rewrite the elasticity formula conveniently as:

$$E_P = -b(P/Q).$$

Using the two demand equations above (one in dollars, the other in cents), at P = \$10 and Q = 75,000, the elasticity is:

$$E_P = \frac{10}{75{,}000}(-2{,}500) = -0.33 \quad \text{(with units as dollars)},$$

$$\text{and } E_P = \frac{1000}{75{,}000}(-25) = -0.33 \quad \text{(with units as cents)}.$$

We get the same answer, since elasticity is unit-free.

The elasticity is *not* the same as the slope. Although linear demand curves have constant slopes, the elasticity changes as we move along the demand curve. In the example above, at P = \$10, $E_P = (10/75{,}000)(-2{,}500) = -0.33$, but at P = \$30, we find that $E_P = (30/25{,}000)(-2{,}500) = -3$.

Since the demand elasticity is always less than zero (demand curves slope down), the distinction between *elastic* and *inelastic* demand depends on whether E_P is less than or greater than –1. If $|E_P| < 1$ then demand is inelastic. This means that the quantity demanded responds very little to changes in price. If price goes up by one percent, quantity demanded will fall by less than one percent. The term "completely inelastic" (or perfectly inelastic) implies that quantity does not respond at all to changes in price. In that case, the demand curve is vertical and $E_P = 0$. If $|E_P| > 1$, demand is elastic. This means that the quantity demanded is sensitive to changes in price. If price goes up by one percent, quantity demanded will fall by more than one percent. The term "completely elastic" (or perfectly elastic, or infinitely elastic) implies that the demand curve is horizontal and $E_P = -\infty$: there is one price at which consumers will demand whatever is supplied, but for a price one penny higher than that, their demand goes to zero.

A few important notes about own-price elasticity of demand before we go on:

1. Don't be confused if you hear someone refer to demand elasticity as a positive number. When discussing demand elasticities, it is often easier not to say "minus" each time. However, when working with elasticities in a mathematical equation, you must always keep track of the negative sign.

2. In the paragraph above, we reviewed the concepts of zero and infinite elasticity. When thinking about the solution to a general problem, you should never assume a perfectly vertical or perfectly horizontal demand curve unless the problem specifically tells you (or leads you) to do so. These are extreme assumptions.

Figure 2.5 shows how the price elasticity for a linear demand curve varies in a systematic way: it is $-\infty$ where the demand curve hits the price axis, less than –1 (elastic) between the vertical intercept and the midpoint, –1 at the midpoint, between –1 and zero (inelastic) between the midpoint and the horizontal axis, and 0 where the demand curve hits the quantity axis. This pattern occurs because the elasticity is the percentage change in quantity divided by the percentage change in price. Although the slope of the demand curve remains the same as we move down a demand curve, the "base" price and quantity that go into the elasticity formula change continuously.

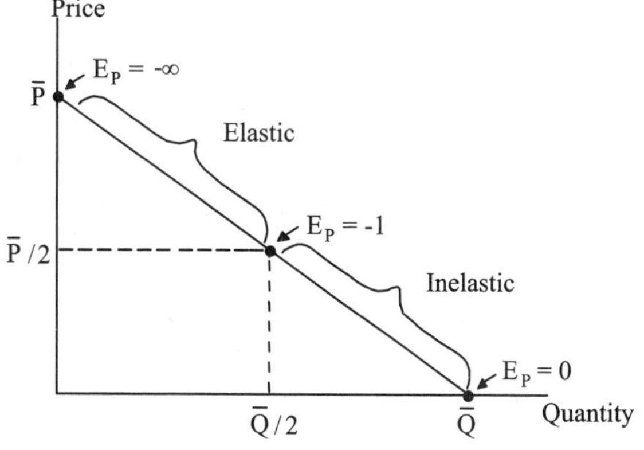

Figure 2.5

Exercise: ◗ ◗ ◗ ◗ ◗ ◗ ◗

7. The demand curve for frozen pizzas is given by $Q_D = 8 - 2P$. What is the demand elasticity at P = 0? P = 2? P = 4?

The *income elasticity of demand* is the percentage change in the quantity demanded in response to a one-percent change in income:

$$E_I = \frac{\%\Delta Q}{\%\Delta I} = \frac{\Delta Q/Q}{\Delta I/I} = \frac{I}{Q} \times \frac{\Delta Q}{\Delta I}.$$

The *cross-price elasticity of demand* is the percentage change in the quantity demanded of one good in response to a one-percent change in the price of a *related good*:

$$E_{Q_x P_y} = \frac{\%\Delta Q_x}{\%\Delta P_y} = \frac{\Delta Q_x / Q_x}{\Delta P_y / P_y} = \frac{P_y}{Q_x} \times \frac{\Delta Q_x}{\Delta P_y}$$

The cross-price elasticity of demand is positive if the two goods are substitutes and it is negative if the two goods are complements. Within this classification, we can still talk about an inelastic or elastic response of quantity to price, depending on whether the cross-price elasticity is greater than or less than one in absolute value.

The *price elasticity of supply* is the percentage change in the quantity supplied in response to a one-percent change in price:

$$E_s = \frac{\%\Delta Q_s}{\%\Delta P} = \frac{\Delta Q_s / Q_s}{\Delta P/P} = \frac{P}{Q_s} \times \frac{\Delta Q_s}{\Delta P}$$

If the linear supply curve is $Q_S = c + dP$, then $\Delta Q/\Delta P = d$. The supply elasticity formula becomes:

$$E_S = d(P/Q).$$

The elasticity of supply is a positive number: a supply curve is elastic if $E_S > 1$ and it is inelastic if $0 < E_S < 1$.

SHORT-RUN VERSUS LONG-RUN ELASTICITIES (Section 2.5)

For non-durable goods, short-run demand is less elastic than long-run demand. Once a price increase occurs, consumers need time to adjust and learn how to use less of the good. Thus, the demand is more responsive to a given price change over the long run, after consumers have had time to adapt to alternatives and change their behavior. For durable goods, the short-run demand is *more* elastic. For example, if the price of washing machines falls, more households will want washing machines. For a short time, many washing machines will be purchased. In the long run, most sales will return to being replacements of old machines.

With some exceptions, such as scrap metal, long-run supply is generally more elastic than short-run supply. In the short run, capacity constraints limit the rate at which firms can expand production, putting a cap on the short-run responsiveness of supply to price.

Exercise: ▶ ▶ ▶ ▶ ▶ ▶ ▶

8. The price of first-class mail has gone up steadily over the years. At the same time, faxes, e-mail, and different forms of automatic online bill payments have become less expensive and more convenient. The U.S. Postal Service is thinking of raising the price of a stamp by 3 cents. Depict the short-run and long-run change in quantity demanded of first-class letters in response to the price increase.

*UNDERSTANDING AND PREDICTING THE EFFECTS OF CHANGING MARKET CONDITIONS (Section 2.6)

By how much will the equilibrium price and quantity change in response to a shift in demand or supply? In order to answer this kind of question, it is necessary to have the equations for demand and supply. We will assume for simplicity that the demand and supply curves are linear. Then, by knowing one point on the demand curve and the price elasticity of demand at that point, we can derive the demand curve. Similarly, with a point on the supply curve and the price elasticity of supply at that point, we can derive the equation of the supply curve.

We can write a linear demand curve as $Q_D = a - bP$, and the formula for the elasticity as $E_P = -bP/Q$, or $b = -E_PQ/P$. Suppose the elasticity of demand is –6, at the current price of $12 and a quantity of 15,000. In this case, $b = -(-6)(15{,}000)/12 = 7{,}500$. Given the slope of the demand curve, we can now find the intercept. Since $Q_D = a - bP$, then $a = Q_D + bP$, or $a = 15{,}000 + (7{,}500)12 = 105{,}000$.

The approximate demand curve is therefore $Q_D = 105{,}000 - 7{,}500P$. Why is this only an approximation? Recall that the elasticity changes as we move along a linear demand curve. Therefore, we do not really know the elasticity without knowing where we are on the curve.

We have used a point elasticity, –6, which is actually only relevant *at the point* Q = 15,000 and P = $12, to derive the *entire* demand line. Therefore, the equation of the line is only an approximation.

For a linear supply curve, $Q_S = c + dP$, we can perform a similar procedure. Since $E_S = dP/Q$, then $d = E_SQ/P$. Using the supply curve, we can then solve for the intercept: $c = Q_S - dP$.

Exercise: ▶ ▶ ▶ ▶ ▶ ▶ ▶

***9.** a) If the elasticity of supply is equal to 4 at P = $12 and Q = 15,000, what is the equation of the supply curve?

b) Using the supply curve from part a) and the demand curve, $Q_D = 105{,}000 - 7{,}500P$, what is the equilibrium price and quantity?

c) What will the new equilibrium price and quantity be if supply increases by 20 percent at all prices?

EFFECTS OF GOVERNMENT INTERVENTION—PRICE CONTROLS (Section 2.7)

So far, we have answered questions by assuming that the market is in equilibrium. When is it not correct to assume that the market is in equilibrium? One important exception is when the government sets a maximum or minimum price in a market. The term *price ceiling* is used when the government sets a price in the market that is below the equilibrium price. When the government sets a price that is above the equilibrium price it is called a *price floor*. Price ceilings create situations of *excess demand* (a shortage at the government-regulated price), while price floors create *excess supply* (a surplus at the government-regulated price). A price ceiling or price floor prevents the market from being in equilibrium, although it presumably achieves other social goals.

Exercise: ◗ ◗ ◗ ◗ ◗ ◗ ◗

10. a) If the supply curve for Frisbees is $Q_S = -10{,}000 + 5{,}000P$, and the demand curve is $Q_D = 40{,}000 - 2{,}000P$, what will be the effect of a price ceiling of \$5? Will the market be in equilibrium? If not, how much excess demand will there be at the ceiling price?

b) Frisbees have fallen out of fashion recently, and the demand curve for Frisbees is now $Q_D = 20{,}000 - 2{,}000P$. What will be the effect of the \$5 price ceiling now? Will the market be in equilibrium? If not, how much excess demand or excess supply will there be at the ceiling price?

PROBLEM SET

11. a) Using the original supply and demand curves for Frisbees from Exercise 10 ($Q_S = -10{,}000 + 5{,}000P$ and $Q_D = 40{,}000 - 2{,}000P$), compute the market equilibrium price and quantity. What is the elasticity of demand and supply at the equilibrium price?

b) If Frisbee manufacturers switch to recycled plastic, which lowers their cost of production, what will happen to the equilibrium price and quantity of Frisbees?

c) If Frisbees come back in fashion after the public learns that Frisbees are now "environmentally friendly," what will happen to the equilibrium price and quantity?

12. *[Mathematical] In Figure 2.6 (a and b), a pair of supply or demand curves are given with particular points indicated on each curve. For each set of curves, indicate whether the supply or demand curve is more elastic, less elastic, or equally elastic at point A or B. (Hint: In each case, write down the definition of elasticity and use the available information to make the comparison.)

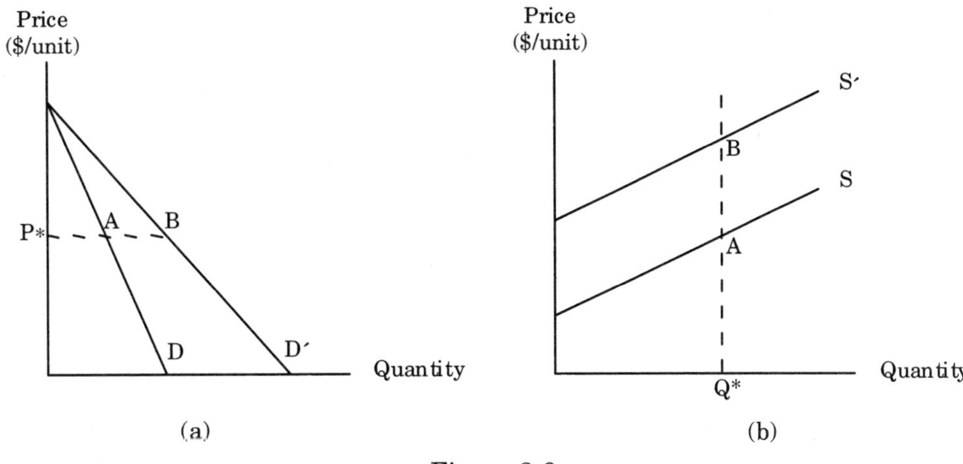

Figure 2.6

13. *[Predicting Effects of Changing Market Conditions] Podunk State University (PSU) is located in the small town of Podunkville. Currently, a typical student apartment rents for $300 per month, and 15,000 apartments are rented. The University is considering expanding enrollment by lowering its current academic standards. A local economist estimates that, at the *current* price and quantity, the price elasticity of demand for apartments is –1/4 and the long-run price elasticity of supply is 1/2.

a) What are the equations of demand and supply?

b) Suppose there is a 20-percent increase in the demand for apartments as a result of the enrollment increase at PSU. What will be the new long-run equilibrium price and quantity in this market? Compute the elasticity of demand at the new equilibrium.

14. You are the manager of a store that carries generic soft drinks. Due to a local economic boom, your customers' incomes have risen by five percent.

a) The income elasticity of demand for these generic soft drinks is estimated to be –2. Estimate the change in the quantity of soft drinks you should order to satisfy the decrease in demand without a surplus or shortage of inventory.

b) Suppose that you have decided to stop carrying generic soft drinks. Your current inventory was acquired to meet the expected demand at the old income level. If own-price demand elasticity for generic soft drinks is –1/3, estimate the change in price required so that the quantity demanded will increase by 10%. .

15. In December 1996, Mexico announced that it would increase import tariffs on wooden furniture from the United States. (While the actual tariff increase was not large, this question explores its effects assuming that it was significant.)

a) Assuming that domestic producers of the wooden dinette sets export them to Mexico, what effect does the tariff increase have on their price in Mexico? Use a graph of supply and demand in the Mexican market to explain your answer.

b) What would you expect to happen in the domestic market for the dinette sets? Use a supply and demand diagram for the U.S. market in your explanation. Would you expect this effect to be more pronounced in the short run or the long run?

c) If you were the manager of a firm that exported to Mexico dinette sets made of metal and glass, what would you expect to happen to your orders?

16. Draw two straight-line parallel demand curves. Then draw an upward-sloping line through the origin to intersect both curves. Compare the elasticities at these two points. (Hint: Recall the formula $E_P = -b(P/Q)$.)

SELF-TEST

17. Which of the following will *not* cause a shift in the demand for baseballs?
    a) Very good weather
    b) A decrease in the price of baseball bats
    c) An increase in the number of nine-year olds
    d) An increase in the price of baseballs
    e) All of the above will shift the demand curve for baseballs.

18. If a market is in equilibrium:
    a) buyers and sellers can buy and sell all they wish at the current price.
    b) there is no tendency for the price to rise or fall.
    c) the quantity supplied equals the quantity demanded.
    d) All of the above are correct.
    e) None of the above is correct.

19. Last month you sold 10,000 stereos nationwide at $400 each. The month before that you sold 9,000 stereos at $410 each. Next month, you are thinking of cutting the price even further to $389.99. Assuming that (i) the market demand for your product is linear, and (ii) all else remains equal, what is your prediction for next month's sales?
    a) 10,100 units
    b) 11,000 units
    c) 11,001 units
    d) 11,051 units
    e) 12,000 units

20. If demand is inelastic:
    a) a two-percent increase in price will result in less than a two-percent decrease in the quantity demanded.
    b) a two-percent increase in price will result in a two-percent decrease in the quantity demanded.
    c) a two-percent increase in price will result in more than a two-percent decrease in the quantity demanded.
    d) a two-percent increase in price will result in less than a two-percent increase in the quantity demanded.
    e) None of the above is correct.

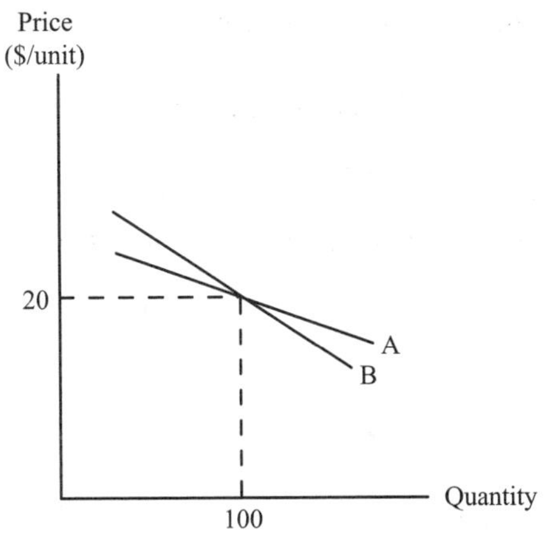

Figure 2.7

21. In Figure 2.7, which comparison of the price elasticity of demand on curves A and B is correct?
a) At P = 20 and Q = 100, demand is more elastic on curve A than curve B.
b) At P = 20 and Q = 100, demand is less elastic on curve A than on curve B.
c) At P = 20 and Q = 100, the elasticity of demand is the same on both curves.
d) More information is needed to compare the elasticities on curves A and B.

22. If the price elasticity of demand for coffee is estimated to be –0.25 in the short run, which is the most likely value of the long-run elasticity?
a) –0.10
b) –0.25
c) –0.40
d) $-\infty$
e) None of the above—the elasticity of demand in the long run is always positive.

23. The demand curve for peanuts is $Q_D = 20{,}000 - 5P$, where Q_D is measured in tons and P is the price per ton. The price elasticity of demand at P = $800 is:
a) – 4.
b) + 4.
c) – 0.25.
d) + 0.25.
e) None of the above is correct.

The next three questions refer to the following demand and supply curves:

$$Q_D = 189 - 2.25P$$
$$Q_S = 124 + 1.5P$$

Your answers should be correct to two decimal places.

24. The equilibrium price is:
a) $84.00
b) $82.67
c) $17.33
d) $150.00
e) None of the above is correct.

25. The equilibrium quantity sold is:
a) 65
b) 150
c) 313
d) 84
e) None of the above is correct.

26. At the market equilibrium, the price elasticity of demand equals:
a) – 2.25
b) + 2.25
c) – 0.26
d) – 0.17
e) None of the above is correct.

27. Which of the following is true?
a) The demand curve for electricity is generally steeper in the long run than in the short run.
b) The demand curve for televisions is generally steeper in the long run than in the short run.
c) The supply curve for sailboats is generally steeper in the long run than in the short run.
d) The supply curve for secondary aluminum is generally flatter in the long run than in the short run.

ANSWERS TO CHAPTER 2

EXERCISE ANSWERS

1. If the price is initially set above the market-clearing price, sellers will produce more compact cars than consumers are willing to buy. Sellers would find that they had a surplus of cars, i.e., excessive inventories would begin to accumulate. In order to get rid of this surplus, sellers will have to lower the price on compacts (or offer rebates or coupons). As they lower the price, demand will increase and the surplus will begin to fall. This will continue until the price reaches equilibrium at P_0.

If the price is initially set below the market-clearing price, consumers will demand more than sellers are willing to sell at that price. A shortage will develop. Consumers who are set on having a compact will begin to bid against each other for the existing supply. This will put upward pressure on the price, and as this happens sellers will begin to expand output. This will continue until the price reaches equilibrium at P_0.

2. a) If production costs increase, the supply curve will shift up (to the left). The equilibrium price increases and the equilibrium quantity decreases. See Figure 2A.1a.

b) The flood will shift the supply curve to the left, as shown in Figure 2A.1b. The decrease in the price of oats and oat bran (a substitute for wheat) will shift the demand for wheat to the left. The equilibrium price may increase or decrease, but the equilibrium quantity will definitely decrease. (To see that the effect on the equilibrium price is ambiguous, draw demand and supply shifts of different sizes.)

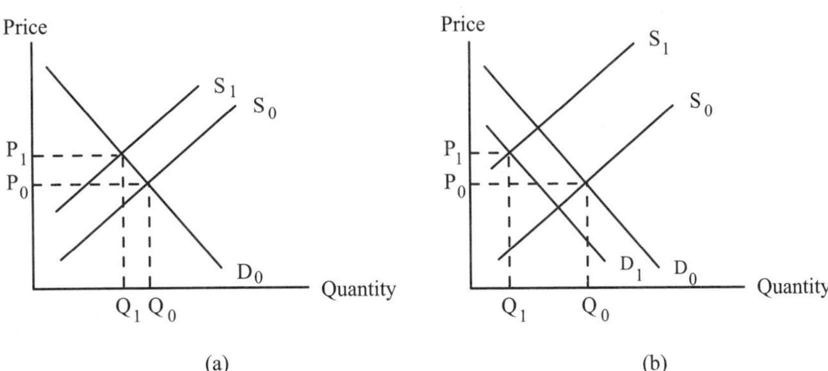

Figure 2A.1

c) The effect of rationing is to limit supply as shown in Figure 2.A.1c (on the next page). The equilibrium quantity declines, by law, and the equilibrium price increases (shown as a movement along the demand curve).

d) By accepting a wage decrease, the union has lowered the costs of production for the steel companies. This will shift their supply curves out (to the right) as shown in Figure 2A.1d. The equilibrium price will decline and the equilibrium quantity will increase.

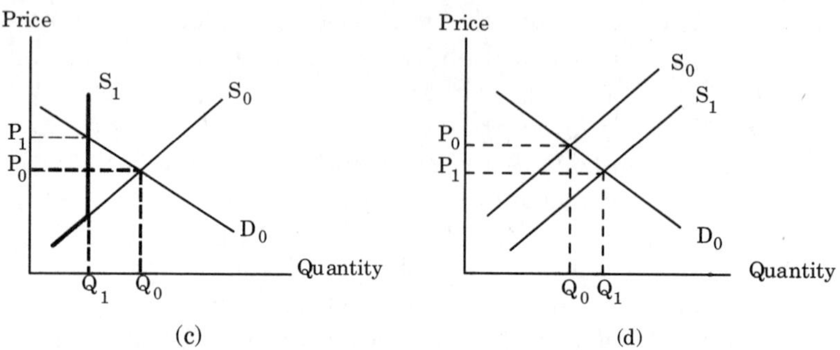

Figure 2A.1

3. The slope of the line $Q_S = c + dP$ is $d = \Delta Q_S/\Delta P = (500 - 350)/(1.00 - 0.75) = 600$. (Note that you can use any combination of the points in Table 2.1 to find d.) The intercept is, therefore, $500 = c + 600(1)$, or $c = -100$. The supply equation is $Q_S = -100 + 600P$.

4. The slope is $(6{,}750 - 5{,}250)/(0.40 - 0.70) = 1{,}500/(-0.30) = -5{,}000$, the same as before.

5. a) See Figure 2A.2.

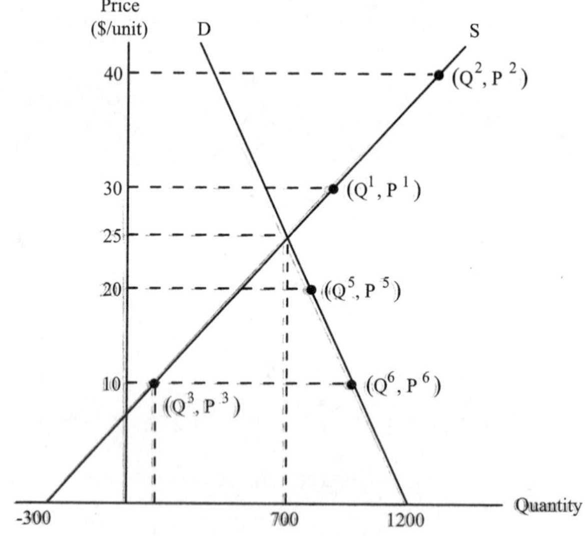

Figure 2A.2

b) First, consider the supply curve. From points (Q^1, P^1) and (Q^2, P^2), we can derive the slope: $d = \Delta Q_S/\Delta P = (Q^2 - Q^1)/(P^2 - P^1) = (1{,}300 - 900)/(40 - 30) = 400/10 = 40$. The intercept c equals $Q_S - dP = 1{,}300 - 40(40) = -300$. So, the supply curve is $Q_S = -300 + 40P$.

The slope of the demand curve is

$$b = \Delta Q_D/\Delta P = (Q^5 - Q^6)/(P^5 - P^6) = (800 - 1{,}000)/(20 - 10) = -200/10 = -20,$$

so b = 20. The intercept is $a = Q_D + bP = 800 + 20(20) = 1{,}200$. So, the demand curve is $Q_D = 1{,}200 - 20P$.

c) For supply, at P = 10, $Q_S = -300 + 40(10) = -300 + 400 = 100$.
At P = 40, $Q_S = -300 + 40(40) = 1{,}300$.
For demand, at P = 10, $Q_S = 1{,}200 - 20(10) = 1{,}000$.
At P = 40, $Q_D = 1{,}200 - 20(40) = 400$.

d) Set $Q_S = Q_D$ or $-300 + 40P = 1200 - 20P$. Combining terms we get, $60P = 1{,}500$, or $P^* = 25$. Substituting back into the supply curve, we obtain $Q_S^* = -300 + 40(25) = 700$. As a check, substitute back into the demand curve to get $Q_D^* = 1{,}200 - 20(25) = 700$. We have verified that $P^* = 25$ is the equilibrium price, since $Q_S^* = Q_D^* = 700$ at that price.

6. a) See Figure 2A.3. If I = 20,000 and R = 15, then $Q_D = 30 - 5P + 0.01(20{,}000) - 2(15)$ or $Q_D = 200 - 5P$. $Q_S = -100 + 20P$. Equating supply and demand:

$$200 - 5P = -100 + 20P \Rightarrow 25P = 300, \text{ or } P^* = \$12.$$

Substitute $P^* = \$12$ into either the demand or supply equation to find $Q^* = 140$.

(Note that in Figure 2A.3 we have drawn the supply curve only for positive quantities. This is the convention that we will follow from this point on.)

b) If R = 10, then $Q_D = 30 - 5P + 0.01(20{,}000) - 2(10) = 210 - 5P$. Set the new demand equation equal to supply: $210 - 5P = -100 + 20P$ or $25P = 310$. Thus, $P^* = \$12.40$ and $Q^* = 148$. Both the equilibrium price and quantity have increased. This makes intuitive sense since the demand for beer during the summer will increase if there are fewer rainy days, which will put upward pressure on the price. It is not necessary (i.e., it is not correct) to shift the supply curve to see the equilibrium supply response. When the demand curve shifts, there is a movement along the supply curve in response to the price increase.

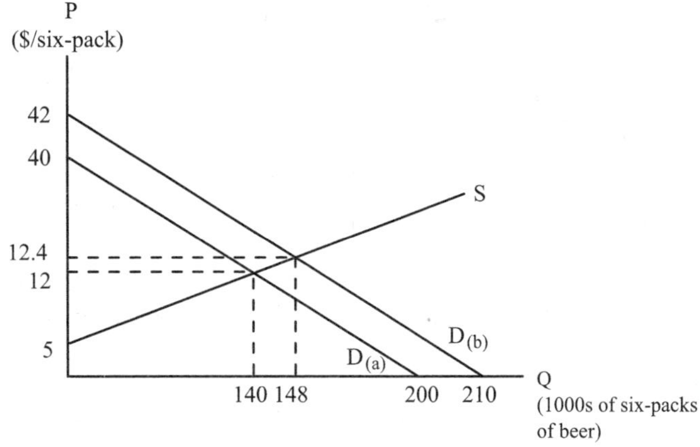

Figure 2A.3

7. Use the formula, $E_P = -bP/Q$: if P = 0, $E_P = 0$; if P = 2, $E_P = -2(2/4) = -1$; if P = 4, $E_P = -2(4/0) = -\infty$.

8. See Figure 2A.4. Starting from the price of P_0, an increase in price of 3 cents to P_1 will bring about a short run response that is less elastic than the long run response. The original equilibrium quantity is Q*. Initially, in the short run, consumers will only cut back on quantity by a small amount (to Q_{SR}) when the price goes up. In the long run, holding everything else constant, they will substitute other forms of communication and demand will fall even further (to Q_{LR}).

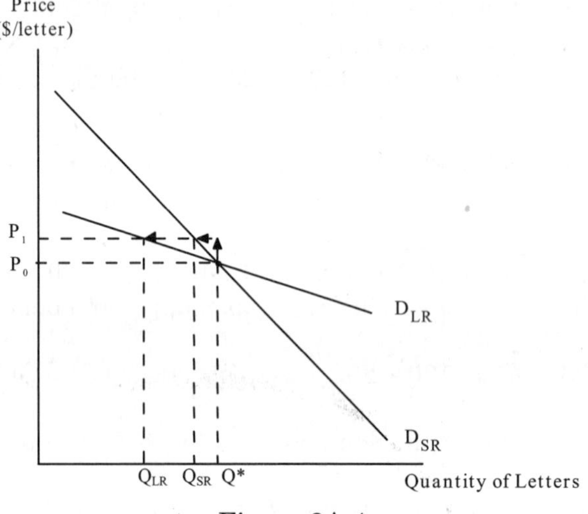

Figure 2A.4

9. a) The price elasticity of supply for the linear supply curve $Q_S = c+dP$ can be written $E_S = dP/Q$, since $d = \Delta Q_S/\Delta P$. Using the information given, $4 = 12d/15{,}000$, so $d = 4(15{,}000)/12$ or $d = 5{,}000$. Plugging this back into the equation yields $15{,}000 = c + 5{,}000(12)$ or $c = -45{,}000$. The linear approximation to the supply curve is then $Q_S = -45{,}000 + 5{,}000P$.

b) The original equilibrium P and Q can be found by setting demand equal to supply: $105{,}000 - 7{,}500P = -45{,}000 + 5{,}000P$. Solving, we get $P^* = \$12$, $Q^* = 15{,}000$.

c) After the 20-percent increase in supply, $Q_S' = 1.2(-45{,}000 + 5{,}000P) = -54{,}000 + 6{,}000P$. Equating demand and new supply, $105{,}000 - 7{,}500P = -54{,}000 + 6{,}000P$, so $P^* = \$11.78$ and $Q^* = 16{,}680$. (Note that if you do not round the answer to P*, which is really $11.7\overline{7}$, you will get $Q^* \approx 16{,}667$. Also note that we are following the convention used in the text regarding percentage changes in demand or supply by shifting the entire curve. An alternative would be to rotate the curve around the y-intercept.)

10. a) At P = \$5, $Q_S = -10{,}000 + 5{,}000(5) = 15{,}000$, and $Q_D = 40{,}000 - 2{,}000(5) = 30{,}000$. The market is *not* in equilibrium at P = \$5, since demand and supply are not equal at that price. Excess demand at P = \$5 is equal to 30,000 – 15,000, or 15,000.

b) To find the new equilibrium price, set $Q_S = Q_D$ or $-10{,}000 + 5{,}000P = 20{,}000 - 2{,}000P$, or $P^* = \$4.29$ (rounding off). This means that the price ceiling of \$5 is ineffective (i.e., not binding) because the market price lies below the price ceiling. There is no excess demand or excess supply.

PROBLEM SET ANSWERS

11. a) Equating supply and demand, $-10{,}000+5{,}000P=40{,}000-2{,}000P$, or $50{,}000=7{,}000P$. Thus, P* = \$7.143 and Q^* = 25,715. (In rounding to P* = \$7.143 one actually gets $Q^*=25{,}715$ from the demand curve and Q* = 25,714 from the supply curve. As long as you are consistent throughout the problem in the Q* you use, your answer will be correct, allowing for rounding error.) The supply elasticity at P* is

$$E_S = d(P/Q) = 5{,}000\ (7.143/25{,}715) = 1.39,$$

and the demand elasticity at P* is

$$E_D = -b(P/Q) = -2{,}000\ (7.143/25{,}715) = -0.56.$$

b) The reduction in the cost of production will shift the supply curve outward, resulting in a lower equilibrium price and a higher equilibrium quantity.

c) If the demand and supply curves shift out at the same time, the equilibrium quantity will rise by even more than part b). The equilibrium price may rise or fall compared to part a), but it will definitely rise compared to part b).

12. In Figure 2.6a, the curves have the same vertical intercept. Substitute the demand equation, Q = a – bP, into $E_P = -bP/Q$ to find $E_P = -bP/(a - bP) = -P/[(a/b) - P]$. This new equation shows that the value of E_P depends on the vertical intercept, a/b, and the price. But both the vertical intercept and the price are the same for A and B. Therefore, the elasticities at A and B are equal.

In Figure 2.6b, the slopes are equal, and the elasticities are measured at the same quantity. If $Q_S = c + dP$, then $E_S = dP/Q$. Since d and Q are the same, but the price is higher at B, the elasticity of supply is greater at B.

13. a) Start with the general linear equations $Q_D = a - bP$ and $Q_S = c + dP$. Since $E_D = -bP/Q$, then $-1/4 = -b(300)/15{,}000$. So b = 12.5. $E_S = dP/Q$, or $1/2 = d(300)/15{,}000$. So d = 25. Plugging the slopes into the linear equations, $Q_D = a - 12.5P$, or $15{,}000 = a - 12.5(300)$, so a = 18,750. Similarly, $Q_S = c + dP$ or $15{,}000 = c + 25(300)$, so c = 7,500. The demand and supply equations are therefore $Q_D = 18{,}750 - 12.5P$ and $Q_S = 7{,}500 + 25P$.

b) The 20-percent increase in demand generates a new demand curve

$$Q'_D = 1.2(18{,}750 - 12.5P) = 22{,}500 - 15P.$$

Equating Q'_D to Q_S, we get $22{,}500 - 15P = 7{,}500 + 25P$, so $P^* = 375$ and $Q^* = 16{,}875$. At the new equilibrium, $E_D = -15(375)/16{,}875 = -0.33$.

14. a) Orders must be reduced by 10 percent because demand falls by twice the percentage change in income. Mathematically, $E_I = \dfrac{\%\Delta Q_D}{\%\Delta I}$, so $-2 = \dfrac{\%\Delta Q_D}{5\%}$ or $\%\Delta Q_D = -10\%$.

b) Price must be reduced enough to stimulate demand 10 percent to compensate for the decline due to the change in income (as shown in part (a)). This means price must fall 30 percent because the percentage increase in quantity is only one-third the size of the percentage fall in price.

15. a) The tariff increases the price that U.S. manufacturers must receive for any set sold in Mexico, shifting the supply curve to the left. This leads to a higher price in Mexico and a lower equilibrium quantity. See Figure 2A.5a.

Mexican Market for
Wooden Dinette Sets

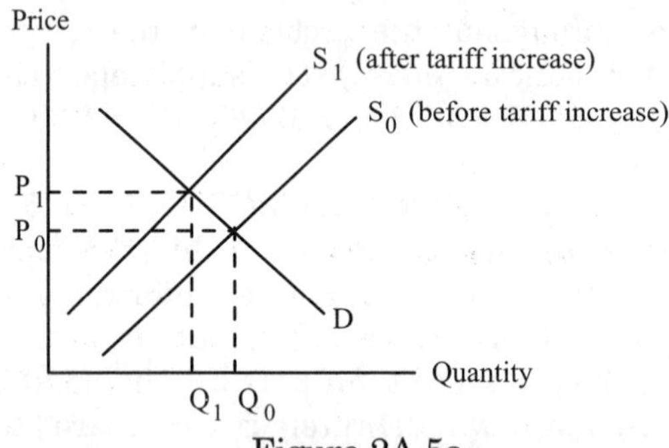

Figure 2A.5a

b) United States manufacturers would now find it profitable to substitute sales in the United States for sales in Mexico, shifting United States supply to the right. This leads to a lower U.S. price and higher sales. See Figure 2A.5b. This effect would probably be the largest in the short term as suppliers diverted away from Mexico units already produced or in production . In future periods, this effect would be moderated by an overall cutback in production.

U.S. Market for
Wooden Dinette Sets

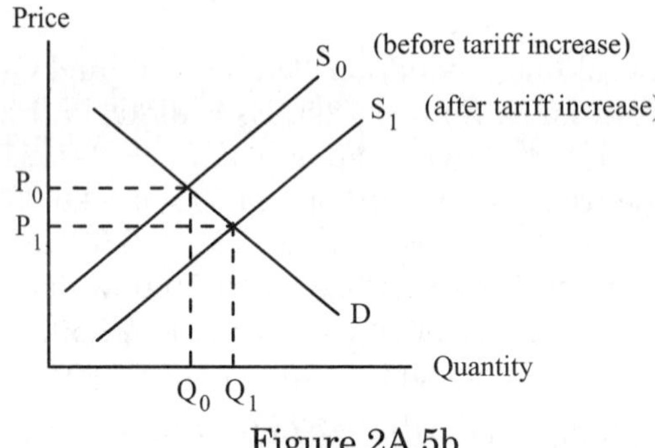

Figure 2A.5b

c) Orders will increase if these sets are substitutes for the wooden ones.

16. See Figure 2A.6. Because (P_1, Q_1) and (P_2, Q_2) lie on a straight line through the origin, $P_1/Q_1 = P_2/Q_2$. Since the demand curves are parallel lines, $b_1 = b_2$, so the elasticities are the same at the two points. (Note: $Q = a - bP$).

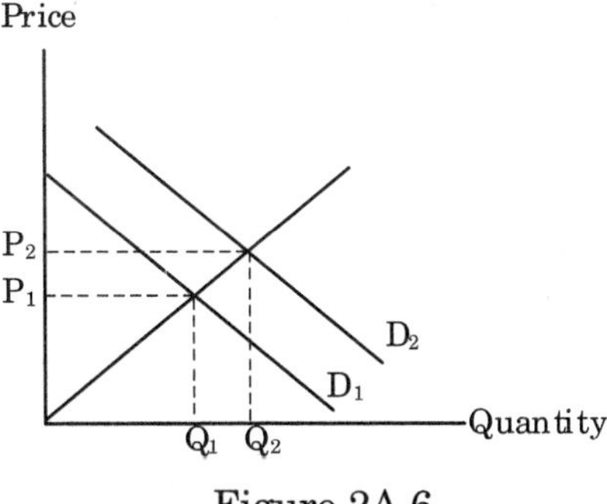

Figure 2A.6

SELF-TEST ANSWERS

17. d) A change in the price of baseballs reflects a movement along the demand curve for baseballs. Good weather shifts the demand curve out, as does an increase in the number of nine-year olds and a decrease in the price of baseball bats.

18. d) Choice a) is a characteristic of a competitive market, while b) and c) are the definition of a market equilibrium.

19. c) Using the two data points, find the slope and intercept of the demand curve: $(9{,}000 - 10{,}000)/(410 - 400) = -100$ and $10{,}000 = a - 100(400)$, or a = 50,000. Thus, the equation of the line is $Q = 50{,}000 - 100P$. When P = \$389.99, Q = 11,001.

20. a) $E_P = \%\Delta Q/\%\Delta P$. Inelastic demand means that $|E_P| < 1$.

21. a) The point (100, 20) is on both demand curves. Intuitively, the flatter curve is the more price-sensitive one. A is more elastic than B because a given price change will result in a larger quantity change along A than along B. Algebraically, since $E_P = -bP/Q$, where b is the slope of the demand curve ($Q_D = a - bP$), the curve with the larger value of b (holding P and Q constant) is more elastic.

22. c) For most goods (except those that are durable), the long-run elasticity is greater in absolute value than the short-run elasticity.

23. c) At a price of \$800 per ton, 16,000 tons are demanded.
$E_P = -bP/Q = -5(800)/16{,}000 = -4{,}000/16{,}000 = -0.25$.

24. c) Setting $Q_S = Q_D$, we obtain $124 + 1.5P = 189 - 2.25P$. Collecting terms, $3.75P = 65$, or P = \$17.33.

25. b) Using P* = \$17.33 (from above), $Q_S = 124 + 1.5(17.33) = 150$.

26. c) $E_P = -bP/Q = -2.25(17.33)/150 = -0.26$.

27. b) In general, long-run demand for a durable good is less elastic than short-run demand. To understand why d) is not true, see the discussion in the text surrounding Figure 2.13.

CHAPTER 3
CONSUMER BEHAVIOR

IMPORTANT CONCEPTS

- Preference Assumptions
  - Completeness
  - Transitivity
  - More is Better
- Indifference Curve
- Budget Constraint
- Marginal Rate of Substitution
  - Diminishing MRS
- Utility Maximizing Market Basket
- Revealed Preference
- Cost-of-Living Indexes

CHAPTER HIGHLIGHTS

A theory of preferences is developed in this chapter that allows us to study consumer behavior and make predictions about a typical consumer's reaction to price changes, income changes, or alternative policies offered by business or government. The two basic tools of analysis are the *indifference curve* and the *budget constraint*. An indifference curve maps out all of the market baskets that yield the same amount of utility to the consumer. The slope of the indifference curve at a point is called the *marginal rate of substitution* (MRS). The MRS describes the rate at which the consumer is willing to trade one good for another and remain indifferent. Three basic *preference assumptions* are required in order to use indifference curves in a consistent manner: *completeness, transitivity,* and *more is better.* In addition, we generally assume that indifference curves have a *diminishing marginal rate of substitution.* The last assumption ensures that indifference curves will be convex to the origin, and this in turn leads to consumer preferences for balanced bundles rather than all-or-nothing allocations between goods.

The *budget constraint* describes the rate at which the consumer is able to trade, given market prices and the level of the consumer's income. We assume that the consumer will always spend all of his or her income.

Indifference curves and budget constraints together determine the consumer's *utility-maximizing* bundle of goods. The consumer strives to choose a market basket on the highest indifference curve that still satisfies the budget constraint.

Utility maximization is achieved when the budget constraint is tangent to an indifference curve. At this tangency point, the marginal rate of substitution between the two goods is equal to the ratio of the prices.

Analyzing consumer choices using indifference curves requires a full description of consumers' preferences over all possible combinations of goods and services. Sometimes we can make predictions about consumer behavior with much less information by simply observing the choices that a consumer makes in response to changing income and prices. This type of analysis, called *revealed preference* analysis, is often used to check whether individual choices are consistent with the assumptions of consumer theory.

Using utility theory, one can ask how much income would be needed to keep a consumer at the same level of satisfaction as price levels change over time. In particular, *cost-of-living indexes* attempt to measure how our purchasing power changes in an inflationary environment. The *ideal* cost-of-living index measures how income must change to keep utility constant. Utility is difficult to measure, however, and therefore economists use a variety of other price indexes to approximate changes in satisfaction. The *Laspeyres* price index measures the cost of buying a particular base-year basket of goods, both at base year prices and current year prices. The *Paasche* price index instead measures the cost of buying the current-year basket of goods, both at base-year prices and current-year prices.

CONCEPT REVIEW AND EXERCISES

CONSUMER PREFERENCES (Section 3.1)

In studying consumer behavior, it is important to distinguish between what a consumer *would like to do* and what a consumer *can do*. The first part of the chapter deals with preferences, which describe a consumer's choices without regard to cost. To understand preferences, think about comparisons between two different market baskets of consumer goods. A market basket is a combination of different quantities of goods or services. The basic assumptions underlying the theory of consumer preferences are as follows:

1) *Completeness*: for any two market baskets, either the consumer prefers one to the other or is indifferent between them;

2) *Transitivity*: for any three market baskets, if the first basket is preferred to a second one, and the second one is preferred to a third one, then the first basket must also be preferred to the third one; and

3) *More is better*: if the first basket contains more of any good than the second basket, the first basket is preferred to the second.

What do these assumptions rule out? *Completeness*, the first assumption, says that the consumer is capable of choosing between any two baskets. For example, would you prefer a basket with 100 gallons of milk and 1 pair of blue jeans or one with 200 pairs of blue jeans and 2 gallons of milk? Completeness means that the consumer can compare any two market baskets, preferring one to the other or being indifferent between the two.

Transitivity, the second assumption, links together comparisons of different pairs of market baskets. It means that a consumer is rational or consistent in his preferences. The following exercise highlights the difference between transitive and intransitive preferences.

Exercise: ◗ ◗ ◗ ◗ ◗ ◗ ◗

1. William prefers market basket P to Q, basket Q to R, and basket P to R. Rather than offering to let William choose among P, Q, and R, offer only two baskets at a time.

a) Offer a choice between P and Q; then offer a choice between the one selected and R. Which basket would be William's final choice?

b) Now first offer a choice between Q and R; then offer a choice between the basket selected and P. Which would be chosen?

c) Compare your answers to a) and b). Are William's preferences transitive?

d) What happens in a) and b) if William prefers P to Q, Q to R, and R to P? Are these preferences transitive?

In your answer to part (d) of Exercise 1, you should have found that the order in which the choices were presented to William changed his decision. This doesn't seem rational. This is because William's preferences in part (d) are intransitive. The transitivity assumption assures us that the same decision will be reached regardless of how the choices are presented.

The third assumption, that *more is better*, means that goods have a positive value. This assumption is made to simplify the exposition; it can be modified easily to cover cases in which goods are undesirable.

What do our preference assumptions tell us about indifference curves? Completeness tells us that every basket has an indifference curve going through it. Transitivity and "more is better" together assure us that a consumer's indifference curves cannot cross. "More is better" also tells us that an indifference curve must be downward sloping.

INDIFFERENCE CURVES

With only two goods in a market basket, we can represent our hypothetical consumer's preferences by drawing a two-dimensional indifference curve. A single indifference curve, such as the one drawn in Figure 3.1, is a collection of market baskets that give a consumer equal satisfaction (i.e., equal utility).

Let the horizontal axis measure the number of units of food (F), and the vertical axis measure the number of units of clothing (C). Every basket on the indifference curve drawn in Figure 3.1 gives the consumer equal satisfaction. Basket A is just as desirable as basket B or basket D.

However, every basket lying *above* the curve in Figure 3.1 (on the next page) has to have more units of F, more units of C, or more of both, and must be better than basket A. Every basket lying *below* the curve has to have fewer units of F or C or both, and must be worse than A.

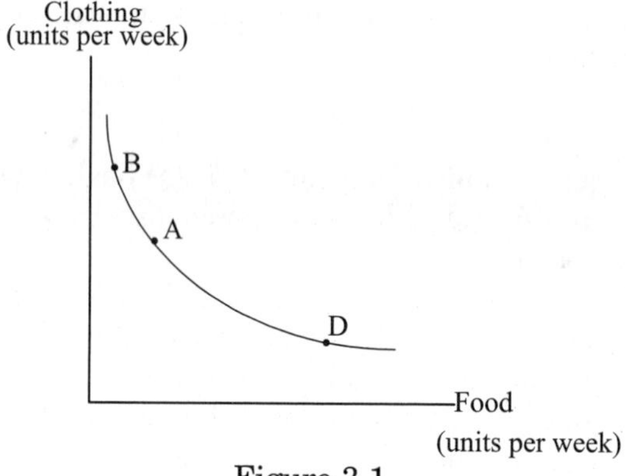

Figure 3.1

Indifference curves only display an *ordinal ranking of preferences*. A basket on a higher indifference curve is preferred to any basket on a lower indifference curve, but we do not know how much more satisfaction it provides. Some economists in the past used a *cardinal ranking* of preferences, attaching specific numbers to different levels of satisfaction. However, we only need an ordinal ranking to describe much of consumer behavior.

Exercise: ◗ ◗ ◗ ◗ ◗ ◗ ◗

2. Draw indifference curves to represent the following descriptions of consumer preferences:

a) I can't taste the difference between apple and grape jelly, but I like them both.

b) I only like grape jelly and never eat apple jelly.

c) Apple and grape jelly are better mixed, although I don't care too much about the proportions.

THE MARGINAL RATE OF SUBSTITUTION

The slope of the indifference curve is the rate at which the consumer is willing to trade. As we move along an indifference curve between food and clothing, we see that the consumer is willing to give up different amounts of clothing to obtain an additional unit of food at different market baskets. We quantify this trade-off the consumer is willing to make as the *marginal rate of substitution* (MRS).

The MRS of food for clothing is the maximum amount of clothing a consumer would give up to obtain one more unit of food. Formally, the MRS equals $-\Delta C/\Delta F$ along a given indifference curve.

Starting at market basket J in Figure 3.2 (on the next page), the consumer is willing to give up 2 units of clothing to obtain 3 units of food. In other words, the MRS between points J and L equals 2/3. For very small changes in clothing and food, we can measure the MRS at a single point on the indifference curve. For example, the MRS at point M is the negative of the slope of the tangent line to the indifference curve at M.

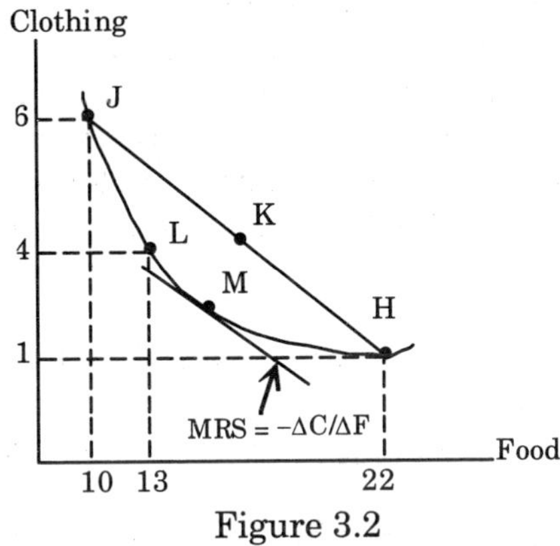

Figure 3.2

One last assumption about consumer preferences that we like to add (although we don't have to) is that indifference curves are convex—they get flatter as we move down the curve. This means the MRS (a positive number) decreases as F increases. We call this a *diminishing marginal rate of substitution*. The more you have of a good, the less value you attach to having one more unit of that good. For example, we just calculated the MRS from J to L as 2/3. The MRS from L to H is 3/9 = 1/3. This demonstrates that the MRS is diminishing as we move down the curve. An implication of diminishing MRS is that "balanced bundles" are preferred to bundles with an extreme allocation of goods. For example, look at market baskets J, K, and H in Figure 3.2. J and H are "unbalanced" in terms of the allocation of goods, while basket K (halfway between H and J) is "balanced." With convex indifference curves the consumer will clearly prefer K, since K lies on a higher indifference curve (draw an indifference curve through point K to convince yourself that this is true). This is one reason why economists believe that the assumption of convex indifference curves is a reasonable one: observation of real consumer choices tells us that consumers prefer variety.

Exercise: ◗ ◗ ◗ ◗ ◗ ◗ ◗

3. Steve consumes only pasta and wine. The following three market baskets are on his indifference curve: A = (1, 8), B = (2, 4), and C = (3, 2), where (1, 8) = (1 pound of pasta, 8 bottles of wine), etc.

a) Draw Steve's indifference curve, with pounds of pasta per week on the horizontal axis and bottles of wine per week on the vertical axis. Label points A, B, and C.

b) What is the MRS between A and B? Between B and C? Does Steve's indifference curve satisfy the assumption of diminishing MRS?

PERFECT SUBSTITUTES AND PERFECT COMPLEMENTS

There are two special cases of preferences that deserve attention. With *perfect substitutes*, indifference curves are straight lines. The consumer's MRS is the same no matter how much of each good he has. For example, think about the rate at which you would trade nickels for dimes. That rate should not depend on how many nickels and dimes you have. You will always want to trade two nickels for one dime.

With *perfect complements*, the indifference curves form right angles. For example, think about your preferences between different combinations of right and left shoes. In order to increase your satisfaction you need more of both goods—having just one more left shoe will not put you on a higher indifference curve. In this case, the MRS is either infinity (on the vertical part of the indifference curve) or zero (on the horizontal part), except at the kink where it is not well defined.

Exercise: ▶ ▶ ▶ ▶ ▶ ▶ ▶

4. Draw two typical indifference curves for each of the following cases. Describe the MRS in each case.

a) Name-brand aspirin and generic aspirin for a consumer who considers the two goods equal in every way.

b) Right gloves and left gloves for a consumer who only wants to wear gloves in pairs.

c) Right gloves and left gloves for a rock star who regards right gloves as useless. That is, it does not matter to him whether he has right gloves or not, since he only wears left gloves.

BUDGET CONSTRAINTS (Section 3.2)

The second part of Chapter 3 discusses what a consumer is able to purchase given market prices and her income level. The *budget constraint* faced by the consumer limits her spending to a maximum of what her income will allow. If F and C are the quantities of the two goods, the *budget line* is $P_F F + P_C C = I$, where P_F is the price per unit of food, P_C is the price per unit of clothing, and I is the total income available. We write the constraint as an equality rather than writing $P_F F + P_C C \leq I$. This is done because "more is better" means that the consumer will always increase her satisfaction by choosing a point *on* the budget line rather than a point below it.

Figure 3.3 shows a typical budget line. The intercepts of the budget line are I/P_C and I/P_F (the maximum amount of clothing or food that can be purchased if all income is spent on clothing or food). The slope of the budget line is minus the price ratio, $-P_F/P_C$. A change in income causes a parallel shift in the budget line. A change in prices alters the slope of the budget line.

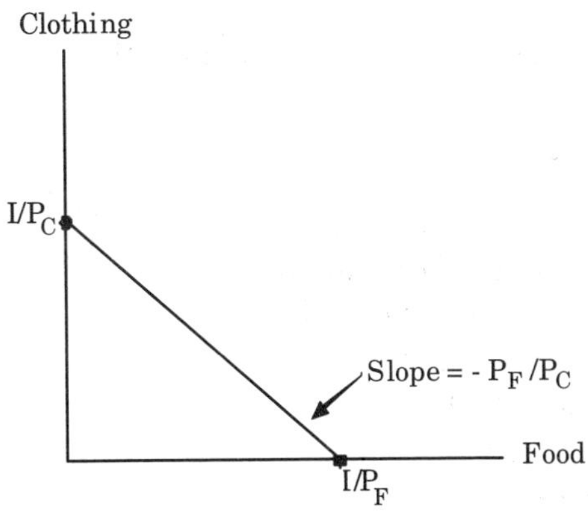

Figure 3.3

It is often easiest to rewrite the equation of the budget line with the good you are plotting on the vertical axis on the left-hand side of the equation. In this case, since we have been plotting clothing on the vertical axis, we will rearrange the equation from

$$P_F F + P_C C = I$$
to
$$C = I/P_C - (P_F/P_C)F.$$

Immediately, you can see that the vertical intercept is I/P_C, and the slope of the budget line is $-P_F/P_C$. The horizontal intercept, I/P_F, is found by setting $C = 0$.

Exercise: ◗ ◗ ◗ ◗ ◗ ◗ ◗

5. Graph the following budget lines:

a) $10F + 20C = 400$
b) $5F + 10C = 400$
c) $10F + 10C = 400$
d) $20F + 20C = 400$

Compare a) to b), a) to c), and a) to d). Which comparisons represent income changes and which represent price changes?

CONSUMER CHOICE (Section 3.3)

Faced with the opportunity to buy any market basket satisfying his budget constraint, what will a consumer choose to do? First, he will spend all his income, since more is preferred to less. Second, he will choose the market basket that gives him the most preferred combination of goods. This most preferred basket is on the highest indifference curve that still satisfies the budget constraint. With smooth indifference curves, the market basket that maximizes utility subject to the budget constraint is at a point where the budget line and the indifference curve are tangent to each other. At this tangency point, the slope of the budget line equals the slope of the indifference curve, or MRS = P_F/P_C. In other words, at this point the rate at which the consumer is *willing* to trade equals the rate at which the consumer is *able* to trade, given market prices.

Exercise: ▶ ▶ ▶ ▶ ▶ ▶ ▶

6. Suppose the consumer is *not* at a tangency point. The comparison between the slope of the budget line and the MRS tells us in which direction along the budget line the consumer will wish to move.
   a) Suppose MRS = 5 and $P_F/P_C = 3$. Is the consumer at a tangency point? If not, will the consumer prefer a market basket on the budget line with more food or more clothing?
   b) Suppose MRS = 2 and $P_F/P_C = 3$. Is the consumer at a tangency point? If not, will the consumer prefer a market basket on the budget line with more food or more clothing?
   c) Suppose MRS = 3 and $P_F/P_C = 3$. Is the consumer at a tangency point?
   d) Draw a budget line and indifference curves to show where the consumer would be if a) were true, if b) were true, and if c) were true.

In some special cases where the indifference curves are not smooth curves, there may not be a tangency between the indifference curve and the budget line. The next two exercises look at cases where the MRS does not equal the price ratio at the most preferred market basket.

Exercise: ▶ ▶ ▶ ▶ ▶ ▶ ▶

7. For the case of perfect complements, draw a budget line and a family of indifference curves. What is the consumer's most preferred market basket?

8. For the case of perfect substitutes, draw a budget line and a family of indifference curves. What is the most preferred market basket? (Hint: The indifference curves, which are straight lines in this case, can have a different slope than the budget line.)

REVEALED PREFERENCE (Section 3.4)

Even if we don't know a consumer's preferences in detail, observing a consumer's choices can give us some description of her indifference curves. This is called *revealed preference* analysis. The consumer reveals her preferences by her purchases in response to price changes.

First, consider the situation in Figure 3.4a where the consumer chooses market basket A. What does that tell us? We already knew that the consumer preferred A to any basket with less of both goods. Now we also know that A is preferred to any market basket in the shaded area of Figure 3.4a *and* to any market basket on the same budget line as A. Because the consumer chose A when every market basket on the budget line was available, *A has been revealed to be preferred* to the other baskets. In general, if market basket A is chosen when both A and B were available, then the consumer prefers A to B.

As we vary prices and the consumer's income (moving the budget line around in various ways), we can discover more about the consumer's preferences. So far, we know very little about the indifference curve through A. We do not yet know whether it looks like the one in Figure 3.4a or like the one in Figure 3.4b.

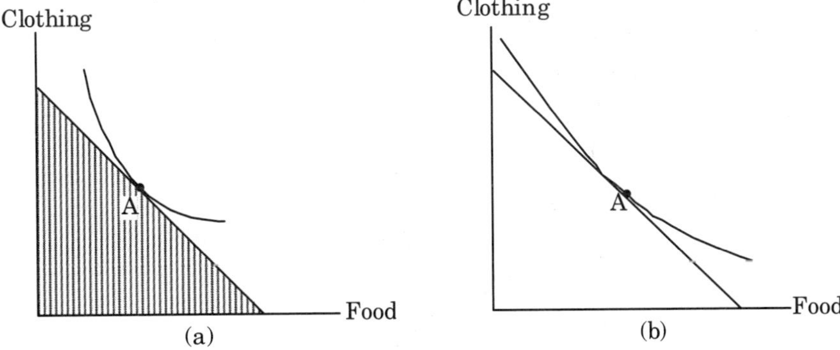

Figure 3.4

Now suppose that we observe the consumer choosing A when the budget line is l_1 and B when the budget line is l_2 in Figure 3.5. Since A and B are both on l_1, A is preferred to B, and B is preferred to all market baskets on or under l_2. This implies that A is preferred to all baskets lying under l_1 and all baskets in the shaded area in Figure 3.5 (on the next page). We can continue to trace out baskets that are not preferred to A in this manner.

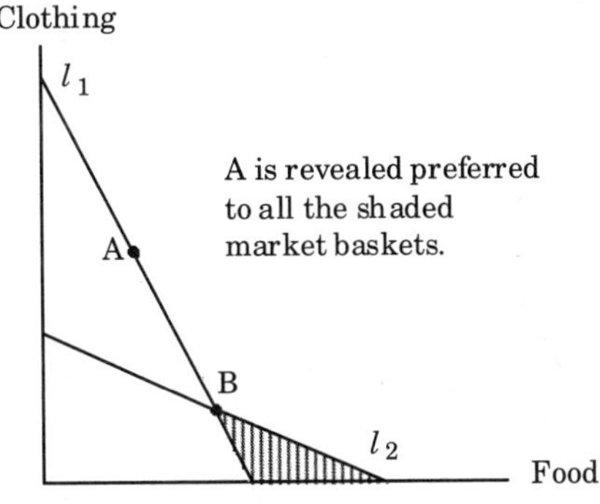

Figure 3.5

We can also try to find baskets that are preferred to A. Consider bundle G in Figure 3.6. G is preferred to A. With the assumption of diminishing MRS, every basket between A and G is also preferred to A. (Draw several possible indifference curves to convince yourself of this. Remember that indifference curves cannot intersect.) Thus, we can narrow down the shape of the indifference curves by using revealed preference analysis, although we cannot determine the shape completely.

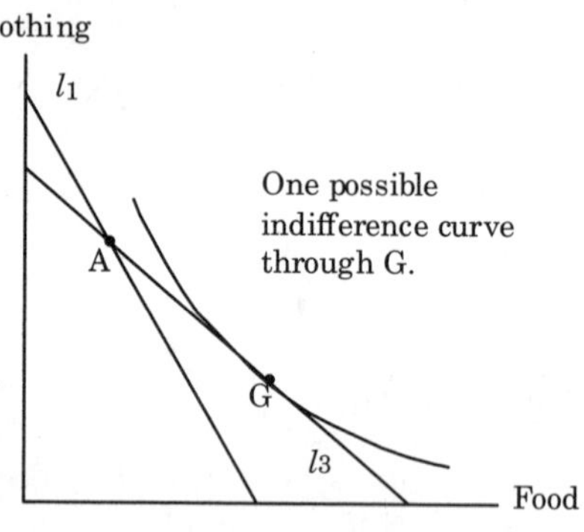

Figure 3.6

Exercise:

9. Food and clothing both cost \$10 per unit. Susan has an income of \$400 per month. At this income level, she buys 25 units of food and 15 units of clothing.

a) Draw the original budget constraint and label Susan's current market basket as point A.

b) Next year, Susan's income falls to \$350 per month. The price of food is \$7 per unit, and the price of clothing is \$14 per unit. She buys 28 units of food and 11 units of clothing. Label this point B. Is she better off before or after the price change?

c) In the following year, her income rises to \$588 per month, and the prices are still \$7 for food and \$14 for clothing. She buys 36 units of food and 24 units of clothing. Label this point C. Is she better off now or when her income was \$400 and both prices were \$10?

MARGINAL UTILITY AND CONSUMER CHOICE (Section 3.5)

Every market basket on an indifference curve gives the same utility. *Utility* is simply a measure of the satisfaction that an individual gets from consuming a particular market basket. A utility function assigns numbers to market baskets such that a higher number for basket A than for basket B means that A is preferred to B. The amount of utility increases as the consumer obtains more of both goods and moves to a higher indifference curve. The actual values of the utility numbers are unimportant for indifference curve analysis, since utility is only an ordinal ranking. The preferences graphed in Figures 3.7a and 3.7b are identical, even though the utility numbers differ.

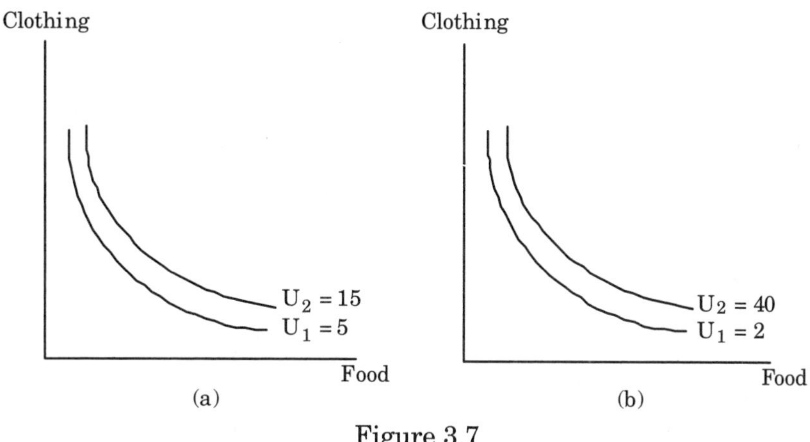

Figure 3.7

For *marginal utility* analysis, the actual utility numbers do matter. The marginal utility of food, MU_F, is the additional utility the consumer will get from adding an additional unit of food to his market basket. MU_C is the additional utility derived from adding a unit of clothing to the market basket. Recall that the more you have of a good the less you value an additional unit. This implies that marginal utility depends on how much of both goods are currently in the market basket.

The MRS equals the ratio of marginal utilities, i.e., MRS = MU_F/MU_C. Our rule for utility maximization, MRS = P_F/P_C, therefore, becomes $MU_F/MU_C = P_F/P_C$. Rearranging terms yields $MU_F/P_F = MU_C/P_C$. Thus, at the most preferred market basket, the consumer gets equal marginal utility from the last dollar spent on each good. To maximize utility, subject to a budget constraint, the consumer should choose the market basket where the last dollar, whether allocated to F or C, would produce the same increase in utility. Once the consumer is at this point, it does not matter where the last dollar is spent. This implies that the consumer has found a point from which he has no desire to move. This is the point of maximum utility. We can use this rule for any number of goods.

Exercise: ◗ ◗ ◗ ◗ ◗ ◗ ◗

10. Use the information in the table below to answer the following questions concerning a consumer's choice between food and clothing.

Clothing	MU_C	MU_C/P_C	Food	MU_F	MU_F/P_F
1	60	6	1	115	5.75
2	55	—	2	105	—
3	51	—	3	98	—
4	48	—	4	94	—
5	47	—	5	92	—
6	46	—	6	90	—

a) Fill in the blanks that remain in the table.

b) Let I = \$130, P_F = \$20, and P_C = \$10. Does the market basket C = 1 and F = 6 satisfy the budget constraint? Could this be the utility maximizing market basket? If not, in which direction would the consumer like to reallocate his purchases (i.e., more food or more clothing)?

c) Given I = \$130, P_F = \$20, and P_C = \$10, and using the information in the table, what is the consumer's utility maximizing market basket, subject to his budget constraint?

*COST-OF-LIVING INDEXES (Section 3.6)

The Consumer Price Index or CPI (introduced in Chapter 1) is an example of a *cost-of-living index*. It measures the overall price level. Of course, it is difficult to define what is meant by "overall." It is defined in practice as the price level associated with a typical bundle of consumer goods and services. The Bureau of Labor Statistics, the government office responsible for calculating the CPI, surveys consumers periodically to find out what goes into a typical consumer's bundle and how much of a typical consumer's budget is spent on each item. By following the cost of that bundle, the BLS tries to measure how much money would be needed to keep consumers at the same level of satisfaction as prices rise.

The best measure of purchasing power is not the CPI, but an *ideal cost-of-living index*, defined as the cost of attaining a given level of utility at current-year prices relative to the cost of attaining the same utility at base-year prices. This index, although ideal, is not easy to put into practice. It would be impossible to measure consumer satisfaction levels and preferences. Therefore, approximate cost-of-living indexes are used to try to get at the same idea with more easily available data.

The two most popular are the *Laspeyres price index* (such as the CPI) and the *Paasche price index*. These indices measure the cost, relative to a base year, of purchasing the base-year bundle of goods and services and current-year prices. The formula for the Laspeyres index can be written as follows:

$$\text{LI} = \frac{\sum P_2 Q_1}{\sum P_1 Q_1}$$

The subscript "1" refers to the consumption bundle and prices in year 1 (the base year), and "2" refers to the current year. Consider a simplistic example: suppose a consumer earns \$10,000 in 2010 and in that year he only buys food (at \$10 per pound) and clothing (at \$30 per item). In 2010, he bought 400 pounds of food and 200 items of clothing. Prices rise the next year—food is now \$12 per pound and clothing is \$35 per item. The Laspeyres index would be

$$LI = \frac{\sum 12(400) + 35(200)}{\sum 10(400) + 30(200)} = \frac{11{,}800}{10{,}000} = 1.18$$

In this example, there has been an 18 percent increase in the cost of living from 2010 to 2011.

The Paasche index is defined similarly, except that instead of holding the consumer's bundle of goods and services fixed at the base year, it looks at current-year quantities. In particular, the Paasche index measures the cost of purchasing the current-year bundle at current-year prices, relative to the cost of this bundle at base-year prices. It can be written as follows:

$$PI = \frac{\sum P_2Q_2}{\sum P_1Q_2}$$

Neither the Laspeyres nor the Paasche price index is an ideal index for one important reason: both of these indexes assume that consumers will continue to consume the same bundle when prices change. While that is a necessary assumption to simplify the calculations and data-gathering cost, it is unrealistic. Consumers will substitute from one good to another, or change the quantities consumed of certain goods, as prices change. For this reason, the Laspeyres index overstates the true change in the cost-of-living and the Paasche index will understate it. The government statistical offices are aware of this problem (and others) and continue to work to improve the accuracy of the cost-of-living indexes that they publish.

Exercise: ▶ ▶ ▶ ▶ ▶ ▶ ▶

11. Susan bought 30 DVDs and 600 pounds of food in 2000 when DVDs cost $30 each and food cost $4 per pound. In 2010, the price of DVDs falls to $20 each and the price of food rises to $5 per pound.

a) Compute the Laspeyres price index for Susan for the year 2010, using 2000 as the base year.

b) In 2010, Susan's income changes and she buys 40 DVDs and 550 pounds of food. Compute the Paasche price index for Susan for 2010 using 2000 as the base year.

c) Can we say for sure if Susan was better off in 2000 or 2010?

PROBLEM SET

12. One week, a snack bar charges Philip $0.30 per bottle of soda and $0.10 per ounce of tortilla chips. Philip spends all his income on soda and tortilla chips and chooses to consume 6 sodas and 30 ounces of tortilla chips that week. A week later, prices have risen to $0.75 per soda and $0.25 per ounce of tortilla chips. Philip's income has also changed. Philip now purchases 3 sodas and 36 ounces of tortilla chips. Is his behavior in the two weeks consistent? In which week is Philip better off?

13. An individual consumes only two commodities, pears and chestnuts. This individual prefers a bundle with 6 pears and 2 chestnuts over a bundle with 4 pears and 7 chestnuts. However, she also prefers a bundle with 2 pears and 8 chestnuts over the one with 6 pears and 2 chestnuts. Are these preferences consistent with our assumptions about consumer preferences? (Hint: Draw a diagram and plot these consumption bundles; then try to fit indifference curves that satisfy the assumptions of consumer theory.)

14. Joan buys gasoline and food. When the price of gasoline is $1.00 per gallon, she buys 50 gallons of gas per week and spends $50 on food per week. The government wants to reduce consumption of gasoline as part of an environmental policy and is considering two alternatives. They are: (1) Restrict the number of gallons of gasoline anyone can buy to 40 gallons per week, and (2) Raise the price of gasoline to $1.25 per gallon. Assume for simplicity that food always costs $1 per unit.

a) Show on a graph Joan's initial budget line and the budget lines under policy (1) and policy (2).

b) Suppose that Joan's most preferred market basket under policy (2) is to consume 40 gallons per week. Show this on the consumption diagram. Would Joan be better off under policy (1) or (2)?

c) Suppose instead that Joan's preferred market basket under policy (2) is to consume 70 gallons per week (we do not know what her original preferred market basket was). Would your answer to b) change?

15. Karen's marginal rate of substitution of food for clothing is 3/2, no matter how many units of each she is currently consuming. Draw several of her indifference curves. If her income is $100, P_F = $5, and P_C = $10, what is her budget line? What will be her preferred market basket?

16. Arthur consumes two goods, iced tea and sugar. Arthur has very discriminating tastes and will only enjoy his beverage if it has two teaspoons of sugar per pint of iced tea.

a) Graph Arthur's preferences over pints of iced tea and teaspoons of sugar.

b) If Arthur has $4.00 to spend and sugar costs $0.05 per teaspoon and iced tea costs $0.15 per pint, what is his preferred market basket?

c) Suppose, instead, that sugar costs $0.10 per teaspoon and iced tea costs $0.05 per pint. What is Arthur's utility maximizing consumption now?

17. George enjoys playing tennis and eating cheese. Cheese currently costs him $4/pound and he has $250 per week to spend. George plays tennis 5 hours per week. Sadly, George lives in a rainy New England town, so he must play tennis on indoor courts. Currently, he pays $11/hour for court rentals.

a) Draw his budget line and an indifference curve showing his current preferred basket.

b) A new club opens and makes George this offer: for a $30/week membership fee, he can play all the tennis he wants by paying only an additional $5/hour for court rental. Draw the budget line for this offer, assuming that George takes the offer.

c) Will George join the new club? Explain.

d) Suppose instead that the membership fee at the new club is $25/week and that George can still rent court time for $5/hour. Will George definitely join the new club, definitely not, or is this uncertain? If he joins, will he play more tennis, less tennis, or is this uncertain?

e) Suppose the membership fee at the new club is $40/week and court time rental rate remains at $5/hour. Will George definitely join the new club, definitely not, or is this uncertain? If he joins, will he play more tennis, less tennis, or is this uncertain?

18. *[Kinked Budget Line] Ken has a job that pays $15 per hour. If he works more than 40 hours in a week, he gets an overtime premium of 50 percent, increasing his wage to

$22.50/hour. He has preferences for a single consumption good and leisure. Assume that he has 80 hours available per week (he spends the other 88 hours sleeping and commuting). Draw his budget line, assuming that the single consumption good costs $6 per unit. Will Ken ever work exactly 40 hours per week? Why or why not?

19. Consider a case where the two goods are food and clothing, and suppose that the MRS is increasing everywhere (i.e., the indifference curves are concave to the origin). What pattern would you expect for consumption of food and clothing?

20. Consider the college trust fund problem discussed in the text (see Example 3.5 and Figure 3.17). Draw the budget lines with and without the trust fund. Now draw a pair of indifference curves such that the student spends less on education if she benefits from the trust fund. Do your indifference curves exhibit a diminishing MRS?

SELF-TEST

21. Which assumption about preferences is violated with the indifference curves in Figure 3.8?
- a) Completeness
- b) Transitivity
- c) Diminishing marginal rate of substitution
- d) All three assumptions
- e) None of these assumptions

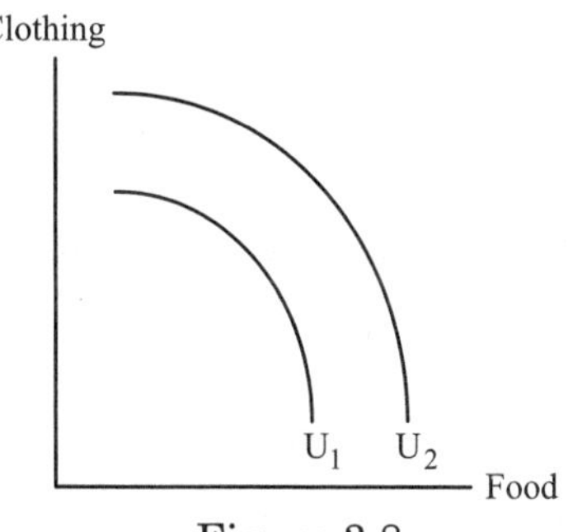

Figure 3.8

22. From the three basic assumptions about preferences, it follows that:
- a) indifference curves cannot cross.
- b) points to the northeast lie on indifference curves with greater satisfaction.
- c) every market basket lies on one indifference curve.
- d) only a) and b) are true.
- e) a), b), and c) are true.

23. Ray cannot tell the difference between Diet Coke and Diet Pepsi. For Ray, these goods are:
- a) perfect substitutes.
- b) perfect complements.
- c) intransitive.
- d) necessities.
- e) None of the above.

24. George Yup insists on drinking his bottled sparkling mineral water with raspberry juice. In addition, he insists that his mix have precisely 1/8 ounce of raspberry juice for every 9 ounces of mineral water. For George, these goods are:

a) perfect substitutes.
b) perfect complements.
c) intransitive.
d) necessities.
e) None of the above.

25. Joe's budget line is 15F + 45C = 900. When Joe chooses his most preferred market basket, he buys 10 units of C. Therefore, he also buys:

a) 10 units of F.
b) 30 units of F.
c) 50 units of F.
d) 60 units of F.
e) None of the above.

26. Kim only buys coffee and compact discs. Coffee costs $0.60 per cup, and CDs cost $12.00 each. She has $18 per week to spend on these two goods. If Kim is maximizing her utility, her marginal rate of substitution of coffee for CDs is:

a) 0.05.
b) 20.
c) 18.
d) 1.50.
e) None of the above.

27. Which assumption about preferences tells us that a consumer's most preferred market basket will lie on the budget line, rather than below the budget line?

a) Completeness
b) Transitivity
c) More is better
d) Diminishing marginal rate of substitution
e) None of these assumptions guarantees this

28. In Figure 3.9, holding income constant, what change must have occurred to rotate the budget line from the old line (1) to the new line (2)?

a) The price of soda fell
b) The price of pizza fell
c) The price of pizza rose
d) The price of soda went up
e) b) and c)

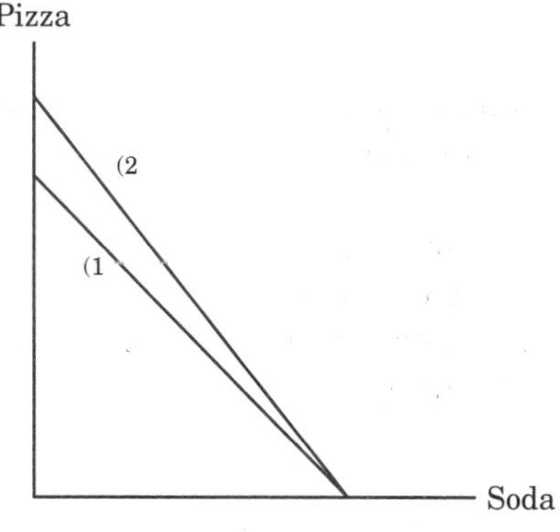

Figure 3.9

29. In Figure 3.10, when the budget line was originally 5F + 10C = 200, Harold purchased 30 units of F and 5 units of C. Budget lines (1) and (2) exist at two later dates. Harold had the same preferences in all three instances. Which market baskets might he have purchased at the later dates?

a) A and B
b) A and D
c) B and E
d) D and E
e) More information is needed

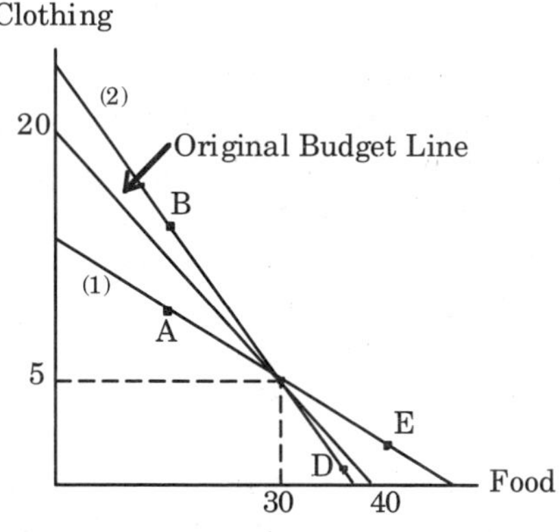

Figure 3.10

30. A wheel of cheddar cheese costs Carl $40 and a night at a Broadway show costs him $100 (including the ticket, parking, etc.). When Carl maximizes his utility, his marginal utility from cheddar cheese is 8 utils. His marginal utility from a Broadway show is therefore:
a) 3.2.
b) 20.
c) 50.
d) 500.
e) None of the above.

31. Lisa likes two different kinds of sandwiches for brown-bag lunches: peanut butter and cream cheese sandwiches, and cream cheese and jelly sandwiches. Which of the following statements is true for Lisa?
a) Peanut butter and jelly are complements
b) Cream cheese and jelly are substitutes
c) Peanut butter and cream cheese are substitutes
d) Peanut butter and jelly are substitutes
e) None of the above is true

32. Sam chooses to spend his entire income on food and buys no clothing. His indifference curves must therefore:
a) be vertical.
b) be horizontal.
c) have a MRS greater than the price ratio where his budget line intersects the food axis.
d) have a MRS less than the price ratio where his budget line intersects the food axis.
e) None of the above is correct.

ANSWERS TO CHAPTER 3

EXERCISE ANSWERS

1. a) From P and Q, William chooses P. Then, from P and R, he chooses P.
b) From Q and R, he chooses Q. Then, from P and Q, he chooses P.
c) Yes, William's preferences are transitive: the order of presentation of the three market baskets does not affect his choice.
d) With these preferences, from P and Q, he chooses P. Then, from P and R, he chooses R. Alternatively, from Q and R, he chooses Q. Then, from P and Q, he chooses P. Here, the order of the choices affects the final market basket because these preferences do not satisfy transitivity.

2. a) See Figure 3A.1a. Since the consumer can't tell the difference between the two flavors, all he would care about is the total amount of jelly he has.
b) See Figure 3A.1b. An increase in the amount of apple jelly doesn't affect the consumer since he never eats it.
c) See Figure 3A.1c. Here, a mixed bundle is better than an extreme one, but the consumer is willing to trade off the different flavors.

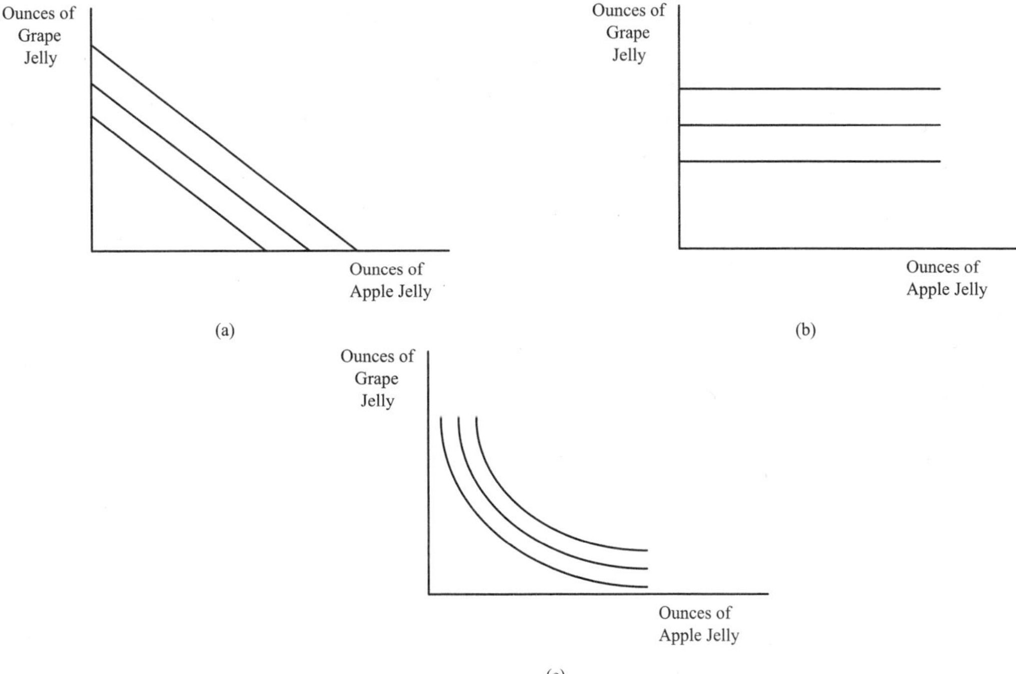

Figure 3A.1

3. a) See Figure 3A.2

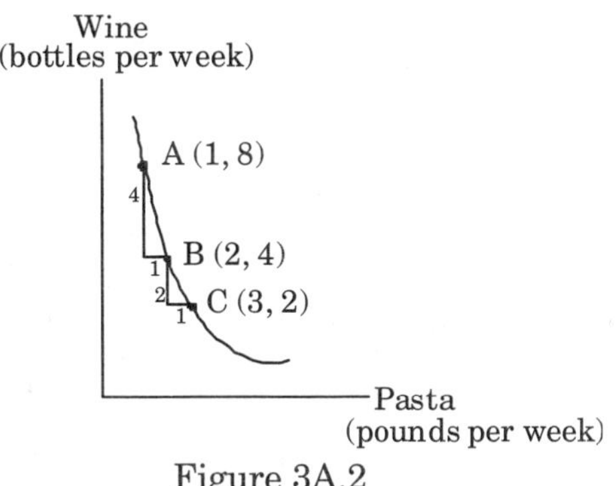

Figure 3A.2

b) $MRS_{A,B} = -(8-4)/(1-2) = 4$; $MRS_{B,C} = -(4-2)/(2-3) = 2$. Yes, this indifference curve satisfies the assumption of diminishing MRS, since MRS is declining as quantity increases along the horizontal axis.

4. a) The two goods are perfect substitutes for the consumer described. See Figure 3A.3a. Notice that the consumer is willing to trade name-brand aspirin for generic aspirin at a constant rate of 1 to 1. Therefore, MRS = 1 along each indifference curve.

b) The two goods are perfect complements. The consumer reaches one level of satisfaction with one pair of gloves and a higher level of satisfaction with two pairs of gloves, but having an unequal number of gloves does not increase utility. See

Figure 3A.3b. MRS = 0 on the horizontal segment of the indifference curve, and on the vertical segment MRS $= \infty$.

c) See Figure 3A.3c. The rock star can reach a higher indifference curve only by having more left gloves. Additional right gloves do nothing to increase or decrease satisfaction (right gloves are a neutral good for this rock star).

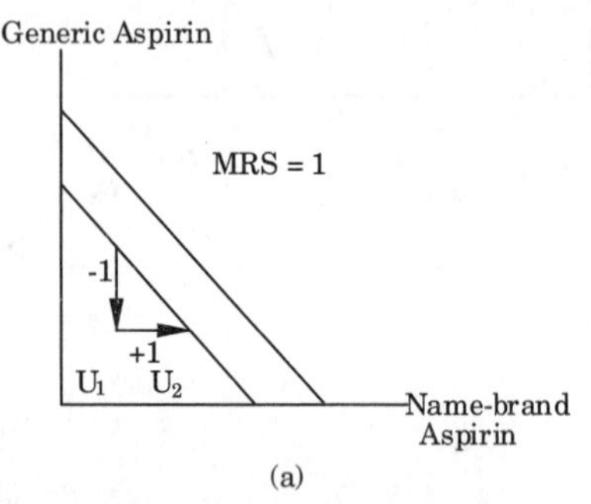

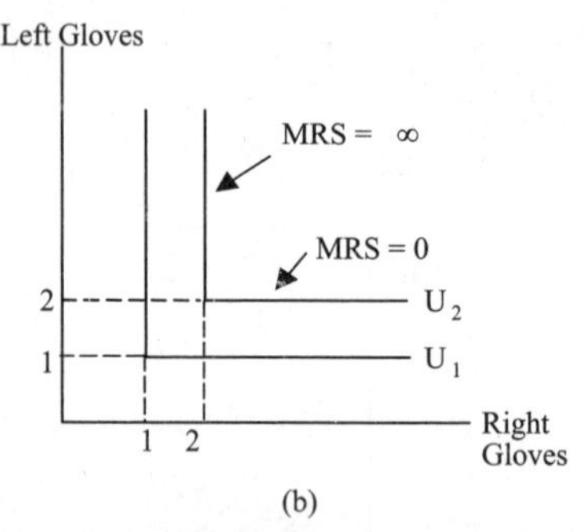

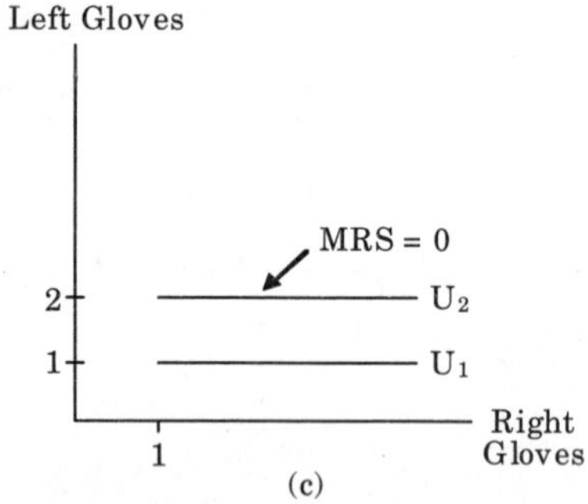

Figure 3A.3

5. Use the equation $C = I/P_C - (P_F/P_C)F$. You can then derive the intercepts and slope as shown in the table below:

Budget Line	Vertical intercept (I/P_C)	Horizontal intercept (I/P_F)	Slope (P_F/P_C)
a)	20	40	1/2
b)	40	80	1/2
c)	40	40	1
d)	20	20	1

Between a) and b), the slope is unchanged, but the budget constraint has moved out. This reflects an income change. Between a) and c), the slope has changed but not the horizontal intercept, so it is a change in the price of good C. Between a) and d), the vertical intercept is unchanged, but the slope has changed, so it is a change in the price of good F.

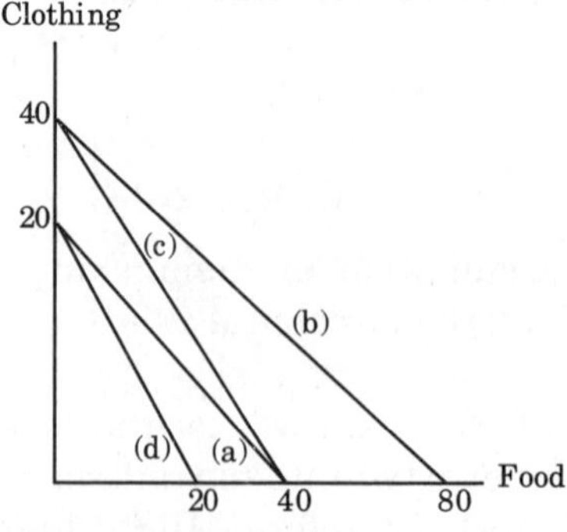

Figure 3A.4

6. a) $MRS > P_F/P_C$: the individual should buy more F and less C (the budget line is flatter than the indifference curve).

b) $MRS < P_F/P_C$: the individual should buy less F and more C (the indifference curve is flatter than the budget line).

c) $MRS = P_F/P_C$: the consumer is at a tangency point.

d) See Figure 3A.5.

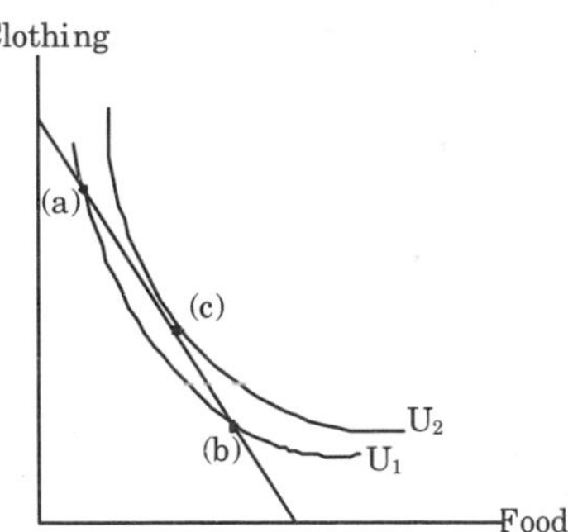

Figure 3A.5

7. See Figure 3A.6. For any budget line, the most preferred market basket must be at the kink point of the indifference curve.

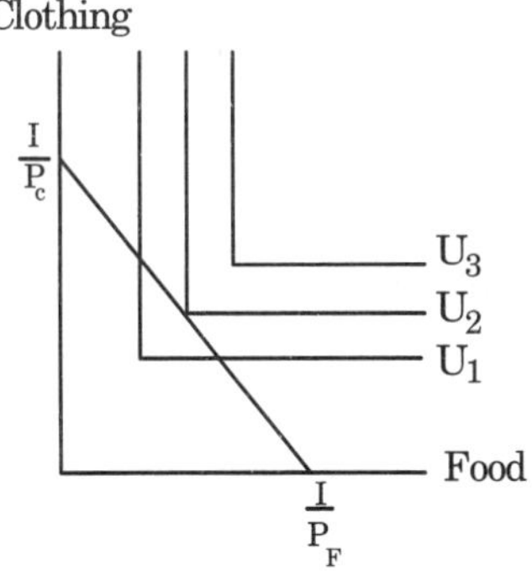

Figure 3A.6

8. See Figure 3A.7. If, as in panel (a), $MRS > P_F/P_C$, the individual will do best to consume only F. If, as in panel (b), $MRS < P_F/P_C$, the individual will do best to consume only C. Panel (c) shows that if $MRS = P_F/P_C$, then any market basket on the budget line is equally good for the consumer.

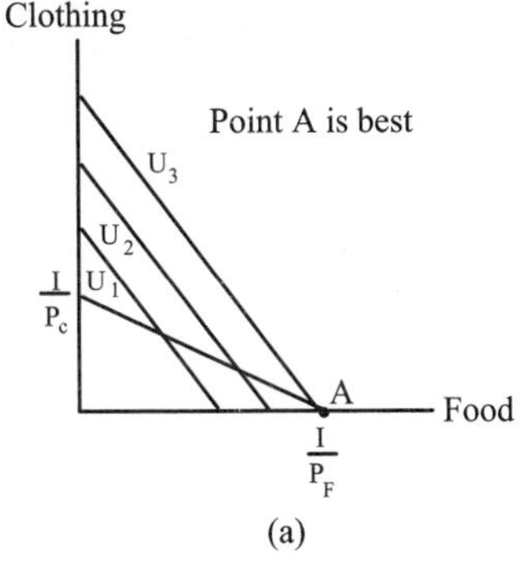

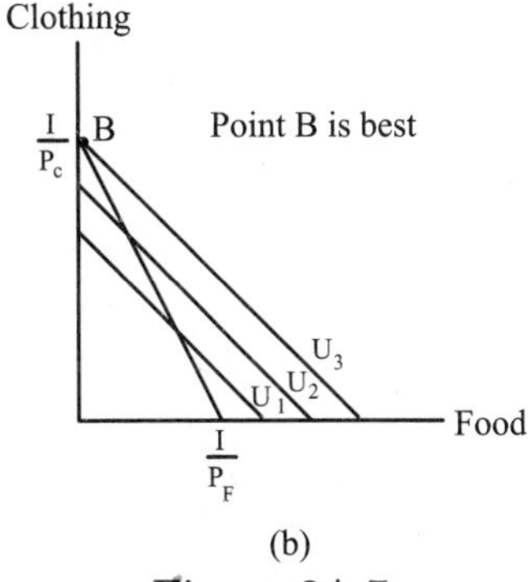

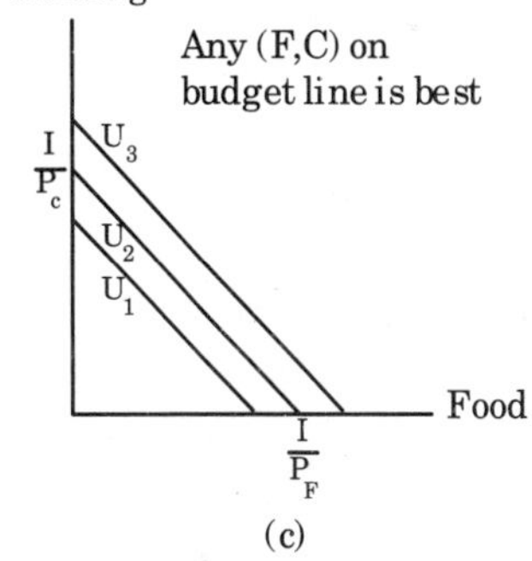

Figure 3A.7

9. a) See Figure 3A.8. The original budget constraint is labeled l_1, and Susan's current market basket is point A. Given that both food and clothing cost \$10, both intercepts of l_1 are 400/10 = 40.

b) The new budget line is l_2. The market basket B (where F = 28, C = 11) costs only \$350 and lies below the original budget line. Since Susan could have bought this market basket before and chose not to, she must be worse off after the change.

c) The final budget line is l_3. The market basket C (where F = 36, C = 24) has more of both goods than the original market basket and clearly lies on a higher indifference curve, so Susan is better off after the price change. This market basket is more expensive than the one purchased originally, but that alone is not enough to establish that the new market basket is preferred, because we don't know the shape of Susan's indifference curves. For example, the market basket labeled D on budget constraint l_3 in Figure 3A.8 (where F = 10 and C = 37) would be more expensive than A, but might lie on the same indifference curve as A, as the dotted line extending U1 suggests.

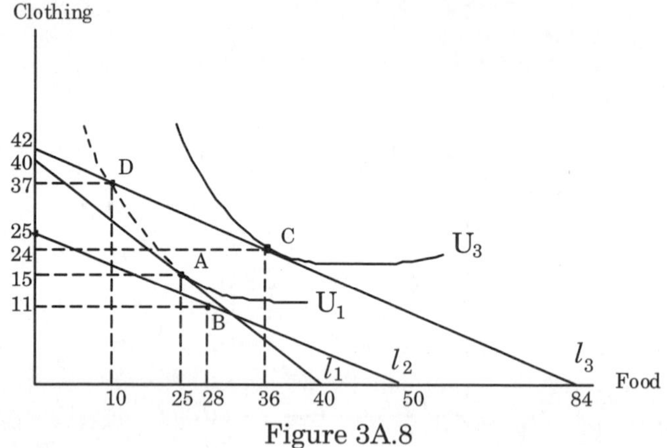

Figure 3A.8

10. a) See Table 3A.1.

b) Yes, 1(10) + 6(20) = \$130 = I, so the budget constraint is satisfied with this market basket. However, this market basket could not be utility maximizing since $(MU_C/P_C) = 6 > (MU_F/P_F) = 4.5$. The consumer can increase utility by spending more money on clothing.

c) The utility maximizing market basket should satisfy the condition that the marginal utility of the last dollar spent on C equals the marginal utility of the last dollar spent on F. From the table, this is true at a market basket of C = 5 and F = 4 (where the ratio of marginal utility to price is 4.7 in both cases). This market basket also satisfies the budget constraint since 5(10) + 4(20) = \$130. Note that at C = 6 and F = 5 we also have $(MU_C/P_C) = (MU_F/P_F) = 4.6$, but this market basket is too expensive, i.e., 6(10) + 5(20) = \$160.

Clothing	MU_C	MU_C/P_C	Food	MU_F	MU_F/P_F
1	60	6.00	1	115	5.75
2	55	5.50	2	105	5.25
3	51	5.10	3	98	4.90
4	48	4.80	4	94	4.70
5	47	4.70	5	92	4.60
6	46	4.60	6	90	4.50

Table 3A.1

11. a) $LI = \frac{20(30) + 5(600)}{30(30) + 4(600)} = \frac{3600}{3300} = 1.09$

b) $PI = \frac{20(40) + 5(550)}{30(40) + 4(550)} = \frac{3550}{3400} = 1.04$

c) Susan's 2000 market basket is less expensive at 2000 prices than her 2010 market basker; her 2010 market basket is also less expensive at 2010 prices than her 2000 market basket. Hence, in 2000 she could not buy her 2010 market basket, and in 2010 she could not buy her 2000 market basket. We cannot determine in which year she is better off.

PROBLEM SET ANSWERS

12. The first budget line is \$0.1T + \$0.3S = \$4.80 since \$4.80 is the cost of 30 ounces of tortilla chips and 6 sodas. The second budget line is \$0.25T + \$0.75S = \$11.25, since \$11.25 is the cost of 36 ounces of tortilla chips and 3 sodas. These budget lines are graphed in Figure 3A.9. Note that the price ratio (P_T/P_S) is 1/3 in both cases, so these lines are parallel. Since he cannot afford to buy the first market basket with the second budget line, no inconsistency is revealed. He is clearly better off in the first week.

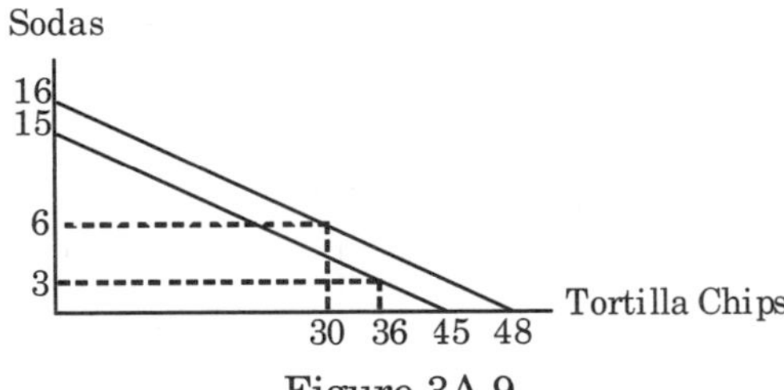

Figure 3A.9

13. With these preferences, more is better, transitivity, and diminishing MRS are inconsistent assumptions. See Figure 3A.10. If basket *1* is preferred to basket *2*, and basket *3* is preferred to basket *1*, the indifference curves must cross if they have the usual shape.

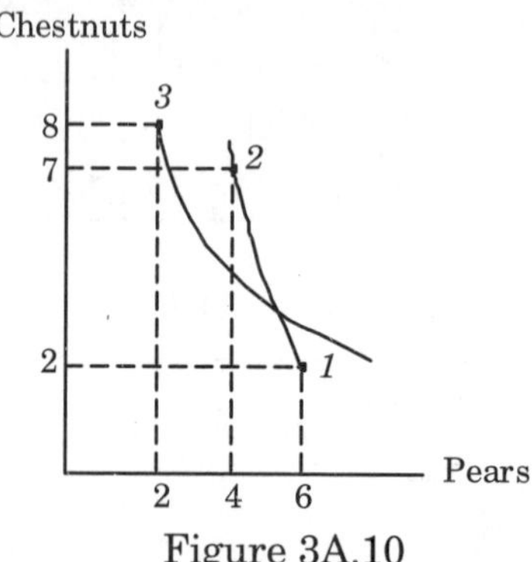

Figure 3A.10

14. a) See Figure 3A.11a. The original budget line is labeled L_0. (Given the information in the problem, we know her total income for food and gas is \$100.) Under the rationing policy, Joan's budget line is L_1, which is the same as her original one, except that it stops at 40 gallons per week. This can be shown graphically by drawing the budget line as vertical at 40. Thus, if she buys 40 gallons of gas she will have \$60 to spend on food. The effect of policy (2) is to rotate the budget line inward to L_2 (the maximum amount of gas she can now purchase is 100/1.25 = 80).

b) With the price increase, if she chooses to buy 40 gallons, she only has \$50 left over to buy food. Since more is better, 40 gallons and \$60 of food are better than 40 gallons and \$50 of food. Hence, Joan prefers the rationing policy. This is shown in Figure 3A.11a by the fact that Joan can reach a higher indifference curve (U_2) under the rationing policy.

c) In this case, Joan would probably prefer *not* to have her gasoline consumption rationed at 40. See Figure 3A.11b for an example.

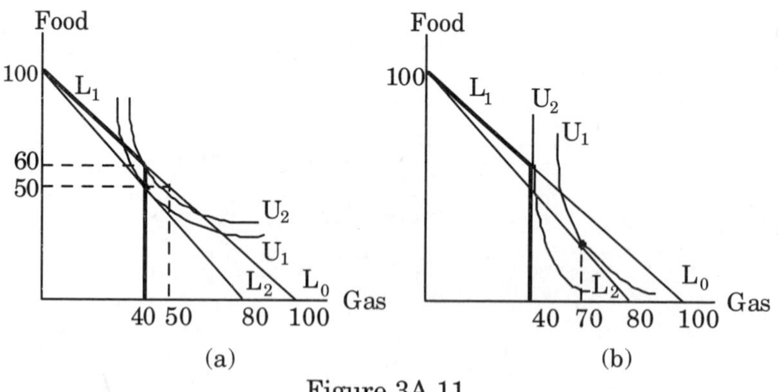

Figure 3A.11

15. Figure 3A.12 displays Karen's indifference curves. The budget line (in bold) is 5F + 10C = 100. Since her MRS is 3/2 and the price ratio is 1/2, Karen will reach the highest indifference curve by buying only food (point A).

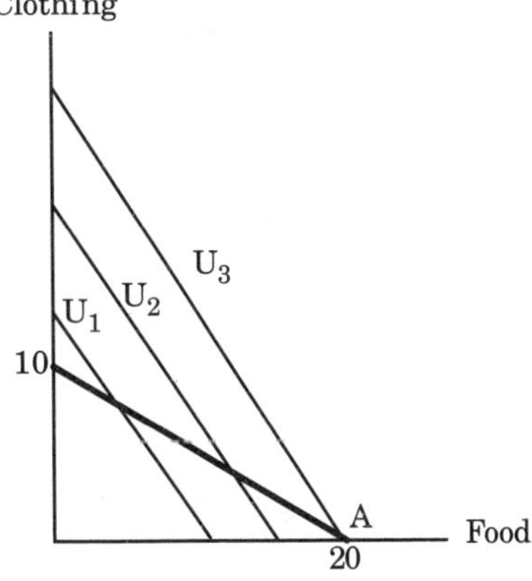

Figure 3A.12

16. a) Figure 3A.13 displays Arthur's indifference curves. Since he will not consume except in the ratio of one pint of iced tea and two teaspoons of sugar, the indifference curves have right angles at that ratio.

b) Given Arthur's preference to consume one pint of iced tea with every two teaspoons of sugar, Arthur's best market basket will always be one with S = 2T. With a budget line 0.05S + 0.15T = 4.0, we can solve for T: 0.05(2T) + 0.15T = 4 or 0.25T = 4, so $T^*=16$. S* then equals 32. We can verify this by plugging our solution back into the budget line: 0.05(32) + 0.15(16) = 4.

c) If $P_S = 0.10$ and $P_T = 0.05$, the budget line is 0.10S + 0.05T = 4. With S = 2T, we find $0.10(2T)+0.05T=4.0$ or $0.25\,T=4$, so $T^*=16$. Again, $S^*=32$. To check, $0.10(32)+0.05(16)=4$. The two budget lines happen to both go through the same "kink" in the indifference curve.

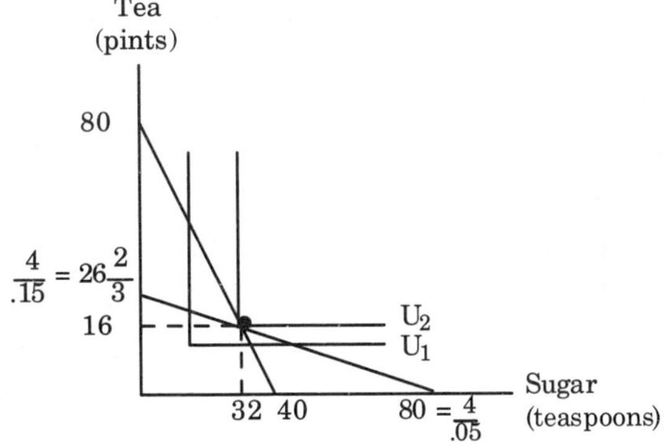

Figure 3A.13

17. a) See Figure 3A.14. George spends \$55 on tennis and therefore has $250 - 55 = \$195$ left over for cheese. Thus, he buys $\$195/4 = 48.75$ pounds of cheese.

b) See Figure 3A.14. The \$30 membership fee comes directly out of George's income before he consumes any cheese or tennis. Thus, his income falls from \$250 to \$220. The new budget line is B1.

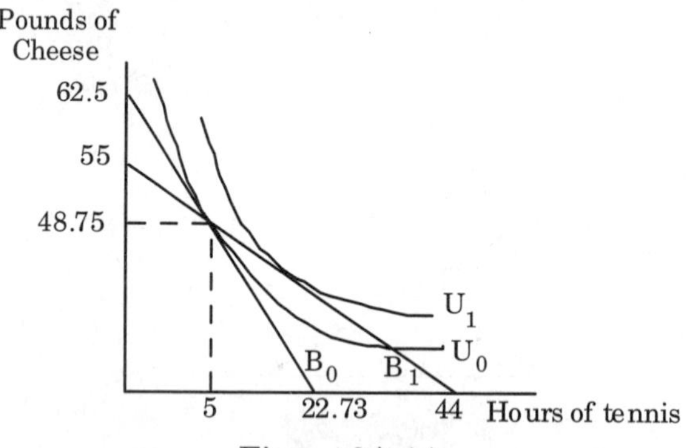

Figure 3A.14

c) Yes, George will be better off to take the new club's offer, so that he can reach a higher indifference curve (U_1), which is tangent to his new budget line, B_1.

d) In this case, his budget line lies above his original market basket of (5, 48.75). Now he can join the club and consume more tennis, more cheese, or both. So we can say for certain that he will join. We cannot establish for certain whether he will consume more tennis.

e) In this case, his budget line lies below his original market basket of (5, 48.75). The only points on the new budget line which lie above the old budget line are ones with more tennis and less cheese. Without knowing George's precise indifference curves, we cannot tell whether he is better or worse off on the new budget line. However, if he joins the club, he will certainly play more than 5 hours of tennis.

18. The two goods are leisure and consumption. Assume Ken's consumption will equal his earnings. *Maximum* earnings are $I = 15(40) + 22.5(40) = 1500$. The equation for the budget line depends on whether Ken is working overtime. Let H = hours worked, L = leisure hours, and C = consumption. Then, if $H < 40$, the budget line will be $15(L - 40) + 6C = 600$, and if $H > 40$, the price of leisure is \$22.50, so the budget line becomes $22.50L + 6C = 1500$.

Figure 3A.15 (on the next page) presents the budget line. The slope is $P_L/P_C = 15/6 = 2.5$ if $H < 40$ and it is $22.5/6 = 3.75$ if $H > 40$. Because it kinks at exactly $H = 40$, either Ken wants to work less than 40 hours or more than 40 hours, depending on the shape of his indifference curves. He would never want to work exactly 40 hours with smooth indifference curves.

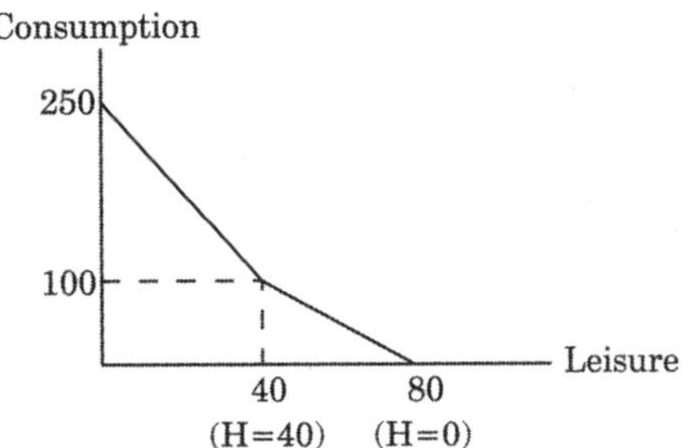

Figure 3A.15

19. If the MRS is always increasing, the consumer will always consume at a corner—the tangency point where the MRS equals the price ratio is the *least* preferred market basket on the budget line. See Figure 3A.16.

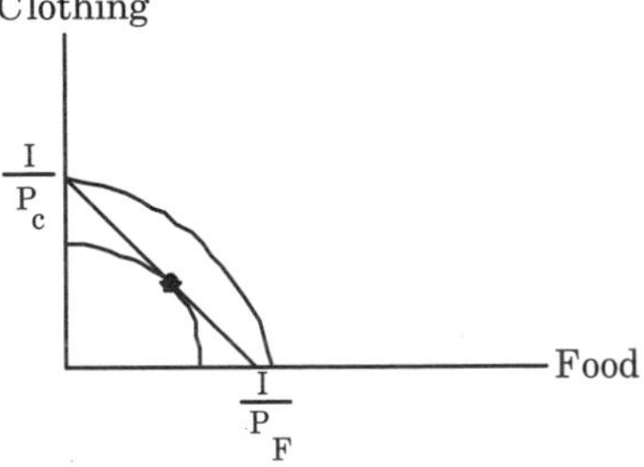

Figure 3A.16

20. See Figure 3A17. As long as E_0 (the amount spent on education without a trust fund) exceeds the amount of the trust fund, we can draw indifference curves such that the consumer is at a corner solution with the trust fund. Clearly, both curves exhibit a diminishing MRS. The small amount of the trust fund may not force the student to increase her spending on education. Only if the trust fund is larger than E_0, must E_1 exceed E_0.

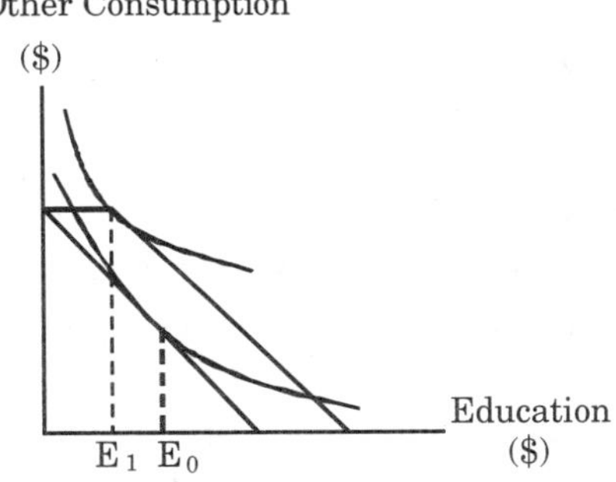

Figure 3A.17

SELF-TEST ANSWERS

21. c) The indifference curves in Figure 3.8 are concave rather than convex. Concave indifference curves have an increasing MRS. A diminishing MRS means that indifference curves get flatter as the quantity on the horizontal axis increases.

22. e) All of the statements are true, given the basic assumptions about consumer behavior.

23. a) Ray would always be willing to trade one Coke for one Pepsi. In other words, he prefers the two goods equally. This means that the two goods are perfect substitutes and the indifference curves are straight lines (the MRS is a constant).

24. b) George must consume raspberry juice and mineral water *together* in just the right proportion. This implies that George's indifference curves are L-shaped.

25. b) We assume that Joe will spend all his income. If C = 10, then 15F = 900 – 45(10) = 450, so F = 450/15 = 30.

26. a) At Kim's most preferred market basket, her MRS equals the price ratio (P_{Coffee}/P_{CD}), which equals 0.60/12 or 0.05.

27. c) Completeness, transitivity, and diminishing MRS describe the shape of indifference curves and their relation to each other. The assumption "more is better" insures that the consumer will continue spending all her income in order to consume more goods (i.e., reach a point *on* the budget line).

28. b) The horizontal intercept, I/P_S, is unchanged, which implies that P_S could not have changed (holding income constant). Since the slope is P_P/P_S, the slope change means that the price of pizza must have fallen. This can also be seen intuitively from Figure 3.9, since the consumer can now buy more pizza than before if he spends all his income on pizza.

29. c) The market basket (30, 5) has been revealed to be preferred to market baskets A and D. These market baskets were within the original budget constraint, but were not chosen. Only B and E would be consistent choices.

30. b) At the utility maximizing point $MU_C/MU_B = P_C/P_B$, where C = cheese and B = Broadway show. Therefore, $8/MU_B = 40/100$ implies $MU_B = 20$.

31. d) Since Lisa is willing to trade peanut butter for jelly in her sandwiches, they are substitutes. In contrast, cream cheese and peanut butter are complements for Lisa (she consumes them together), as are cream cheese and jelly.

32. c) For a corner solution, it is only necessary that the MRS exceed the price ratio.

CHAPTER 4
INDIVIDUAL AND MARKET DEMAND

IMPORTANT CONCEPTS

- Price Consumption Curve
- Income Consumption Curve
- Engel Curve
- Normal and Inferior Goods
- Income and Substitution Effects of a Price Change
- Giffen Good
- Price Elasticity of Demand
  - Point Elasticity
  - Arc Elasticity
- Consumer Surplus
- Network Externalities
  - Bandwagon Effect
  - Snob Effect

CHAPTER HIGHLIGHTS

Using the knowledge of budget constraints and indifference curves that we have built thus far, we can analyze how changes in price and income affect consumer choice. First, consider changes in the price of one good, holding income and all other prices constant. As the price changes, the utility-maximizing market basket will change. From this relationship between changes in the price of one good and demand for that good, we can derive both the *price-consumption curve* (with quantities of two goods on the axes) and the *demand curve* (with quantity on one axis and price on the other). Second, consider changes in income, holding all prices constant. As income changes, the utility-maximizing market basket will again change. We can then derive both the *income-consumption curve* (with quantities of two goods on the axes) and the *Engel curve* (with quantity on one axis and income on the other). If consumption increases as income increases, then we describe the good as *normal*. If consumption decreases as income increases, the good is *inferior*.

A change in the price of a good actually has two effects. First, real purchasing power changes. Second, relative prices change. The *substitution effect* of a price change isolates the effect of the change in relative prices, holding utility constant. The *income effect* of a price change isolates the effect of the change in real purchasing power or real income, holding relative prices constant. The *total effect* of a price change is the sum of the substitution and income effects.

If a good is normal, the substitution and income effects will work in the same direction and the demand curve for that good will slope down. If a good is inferior, the demand curve for that good will still slope down, as long as the substitution effect outweighs the income effect (which goes in the opposite direction from the substitution effect in this case). Only if the good is inferior and the income effect outweighs the substitution effect will the demand curve for that good slope upward. In this case, the good is called a *Giffen good*.

This chapter reviews the *price elasticity of demand*, which is the percentage change in quantity demanded resulting from a percentage change in price. We distinguish between a *point elasticity*, which is measured at one point on the demand curve, and an *arc elasticity*, which measures the elasticity between two points on a demand curve.

Working with indifference curves and budget lines allows us to see directly whether a consumer is better or worse off as the result of a price change or income change. *Consumer surplus* measures consumer welfare directly from the demand curve. Consumer surplus equals the difference between the maximum amount that consumers are willing to pay for a given quantity demanded and the amount that they actually pay when buying that quantity. An increase in consumer surplus implies that consumers are better off.

A *network externality* exists if one person's demand for a good depends on the demands of other people. Two types of network externalities are discussed: the *bandwagon effect* arises when an individual's demand for a good grows in response to purchases by other individuals, while the *snob effect* arises when an individual's demand falls in response to purchases by other individuals. The bandwagon effect makes the demand curve more elastic. The snob effect makes the demand curve less elastic.

CONCEPT REVIEW AND EXERCISES

INDIVIDUAL DEMAND (Section 4.1)

PRICE CHANGES

Economists rarely use the model of consumer behavior to explain exactly what a consumer will buy. More commonly, the model of consumer behavior is used to explain how consumers respond to changes in their set of consumption possibilities. For example, consider the consumer with the indifference curves given in Figure 4.1. The two goods are food and clothing, where P_F = \$2, P_C = \$10, and I = \$100. As the price of food decreases from \$2 to \$1, the budget line will rotate, keeping the same vertical intercept. For any level of clothing consumption, more food can be purchased than before. Clearly, the individual will be better off because new opportunities are now available (and all previous opportunities remain available). The consumer will move to a new utility-maximizing market basket. As drawn in Figure 4.1 (on the next page), the consumer now consumes more food and less clothing.

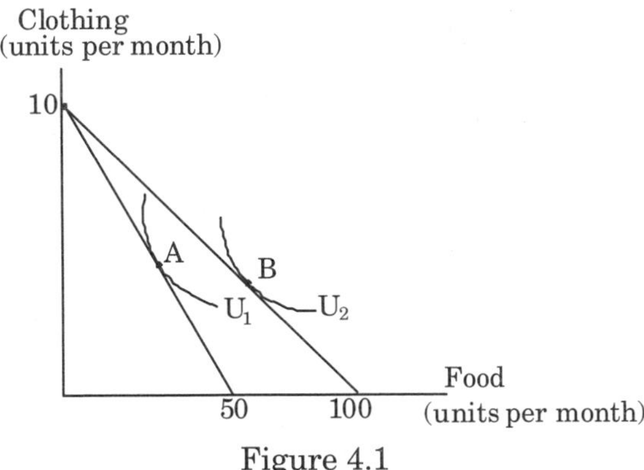

Figure 4.1

Exercise:

1. In Figure 4.1 if the price of food rises, does consumption of food necessarily rise or fall? Does consumption of clothing necessarily rise or fall?

Now suppose that the price of food is set at a variety of levels, while the price of clothing and income are held constant. The consumer will choose a new preferred market basket for each price of food. The locus of all these points that maximize the consumer's satisfaction is the *price-consumption curve*, which is drawn in Figure 4.2. The price-consumption curve is the line connecting the tangencies between the indifference curves and the budget lines with a varying price of food.

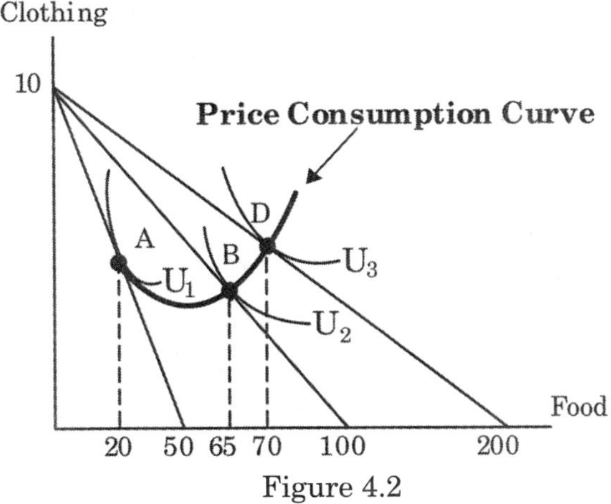

Figure 4.2

Although the price consumption curve shows how food consumption changes as the price of food changes, it is awkward to use because the price of food can only be seen implicitly by looking at the slope of the budget line. A *demand curve* for food explicitly graphs the price of food against the consumption of food.

To move from the price consumption curve to the demand curve, we plot P_F, the price of food, and F, the quantity of food, for each market basket. (Recall that P_C and I are being held constant.) Each budget line in Figure 4.2 has a value for P_F associated with it. The demand curve shows the amount of food the consumer would like to purchase at each price of food, as in Figure 4.3 . If P_C or I were to change, we would derive a different demand curve, lying to the right or left of the original demand curve.

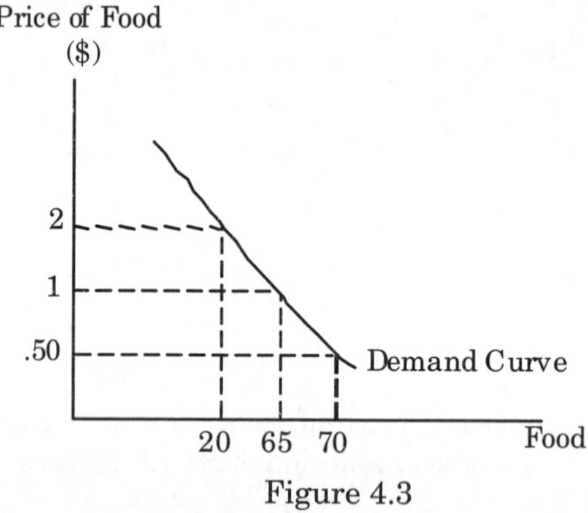

Figure 4.3

INCOME CHANGES

A change in the consumer's income causes a parallel shift in the budget line. The most preferred market basket after an income change is the tangency between an indifference curve and the new budget line. The locus of all points of tangency that maximize the consumer's satisfaction for changing income levels is the *income-consumption curve*. An example of an income consumption curve is shown in Figure 4.4, where P_F = \$10, P_C = \$10, and I = \$100, \$200, and \$300. Like the price-consumption curve, the income-consumption curve is drawn with the quantities of food and clothing on each axis. We can also draw the *Engel curve*, which relates the consumption of one good directly to the consumer's income. Typically, the vertical axis is the income level and the horizontal axis is the consumption level, as in Figure 4.5. Both the Engel curve and the income-consumption curve are drawn on the assumption that prices are fixed. The Engel curve will shift if the price of either good changes.

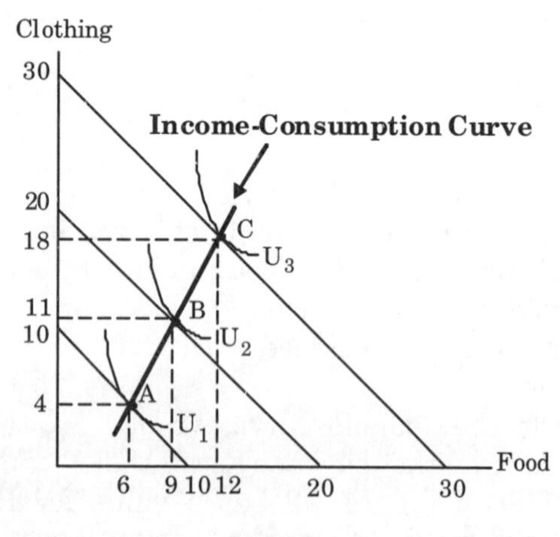

Figure 4.4

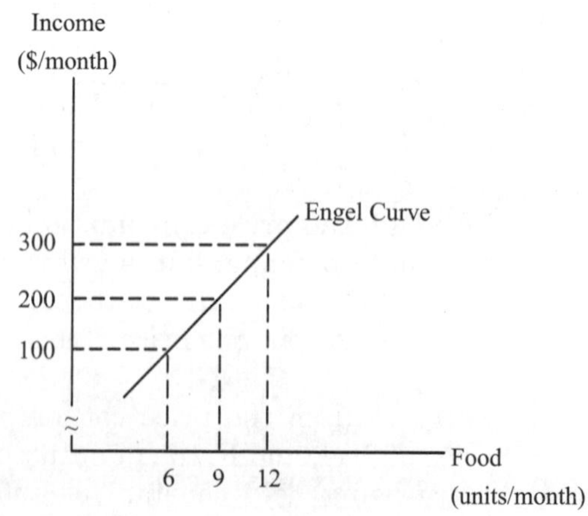

Figure 4.5

If income increases, the consumer may buy either more or less of a good. When consumption rises with income, we call that good a *normal good* (air travel, for example). If consumption falls when income rises, we call that good an *inferior good* (travel by bus, for example). A good is normal if the Engel curve slopes upward, and it is inferior if the Engel curve slopes downward. A good may be inferior over some income ranges, but normal over others, so it is important to define the income range in which a good is normal or inferior.

Exercise:

2. a) Is the slope of the income-consumption curve positive or negative if both food and clothing are normal goods?

b) Is the slope of the income-consumption curve positive or negative if food is normal and clothing is inferior?

c) With only two goods, can both goods be inferior in the same range? Why or why not?

INCOME AND SUBSTITUTION EFFECTS (Section 4.2)

This section looks at how the demand of one good is affected by changes in prices of other goods. In Figure 4.6, when the price of food equals P_F^1, the consumer is initially consuming at point A. Suppose the price of food *decreases* to P_F^2. When the price of a good decreases, two changes occur. We call these two changes the *income effect* and the *substitution effect* of a price change. The first implication of a decline in P_F is that the consumer's budget line lies farther out since the consumer's real income or purchasing power has gone up. Second, the slope of the budget line becomes flatter. That is, the endpoint of the budget line along the horizontal axis moves out. (Recall that the endpoint is expressed mathematically as I/P_F, so as P_F falls the endpoint must move out.) The first change makes the consumer better off because market baskets with more of both goods are now available.

The second change means that the relative market prices have changed so that the consumer's MRS will now be different at the most preferred market basket.

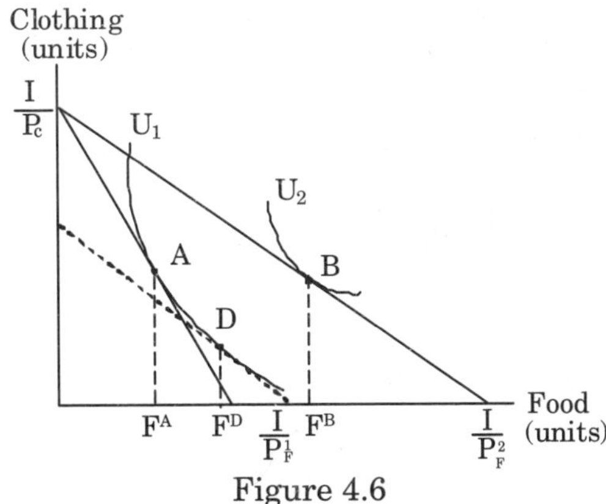

Figure 4.6

To analyze the response to a price change, we can look at these two effects separately. The substitution effect is the change in the consumption of food that would occur if *both* income and the price of food changed in just the right way so that the consumer's most preferred market basket would still lie on her *original* indifference curve. The substitution effect is found by drawing a hypothetical budget line parallel to the *new* budget line (the one with a lower price of food in this case), but just tangent to the *original* indifference curve. In Figure 4.6 the change in food consumption from point A to point D, or $F^D - F^A$, is the substitution effect of a decrease in the price of food. The substitution effect is always in the direction opposite to the price change. *Holding utility constant*, an increase in price will cause a decrease in consumption and vice versa. If P_F falls, F rises along the indifference curve. If P_F rises, F falls along the indifference curve.

We know that the consumer cannot actually stay at point D, given that we *hypothetically* altered income to balance out the price change in order to show a pure substitution effect, holding utility constant. The income effect shows how consumption changes when income is changed from this hypothetical level to its real, final level. The income effect is the change in the consumption of food that would occur if income changed from the hypothetical level at point D in Figure 4.6 to the income level corresponding to the true budget line after the price change: This is market basket B in Figure 4.6. The income effect is therefore $F^B - F^D$. The income effect of a price decrease is positive for a normal good and negative for an inferior good.

By putting these two effects together we can derive the *total effect* of a price change. Three types of goods are defined according to the total effect of a price change and the accompanying income effects, and they are *normal*, *inferior*, and *Giffen*.

CONSUMPTION EFFECTS WHEN P_F FALLS

Substitution Effect	Income Effect	Total Effect	Type of Good	Slope of Demand Curve
F rises	F rises	F rises	normal	down
F rises	F falls	F rises	inferior	down
F rises	F falls	F falls	Giffen	up

Consumption of a normal good always increases when its price falls and decreases when its price rises. *The demand curve for a normal good always slopes downward.*

For an inferior good, the total effect depends on the magnitudes of the income and substitution effects. The total effect of a price decrease can still be an increase in demand if the good is inferior, as long as the income effect is less than the substitution effect. However, when the income effect for an inferior good outweighs the substitution effect, the good is called a Giffen good. Since the quantity demanded rises when the price rises, the demand curve slopes upward for a Giffen good.

Exercise: ▶ ▶ ▶ ▶ ▶ ▶ ▶

3. a) Consider the effect of a sales tax of 10 percent on good X, when X and Y are the only two goods in the economy. Start at an initial utility maximizing point and graph the substitution and income effects of the change in the price of X. Assume X and Y are normal goods.

b) Now suppose that a sales tax of 10 percent is imposed on X and at the same time an income-tax rebate is given to the consumer in just the right amount so that she could continue consuming her original market basket if she wanted to. Graph the effect of the combined sales tax and income tax rebate on the budget line and the consumer's utility maximizing choice. Is the difference between the original and the new market basket the same as the income effect in part a)? Why or why not?

MARKET DEMAND (Section 4.3)

The *market demand curve* for a good is simply the horizontal summation of the individual demand curves. The summation is horizontal to reflect the fact that we add together the quantity demanded by each consumer in the market for each given price in order to find the market demand at each price.

Exercise: ▶ ▶ ▶ ▶ ▶ ▶ ▶

4. Abbott's demand curve for pineapples is: $Q_A = 15 - 5P$, where Q_A is the quantity consumed by Abbott and P is the price. Costello's demand curve for pineapples is $Q_C = 20 - 2P$, where Q_C is the quantity consumed by Costello. Suppose these are the only two consumers of pineapples in the market. Graph the two individual demand curves on two separate diagrams and then graphically derive the market demand curve.

ELASTICITY OF DEMAND

Chapter 2 introduced the *price elasticity of demand*, $E_P = \%\Delta Q/\%\Delta P$. The elasticity of demand can provide us with information about how total revenue changes when price changes. If demand is *elastic*, total revenue increases when price falls. In this case, demand is very sensitive to price changes. Total revenue rises as price falls because enough new customers are attracted by the lower price so that they more than make up for the lost revenue resulting from lowering the price per unit sold. If demand is *inelastic*, total revenue falls when price falls. Consumers are very insensitive to price when demand is inelastic. A decrease in price decreases revenue because relatively few new customers are attracted to the market by the lower price. In the special case where demand is *unit elastic*, a decrease in price attracts just enough new customers so that total revenue is unchanged.

Exercise: ▶ ▶ ▶ ▶ ▶ ▶ ▶

5. On April 29, 1991, the *Wall Street Journal* reported on the effects of a new luxury goods tax, enacted at the beginning of the year. The 10-percent luxury tax operated like an excise tax on amounts paid for luxury items over

$30,000. For example, buyers of a $50,000 Mercedes-Benz would pay an additional $2,000. Between January and April of 1991, Mercedes-Benz sales dropped 27 percent, compared to the same period in 1990.

a) Estimate the price elasticity of demand for Mercedes-Benz cars at a price of $50,000. Assume the luxury tax was the only change in the market between 1990 and 1991.

b) Will total expenditures (revenue) earned by Mercedes-Benz rise, fall, or stay the same as a result of the tax?

6. Draw a linear demand curve. Recall that demand is elastic on the upper portion of the demand curve, unit elastic at the midpoint of the demand curve, and inelastic on the lower portion of the demand curve. Draw a price and corresponding quantity at the midpoint on your demand curve. Shade in the area of total revenue. Show how this area changes in size as you double the price or cut the price in half.

When economists talk about the elasticity of demand, they are usually referring to the *point elasticity*. A point elasticity will change as you change the base P and Q that you use to calculate the percentage changes. The *arc elasticity* provides an alternative measure: it measures the elasticity *between* two points. For the change in price from P_1 to P_2, the arc elasticity equals:

$$E_P = \frac{(Q_2 - Q_1)/[(Q_1 + Q_2)/2]}{(P_2 - P_1)/[(P_1 + P_2)/2]} = \frac{\Delta Q}{\Delta P}\frac{\overline{P}}{\overline{Q}}$$

The arc elasticity uses the average of the old and new prices $P = (P_1 + P_2)/2$ and quantities $Q = (Q_1 + Q_2)/2$ to calculate the elasticity. The arc elasticity has the property that it is the same for a price increase from P_1 to P_2 as it is for a price decrease from P_2 to P_1. For small price changes, the arc elasticity and point elasticity will be roughly the same. For large changes, it is often better to use the arc elasticity.

Exercise: ▶ ▶ ▶ ▶ ▶ ▶ ▶

7. Consider the demand curve $Q_D = 2{,}000 - 40P$. If $P = \$10$, calculate the point elasticity of demand. If $P = \$30$, calculate the point elasticity of demand. What is the arc elasticity for a price increase from $10 to $30? Verify that the arc elasticity for a price decrease from $30 to $10 is the same.

CONSUMER SURPLUS (Section 4.4)

Figure 4.7 presents the Smith family's demand curve (their willingness to pay function) for tennis court time per week. If court time costs $15/hour, they will only rent a court for one hour. At $12/hour, they will rent two hours of court time. If court rentals are $1/hour or less, they will rent five hours of court time per week.

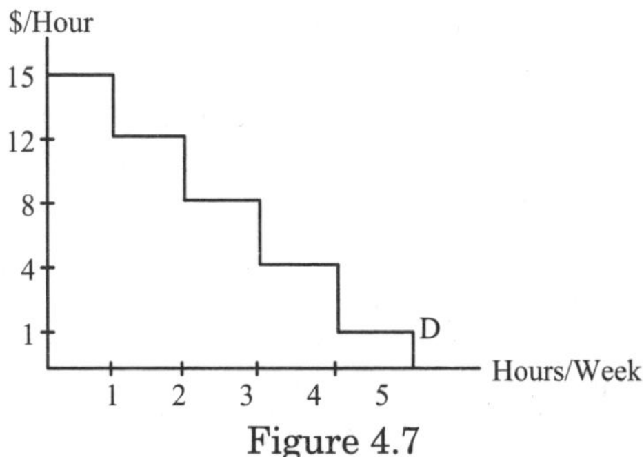

Figure 4.7

Suppose the local tennis court charges $10/hour. The Smith family will rent two hours and pay $20. But, if this is the only tennis court on which the Smiths can play, what is the maximum they would be willing to pay for two hours per week of court time? From their demand curve we see that they are willing to pay $15 for the first hour and $12 for the second hour, so they would be willing to pay a maximum of $27 for the two hours.

Since their actual payment of $20 is $7 ($27 – $20) less than the *maximum* they are willing to pay, they have $7 left to buy other goods. We refer to this difference between the maximum amount the consumer is willing to pay and the amount actually paid for a good as *consumer surplus*. We can calculate consumer surplus as the difference between the consumer's reservation price and the price actually paid and add this up for each unit purchased. In this case, from the first hour, they gain $15 – $10 = $5, and from the second hour they gain $12 – $10 = $2, for a total of $7 in consumer surplus.

Exercise: ◗ ◗ ◗ ◗ ◗ ◗ ◗

8. The Andersons have the following demand for tennis court time:

P ($/hour)	Q (hours/week)
24	1
17	2
8	3
2	4
0	4

a) What is the maximum that they are willing to pay for one hour/week; 2 hours/week; 3 hours/week; 4 hours/week?

b) What is their consumer surplus if the market price is $20; $15; and $7?

c) The tennis court management company is thinking of letting members play as much tennis as they wish for a flat weekly fee with no hourly rental. What is the maximum weekly fee the Andersons would be willing to pay?

Suppose for simplicity we smooth out the demand curve in Figure 4.7 to a straight line, such as the demand curve for food shown in Figure 4.8. (The underlying assumption behind a smoothed demand curve is that the consumer can buy fractions of units of the good.) In Figure 4.8, the consumer will buy 15 units of F when P_F = $30. Since the consumer is willing to buy a positive amount of good F at prices above $30, she must value the first 15 units of the good at more than $30 per unit. The amount she is willing to pay for a given quantity of good F is the entire area under the demand curve between the vertical axis and the quantity consumed. The amount actually paid is just price times quantity, which is a rectangle. Consumer surplus, the difference between these two amounts, equals the area of the triangle bordered by the vertical axis, the demand curve, and the market price. Since the area of a triangle is 1/2(base)(height), consumer surplus at P = $30 equals (1/2)(15)($50) = $375. In order to calculate or draw consumer surplus at a given price, you must first figure out what quantity will be demanded at that price.

Consumer surplus is the area above the market price and below the demand curve, but only up to the quantity demanded at that price.

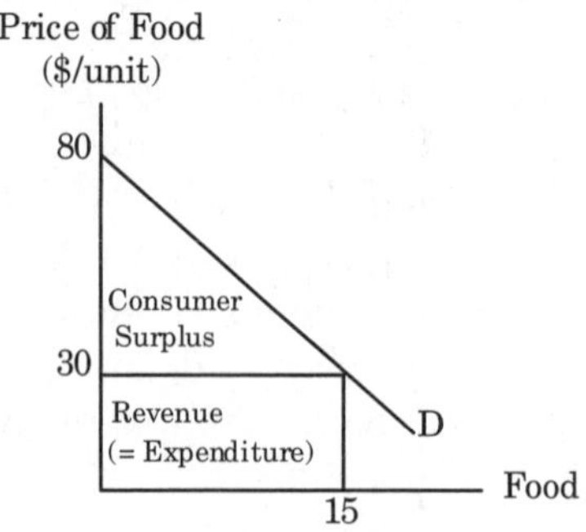

Figure 4.8

Exercise:

9. A phone company is currently charging 20 cents per minute for long-distance calls anywhere in the United States, under its new "Anywhere Plan." It has learned that consumers who use this plan are of two types. Type A consumers have the demand curve $Q = 40 - 0.5P$ and Type B consumers have the demand curve $Q = 120 - P$, where Q is the number of minutes of long-distance calls per month and P is measured in cents per minute. There are an equal number of Type A and Type B consumers.

a) Draw each demand curve. Calculate consumer surplus for Type A consumers and for Type B consumers, and total revenue for the phone company.

b) The phone company is thinking about charging $10 per month in addition to the current charge of 20 cents per minute. Would revenues increase or decrease? Why?

NETWORK EXTERNALITIES (Section 4.5)

Consumer demands are likely to vary with respect to more than just price and income. In fact, in some cases the choices of other consumers can affect our demand for a good. The *bandwagon effect* is present when an increase in other people's consumption of a good causes a consumer's demand curve to shift to the right. For example, when one child has the hottest toy of the year, then all the children in the neighborhood want that toy, too. A price decrease causes each consumer to buy more, even if other consumers buy the same amount, and each consumer's demand curve shifts to the right because other consumers are buying a greater quantity. Thus, compared to the demand curve that holds fixed the consumption of others, a market demand curve with a bandwagon effect will be flatter.

The *snob effect* is present when an increase in others' consumption of a good causes a consumer's demand curve to shift to the left. If everyone had a Cadillac car, the elite would find it less appealing to own a Cadillac. Compared to the demand curve holding fixed others' consumption, a market demand curve with a snob effect will be steeper.

Exercise:

10. There are reasons other than fads, fashions, and consumer insecurity for bandwagon and snob effects. Various types of externalities in the consumption of certain goods also exist. Explain which of these effects (bandwagon or snob) might be present in the following cases:

a) A restaurant that is often crowded
b) A personal computer software product
c) A rock concert

*EMPIRICAL ESTIMATION OF DEMAND (Section 4.6)

Statistical estimation of demand curves is an important part of applied microeconomics. An important consideration for estimation is the functional form. Two convenient forms are the linear demand curve:

$$Q_D = a - bP + cI,$$

where Q_D is quantity demanded, P is price, I is income and a, b, and c are positive constants; and the logarithmic demand curve:

$$\log(Q_D) = \alpha - \beta\log(P) + \gamma\log(I),$$

where α, β, and γ are positive constants. The logarithmic form is also known as an isoelastic (constant elasticity) demand curve. To see that the elasticity of demand does not vary with price in this case, first convert the log form of the demand curve back to quantity and price:

$$Q_D = e^{\alpha}P^{-\beta}I^{\gamma}.$$

Using calculus, the slope of this demand curve is:

$$\partial Q_D / \partial P = -\beta e^{\alpha} P^{(-\beta-1)} I^{\gamma}$$

The elasticity of demand E_P then equals:

$$E_P = \left(\frac{\partial Q_D}{\partial P}\right)\left(\frac{P}{Q}\right) = \frac{-\beta e^{\alpha} P^{(-\beta-1)} I^{\gamma} P}{e^{\alpha} P^{-\beta} I^{\gamma}} = -\beta\ .$$

For a demand function of this form, the price elasticity, $-\beta$, is the same value everywhere on the demand curve. The income elasticity is also constant and equal to γ.

Exercise: ◗ ◗ ◗ ◗ ◗ ◗ ◗

***11.** The marketing department of your firm, which manufactures energy drinks, estimated the demand for your product as $Q_E = e^{0.5} P_E^{-3} P_C^{1.5} I^{1.1}$ where E = energy drinks, C = coffee, and I = aggregate income.

a) What is the estimated own-price elasticity of energy drinks? The cross-price elasticity between energy drinks and coffee? The income elasticity of energy drinks?

b) Do these estimates make economic sense?

PROBLEM SET

12. Wimpy buys fewer hamburgers when his income increases. However, when the price of hamburgers rose, Wimpy bought more hamburgers. Is this behavior possible? If not, what basic assumptions of consumer behavior are violated? Can you determine what type of good (normal, inferior, or Giffen) hamburgers are for Wimpy?

13. Connie's demand for electricity is given by $Q = 2{,}000 - 100P$, where Q is measured in kilowatt-hours per month and P is measured in cents per kilowatt-hour.

a) Calculate Connie's price elasticity of demand at the points $P = 9$, $P = 10$, and $P = 11$.

b) If costs were zero and the price were currently set at $P = 11$, would you advise the local electric utility company to raise or lower the price?

c) Many local electric utilities charge a higher rate for large quantities of kilowatt-hours (KWH) consumed per month in order to encourage conservation. Suppose $P = 5$ for the first 500 KWH consumed per month and $P = 10$ for all remaining KWH demanded. What would be Connie's consumer surplus? Illustrate.

14. Consumption of pounds of hamburger per year by a typical consumer has been estimated as follows:

	Income	
Price	\$20,000 per year	\$30,000 per year
\$0.50	1,000 pounds	1,500 pounds
\$1.00	900	1,100
\$1.50	800	900

a) Suppose the Hamburger Manufacturers' Association asks you to compute the price elasticity of demand. Will you use arc or point elasticities? Why? Calculate these elasticities at I = \$20,000 and I = \$30,000. What pattern do you observe?

b) Sketch the Engel curves implied by these data.

15. Suppose that a consumer has \$600 income per month and spends it all on two goods, X and Y. The price of good Y is \$20. When P_X = \$2, her consumption of X is 240; when P_X = \$3, her consumption of X is 160; and when P_X = \$4, her consumption of X is 120 units per month.

a) Graph the price consumption curve for this consumer. What is the expenditure on X as price varies?

b) Is the demand for X elastic, inelastic, or unitary elastic?

16. Describing the type of jelly sandwiches she prefers, a consumer says she only likes a half-and-half mixture of apple and grape jelly. Graph and determine the optimal combinations of apple and grape jelly as income and prices change for this consumer. Trace out the demand curve for grape jelly as a function of the price of grape jelly.

17. The Federal Communications Commission, television broadcasters, and manufacturers have not yet agreed upon a standard for three-dimensional television broadcast (3D TV). Currently, several formats exist. Watching 3D TV will require a new type of TV set, and new TV channels will be used for these broadcasts.

a) Will the demand curve for 3D TV sets exhibit a network externality effect? Will it be a bandwagon effect or a snob effect? Explain.

b) When complete plans for 3D TV are announced (the timetable for the introduction of new stations, estimates of prices of 3D TV sets, etc.), what do you think will happen to the sales of ordinary TV sets in the few years prior to the introduction of 3D TV?

18. Suppose a consumer has indifference curves that have a constant slope on any ray through the origin (so that doubling the consumption of both goods leaves the MRS unchanged). Draw a budget line and indifference curve with food on the horizontal axis and clothing on the vertical axis.

a) Show that, if the price of clothing rises and the consumer's money income remains the same, the consumer will purchase fewer units of clothing.

b) With these indifference curves, are food and clothing both normal goods?

SELF-TEST

19. John currently buys 40 cans of soda per month. To discourage litter, the government imposes a tax, t, per can of soda and uses the revenue to pay tax rebates to consumers. After the tax is imposed, but before he receives the rebate, John would buy 34 cans per month. John receives a rebate of r = 34t per month. Which of the following is true?

a) He was better off with no tax and no rebate.
b) He is equally well off before and after the tax.
c) He is worse off with no tax and no rebate.
d) b) or c) might be true.
e) More information is needed.

20. Andy buys 10 pounds of onions per month when the price is $0.75 per pound. If the price falls to $0.50 per pound, he buys 30 pounds of onions. What is his arc elasticity of demand over this price range?

a) – 1.33
b) – 2
c) – 2.5
d) – 6
e) None of the above is correct.

21. The demand for laptop computers is price elastic. As the price of laptop computers fell through the early 2000s, all else remaining equal,

a) consumer surplus rose and total expenditures fell.
b) consumer surplus fell and total expenditures fell.
c) consumer surplus rose and total expenditures rose.
d) consumer surplus fell and total expenditures rose.
e) no change occurred in either consumer surplus or total expenditures.

22. An Engel curve for a good has a positive slope if the good is:

a) an inferior good.
b) a Giffen good.
c) a normal good.
d) a), b), and c) are true.
e) None of the above is true.

23. Which of the following pairs of goods are complements?

a) Hot dogs and chicken
b) Iced tea and lemonade
c) Hot dogs and hot dog buns
d) Chicken and steak
e) All of them are complements.

24. If the demand curve for steak slopes downward, which of the following is true?
a) The substitution and income effects work in the same direction.
b) The substitution and income effects work in opposite directions, with the income effect being larger in magnitude.
c) The substitution and income effects work in opposite directions, with the substitution effect being larger in magnitude.
d) a) or b)
e) a) or c)

The next two questions refer to Jane's demand curve for racquetballs, which is displayed in Figure 4.9.

25. If racquetballs cost \$3 each, Jane's consumer surplus is:
a) \$0
b) \$7
c) \$15
d) \$22
e) \$31

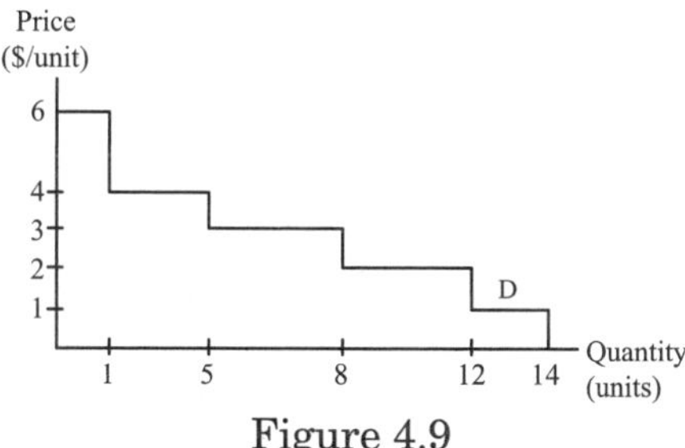

Figure 4.9

26. If racquetballs cost \$2.00 each, Jane's consumer surplus is:
a) \$15
b) \$21
c) \$24
d) \$39
e) None of the above is correct.

27. When a freeze in Florida increased the price of oranges in a recent year, total revenue earned by orange producers increased. We can infer from these facts that the demand for oranges is:
a) inelastic.
b) unit elastic.
c) elastic.
d) upward sloping.
e) infinitely elastic.

The next two questions refer to the following information: Sophie and Mark are the only two consumers in the DVD rental market in their small town. Their demand curves per week are pictured in Figure 4.10.

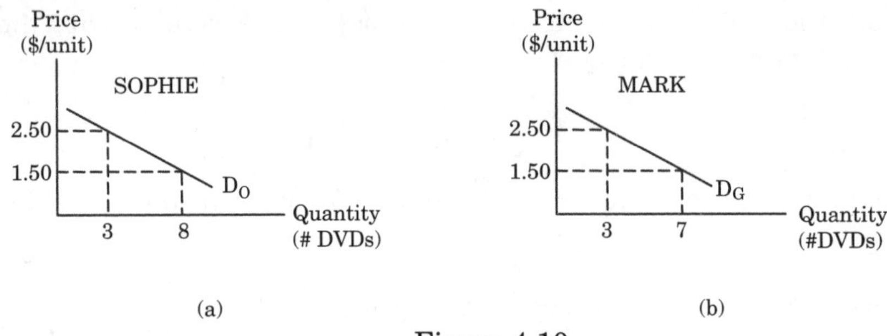

Figure 4.10

28. If rentals cost $2.50 each, the total quantity demanded each week in the market is:
a) 3
b) 6
c) 15
d) 10
e) None of the above is correct.

29. For a decrease in price from $2.50 to $1.50, market demand is:
a) elastic.
b) unit elastic.
c) inelastic.
d) perfectly inelastic.
e) More information is needed.

ANSWERS TO CHAPTER 4

EXERCISE ANSWERS

1. As the price of F rises, consumption of F would ordinarily fall; however, it is possible that food is a Giffen good and consumption rises when the price rises. As the price of F rises, consumption of C may rise or fall without any need for food or clothing to be Giffen goods.

2. a) Figure 4A.1a (on the next page) shows that the income-consumption curve slopes upward (positive slope); more income means that more of both goods are purchased.
b) If clothing is inferior, then the income-consumption curve is negatively sloped; with more income, food consumption rises, but clothing consumption falls. See Figure 4A.1b.
c) No, if both goods were inferior, then food and clothing consumption would both fall as income rises. The consumer would then be spending less as income rises. This violates the "more is better" assumption.

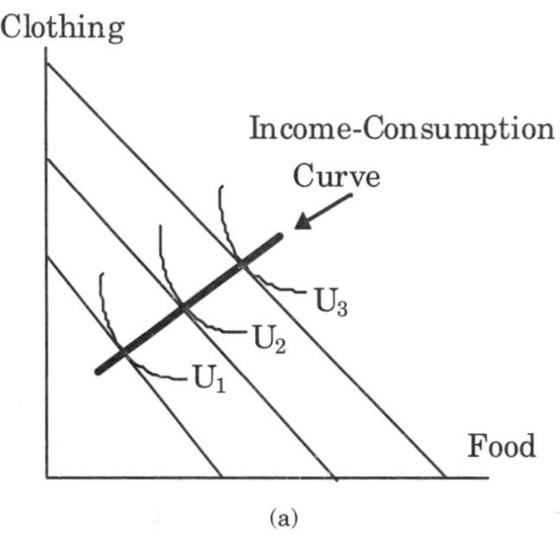

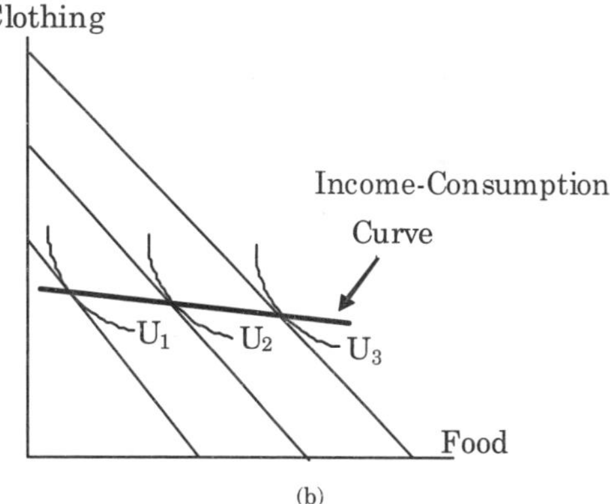

Figure 4A.1

3. a) A 10 percent sales tax on X rotates the budget line inward along the x-axis in Figure 4A.2a. The substitution effect is the movement from the original utility maximizing point, A, to the hypothetical utility maximizing point, D. This point D is found by drawing a new budget constraint tangent to the original indifference curve U_1, but reflecting the new price of X (i.e., parallel to the actual new budget line). The income effect is the movement from point D to the actual new utility maximizing point B, which reflects the decrease in real income resulting from the increase in the price of X. Assuming that X and Y are normal goods, consumption of both X and Y must fall from D to B. The total effect of the price change is a reduction in the consumption of X from X_1 to X_2.

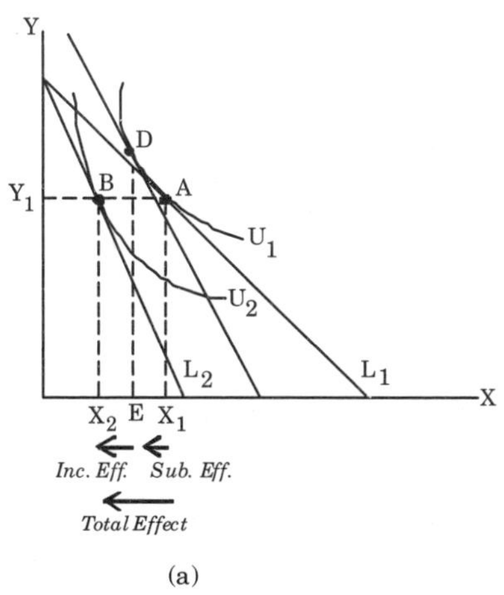

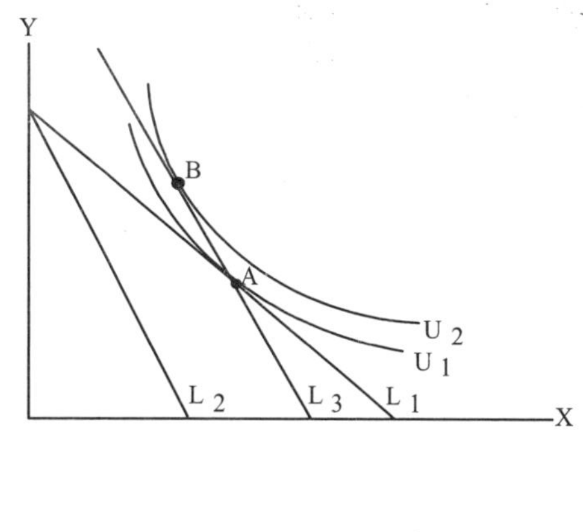

Figure 4A.2

b) An income-tax rebate given to this consumer allowing her to consume her original market basket A implies that we must draw the new budget line going *through* A, as shown in Figure 4A.2b. This is not the same as the budget line we constructed in Figure 4A.2a to be tangent to U_1. The new utility maximizing market basket will be a point such as B on a higher indifference curve U_2. Given enough income to purchase market basket A, the consumer chooses to use some of that income to substitute out of X and into the relatively cheaper good, Y.

4. If the market price goes above three, Abbott will demand zero pineapples. Therefore, the total quantity demanded at each price is:

$$Q_T = 35 - 7P \text{ if } P \leq 3 \text{ (adding together } Q_A \text{ and } Q_C\text{)},$$
and
$$Q_T = 20 - 2P \text{ if } P > 3.$$

See Figure 4A.3.

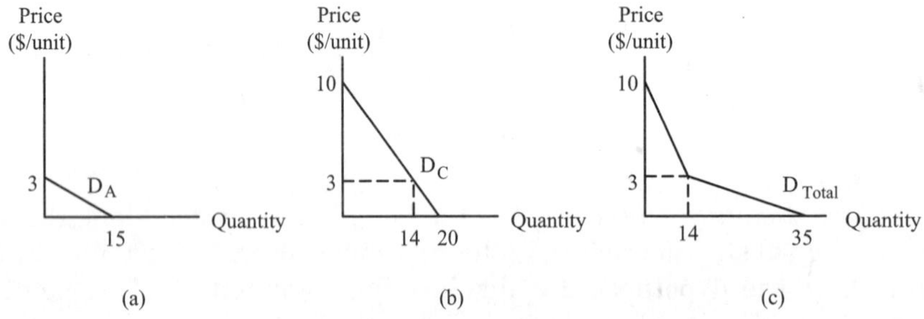

Figure 4A.3

5. a) The $2000 price increase due to the tax is a 4% increase in the final price of the car, since the 10% tax only applies above a threshold: $E_P = \%\Delta Q/\%\Delta P = -27/4 = -6.75$.

b) Since $|E_P| > 1$, total revenue will fall as price rises.

6. Total revenue is given by the area of the rectangle between the origin and the point on the demand curve. See Figure 4A.4. The rectangle grows as P falls until halfway down the curve. Then the area falls as P continues to decline toward zero.

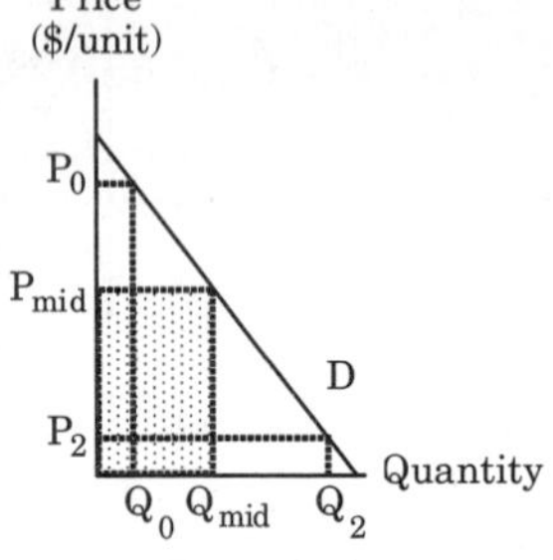

Figure 4A.4

7. The point elasticity is $E_P = -bP/Q$ where $-b$ is the slope of the demand curve.
At P = 10, $E_P = -40(10)/[2{,}000 - 40(10)] = -400/1{,}600 = -1/4$.
At P = 30, $E_P = -40(30)/[2{,}000 - 40(30)] = -1{,}200/800 = -1.5$.
For the arc elasticity, we use the formula:

$$E_P = \frac{\Delta Q}{\Delta P} \cdot \frac{(P_1 + P_2)/2}{(Q_1 + Q_2)/2} = \frac{-b(P_1 + P_2)/2}{(Q_1 + Q_2)/2}.$$

Therefore, for a change from P=10 and $Q = 2{,}000 - 40(10) = 1{,}600$, to $P = 30$ and Q=2,000 – 40(30)=800 , the arc elasticity is:

$$E_P = \frac{-40(10+30)/2}{(1{,}600+800)/2} = \frac{-800}{1{,}200} = -0.67.$$

For a price change in the opposite direction, the arc elasticity formula is exactly the same.

8. a) For one hour per week, they are willing to pay \$24. For two hours they are willing to pay \$24 for the first hour plus \$17 for the second, for a total of \$41. For three hours it is \$24 for the first hour plus \$17 for the second plus \$8 for the third, for a total of \$49. For four hours it is \$24 for the first hour plus \$17 for the second plus \$8 for the third plus \$2 for the fourth, or \$51 total.

b) If P = \$20, they play for one hour. Since they are willing to pay \$24, they receive a surplus of \$4.
If P = \$15, they purchase two hours and pay \$30. Since they are willing to pay \$41, they receive \$11 in surplus.

If P = \$7, they purchase three hours and pay \$21. Since they are willing to pay \$49, they receive \$28 in surplus.

c) At P = 0, they would play four hours. Since they are willing to pay \$51 for four hours, the weekly fee could be as much as \$51 per week.

9. a) For consumer A: Q = 40 – 0.5P. See the demand curve drawn in Figure 4A.5a. At P = 20, Q = 30. Thus, CS_A = 0.5(30)(80 – 20) = 900 cents or \$9.

For consumer B: Q = 120 – P. See the demand curve drawn in Figure 4A.5b. At P = 20, Q = 100. Thus, CS_B = 0.5(100)(120 – 20) = 5,000 cents or \$50.

Total Revenue = 20(30) + 20(100) = 2,600 cents or \$26.

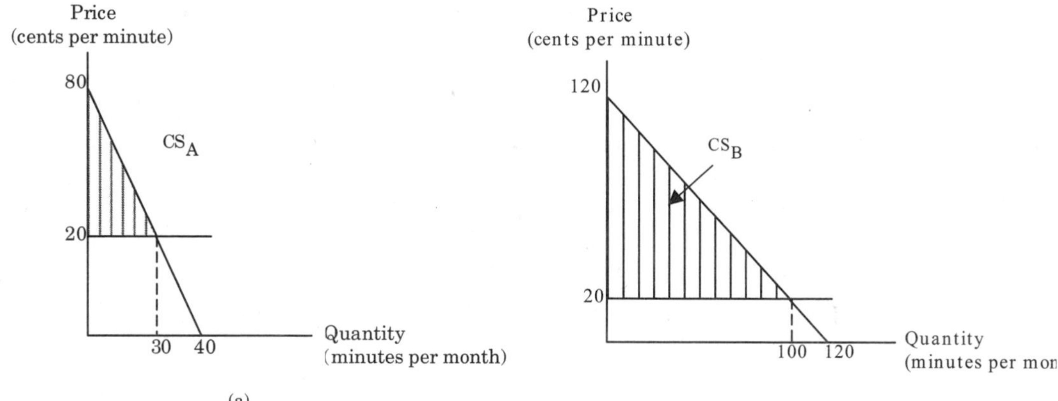

Figure 4A.5

b) Assume that the income effect of the $10 monthly fee is small enough so that the demand curves do not shift. Since CS_A is only $9, the Type A consumers are unwilling to pay the $10 monthly fee and will drop out of the market. Type B consumers who have a consumer surplus of $50 at a price per minute of 20 cents, are willing to pay the increased price and will continue to maximize utility by consuming Q = 100 (since optimal quantity demanded is based on the per unit price and not on the lump-sum fee). Therefore, each Type B consumer now spends 20(100) + 1,000 = 3,000 cents or $30. Previously, the company obtained $6 from each Type A consumer and $20 from each Type B consumer. With equal numbers of A and B consumers, total revenue would increase with the fee (from $26 per pair of consumers to $30), despite the fact that some consumers drop out of the market.

10. a) A price decrease will attract more customers, but the crowding (longer lines, poorer service) will discourage others. This would resemble a snob effect.

b) The more people you expect to buy a software product, the more likely you can find another experienced user to ask questions about it. Also, the more likely it is that a computer bookstore will carry publications about how to use the software. Thus, we would expect to see a bandwagon effect.

c) Here, crowding might discourage some customers. But, since part of the enjoyment of a concert is seeing the band with other fans, we might observe a bandwagon effect.

11. a) $E_E = -3$; $E_{E,C} = 1.5$; $E_I = 1.1$

b) One would expect the demand for energy drinks to be elastic (since there are many substitutes, such as coffee and energy bars). The cross-elasticity between energy drinks and coffee should be positive, indicating that they are substitutes, but it is not surprising that it is not highly elastic, given that coffee has other features that consumers value (i.e., most often served hot). The income elasticity is positive, indicating that energy drinks are a normal good, and it is slightly greater than one, showing that energy drink purchases are slightly income elastic.

PROBLEM SET ANSWERS

12. For Wimpy, hamburgers are a Giffen good, since his quantity demanded increases as price increases. This can happen if hamburgers are a strong inferior good for Wimpy (i.e., the income effect outweighs the substitution effect). There is no need to violate our basic preference assumptions to generate this demand behavior.

13. a) If $Q = a - bP$, then $E_P = -b(P/Q)$. At $P = 9$, $E_P = -100(9/1{,}100) = -0.82$. At $P = 10$, $E_P = -100(10/1{,}000) = -1.00$. At $P = 11$, $E_P = -100(11/900) = -1.22$.

b) At $P = 11$, $E_P = -1.22$. Therefore, revenues will increase if price were lowered (since demand is elastic at P = 11). In fact, you could recommend that they lower the price to 10 cents or KWH. If they lowered it any further, revenues would begin to fall as demand became inelastic.

c) Consumer surplus is the shaded area in Figure 4A.6.

$$CS = (10 - 5)\,500 + 0.5(1{,}000)(20 - 10) = 7{,}500 \text{ cents or } \$75.$$

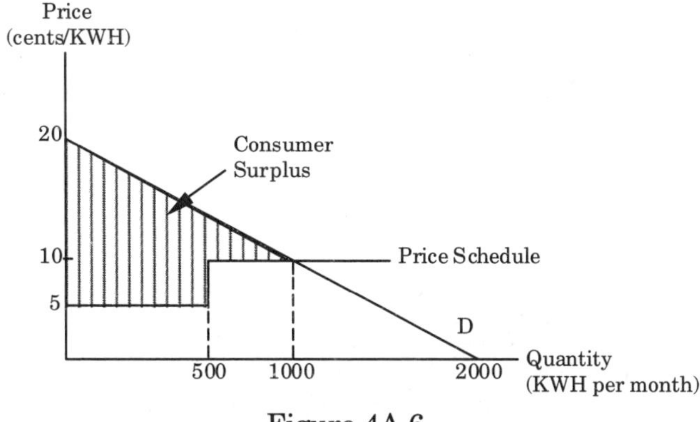

Figure 4A.6

14. a) The data only allow us to look at 50-cent changes in price. Computing arc elasticities would be best. At I = $20,000:

$$E_P = \frac{\Delta Q}{\Delta P} \cdot \frac{\overline{P}}{\overline{Q}} = \left(\frac{1{,}000 - 900}{0.50 - 1.00}\right)\left(\frac{0.75}{950}\right) = -0.16 \text{ from P = 0.50 to 1.00.}$$

$$E_P = \left(\frac{900 - 800}{1.00 - 1.50}\right)\left(\frac{1.25}{850}\right) = -0.29 \text{ from P = 1.00 to 1.50.}$$

At I = $30,000:

$$E_P = \left(\frac{1{,}500 - 1{,}000}{0.50 - 1.00}\right)\left(\frac{0.75}{1{,}300}\right) = -0.46 \text{ from P = 0.50 to 1.00.}$$

$$E_P = \left(\frac{1{,}100 - 900}{1.00 - 1.50}\right)\left(\frac{1.25}{1{,}000}\right) = -0.50 \text{ from P = 1.00 to 1.50.}$$

Therefore, demand is inelastic. However, demand is less inelastic at higher income levels.

b) See Figure 4A.7.

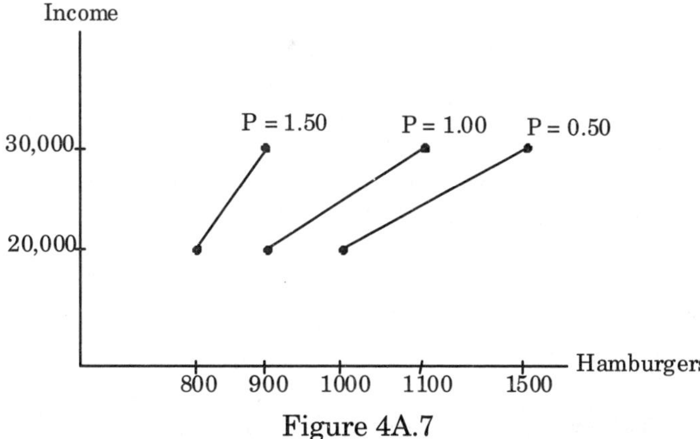

Figure 4A.7

15. a) See Figure 4A.8. Expenditure on X is always \$480, and, therefore, Y consumed must always equal 6. The corresponding price consumption curve is horizontal.

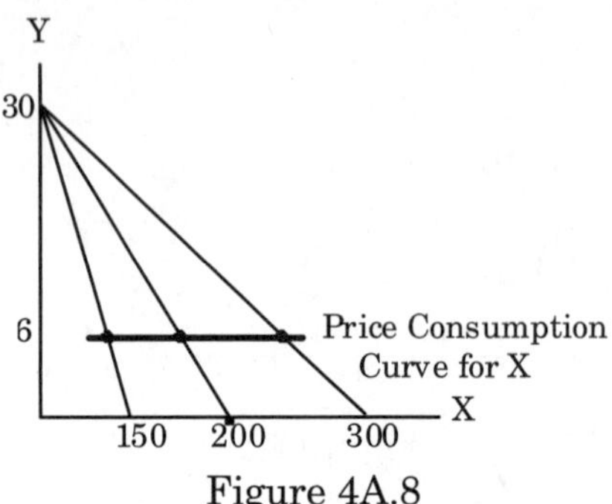

Figure 4A.8

b) The demand for X is unitary elastic because total expenditure remains constant as the price of X is varied.

16. Since the consumer eats only equal amounts of apple and grape jelly, they are perfect complements. Therefore, A=G when the consumer chooses her optimal market basket for any income level and price ratio. Thus, the income-consumption curve and the price-consumption curve are a 45° line. Substituting A=G into the budget constraint $P_A A + P_G G = I$, we obtain $G = I/(P_A + P_G)$. See Figure 4A.9(a–c).

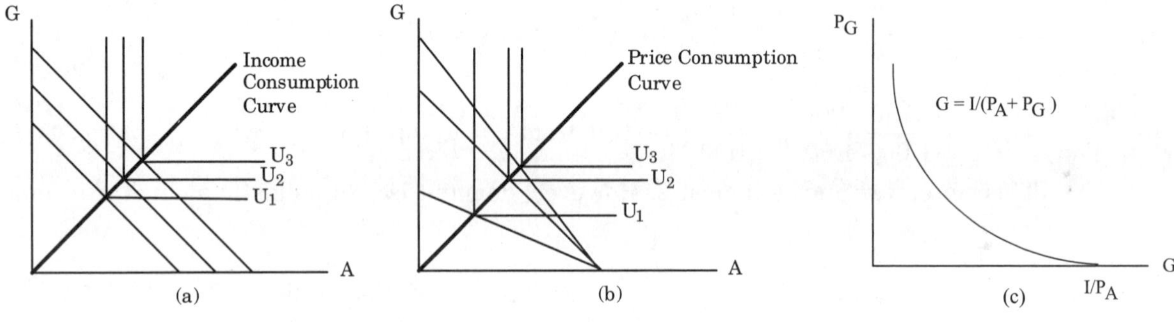

Figure 4A.9

17. a) Broadcasters will only start using 3D TV if there is a market of consumers to watch programs in the new format. The more consumers that buy 3D TV sets, the more 3D TV programming there will be. This is a bandwagon effect (a positive network externality).

b) Once the future of 3D TV is clear, at least some consumers will delay buying new TVs which lack 3D capability. Thus, sales of such ordinary TV sets might drop until 3D TV sets become available.

18. a) Figure 4A.10 shows that the tangency on the budget line after the price of clothing increases must lie below the ray connecting the origin and the original preferred market basket. Since indifference curves have the same slope everywhere on the ray through the original preferred market basket, the consumer will purchase more food and less clothing than at the point on the ray.

b) The income effect is found from a parallel shift in the budget line. Since the MRS stays the same along a ray through the origin, the consumer buys less of both goods if her income falls. Thus, both goods are normal.

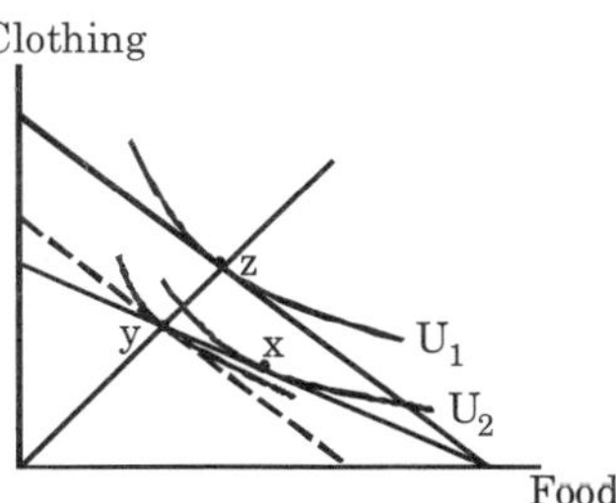

Figure 4A.10

SELF-TEST ANSWERS

19. e) John is unambiguously worse off after the tax is imposed. However, we can't tell whether he is better off or worse off after the rebate is given because we don't know the amount of the rebate.

20. c) Using the arc elasticity formula,

$$E_P = \frac{\Delta Q}{\Delta P} \times \frac{\overline{P}}{\overline{Q}} = \frac{(30-10)}{(0.50-0.75)} \times \frac{(0.50+0.75)/2}{(30+10)/2} = -2.5$$

21. c) Consumer surplus rises as price falls (as long as we know that the demand curve is stable, which is why the all else equal assumption is important). When demand is price elastic, a decrease in price increases total expenditure on the product.

22. c) Inferior and Giffen goods have negatively sloped Engel curves.

23. c) Hot dogs and hot dog buns are often consumed together (they are complements in consumption). A fall in the price of one would increase demand for both. The other pairs are alternatives, or substitutes, in consumption.

24. e) Downward-sloping demand can hold if either the income and substitution effects move together (which will happen for normal goods) or for the case of an inferior good, as long as the substitution effect outweighs the income effect.

25. b) At P = \$3, Jane buys 8 racquet balls and spends \$24. Her total willingness to pay is $\$31(6(1)+4(5-1)+3(8-5))$. The difference is her consumer surplus: $CS = 31 - 24 = \$7$.

26. a) At $P = \$2$, Jane buys 12 balls and spends \$24. Her total willingness to pay is \$39 (31+2(12 – 8)). The difference is her consumer surplus: $CS = 39 - 24 = \$15$.

27. a) If revenue rises as price rises, then demand is inelastic.

28. b) Add horizontally to get the market demand curve. At $P = \$2.50$, $Q_O = 3$ and $Q_G = 3$ for a total of 6 units demanded.

29. a) Demand is price elastic:

$$E_P = \%\Delta Q / \%\Delta P = \left[(6-15)/6\right] / \left[(2.50-1.50)/2.50\right] = -3.75$$

CHAPTER 5
UNCERTAINTY AND CONSUMER BEHAVIOR

IMPORTANT CONCEPTS

- Probability
- Payoff
- Expected Value
- Variance (Standard Deviation)
- Expected Utility
- Risk Preferences (Risk-Averse, Risk-Loving, Risk-Neutral)
- Risk Premium
- Risk-Return Relationship
- Behavioral Economics

CHAPTER HIGHLIGHTS

Decisions made under conditions of perfect certainty are rare. It is much more common for people to find themselves in a situation involving more than one possible future outcome. This chapter examines choice under uncertainty: how to describe risk, how people differ in their attitudes towards risk, and how people can deal with risk.

Risky situations are described by listing the possible outcomes (also called events or states of nature) that might occur and then assessing the likelihood that each outcome will occur. *Probability* refers to the chance that an outcome will occur. The probability attached to each outcome must have a value between zero and one. The *payoff* associated with each outcome is simply the value (measured in dollar terms) of that outcome. The two measures of risk that are the focus of this chapter are *expected value* and *variance*. Expected value measures the average payoff and the variance measures the variability of the possible payoffs.

Attitudes toward risk differ between individuals, and these attitudes will affect their decisions. We distinguish between different attitudes towards risk by focusing on the utility that consumers obtain from making different choices. In particular, we look at the utility of a certain (guaranteed) income and compare that to the *expected utility* obtained by entering into an uncertain situation. Expected utility is the weighted average of the utilities for each outcome, where the weights are the probabilities associated with each outcome. It is the average payoff in utility terms, rather than dollar terms. A *risk-averse* person prefers a certain income to entering into a gamble that will yield the same expected income. A *risk-loving* person prefers taking the gamble to having the equivalent amount of income with certainty.

A *risk-neutral* person is indifferent between having a certain income and an uncertain income with the same expected value.

Most people are willing to pay to avoid risk, particularly if there is a large downside risk in certain states of the world (in case of a fire or an earthquake, for example). The *risk premium* is the amount of money that a risk-averse person would pay to avoid taking a risk. The more risk averse a person is or the greater the variance in outcomes, the higher the risk premium (holding everything else equal).

Different risky assets have different expected returns. The risk-averse investor chooses a portfolio of assets to balance expected return against risk. The higher the expected return on an investment, the more risk (measured by the standard deviation of the return) the investor has to accept. This tradeoff can be expressed in terms of a budget line. Indifference curves can be used to describe the different combinations of risk and return that leave the investor equally satisfied. The investor maximizes utility by choosing a combination of risk and return where the indifference curve and budget line are tangent.

The chapter concludes with a brief discussion of the growing field of *behavioral economics*. The basic theory of consumer behavior is a powerful tool for understanding and analyzing many apects of consumer decision-making. Still, consumer preferences are complex and there are many aspects of it that basic theory cannot explain. Research from psychology and sociology can help explain such phenonmenon as *loss aversion* – the tendency of individuals to prefer avoiding losses over acquiring gains – and *anchoring* – when the context in which the decision is made can affect the consumer's final decision.

CONCEPT REVIEW AND EXERCISES

DESCRIBING RISK (Section 5.1)

Probability is the basic tool for describing situations involving risk. The probability of an event is simply the frequency with which it is expected to occur. In some cases, such as tossing a coin, the (objective) probability of heads can be determined directly by repeated trials. In other cases, such as whether the Dow Jones average of 30 stocks will rise tomorrow, the probability may only be a subjective measure of the likelihood of an event. For most economic problems, we can only find subjective probabilities (which may vary between individuals). Either type of probability can be used for decision making.

The basic description of an event subject to risk consists of a list of all possible outcomes (which are mutually exclusive) and the probability of each outcome occurring. Since one of these events *must* occur in the future, the probabilities of all possible events must sum to one. For example, consider a farmer faced with the decision of whether to incur the cost of having his crop sprayed with insecticide. In the simplest case, the two possible outcomes are (1) the insects do not damage his crop this year, and (2) the insects destroy his crop. The probability of the good outcome might be 70 percent (0.70). That would mean that the probability of the bad outcome must be 30 percent (0.30), so that 0.70 + 0.30 = 1. If we looked at the problem more realistically, it might be that there are six possible outcomes: (1) no insect damage to the crop, (2) the insects destroy 20 percent of his crop, (3) the insects destroy 40 percent of his crop, (4) the insects destroy 60 percent of his crop, (5) the insects destroy 80 percent of his crop, and (6) the insects destroy 100 percent of his crop. The sum of the probabilities across all six events must add up to one. For example, if the probability of the first event were 25 percent and events (2) – (6) were equally likely, we would have 0.25 + 0.15 + 0.15 + 0.15 + 0.15 + 0.15 = 1.

The *expected value* associated with an uncertain situation is the sum of the payoffs in each possible state of the world weighted by their associated probabilities. If Pr_i is the probability of receiving X_i dollars and there are three possible outcomes, the expected value is given by:

$$\text{Expected Value} = E(X) = Pr_1X_1 + Pr_2X_2 + Pr_3X_3 .$$

The *variance* measures the dispersion of possible outcomes. For example, if there are three possible outcomes, the variance is:

$$\text{Variance} = \sigma^2 = Pr_1[X_1 - E(X)]^2 + Pr_2[X_2 - E(X)]^2 + Pr_3[X_3 - E(X)]^2 .$$

The *standard deviation* is simply the square root of the variance:

$$\text{Standard Deviation} = \sigma = \sqrt{\sigma^2}$$

For instance, if a lottery ticket pays \$500,000 with probability 0.001, \$200 with probability 0.02, and \$0 with probability 0.979, the expected value of the ticket is:

$$E(X) = 0.001(\$500{,}000) + 0.02(\$200) + 0.979(\$0) = \$500 + \$4 + \$0 = \$504.$$

The variance of the lottery ticket outcomes would be:

$$\sigma^2 = 0.001(\$500{,}000 - \$504)^2 + 0.02(\$200 - \$504)^2 + 0.979(\$0 - \$504)^2 = \$249{,}746{,}784.$$

Exercise: ▶ ▶ ▶ ▶ ▶ ▶ ▶

1. Jeff lives in California. His total wealth next year, including his house, will be $500,000. There is a 10-percent chance that a big earthquake will occur next year and destroy his house, valued at $200,000. What is Jeff's expected wealth next year if he chooses not to purchase insurance?

2. Lauren is graduating from college this semester. She has been offered a job paying a salary of $24,000. She has also applied for a job with an annual salary of $32,000. If her probability of being offered the better job is 3/4, what is her expected income next year? What is the variance and standard deviation of her income next year?

PREFERENCES TOWARD RISK (Section 5.2)

To evaluate an individual's attitude toward risky situations, we calculate the *expected utility.* If u(X) is the utility that an individual receives from $X of income, expected utility will be:

$$E(u) = Pr_1 u(X_1) + Pr_2 u(X_2) + Pr_3 u(X_3),$$

where X_1, X_2, and X_3 are the three possible outcomes. Calculating expected utility is exactly like calculating expected value. The only difference is that you must multiply each probability by the *utility* of the outcome rather than the dollar value of the outcome.

Tastes for risk are diverse, just as tastes for goods vary between individuals. We can classify three types of preferences for risk: *risk-averse, risk-neutral, and risk-loving.* If a risk-averse person is offered the choice between a gamble with an expected payoff of $100 and a sure $100, they will always take the sure thing. All other things equal, they prefer the "safe" choice to the risky choice. In other words, risk-averse individuals attach negative utility to risky situations. If a risk-neutral person were offered the same two choices (a gamble with an expected payoff of $100 or a sure $100), they would be indifferent—the dollar payoff is *all* that matters to a risk-neutral person, not the risk attached to the outcome. A risk-loving person offered the same two choices would always take the gamble. They attach positive utility to risky situations.

Both risk-averse and risk-loving consumers will choose the option that gives them the highest expected utility. In contrast, a risk-neutral person will always choose the option that gives them the highest expected dollar value. The utility curves that describe these three different types of risk preference are shown in Figure 5.1.

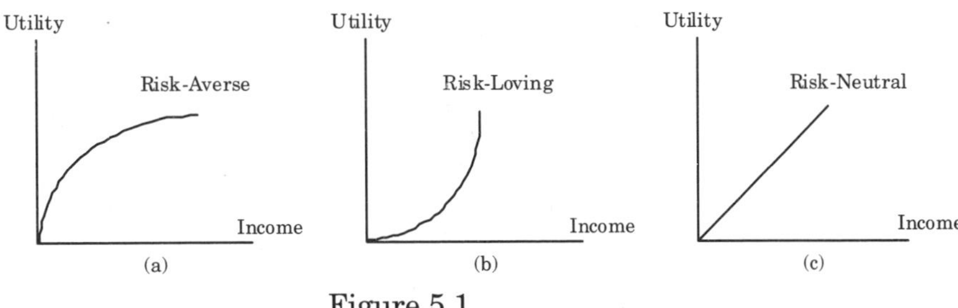

Figure 5.1

Note that risk-averse individuals have a *diminishing marginal utility of income*—although total utility always rises as income rises, the rate of increase in utility falls with increased income levels. Imagine a risk-averse person at a particular point on Figure 5.1(a). A loss in income from that point results in a large decline in utility. A gain in income from that point results in a small increase in utility. This helps explain why convex utility curves describe risk-averse preferences: risk-averse people don't like "downside" risk.

An individual's risk preferences may vary depending on her income level. The individual whose risk preferences are depicted in Figure 5.2 is risk-averse at low income levels and risk-loving at high income levels.

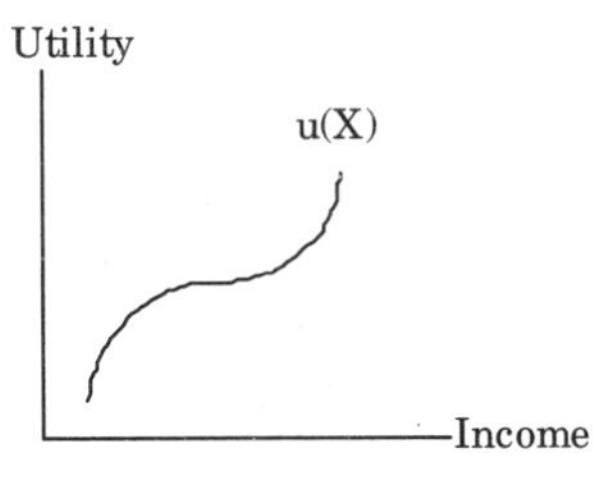

Figure 5.2

Exercise:

3. Suppose that Jeff's utility function is given by $u(W) = W^{0.5}$, where W represents total wealth in thousands of dollars. Is Jeff risk-averse, risk-loving, or risk-neutral?

Many people buy insurance or warranties. How high a price will they pay for such insurance? One measure of the level of risk aversion is the *risk premium*. Suppose you have the utility function u(X) in Figure 5.3 with two possible income levels, X_1 and X_2. E(X) is the expected value of income, which equals $Pr_1X_1 + Pr_2X_2$. Point F on the curve gives the utility of having E(X) *guaranteed* to you. But you don't actually get E(X) with certainty. The expected utility, E(u), which you get from gambling between points A and B, is shown by point D. Since $E(u) = Pr_1u(X_1) + Pr_2u(X_2)$, point D tells us the expected utility of a gamble over X_1 and X_2 with an expected value of E(X). Now look at the income level shown on the graph as X*. At the *certain* income level X*, the consumer is *on* her utility curve: her utility from a sure thing of X* is u(X*). At point D, the consumer's utility from a gamble between X_1 and X_2 is E(u) which is the same as u(X*). Notice that we have picked X* so that points C and D line up horizontally. The value of X* satisfies u(X*) = E(u). *The risk premium equals* *the horizontal distance between* C *and* D *or* E(X) – X*; it measures the maximum amount of income an individual would give up which would leave her just indifferent between a risky choice and a certain one. The vertical distance from D to F measures this consumer's aversion to risk. The horizontal distance from D to C captures this same risk aversion factor in monetary terms.

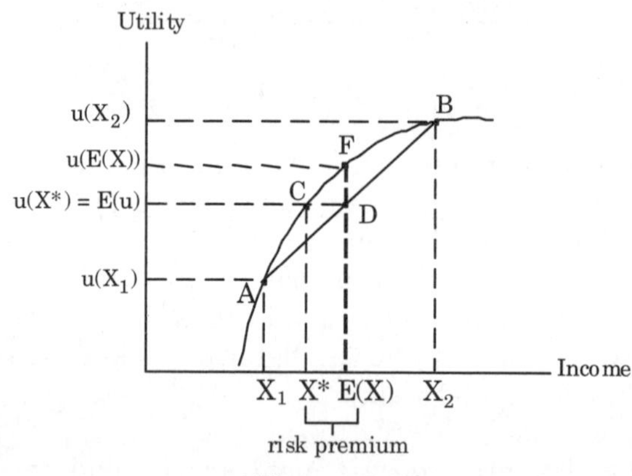

Figure 5.3

Exercise:

4. Let's continue with Jeff's problem. His wealth next year if he chooses not to buy insurance is $500,000 without an earthquake, and $300,000 with an earthquake and the loss of his house. The probability of an earthquake is 10 percent. His utility function is $u(W) = W^{0.5}$, where W represents his total wealth next year.

   Jeff has an opportunity to insure himself against the potential $200,000 loss. What is Jeff's risk premium?

REDUCING RISK (Section 5.3)

When individuals are willing to give up income to avoid risk, they have a positive risk premium. The decision to purchase insurance is a way of smoothing out their expected income stream. Although they give up a certain amount of income in insurance premiums no matter what, they are guaranteed that if a "bad" event happens, the insurance company will compensate them for their losses. Purchasing insurance decreases the variance of future income, and this raises the expected utility for risk-averse individuals.

How do the insurance companies make money? In order to avoid risk, risk-averse individuals are willing to pay more for insurance than the expected value of their losses. As a consequence, insurance companies can be compensated for bearing this risk, plus the costs of processing claims, and so on. Also, an insurance company engages in risk pooling, so that the variance of its losses is small relative to the total number of risks insured.

Exercise: ▶ ▶ ▶ ▶ ▶ ▶ ▶

5. Suppose a small business owner faces a five-percent probability that one of his employees will be injured on the job this year and will need medical care. The medical expenses for this employee will be \$400. Assume that the owner will earn \$15,000 in profits this year and that the cost of fully insuring against the possibility of injury is equal to the expected dollar loss (expected medical expenses). Show that the decision to purchase insurance does not alter the owner's expected wealth.

Purchasing insurance is one way of reducing risk. Another way is to purchase information. One can then use the information to reduce the amount of uncertainty before making a choice. The *value of complete information* is the difference between the expected value of a choice under complete information and the expected value under incomplete information.

The easiest way to understand how to calculate the value of complete information is to work through a problem. We will review the problem given in Table 5.7 in the text, and then follow this with an exercise where you can work through the same problem with different probabilities. Suppose that you are a store manager selling suits at a price of \$300 per suit. You are trying to decide how many suits to order for the fall season, but you are not sure whether it will be a good season (or good economy, in general) or a bad season. The quantity of suits you will sell will be 100 if the economy is good and 50 if the economy is bad. It will cost you \$180 per suit to order 100 suits and \$200 per suit if you order only 50 suits. If you order 100 and sell only 50, you can return the other 50 and get back \$90 per suit. You believe that there is a 0.5 probability that 100 suits will be sold and a 0.5 probability that sales will be 50. Assuming you are risk neutral, how much would you be willing to pay to get an accurate sales forecast?

Table 5.1 shows profits under each outcome:

Decision	Sales of 50 (Pr = 0.5)	Sales of 100 (Pr = 0.5)	E(Profit)
Buy 50 suits	\$5,000	\$ 5,000	\$5,000
Buy 100 suits	\$1,500	\$12,000	\$6,750

Table 5.1

Since you are risk neutral, you will make the choice that maximizes your expected payoff. Therefore, with incomplete information, you will choose to buy 100 suits (\$6,750 > \$5,000), and your expected profits are \$6,750.

In order to calculate expected profits with complete information, think about the following: The information for which you are paying will give you an accurate forecast of whether sales will be good or bad for the upcoming fall season. However, there will still be good and bad years. If you think of yourself as being in business over a 10-year period, there could be five good years and five bad years.

The advantage of having complete information is that you will know ahead of time which is which, but you still must weight the profits in each year by the probabilities. Therefore, expected profits with complete information are: 0.5(5,000) + 0.5(12,000) = \$8,500. (If it helps, think of taking the expected value along the diagonal of Table 5.1. If you *know* that it will be a bad year, you will order 50 suits and earn \$5,000. If you *know* that it will be a good year you will order 100 suits and earn \$12,000.) *The value of complete information is the difference between the expected value of profits with complete information and without:* 8,500 – 6,750 = \$1,750. This is the maximum amount you would be willing to pay (for a marketing study or economic forecast) to decrease the uncertainty you face.

Exercise: ◗ ◗ ◗ ◗ ◗ ◗ ◗

6. Work through the identical problem to the one above, assuming that there is a 0.6 probability that 100 suits will be sold in the fall and a 0.4 probability that sales will be 50 suits. Assuming you are risk neutral, how much would you be willing to pay to get an accurate sales forecast?

*THE DEMAND FOR RISKY ASSETS (Section 5.4)

A *risky asset* is an investment that pays a flow of money that is subject to risk. If the risk of two assets is equal, a risk-averse investor will prefer the asset that pays a higher expected return. If two assets have the same expected return, a risk-averse investor will also prefer the asset with less risk. The relevant choices are between assets with low (or zero) risk and low return, and those with high risk and high return. *Even a risk-averse investor can decide to invest in a risky asset if the expected return is high enough compared to the return on a safe asset.*

The expected return on a portfolio with one completely safe asset and one risky asset is the weighted average of the two returns:

$$R_p = bR_m + (1-b)R_f,$$

where R_m is the expected return on the stock market portfolio (a risky asset), R_f is the return on the risk-free asset, and $0 \leq b \leq 1$ describes the fraction of the portfolio invested in the stock market.

The standard deviation of the return on the portfolio is:

$$\sigma_p = b\sigma_m + (1-b)0 = b\sigma_m,$$

since only the market portfolio is subject to risk. This implies that $b = \sigma_p/\sigma_m$.

Rewriting the expected return on the total portfolio as $R_p = R_f + b(R_m - R_f)$, we can substitute in the expression for b to derive the budget line:

$$R_p = R_f + \frac{R_m - R_f}{\sigma_m}\sigma_p.$$

The expected return of the portfolio increases with increases in the standard deviation of the portfolio return. In *risk-return diagrams* such as Figure 5.4, the budget line is a positively sloped straight line, and the indifference curves are upward sloping and convex. The convex shape of the indifference curves comes from the fact that for a fixed increase in risk, a risk-averse investor demands a larger increase in the expected return the more risk he is currently bearing.

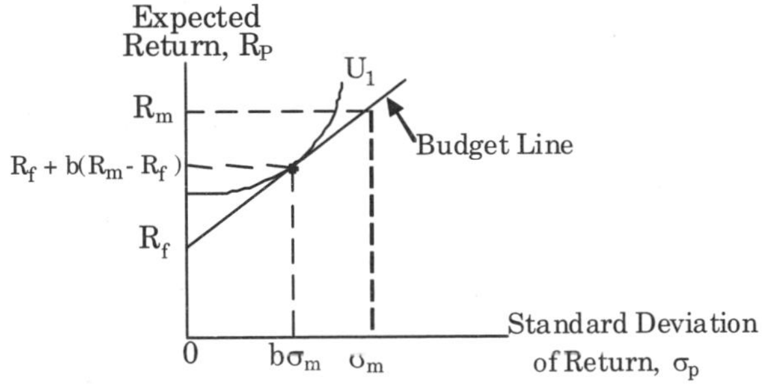

Figure 5.4

As with the demand for ordinary goods, the consumer's optimal portfolio is a point of tangency between the indifference curve and the budget line. As shown in Figure 5.5 (on the next page), the precise shape of the indifference curves determines whether the investor places more or less wealth in the risky assets. Investor A is very risk averse: increases in risk require a relatively large increase in expected return in order to keep the same level of utility. Investor B is less risk averse and chooses an optimal portfolio that carries more risk (point B).

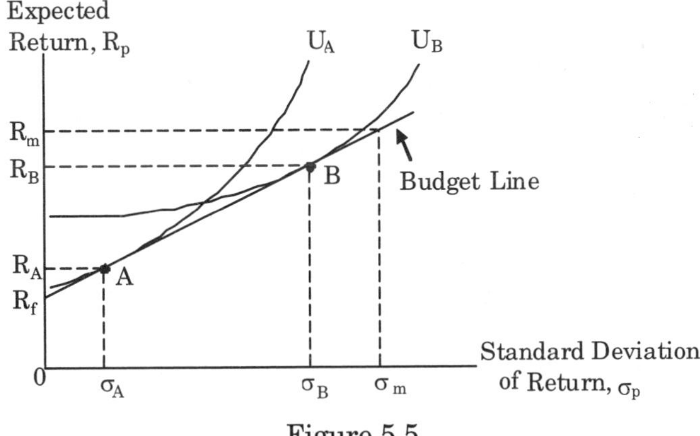

Figure 5.5

BEHAVIORAL ECONOMICS (Section 5.6)

The growing field of *behavioral economics* is deepening our understanding of consumer behavior by examining those instances when actual consumer decision-making is at odds with traditional utility theory. For example, psychologists and sociologists have found that a consumer's perceived value of a good or service can depend on the context surrounding the decision. In these cases, individuals may care about *reference points* such as relative wealth rather than absolute wealth (e.g., it matters more to you how you compare relative to your neighbor than your actual dollar income or wealth). There are other complexities in consumer behavior that can only be explained by reaching beyond our traditional models, such as *loss aversion*, where individuals tend to prefer avoiding losses to obtaining gains. Or, when decisions are particularly complex, consumers may use a *rule of thumb* or adopt an *anchoring* approach, where a suggested piece of information can influence the consumer's decision (such as a suggested donation amount). These and other adjustments to the economist's standard models enrich our understanding of consumer behavior and demand and allow us to make better predictions.

Exercise:

7. Many charities tailor their solicitations based on an individual's previous giving. An unnamed university lists several dollar amounts and "other" as potential gift options. If you had donated $500 in past years, the options listed are: $750, $1000, $2000, and Other. If you had donated $1500 in past years, the options listed are: $2000, $2500, $5000, and Other. Does this strike you as an example of taking advantage of anchoring in decision-making?

PROBLEM SET

8. A fair die has the numbers one through six on its six sides. On any roll, each side has an equal probability of being thrown. What is the expected number of points thrown on one roll? What are the variance and standard deviation in the number of points on one roll?

9. An executive has the option of choosing investment A, which has a 60-percent chance of earning a $30,000 profit and a 40-percent chance of breaking even ($0 profit). Or, the executive can choose investment B, which will yield a sure $10,000 profit. She chooses investment B. Can the risk preference of this person be determined?

10. *[Mathematical] A consumer has an income for the next year of $14,400, but faces a 1/2 probability of a monetary loss of $4,400 due to illness. There are no other losses in utility caused by the illness. Her utility function is $\sqrt{X}$ where X is the amount of income, net of any loss she suffers.
    a) What is this consumer's expected utility?
    b) What is the expected dollar loss? What is her expected income? What is the minimum certain income she would accept to avoid this risk (i.e., to be completely insured)? What is the risk premium? Graph your answer.
    c) Redo the calculations in (a) and (b) where the probability of the loss is 1/4.

11. The management of Free & Lite products is considering introducing a fat-free breakfast sausage. Based on a few consumer tests, which produced mixed results, F&L estimates that there is a 60-percent chance that the product will be a hit. If the product is a hit they will sell 500,000 sausages per year, and if the product is not a hit they will sell 250,000 sausages per year. F&L has estimated its profits for the first year of sales depending on the plant size they decide to build. If they build a small plant, profits will be $62,500 regardless of whether demand for the fat-free sausages is 250,000 or 500,000. If they build a large plant, profits will be –$12,500 if demand is only 250,000 and $150,000 if demand is 500,000. Assuming that F&L's management is risk neutral, how much would they be willing to pay a marketing company for complete information on sales of their product?

12. *[Demand for Risky Assets.] Financial analysts often suggest that individuals should put most of their savings in stocks when they are under 40 years of age, split their savings

between stocks and bonds in middle age, and invest most savings into bonds as they near retirement. The model of risk and return shows that individuals should allocate their investments depending on their degree of risk aversion. If the advice from financial analysts is appropriate, is it because individuals' degree of risk aversion changes over their lifetime? Or, is there an explanation that is consistent with individuals' risk aversion remaining the same throughout their lifetimes?

SELF-TEST

13. If Martha is willing to pay up to $300 for insurance against a loss of $8,000 that will occur with a four-percent probability, she is:
a) risk neutral.
b) risk averse.
c) risk loving.
d) irrational.
e) Not enough information is given.

14. Nanette has an uncertain income next year. If her expected utility is less than her utility of expected income, she is:
a) risk averse.
b) risk loving.
c) risk neutral.
d) a) or c)
e) b) or c)

15. Figure 5.6 graphs Tom's utility as a function of his income. Which statement is true?
a) At low income levels he is risk neutral; at higher income levels he is risk loving.
b) At low income levels he is risk loving; at higher income levels he is risk averse.
c) At low income levels he is risk averse; at higher income levels he is risk loving.
d) At low income levels he is risk loving; at higher income levels he is risk neutral.

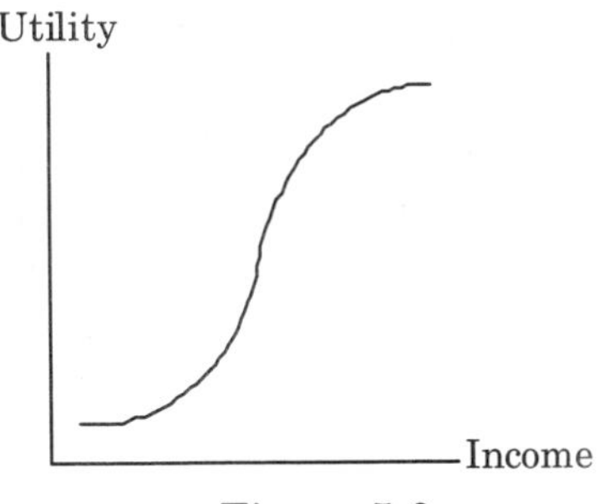

Figure 5.6

16. Most investors are risk averse (at least to some degree). Therefore, assets with higher expected returns have:
    a) lower variances.
    b) higher variances.
    c) no particular pattern of variances.
    d) a) or c)
    e) None of the above is correct.

The next two questions refer to the following problem: An investor has $60,000. Opening a small clothing store or a sporting goods store will cost $30,000. This summer's profits from each type of store depend on the weather. If the weather is good this summer, each clothing store will earn $40,000 in profits and each sporting goods store will earn $90,000 in profits. If the weather is bad this summer, each clothing store will earn $80,000 in profits and each sporting goods store will earn $30,000 in profits.

17. If the probability of bad weather is 1/2, a risk-averse investor will open:
    a) two clothing stores.
    b) one clothing store and one sporting goods store.
    c) two sporting goods stores.
    d) a) or c)
    e) More information is needed.

18. A risk-neutral investor will open two sporting goods stores if the probability of good weather is:
    a) greater than 1/2.
    b) greater than 3/4.
    c) less than 1/2.
    d) less than 1/4.
    e) More information is needed.

19. Which of the following are examples of loss aversion?
    a) Existing-home prices may rise rapidly with a high volume of sales, but prices fall only a slow ratewith a low volume of sales.
    b) Investors choose not to buy risky stocks which may become worthless.
    c) Consumers often wait to trade in an automobile until the loan is paid off, even if they must pay repair costs to continue to drive the old car.
    d) a) and b).
    e) a) and c).

ANSWERS TO CHAPTER 5

EXERCISE ANSWERS

1. Jeff's expected wealth is a weighted average of the probability that no earthquake occurs, times his wealth in that case, plus the probability an earthquake does occur, times his wealth after losing the house:

   E(wealth) = 0.90(500,000) + 0.10(300,000) = $480,000.

2. Her expected income is:

   E(X) = (1/4)($24,000) + (3/4)($32,000) = $30,000.

   The variance of her income is:

   $\sigma^2 = (1/4)(24{,}000 - 30{,}000)^2 + (3/4)(32{,}000 - 30{,}000)^2 = \$12{,}000{,}000.$

   The standard deviation of her income is: $\sqrt{\sigma^2} = \$3{,}464.10$.

3. Jeff is risk-averse. There are two ways to find the answer:

   a) Plot the function for a few values, as shown in Figure 5A.1, and see that the curvature is characteristic of risk averse individuals.

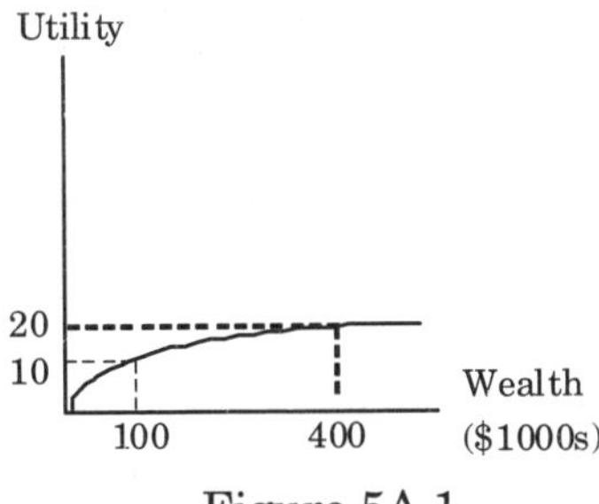

Figure 5A.1

   b) *[Calculus] Find the first and second derivative of $u(W) = W^{0.5}$:

$$\frac{\partial u}{\partial I} = .5W^{-.5}, \quad \frac{\partial^2 u}{\partial W^2} = -.25W^{-1.5}.$$

Since the first derivative is positive and the second derivative is negative, the utility curve is characterized by diminishing marginal utility. In other words, the slope of the utility curve increases at a decreasing rate causing it to become flatter at higher levels of wealth. This occurs only for risk-averse individuals.

4. Jeff's expected wealth was calculated in Exercise 1 as \$480,000. Given Jeff's utility function of $u = \sqrt{W}$, his expected utility is (rounding to the second decimal place):

$$E(u) = 0.90u(500{,}000) + 0.10u(300{,}000)$$
$$= 0.90\sqrt{500{,}000} + 0.10\sqrt{300{,}000}$$
$$= 0.90(707.11) + 0.10(547.72) = 691.17$$

Figure 5A.2 shows that the risk premium we need to find is the distance between points C and D.

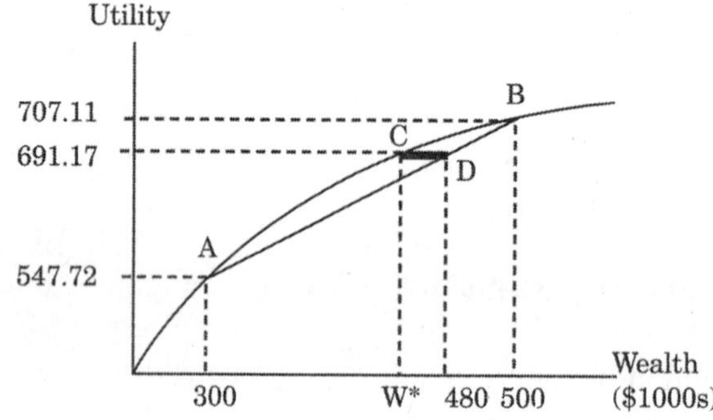

Figure 5A.2

At point C, $u(W^*) = 691.17$

or, $\sqrt{W^*} = 691.17$

or, $W^* = 477{,}715.96$ (with rounding)

Therefore, Jeff's risk premium is 480,000 – 477,715.96 = \$2,284.04.

5. See Table 5A.1. The expected dollar loss is (0.05)(\$400) = \$20. If the owner does not purchase insurance and the employee is injured, his wealth is \$15,000 – \$400 = \$14,600. Without insurance, his expected wealth is, therefore, E(W) = 0.05(14,600) + 0.95(15,000) = \$14,980. If the owner purchases insurance for \$20, his income will be the same in both states of the world. Therefore, the decision to purchase insurance does not alter his expected wealth.

Full Insurance	Injury (Pr = 0.05)	No Injury (Pr = 0.95)	Expected Wealth
No	\$14,600	\$15,000	\$14,980
Yes	\$14,980	\$14,980	\$14,980

Table 5A.1

6. Table 5A.2 shows profits under each outcome:

Decision	Sales of 50 (Pr = 0.4)	Sales of 100 (Pr = 0.6)	E(Profit)
Buy 50 units	$5,000	$ 5,000	$5,000
Buy 100 units	$1,500	$12,000	$7,800

Table 5A.2

With incomplete information, a risk-neutral individual will choose to order 100 suits. The expected profit under incomplete information is 0.4(1,500) + 0.6(12,000) = $7,800. With complete information, expected profits are 0.4(5,000) + 0.6(12,000) = $9,200. Therefore, the value of complete information is 9,200 – 7,800 = $1,400.

7. By listing only suggested amounts that are slightly larger than your previous donation, the university may be trying to anchor your decision on a larger donation. If you do not recall your last donation, you might choose the smallest amount listed. Certainly, the university is subtly trying to get you to consider a larger donation.

PROBLEM SET ANSWERS

8. A fair die has probability 1/6 for each of the six outcomes—1, 2,...6. The expected value of a roll is thus:

E(X) = (1/6)(1 + 2 + 3 + 4 + 5 + 6) = 3.5.

The variance is:

$$\sigma^2 = (1/6)[-(2.5)^2+(-1.5)^2+(-0.5)^2+(0.5)^2+(1.5)^2+(2.5)^2]$$
$$= 2.92$$

The standard deviation is: $\sigma = \sqrt{\sigma^2} = 1.71$.

9. E (return from A) = 0.60(30,000) + 0.40(0) = $18,000.

E (return from B) = $10,000.

The executive is risk averse. If she were risk neutral, she would prefer the $18,000 payoff. A risk-loving executive would also prefer investment A. A risk-averse individual may or may not prefer the high risk-high payoff investment A, depending on *how* risk averse she is. Since B is chosen, it must be because the executive is risk averse.

10. a) If no loss occurs, the consumer will have an income of $14,400, which gives her a utility of $\sqrt{14,400}$ = 120. If she falls ill, her income will be $10,000 with utility equal to 100. Therefore, E(u) = (1/2)(120) + (1/2)(100) = 110.

b) Her expected loss is (1/2)($14,400 – $10,000) = $2,200. Her expected income is (1/2)($14,400 + $10,000) = $12,200. The minimum certain income she would accept to avoid the risk is given by the solution to $u(X^*) = \sqrt{X^*} = 110$ or $X^* = \$12,100$. The risk premium is $12,200 – $12,100 = $100. See Figure 5A.3 (on the next page).

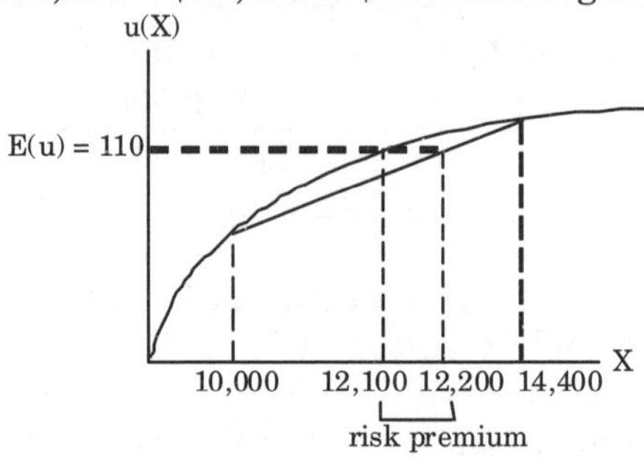

Figure 5A.3

c) With the new probabilities, E(u) = (3/4)120 + (1/4)100 = 115.

The minimum certain income she would accept to avoid the risk is given by the solution to $u(X^*) = \sqrt{X^*} = 115$ or $X^* = \$13,225$.
Her expected income is $(3/4)(\$14,400) + (1/4)(\$10,000) = \$13,300$.
The risk premium is $13,300 – $13,225 = $75. Compared to part (b), the premium she is willing to pay has dropped due to the lower probability of loss.

11. Table 5A.3 shows profits under each outcome:

Decision	Low Demand (Pr = 0.4)	High Demand (Pr = 0.6)	Expected Profit
Small Plant	$62,500	$ 62,500	$62,500
Large Plant	–$12,500	$150,000	$85,000

Table 5A.3

F&L, being risk neutral, will choose to build a large plant under incomplete information. Their expected profits are maximized by doing this and are equal to 0.4(–12,500) + 0.6(150,000) = $85,000. Expected profits with complete information are 0.4(62,500) + 0.6(150,000) = $115,000. Therefore, the maximum amount they will be willing to pay for complete information is $115,000 – $85,000 = $30,000.

12. In microeconomic theory, we are usually reluctant to think about individuals' preferences changing. More often, opportunities or information change. In this case, individuals are probably willing to hold riskier portfolios early in life because they have more opportunity to adjust their portfolio if their returns are low. For example, a younger person who invests heavily in stocks and loses money could save more out of income for several years to make up for the loss in wealth. The older one gets, the fewer years one would have in which to make these adjustments.

SELF-TEST ANSWERS

13. c) Her expected loss is 0.04($8,000) = $320. Since she is only willing to pay $300, which is less than the expected value of her loss, she must be risk loving.

14. a) Nanette has a diminishing marginal utility of income, so she is risk averse.

15. b) His marginal utility of income first rises (risk-loving), then falls (risk-averse).

16. b) In risk-return diagrams, an investor's indifference curves are upward sloping. If different types of assets are held, those assets with higher variances require higher expected returns.

17. b) All three options (2 clothing stores, 2 sporting goods stores, and 1 of each) have expected earnings of $120,000. Expressing all dollar values in thousands,

E(Profit with 2 clothing stores) = 0.5(40 + 40) + 0.5(80 + 80) = 120.

E(Profit with 2 sports stores) = 0.5(90 + 90) + 0.5(30 + 30) = 120.

E(Profit with 1 clothing & 1 sports store) = 0.5(40 + 90) + 0.5(80 + 30) = 120.

However, diversifying with one of each type of store will have a lower variance of earnings:

Variance (2 clothing stores) = $0.5(80 - 120)^2 + 0.5(160 - 120)^2 = 1{,}600$.

Variance (2 sports stores) = $0.5(180 - 120)^2 + 0.5(60 - 120)^2 = 3{,}600$.

Variance (1 clothing & 1 sports store) = $0.5[(40 + 90) - 120)]^2 + 0.5[(80 + 30) - 120]^2 = 100$.

Therefore, the risk-averse investor will choose to open one store of each type.

18. a) The risk-neutral investor will open two sporting goods stores if the expected return from taking that action is higher than the alternatives. Let P = probability of good weather. Then, the two conditions that must hold are:

$$P(180) + (1 - P)(60) > P(80) + (1 - P)(160)$$

and, $P(180) + (1 - P)(60) > P(130) + (1 - P)(110)$.

Solving both equations for P yields:

$$200P > 100, \text{ or } P > 1/2, \text{ and } 100P > 50, \text{ or } P > 1/2.$$

19. e) Loss aversion describes behavior with repsect to assets which have fallen in value.

CHAPTER 6
PRODUCTION

IMPORTANT CONCEPTS

- Production Function
- Short-Run vs. Long-Run
- Total Product, Average Product, Marginal Product
- Isoquants
- Marginal Rate of Technical Substitution
- Law of Diminishing Returns
- Increasing, Decreasing, and Constant Returns to Scale

CHAPTER HIGHLIGHTS

The *production function* shows the relationship between the quantities of various inputs used and the maximum (technically feasible) output that can be produced with those inputs. The inputs that we tend to focus on are capital (buildings, machinery) and labor (skilled and unskilled workers).Other important inputs are materials and land. The production function is written as $Q = F(K, L)$.Production functions will differ across industries and can change over time as technology changes.

In the *short run*, there is at least one factor of production that is fixed (cannot be varied). It is common to think of a firm's capital as being fixed in the short run because it cannot be varied easily. It takes time to build a new factory or even to install a new piece of equipment, for example. The *long run* is the amount of time needed to make all inputs variable.

Restricting our focus to two variable inputs, say labor and capital, we can use an *isoquant* to summarize how different levels of these inputs might be combined to produce a given output level. Each isoquant is a curve showing all the possible combinations of labor and capital that can be used to produce a fixed amount of output—a higher isoquant corresponds to a higher output level. The convex shape of an isoquant implies that the production process is flexible enough to allow labor and capital to be substituted (at some rate) to reach the same output level.

The *marginal rate of technical substitution* (MRTS) describes how capital and labor can be substituted, so that output remains constant. The MRTS is the negative of the slope along a given isoquant at a particular point (or for small changes in capital and labor along an isoquant).If the isoquant is convex, then as we move along an isoquant, substituting one input for another, the MRTS decreases (the isoquant becomes flatter if we are moving along the horizontal axis). In the extreme case of inputs that are perfect substitutes or perfect complements, the isoquant will be a straight line or L-shaped, respectively.

Analyzing a firm's production process involves discovering the exact nature of the technology as inputs vary. The *marginal product* of labor ($\Delta Q/\Delta L$) is the additional output (or *total product*) that is produced when labor is increased by one unit. The *average product of labor* is defined as Q/L. The average product and marginal product of capital can be defined similarly if we hold labor fixed and let capital vary.

The *law of diminishing returns* describes a pattern that we observe in most production processes: holding all inputs fixed except for one, and continually increasing the remaining input, a point will eventually be reached at which the rate of increase in output begins to fall. Note that the law of diminishing returns does not state that output declines as additional input is added. It only says that the rate of increase in output will begin to get smaller, after a point, as additional input is added.

Diminishing returns is not the same as *returns to scale*. The question to have in mind when thinking about returns to scale is "What will happen to output if *all* inputs are increased proportionally?" If doubling all inputs causes output to more than double, there are *increasing returns to scale*. If doubling all inputs causes output to double, there are *constant returns to scale*. If doubling all inputs causes output to go up by less than double, there are *decreasing returns to scale*. It is normal for most firms to experience increasing returns to scale over some initial range of output and then perhaps to experience decreasing returns to scale as they become large-scale operations.

CONCEPT REVIEW AND EXERCISES

FIRMS AND THEIR PRODUCTION DECISIONS Section 6.1)

In economics, the technology of a firm is the process by which inputs (factors of production) are turned into outputs (products for sale in the market).Inputs, which include human resources, machinery, and raw materials, are usually categorized as labor, capital, and materials. The output may be a final good sold to consumers or an intermediate good, i.e., capital or materials used by other firms. We describe this technology with a *production function* that tells us the amount of output for each specified combination of inputs.

To simplify the presentation, we often consider only two inputs, labor and capital. In effect, this means that we are holding constant the material inputs into the final product. Using this simplification, we can write a production function for a given level of technology as $Q = F(K, L)$.

While technical inefficiency (getting less output with the same inputs) is a real possibility, we assume in this chapter that firms are operating efficiently. This means that the firm is getting as much output as is technically feasible with a given level of inputs.

THE SHORT RUN VERSUS THE LONG RUN

The difference between the short run and the long run is not based explicitly on time; rather, it depends on the characteristics of production inputs. In the *short run*, the use of at least one factor of production cannot be adjusted. In the short run, therefore, the firm has some fixed inputs. Typically, capital is the input that is fixed in the short run. In the *long run*, all input levels can be adjusted. The time horizons for these runs will differ across firms and industries. The level of capital at a dry cleaning establishment can be adjusted in two months, whereas a major capital addition at an aluminum plant could take two to three years. But whether the short run is designated as two months or two years, there must be some input level that, by definition, cannot be varied within that time period.

PRODUCTION WITH ONE VARIABLE INPUT (LABOR) (Section 6.2)

To introduce several concepts relating to the technology of the firm, consider the data in Table 6.1.A firm uses two inputs, capital, which is fixed, and labor, which is variable, to produce its output. The table tells us how output changes as the labor input varies.

DAILY PLANT OUTPUT OF COPPER WIRE

(1) Labor (person-hours) L	(2) Capital (machine-hours) K	(3) Output (pounds) Q	(4) Average Product (pounds per person-hour) Q/L	(5) Marginal Product (pounds per person-hour) ΔQ/ΔL
10	40	200	20	—
11	40	231	21	31
12	40	264	22	33
13	40	286	22	22
14	40	294	21	8
15	40	300	20	6

Table 6.1

The first two columns give the input levels. Capital is held constant at 40 units to focus on the effects of changing the level of labor input. The last three columns are productivity measures. Column (3) shows the output produced with these inputs. The fourth column shows the *average product* of labor, AP_L, which is the output per unit of labor. The average product of labor for an industry or the economy is referred to as "labor productivity." Trends in labor productivity growth are important for determining how fast living standards rise.

Column (5) shows the *marginal product* of labor, MP_L, which is the additional output resulting from the addition of one more unit of labor, or $\Delta Q/\Delta L$. For example, the marginal product of labor between 12 and 13 person-hours of labor equals 22 pounds (286 – 264). Thus, if 12 person-hours of labor are currently being hired, employing one more person-hour of labor would raise output by 22 pounds.

The data in the table describe a common relationship between MP_L and AP_L. If $MP_L > AP_L$, AP_L increases as labor input increases. If $MP_L = AP_L$, then AP_L is constant. If $MP_L < AP_L$, then AP_L will fall as labor input increases. For example, at $L = 11$, $AP_L = 21$ and the MP_L of the next worker equals 33. Since 33 is greater than 21, we know that AP_L must rise, which we can verify by looking down column (4).

Since the level of capital input does not change throughout Table 6.1, we can graph the output obtained from various labor inputs in two dimensions. Figure 6.1a displays a graph of output versus labor input for the data of Table 6.1. This curve is called the *total product of labor curve.* Figure 6.1b displays the graph of the marginal product and average product of labor.

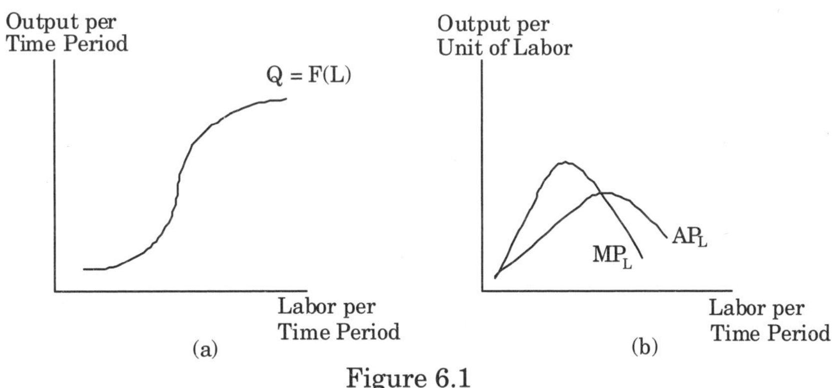

Figure 6.1

Exercise:

1. a) Fill in the blank entries in the following table of production data:

Labor L	Capital K	Output Q	Average Product Q/L	Marginal Product ΔQ/ΔL
3	8	33		n.a.
4	8		9	
5	8			4
6	8		7.5	5

Table 6.2

b) Graph the total product of labor curve with output (Q) as a function of labor input (L), as in Figure 6.1a.

c) Graph the AP_L and MP_L curves as a function of labor input as in Figure 6.1b.

2. If MP_L is declining, is AP_L always declining in that output range? Why or why not?

THE LAW OF DIMINISHING MARGINAL RETURNS

When the level of capital is fixed, it is regularly observed that MP_L eventually starts falling as labor is continually increased. This is the *law of diminishing returns.* Diminishing returns arise in the short run when continual increases in labor, holding the level of capital fixed, result in smaller and smaller increases in total output. Diminishing marginal returns is a short-run concept because it deals with the response of output to changes in a single input; in the long run, a firm may change all of its inputs. Do not confuse it with returns to scale (discussed later in this chapter), that describes how output changes as *all* inputs are varied proportionally.

Exercise: ▶ ▶ ▶ ▶ ▶ ▶ ▶

3. Figure 6.2 shows the total product curve for Quik Image copy shop. The copy shop currently has two copying machines.

a) As Quik Image expands the number of workers, holding the number of copiers fixed, will diminishing returns set in at point A, B, C, D, or E?

b) Draw the new total product curve if Quik Image acquires another copier. Will the point of diminishing returns stay the same? Explain.

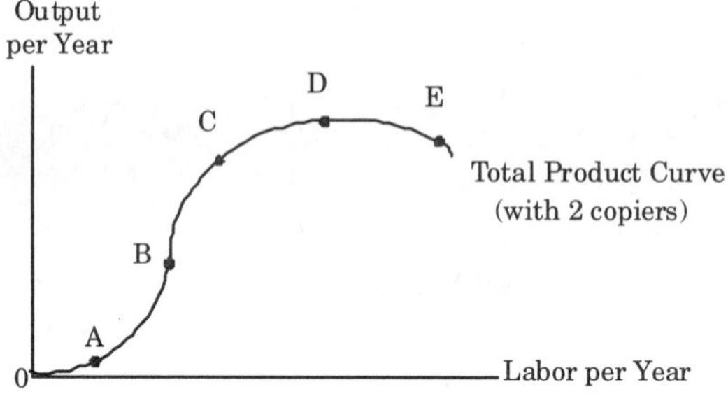

Figure 6.2

PRODUCTION WITH TWO VARIABLE INPUTS (Section 6.3)

When more than one input level is free to be adjusted, a firm faces the question of what is the best input combination to use. This section analyzes the different choices the firm faces when deciding how to produce each particular level of output.

With two inputs, we can graph *isoquants* of the production function in two dimensions. Just as an indifference curve shows all combinations of two goods that give a consumer a particular level of satisfaction, an isoquant displays all combinations of labor and capital that yield the same level of output. Isoquants are different from indifference curves in one important respect: we can observe and measure output, whereas we could not measure utility with ordinal preferences. Isoquants slope downward—a firm can reduce the level of one input while increasing the level of the other input and maintain the same rate of output.

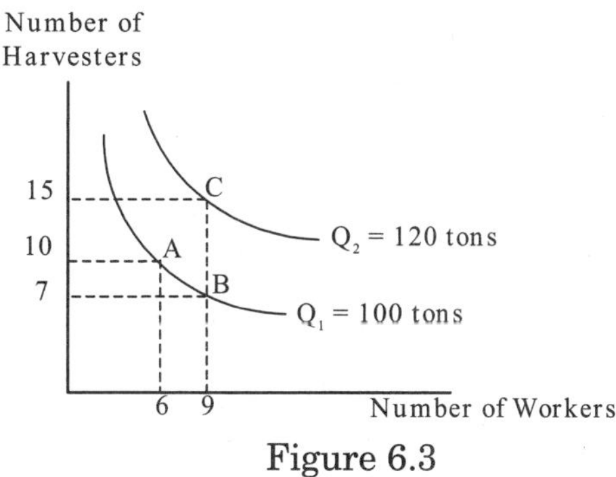

Figure 6.3

Figure 6.3 plots two typical isoquants for wheat harvesting with two variable inputs, harvesting equipment and labor. Isoquant Q_1 is made up of all those combinations of workers and harvesters per year that could be used to produce 100 tons of wheat, e.g., points A and B. Point C, which corresponds to more of *both* labor and capital, lies on a higher isoquant, Q_2.

Exercise: ◗ ◗ ◗ ◗ ◗ ◗ ◗

4. Suppose an isoquant for a particular production process were so tightly curved that it was almost L-shaped. What would this imply about the technology?

SUBSTITUTION AMONG INPUTS

Just as the marginal rate of substitution describes a consumer's willingness to trade goods while obtaining an equally preferred market basket, *the marginal rate of technical substitution* (MRTS) describes how the firm can replace one input with another and still achieve the same output. The MRTS equals the negative of the slope of the isoquant, or $-\Delta K/\Delta L$, holding Q constant. The MRTS also equals the ratio of the marginal product of labor to the marginal product of capital, MP_L/MP_K. As labor increases and capital decreases along an isoquant, the convex shape of the isoquant implies that MRTS falls. (Recall that a negatively sloped curve is convex if it gets flatter as you move down the curve.)

Two special cases involving isoquants are important. In one extreme, if inputs are perfect substitutes, the isoquants are parallel straight lines, and the MRTS is constant. On an assembly line, for example, a part might be easily installed either by a worker or by a machine. In the other extreme, with a fixed proportions production function, the isoquants are L-shaped. For example, one person can type at only one keyboard. A second keyboard without a second worker is useless.

Exercise: ▶ ▶ ▶ ▶ ▶ ▶ ▶

5. Sketch the isoquants corresponding to the following situations:

a) Thermos production, with thermos carafes on the x-axis (as one input) and thermos lids (as the other input) on the y-axis. (Assume capital is held constant.)

b) Office building construction, with labor on the x-axis and capital on the y-axis.

c) Hamburger production using either gas grills (x-axis) or electric grills (y-axis), assuming the two types of grills are perfect substitutes.

RETURNS TO SCALE (Section 6.4)

When all factor inputs are increased in proportion, we describe the magnitude of the resulting output change using the concept of *returns to scale*. If doubling all inputs causes output to more than double, then the production function exhibits *increasing returns to scale*. Specialization of labor is one important source of increasing returns—as the firm grows, workers don't have to perform multiple tasks and can become more efficient. Another important source is more efficient use of large-scale equipment—if you double the diameter of a pipeline, for example, the increase in the cost of the materials to build the larger pipeline will be small compared to the increase in the volume of output you can pump through. If doubling all inputs causes output to double exactly, then there are *constant returns to scale*. Most firms experience some increasing returns to scale as they grow, but there are limits: if doubling all inputs causes output to rise by less than double, then there are *decreasing returns to scale*. One common source of decreasing returns to scale is difficulties in management, as the organization grows increasingly complex.

Exercise: ▶ ▶ ▶ ▶ ▶ ▶ ▶

6. Table 6.3 gives labor, capital, and output data for four different isoquants.

a) Calculate the percentage changes in labor and capital inputs used in moving from the input combinations A to B, B to C, and C to D.

b) Are there increasing, decreasing, or constant returns to scale between A and B? B and C? C and D?

Input Combination	Output	Labor	Capital
A	100	20	40
B	250	40	80
C	600	90	180
D	810	126	252

Table 6.3

PROBLEM SET

7. Why is the total product of labor curve never downward sloping?

8. The production function for fragles is $Q = F(K, L) = 0.5L + \sqrt{K}$.

a) What type of returns to scale does this production function display?

b) If $K = 4$, what is the average product of labor?

*c) If $K = 4$, what is the short-run marginal product of labor?

9. Suppose that a firm currently has 100 machines available for its production process. Output per person-hour when 100 machines are used is described by the function:

$$Q = -50 + 10L - 0.02L^2.$$

With this total product curve, the marginal product of labor is:

$$MP_L = 10 - 0.04L,$$

and the average product of labor is:

$$AP_L = -50/L + 10 - 0.02L.$$

a) Graph the AP_L curve over the range $L = 10$ to $L = 70$ (find AP_L at intervals of 10 person-hours between 10 and 70 and plot the points).

b) At what level of labor input does the AP_L curve reach its maximum? (Use your graph or solve algebraically.) What is the marginal product of labor at this input level?

10. You manage a department in a large corporation. Two years ago, you had 20 workers and produced 40,000 units. The company allocated 10 more workers to your department last year, and output increased to 45,000. You just received a memo from your boss indicating that he is very concerned about the 500-unit fall in the average productivity of your workers. How can you defend yourself?

11. There are two steps in the manufacture of widgets. First, the sheet metal is run through a shear that cuts out the individual parts. Then, the parts are run through a progressive dye press that assembles them into widgets. Each widget requires one unit of sheet metal. Further, the shear can cut parts for 3,000 widgets per week, and the press can assemble 2,000 per week. The machines are available only in integer units.

a) How many of each machine, and how much material, is the minimum needed to produce 9,000 widgets per week? To produce 12,000 per week?

b) Over this range of output, does the production process exhibit increasing, constant, or decreasing returns to scale?

12. In Figure 6.4, identify all the output levels at which $AP_L = MP_L$. At which one of these output levels does AP_L reach its maximum value?

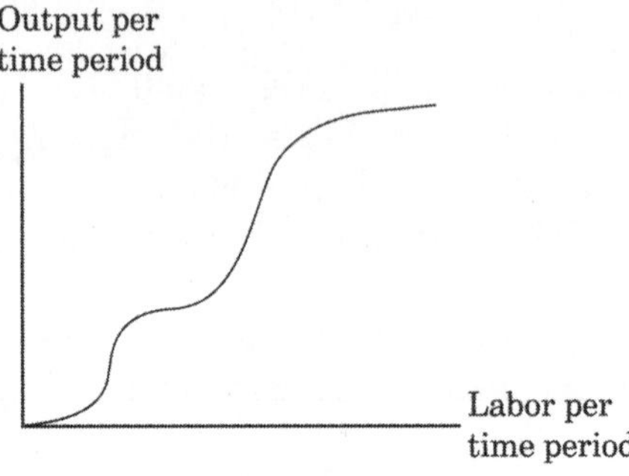

Figure 6.4

SELF-TEST

13. A production function for a firm describes:
- a) the quantity that should be produced to maximize profit.
- b) what is technically feasible when the firm produces efficiently.
- c) the revenue earned from producing efficiently.
- d) the firm's actual production with given inputs.
- e) All of the above are correct.

14. A production isoquant describes:
- a) all the different output levels possible as labor input changes.
- b) all the different output levels possible as capital input changes.
- c) all the combinations of labor and capital that produce the same level of output.
- d) all the combinations of labor and capital that maximize profit.
- e) None of the above is correct.

15. In the short run:
- a) there are no fixed inputs.
- b) all inputs are fixed.
- c) at least one input level cannot be varied.
- d) labor input cannot be varied.
- e) b) and d)

16. The marginal product of labor equals:
- a) output divided by labor input (Q/L).
- b) the additional output from the last unit of labor ($\Delta Q/\Delta L$).
- c) labor input divided by capital input (L/K).
- d) the labor input needed for the last unit of output ($\Delta L/\Delta Q$).
- e) None of the above is correct.

17. Diminishing marginal returns means that:
a) as more capital is used in production, holding labor input constant, MP_K falls.
b) as labor increases and capital decreases along a given isoquant, MRTS increases.
c) if capital and labor inputs double, output increases by less than double.
d) a) and c)
e) a) and b)

The next two questions refer to the following table:

Labor Input (person-hours) L	Capital Input (machine-hours) K	Output (pounds) Q
35	40	210
36	40	252
37	40	266

18. The marginal product of the 36th person-hour is:
a) 42
b) 40
c) 14
d) 6
e) None of the above is correct.

19. The average product of labor when 37 person-hours are employed is:
a) 7
b) 7.2
c) 14
d) 6.65
e) None of the above is correct.

20. Decreasing returns to scale may arise from:
a) specialization of inputs.
b) duplication of plant and equipment at equal cost.
c) inefficiencies in management.
d) using inputs in unequal proportions.
e) None of the above is correct.

21. If labor is the only variable input, marginal product reaches its maximum:
a) at the point where the average product curve is horizontal.
b) at the point where average product equals marginal product.
c) at the inflection point of the total product curve.
d) at the point where the total product curve turns down.
e) None of the above is correct.

22. A production process would exhibit increasing returns to scale if:
- a) adding a complete second shift increased output by less than 100%.
- b) doubling output required less than twice as much energy.
- c) opening a second assembly line increased output by 100%.
- d) planting twice as many acres and doubling all other inputs increased production by less than 100%.
- e) None of the above is correct.

23. If a firm using only capital and labor doubles its labor input and output increases by less than 100%, then:
- a) production exhibits decreasing returns to scale.
- b) production exhibits increasing returns to scale.
- c) production exhibits diminishing returns.
- d) a) and c).
- e) b) and c).

ANSWERS TO CHAPTER 6

EXERCISE ANSWERS

1. a) See Table 6A.1. If L = 3, AP_L = Q/L = 33/3 = 11. If L = 4, AP_L = 9, so Q = (AP_L) L = 9(4) = 36. MP_L between 3 and 4 equals 36 – 33 = 3. Since MP_L between 4 and 5 is 4, Q = 40 when L = 5. AP_L is then 40/5 = 8. Adding another unit of labor increases output by 5 units, so Q = 45 if L = 5. We can also find this from Q = (AP_L) L = 7.5(6) = 45.

Labor L	Capital K	Output Q	Average Product Q/L	Marginal Product ΔQ/ΔL
3	8	33	11	n/a
4	8	36	9	3
5	8	40	8	4
6	8	45	7.5	5

Table 6A.1

b) See Figure 6A.1a.
c) See Figure 6A.1b.

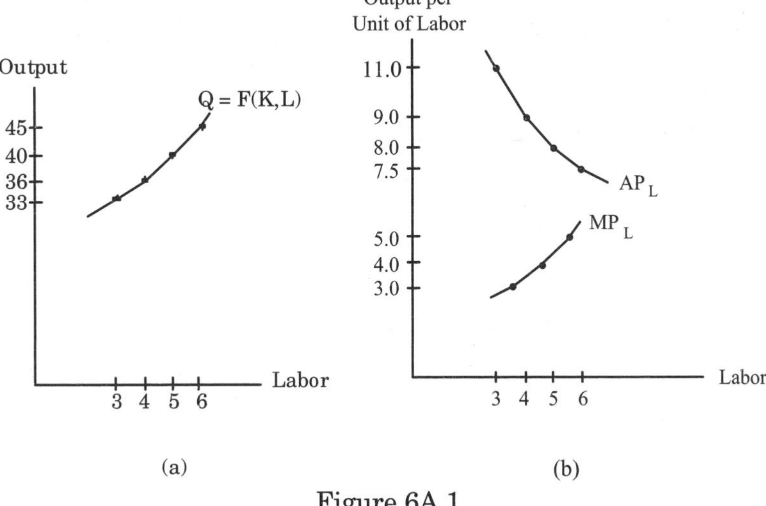

Figure 6A.1

2. When the marginal product of labor is falling, the average product of labor may be rising or falling. The slope of the AP_L curve depends not on the slope of the MP_L curve, but on whether the MP_L curve lies above or below the AP_L curve.

3. a) Diminishing returns set in at point B, when the marginal product of labor (the slope of the total product curve with capital fixed) begins to increase at a decreasing rate. A common wrong answer to this question would be point D, where the MP_L changes from positive to negative. Diminishing marginal returns does not require a negative MP_L. It only requires that additional units of an input become less productive, although still adding to output.

b) See Figure 6A.2 (on the next page). Additional capital shifts the entire total product curve. The point of diminishing returns will occur at a higher level of labor because additional workers will have an extra machine with which to work.

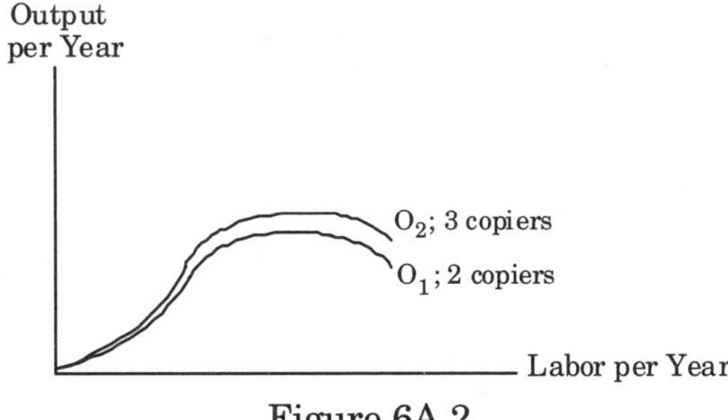

Figure 6A.2

4. Figure 6A.3 shows a tightly curved isoquant. In this case, the firm is relatively inflexible about substituting labor for capital (or vice versa) to maintain an output of Q_1. If the firm were at point A and tried laying off a few workers, it would have to buy a lot of machinery (move to point B) to compensate for the loss in labor while maintaining Q_1. The dotted line isoquant is less tightly curved and therefore represents a more flexible production technology: capital can more easily be substituted for labor while maintaining an output level of Q_1 (moving from point A to point C).

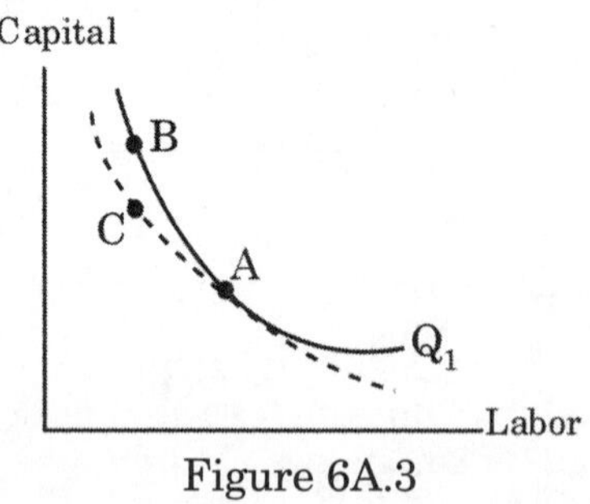

Figure 6A.3

5. a) Lids and carafes are perfect complements. Both inputs are required (in a ratio of 1 to 1) to make the product.

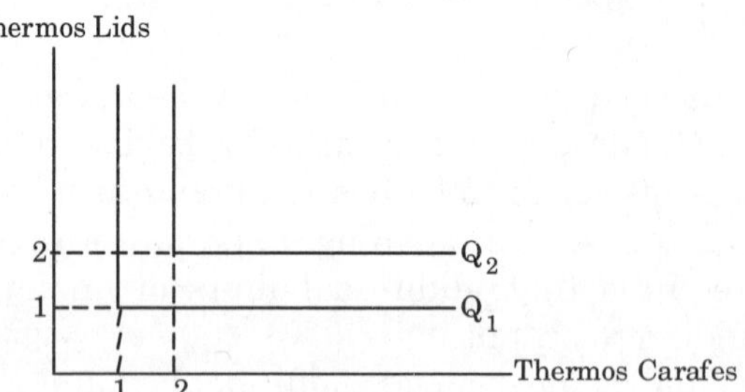

Figure 6A.4a

b) The curvature of these isoquants depends on how substitutable labor and capital are in office building construction.

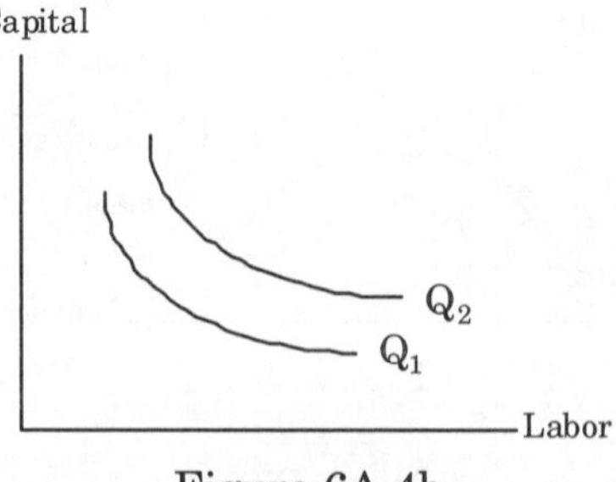

Figure 6A.4b

c) If gas and electric grills are perfect substitutes, the isoquants are straight lines.

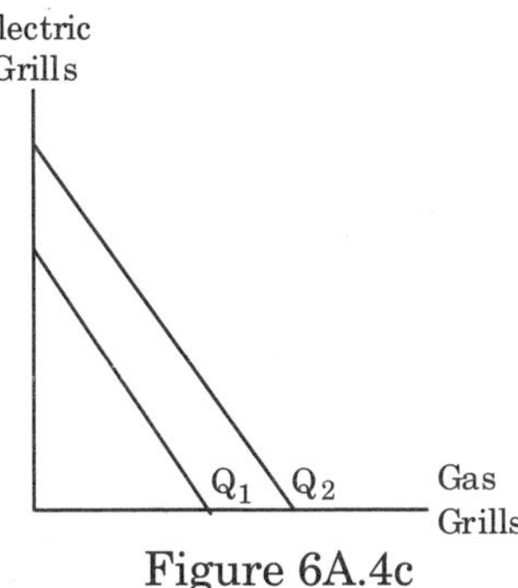

Figure 6A.4c

6. a) Between A and B, both labor and capital increase by 100 percent. Between B and C, they increase by 125 percent, and between C and D, they increase by 40 percent.

b) Output increases by 150 percent, 140 percent, and 35 percent between A and B, B and C, and C and D, respectively. This implies that there are increasing returns to scale between A and B, since inputs increase by 100 percent and output goes up by 150 percent. Using similar logic, there are increasing returns between B and C (140% > 125%) and decreasing returns between C and D (35% < 40%).

PROBLEM SET ANSWERS

7. The total product of labor curve is the graph of the production function with only one variable input. Since a production function tells us the maximum output for each input level and the firm could always choose to use only part of its labor input, maximum output will never fall with an increase in input. In other words, a rational firm would not choose to employ additional labor if it caused a decline in total output.

8. a) The simplest way to determine returns to scale is to compare output at two different input levels, where the second input level has more of both inputs in the same proportion. Analytically, compare $Q^* = F(K^*, L^*)$ and $Q^{**} = F(cK^*, cL^*)$ where c is a constant. In this case, $Q^*=0.5L^*+\sqrt{K^*}$ and $Q^{**}=0.5(cL^*)+\sqrt{cK^*}$. For $c > 1$ (an increase in input levels), $Q^{**} < cQ^*$. (Why? The first term increases proportionately, but the second term only goes up by $\sqrt{c}$ which is less than proportionately.) Since $Q^{**} < cQ^*$, decreasing returns to scale is exhibited. (You could also plug in numbers for different levels of L and K to answer the question.)

b) With K fixed at 4, the short-run production function is $F(4,L) = 0.5L + \sqrt{4} = 0.5L + 2$
$AP_L = F(4, L)/L = 0.5 + 2/L$.

c) The marginal product of labor is the first derivative of total product with respect to labor, or $\partial F(4, L)/\partial L = 0.5$. (You can also find this by measuring F(4, L) and F(4, L – 1).)

9. a) Table 6A.2 shows the values for AP_L and Figure 6A.5 plots these values.

L	$AP_L = Q/L$
10	4.80
20	7.10
30	7.73
40	7.95
50	8.00
60	7.97
70	7.89

Table 6A.2

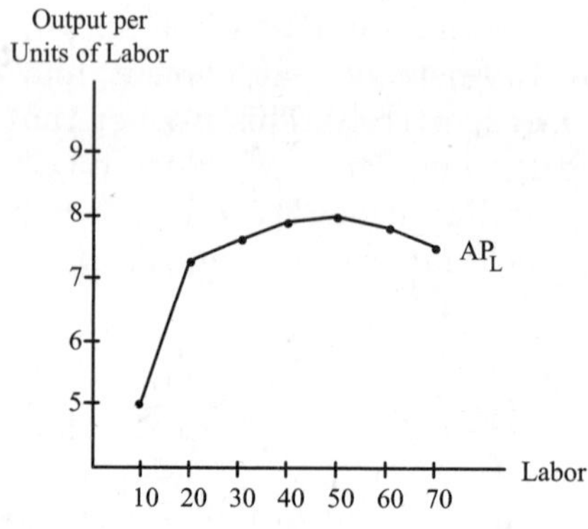

Figure 6A.5

b) The table above shows that AP_L hits its maximum at L = 50. But we should check for the maximum algebraically, just in case it lies between 50 and 60. AP_L reaches its maximum when $AP_L = MP_L$:

$-50/L + 10 - 0.02L = 10 - 0.04L$, or $-0.02L^2 = -500$, so $L^2 = 2{,}500$, or L = 50.

Thus, L = 50 is exactly where AP_L hits its maximum.

At L = 50, $MP_L = 10 - 0.04(50) = 8$.

10. Since your department was allocated more workers but not more capital, the law of diminishing marginal returns indicates that the additional output from these last workers might be lower. If the marginal product were less than the average product, the average product would fall. Thus, the decline is probably simply due to technical matters, not management problems. It would be prudent to consider increasing the capital/labor ratio in the department in the future.

11. a) 9,000 widgets: 9,000 units of material, 3 shears, 5 presses.
12,000 widgets: 12,000 units of material, 4 shears, 6 presses.

b) When materials increase 33 percent, shears increase 33 percent, and presses increase 20 percent, then output will increase by 33 percent. Thus, it takes less than a 33-percent increase in all inputs to increase output 33 percent, so the production process exhibits increasing returns to scale over this output range.

12. See Figure 6A.6. Whenever a ray from the origin (whose slope is AP_L) is also a tangent to the total product curve at a point, $AP_L = MP_L$ at that quantity. The steepest of these rays is then the maximum value of AP_L. In this case, it is when $L = L_3$.

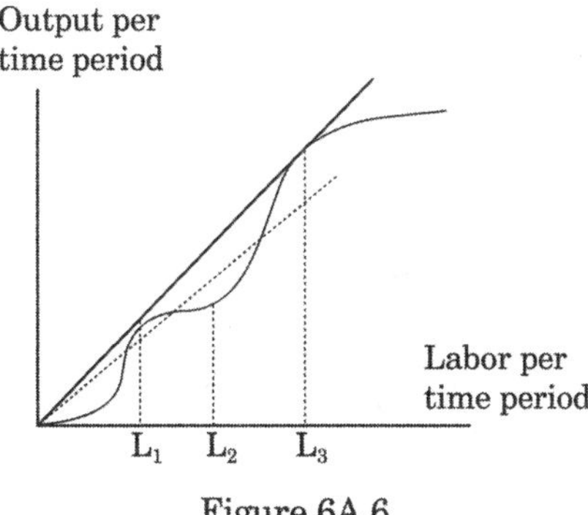

Figure 6A.6

SELF-TEST ANSWERS

13. b) The production function describes the firm's particular technology when used most efficiently.

14. c) This is the definition of an isoquant.

15. c) Some input must be fixed in the short run, according to the basic definition of "short run." In the long run, by definition, all inputs are variable.

16. b) This is the definition of MP_L.

17. a) Diminishing returns refers to increasing one input with the others held fixed. Choice b) is a move along an isoquant, which means that both inputs are being varied, and choice c) describes decreasing returns to scale.

18. a) MP_L = Q(40, 36) – Q(40, 35) = 252 – 210 = 42.

19. b) AP_L = 266/37 = 7.2 (with rounding).

20. c) Choice a) is a source of increasing returns to scale. Choice b) describes constant returns to scale.

21. c) This is the point where the slope of the total product curve, which equals marginal product, is the greatest (or most steep).

22. b) The other choices are all constant or decreasing returns to scale.

23. c) Returns to scale relate to increasing *all* inputs proportionately.

CHAPTER 7
THE COST OF PRODUCTION

IMPORTANT CONCEPTS

- Economic Cost versus Accounting Cost
- Opportunity Cost
- Difference Between Fixed Costs and Variable Costs
- Difference Between Fixed Costs and Sunk Costs
- Marginal Cost, Average Variable Cost, Average Total Cost
- Isocost Line
- Expansion Path
- Economies and Diseconomies of Scale
- Economies of Scope
- Learning Curve

CHAPTER HIGHLIGHTS

Different cost concepts are used to answer an array of different questions that are important to the firm: Should the firm enter the market? What is the optimal short-run output level? What is the optimal long-run output level? When should the firm exit the market? The first cost concept to learn is the distinction between *economic costs* and *accounting costs*. Economic costs are forward-looking, while accounting costs tend to be retrospective. An economist recognizes that every choice carries an *opportunity cost* of the path not taken. The opportunity cost is the cost associated with opportunities that are foregone by not putting the firm's resources to their best alternative use. *Sunk cost* is an expenditure that has already been made and cannot be recovered. Therefore, sunk costs should not be considered in forward-looking decisions (since the past cannot be altered no matter what the current decision).

In the short run, there are both fixed and variable inputs. The short-run/long-run distinction leads to an array of different concepts describing the costs of production: *fixed cost*, *variable cost*, *total cost*, *average fixed cost*, *average variable cost*, *average total cost*, and *marginal cost*. Each of these cost concepts is defined in the review below. The concept of *economies of scale* is linked to the shape of the long-run average cost curve. Economies of scale arise when doubling output causes total cost to go up by less than double, leading to a decrease in average cost. Diseconomies of scale arise when doubling output causes total cost to go up by more than double, leading to an increase in average cost.

If the long-run average cost curve is U-shaped, the firm faces economies of scale at relatively low output levels and diseconomies of scale at higher output levels.

The *isocost line* shows all possible combinations of labor and capital that can be purchased for a given total cost. In order to choose the mix of inputs that minimizes costs, the firm will choose the lowest isocost line that is just tangent to the isoquant for the target output level. At this tangency point, the slope of the isoquant is equal to the slope of the isocost, or MRTS = w/r, where w is the price of labor (the wage) and r is the price of capital (the rental rate for machinery). Connecting the points of tangency for different output levels gives us the firm's *expansion path*.

Economies of scope describe what happens to costs when the firm produces more than one product under the same roof. Economies of scope occur when a single firm producing several products jointly can do so at a lower cost than several firms each producing only one of the products.

In many production processes, particularly those that are complex, the costs of production fall as management and labor become more efficient and gain experience and knowledge of the organization and technology of production. *Learning curve effects* capture what happens to costs as the firm gains experience with the production process over time. A learning curve describes the relationship between a firm's cumulative output (all of the output it has produced since going into business) and the amount of inputs needed to produce a unit of output.

CONCEPT REVIEW AND EXERCISES

MEASURING COST: WHICH COSTS MATTER? (Section 7.1)

Accounting costs (which include actual expenses and depreciation expenses for capital equipment) tend to be historical costs. Firms making forward-looking decisions need to focus on costs that capture relevant future expenses. The key to understanding economic cost is that every decision to do something is implicitly a decision not to do something else. The notion of *opportunity costs* embodies that principle: the opportunity cost of using a resource is the value forgone by not using it in its highest valued use. For example, the economic cost of going to school includes the cost of tuition, books, food, and housing plus the salary that you could have earned if you had gone to work instead. This forgone salary is an opportunity cost of spending your time at school and should be included as part of the economic cost. Two important opportunity costs for firms are the value of the firm owner's time and the value of any capital used in the business.

Exercise: ▶▶▶▶▶▶▶

1. In 1970, an art collector paid $10,000 for an Andy Warhol painting. Warhol's paintings have risen in value since then. True or False: The opportunity cost of owning the painting this year is the interest the collector could have received on the $10,000 invested in the painting.

2. Josh, a second year MBA student, takes three hours off one evening and uses his car to go to a movie with a friend. A ticket to the movie costs Josh $8, gasoline for the trip costs $3, and Josh passed up tutoring a student that night for $20 an hour. He could also have used the three hours to work as a grader for a professor at $15 an hour. What is Josh's economic cost of going to the movie?

A *sunk cost* is an irretrievable past cost. Sunk are expenditures that have already been made and cannot be recovered. Only future benefits and future costs, not sunk costs, should be considered in making current economic decisions. Expenditures on advertising or on research and development are often examples of sunk costs. They cannot be altered or avoided (since they have already been spent!), and thus should have no influence on a firm's future decisions.

Exercise: ▶ ▶ ▶ ▶ ▶ ▶ ▶

3. The Quick Corp. had a great business idea: produce an over-the-counter pain reliever and sell it at a discount compared to the price charged by the market leader. At this price, they would earn a normal return on the start-up costs (primarily advertising) plus some additional economic profit. After they introduced the product, it was so successful that the market leader matched Quick Corp.'s price. Quick's sales fell almost to zero. Then, they learned from market research that selling at a deeper discount would enable them to meet all production costs, but they would earn a below-normal return on their start-up costs, which they now consider to be sunk costs. Should they stay in the business, or should they abandon this product line?

COST IN THE SHORT RUN (Section 7.2)

Recall that the short run for a firm is the time horizon during which one input is held constant. To study short-run costs, we hold fixed the level of capital and study the changes in the quantity of labor hired. It is important to distinguish between two types of costs—*fixed costs*, which do not vary with output, and *variable costs*, which depend on the firm's output level. *Total costs* are the sum of fixed and variable costs. From total costs, we can find *average total cost* (the cost per unit of output), and *marginal cost* (the cost of an additional unit of output). *Average variable cost* is the variable cost per unit of output, whereas *average fixed cost* is the fixed cost divided by total output. Note that fixed costs are *not* the same as sunk costs. A fixed cost is an obligation to pay a certain amount regardless of the output level. For example, interest payments on a loan must be made even if output goes to zero. These interest payments are not sunk, though, because they have not been paid yet.

Fixed costs do not vary with output in the short run (because the firm has, by definition, locked themselves in to certain payments), but they can be avoided in the long run.

Consider the data in Table 7.1 for a steel producer:

(1) Output (tons)	(2) Total Cost ($)	(3) Variable Cost ($)	(4) Fixed Cost ($)	(5) Avg. Total Cost ($/ton)	(6) Avg. Variable Cost ($/ton)	(7) Marginal Cost ($/ton)
Q	TC = FC + VC	VC	FC	ATC – TC/Q	AVC = VC/Q	MC = DTC/DQ
8	2,800	800	2,000	350	100	n.a.
9	2,880	880	2,000	320	97.8	80
10	2,980	980	2,000	298	98	100
11	3,100	1,100	2,000	281.8	100	120

Table 7.1

The two fundamental columns in this table are columns (3) and (4), variable cost and fixed cost. From these two columns we can derive all the other entries. Total cost is simply the sum of fixed and variable cost: TC(Q) = FC + VC(Q). Average total cost, ATC(Q), equals TC(Q)/Q, and average variable cost, AVC(Q), equals VC(Q)/Q. We can also calculate average fixed cost, or AFC(Q), which equals FC/Q. Marginal cost is the increase in cost that results from producing one extra unit of output, or MC = ΔVC/ΔQ. Geometrically, MC at any given output level is the slope of the line tangent to the total cost curve at that output. (Notice that we have written all the cost definitions except total fixed cost as functions of Q. After this point we will usually leave out the function notation, but keep in mind that all costs except fixed costs depend on Q.)

Exercise: ▶▶▶▶▶▶▶

4. From the data in Table 7.1, calculate AFC for Q = 8, 9, 10, and 11. Check that it equals ATC – AVC for each quantity.

5. Does average fixed cost always decline with increases in output? Why or why not?

As output grows, average variable cost typically has a U-shape, i.e., it first declines and then rises. It is falling when $MC < AVC$ and rising when $MC > AVC$. If $MC < AVC$, the average is being "pulled down" by low incremental costs and if $MC > AVC$, the average is being "pulled up" by relatively high incremental costs. (We observed a similar relation between marginal and average products in Chapter 6.) Note also that the ATC curve typically has a U-shape and that ATC is falling when $MC < ATC$ and rising when $MC > ATC$.

Exercise: ▶ ▶ ▶ ▶ ▶ ▶ ▶

6. Table 7.2 presents cost data similar to Table 7.1, but these data come from a different steel producer. Fill in the blanks in Table 7.2 using the information given.

Output Q	Fixed Cost FC	Variable Cost VC	Total Cost TC	Average Variable Cost AVC	Average Total Cost ATC	Marginal Cost MC
13	1,125	975	___	___	___	n. a.
14	___	1,120	___	___	___	___
15	___	1,275	___	___	___	___
16	___	___	___	90	___	___
17	___	___	___	95	___	___

Table 7.2

There is a direct connection between productivity of inputs and costs to the firm. Suppose that labor is the only variable input. For the firm to increase output, it must hire additional labor. Each unit of labor will increase output by the marginal product of labor, MP_L. Thus, to produce one more unit of output, a firm needs to hire $1/MP_L$ units of labor. Therefore, at a wage of w, marginal cost is given by:

$$MC = w/MP_L.$$

Since MP_L eventually declines (recall the law of diminishing marginal returns), MC eventually increases. If labor is the only variable input, AVC = VC/Q = wL/Q, or AVC = w/AP_L. Since AP_L eventually declines, AVC eventually increases. Due to the influence of increasing AVC, ATC will eventually increase even though AFC is always falling.

The typical shape for the average and marginal cost curves is shown in the text in Figure 7.1(b), which is reproduced here:

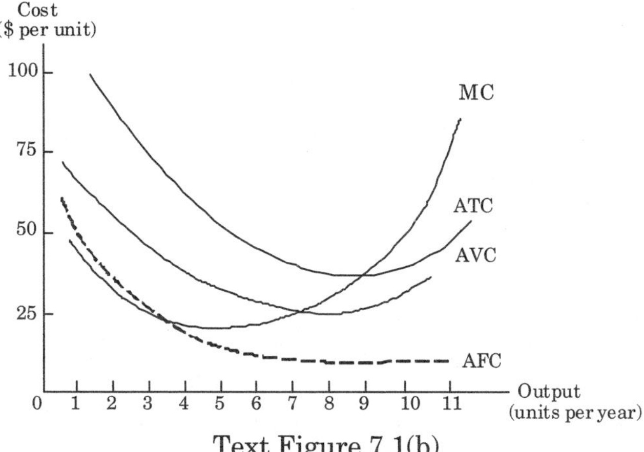

Text Figure 7.1(b)

Notice that in the preceding figure MC crosses both the AVC curve and the ATC curve at their minimum points. Intuitively, if the incremental cost is exactly equal to the current average, then adding it to the average will not change that average. Therefore, when MC and AVC cross (or when MC and ATC cross), the average stops falling. As soon as MC rises above AVC or ATC, these averages start to rise.

COST IN THE LONG RUN (Section 7.3)

In the long run, the firm can change *all* its input levels. The long-run problem that the firm must solve reflects this flexibility. The question is what *mix* of inputs should the firm choose to minimize cost? *Isocost lines* help to solve this problem. Isocost lines show all the input combinations associated with a given total cost.

We assume that the firm hires inputs in competitive markets. The wage rate, w, is the cost per unit of labor (person-hours) and the rental rate, r, is the cost per unit of capital (machine-hours). The rental rate is the opportunity cost of a unit of capital. For any level of inputs, total cost of production is $C = wL + rK$, or $K = C/r - (w/r)L$. For each value of total cost, C, we can draw an isocost line in a labor-capital diagram, like the one in Figure 7.1. No matter what the level of total cost, an isocost line has the slope $-w/r$ (minus the wage-rental ratio). Because input prices are fixed, all isocost lines are parallel (they have the same slope). An isocost line with higher costs is farther from the origin.

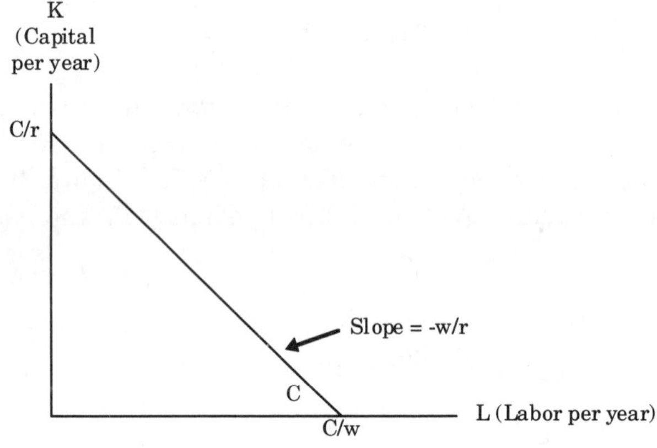

Figure 7.1

Exercise:

7. a) Draw the isocost line for C = 200, w = 20, and r = 40.
   b) Draw the isocost line for C = 300, w = 20, and r = 40.
   c) Draw the isocost line for C = 300, w = 30, and r = 40.

The problem for the firm is how to choose the right combination of inputs to minimize the cost of producing each target level of output, recognizing that technology (the production function) puts limits on how the inputs can be mixed. The firm wants to minimize $C = wL + rK$, subject to producing a target output level $\bar{Q}$.

Graphically, the problem is to find the isocost line closest to the origin (the lowest cost line) which touches the $\bar{Q}$ isoquant. The input choice that minimizes cost is found at a tangency between an isocost line and the $\bar{Q}$ isoquant, as at point A in Figure 7.2. The input mix at points B or D could be used, but it would not minimize cost ($C_1 > C_0$). Only at point A does the slope of the isoquant (the marginal rate of technical substitution) equal the slope of the isocost line.

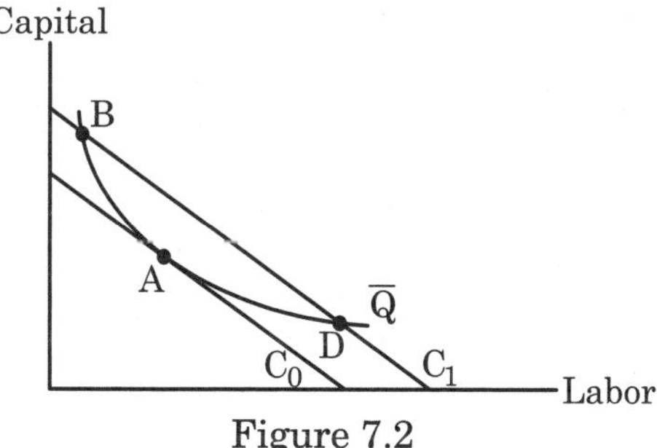

Figure 7.2

In other words, *for any output level, the firm minimizes its cost of production by operating where the* MRTS = w/r. Point B is not optimal because MRTS > w/r at that point, while MRTS < w/r at point D.

Relating this back to the production function yields:

$$MRTS = -\Delta K/\Delta L = MP_L/MP_K = w/r.$$

Rewriting this equation gives $MP_L/w = MP_K/r$. Therefore, costs are minimized when input levels are chosen such that the last dollar allocated to either input adds the same amount of output.

Holding input prices constant, we can vary output to find how the firm mixes inputs to produce different levels of output. Each optimal input mix for a given level of output is a tangency point between an isocost and an isoquant. The curve connecting all of these tangencies is the firm's *expansion path*. It indicates how the firm will choose inputs to produce different levels of output in the long run at minimum cost. If the expansion path is not a straight line, then the cost-minimizing capital-labor ratio changes as output changes.

Exercise: ◗ ◗ ◗ ◗ ◗ ◗ ◗

8. A firm uses two inputs, unskilled labor (L) and capital (K) to produce its product. The wage rate for one unit of labor is \$5, while units of capital cost \$20.

a) Graphically depict the isocost line for a \$1,000 expenditure by the firm on inputs. Label the intercepts. Draw a typical isoquant for an output level Q_0 and depict the optimal input levels L and K.

b) Suppose the federal government institutes a minimum wage for unskilled labor of \$6 per unit. In the short run, with capital fixed at K, show graphically how much it would cost the firm to hold its output constant at Q_0.

c) Show the optimal factor mix the firm will use in the long run to produce Q_0, given the minimum wage.

LONG-RUN VERSUS SHORT-RUN COST CURVES (Section 7.4)

The long-run total cost of producing a given level of output is always the lowest value of the short-run total cost of producing that output. Figure 7.3a shows the case of a firm that could build three possible plant sizes. If the firm knows that output will always be smaller than q_L, it should build plant 1. If output is between q_L and q_H, it should build plant 2, and so on. The long-run average cost curve (LAC) in Figure 7.3a is the heavily shaded parts of the SACs. The LAC takes the best points from each SAC curve because in the long run the firm has the flexibility to choose the optimal plant size, given expected output. The additional flexibility in the long run cannot hurt the firm (flexibility surely cannot raise costs).

Figure 7.3b shows a smooth LAC curve assuming the firm has a continuum of plant sizes to choose from. Notice that the long-run marginal cost (LMC) goes through the minimum of the LAC curve, just like in the short-run. The only difference is that LMC is flatter than SMC, which again is a reflection of the flexibility of plant size in the long run.

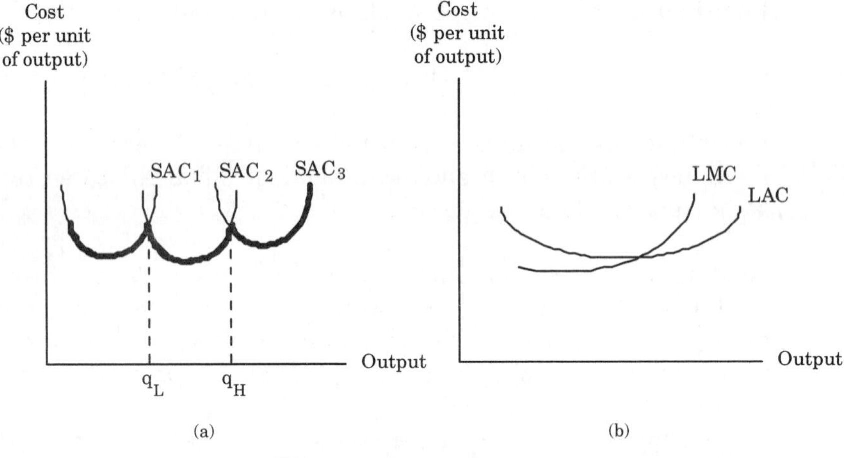

Figure 7.3

The slope of the long-run average total cost curve, LAC, indicates whether there are economies or diseconomies of scale present for each level of output. Thus, when LAC is falling, economies of scale are present, and when LAC is rising, there are diseconomies of scale. If there are constant returns to scale, the long-run average total cost curve is horizontal.

Exercise:

9. A firm with a U-shaped long-run average total cost curve wants to find the production level that minimizes LAC. Currently, the firm is producing at an output level where LMC > LAC. Should the firm increase or decrease output?

10. Suppose the long-run average cost for a firm is given by $LAC = 100 + (150 - Q)^2$. Are there economies or diseconomies of scale for $Q < 150$? For $Q > 150$?

PRODUCTION WITH TWO OUTPUTS—ECONOMIES OF SCOPE (Section 7.5)

Economies of scope are present when the joint output of a single firm is greater than the output that could be achieved by two different firms, each producing a single product. If a firm's joint output is less than that which could be achieved by separate firms, then *diseconomies of scope* exist.

The degree of economies of scope (SC) measures the percentage savings in costs when two (or more) products are produced jointly rather than individually:

$$SC = \frac{C(Q_1) + C(Q_2) - C(Q_1, Q_2)}{C(Q_1, Q_2)},$$

If there are economies of scope, then $SC > 0$, since $C(Q_1,Q_2) < [C(Q_1) + C(Q_2)]$. If there are diseconomies of scope, then $SC < 0$.

Exercise: ▶ ▶ ▶ ▶ ▶ ▶ ▶

11. Example 7.6 in the text discusses economies of scope and scale in the trucking industry. Joint production for a large trucking firm involves operating both quick direct hauls and slower indirect (but less expensive) hauls. A 1985 study estimated that $SC = 1.576$ for a reasonably large firm and $SC = 0.104$ for a very large firm.
    a) Interpret the estimated SC (degree of economies of scope) for "reasonably large" and "very large" trucking firms.
    b) The discussion in the text mentions that there are disadvantages associated with the management of very large firms. Does this explain the drop in the SC for very large firms?

*DYNAMIC CHANGES IN COSTS—THE LEARNING CURVE (Section 7.6)

Learning-by-doing is a salient feature of manufacturing. Workers' skills improve with practice. Better organization of the workplace occurs over time as new ideas are tried and these ideas will be implemented permanently if they succeed in lowering costs. The *learning curve* describes cost reductions that occur as a firm gains experience and develops more efficient production over time. The graph of a learning curve has *cumulative output to date* on the horizontal axis and labor hours per unit of output (or average variable cost) on the vertical axis. In comparison, the graphs of average and marginal costs have *output per period* on the horizontal axis.

The learning curve phenomenon is a dynamic concept that is independent of returns to scale. In graphical terms, if the firm is experiencing increasing returns to scale, they are moving down a negatively sloped average cost curve. On the other hand, if the firm is experiencing a learning effect, the *entire average cost curve shifts down*.

Exercise: ▶▶▶▶▶▶▶

***12.** A chemical processing firm estimated its average cost curve last year and found that AC = 1,000 – 0.05Q. This year it estimated its average costs and found that they were AC = 900 – 0.05Q.

a) Are there increasing or decreasing returns to scale?

b) Is there a learning curve effect?

*ESTIMATING AND PREDICTING COST (Section 7.7)

The variable cost function for a firm can be estimated with data on variable production costs at different output levels. (Although the total cost function could be estimated in principle, it is often difficult to know how to allocate fixed costs across different products for a multiproduct firm.) A variety of functional forms can be used, depending on which best fits the data:

Linear: $VC = \alpha + bQ.$

Quadratic: $VC = \alpha + bQ + \gamma Q^2.$

Cubic: $VC = \alpha + bQ + \gamma Q^2 + \delta Q^3.$

The choice of functional form depends on the shape you wish to allow for AVC and MC. The linear cost curve, for example, implies constant MC. The quadratic and cubic cost curves imply a linear and a U-shaped marginal cost, respectively.

For example, suppose a quadratic long-run average cost function is estimated for the banking industry in a particular country as follows:

$$LAC = 2.38 - 0.6153Q + 0.0536Q^2.$$

Output is measured as total assets of each of the banks studied, and LAC is measured by average operating expense. Both Q and LAC are measured in hundreds of millions of dollars. The next exercise takes a closer look at this estimated cost function.

Exercise: ▶▶▶▶▶▶▶

***13.** a) The estimated long-run average cost function discussed above is U-shaped with a minimum at Q = \$5.74 in total assets (i.e., Q = \$574 million). If two firms in the industry merged, each with assets of \$287 million, would there be a cost savings (based on this LAC)?

b) Suppose you observed a particular bank operating at Q = \$5.74 with LAC = 0.75 (i.e., average operating expense of \$75 million). Is this bank operating efficiently?

PROBLEM SET

14. Your university sells student tickets to football games for $6 each, but you must wait in line for a half-hour to obtain a ticket. Fortunately, you live in a state where scalping is legal. Non-student fans are willing to pay you $20 for your ticket. Attending the game will take approximately four hours. You have a part-time job where you can choose your own hours, which pays $8/hour.

a) What is your economic cost of buying a ticket?

b) Given that you have bought a ticket, what is your economic cost of attending the game?

c) If you know you will have to work the day of the game, should you buy a ticket in order to resell it?

15. A large real estate office wants to rent a new copying machine. One desktop model will cost $200 per month for rental and $0.035 per copy. Another larger model will cost $400 per month for rental and $0.02 per copy. Currently, the office makes about 15,000 copies per month. Which machine should they rent? What is the smallest number of copies per month that would make it desirable to rent the larger model?

16. A firm has the following cost data:

Output	Total Cost	Variable Cost
100	$7,000	$3,000
101	7,400	3,400
102	7,900	3,900

What are ATC, AFC, AVC, and MC at these output levels?

17. *[Calculus] Suppose that a widget producer's short-run total cost function is:

$$TC = 300 + 3Q + 0.02Q^2 \text{ if } Q > 0 \text{ and } TC = 0 \text{ if } Q = 0,$$

where TC is total cost in dollars and Q is the number of cases of widgets produced.

What are the corresponding ATC, AVC, and MC functions?

18. A firm has a long-run total cost function of $C(Q) = 180{,}000 + 30Q + 2Q^2$ for $Q > 0$ and $C(0) = 0$, with $MC(Q) = 30 + 4Q$.

a) What is the average total cost function?

b) At what quantity is ATC minimized?

19. A digital camera company has a cost function which relates its average cost of production (ATC) to its cumulative output (CUMQ) and its production per year (Q):

$$AC = 22{,}000 - 0.5*CUMQ - 0.2*Q$$

This cost curve is relevant within the production range of 10,000 to 30,000 cameras.

a) Are there economies or diseconomies of scale for this firm?
b) Is the firm currently enjoying a learning curve effect?

20. Suppose Wally's Widgets has a fixed-proportions production function. It currently delivers 1000 widgets per month to its only customer. Currently, Wally's costs are $2000 per month per machine and $4000 per month per worker. Wally uses 20 machines and 10 workers to produce 1000 widgets each month. If the cost of the machines falls to $1600 per month and Wally continues to produce 1000 widgets, what happens to its total costs? Show this in a graph, using one isoquant and a pair of isocost lines. (Hint: What are the horizontal intercepts of the old and new isocost lines?)

SELF-TEST

21. Phyllis wants to buy two tickets to a concert. Tickets cost $15 each, and she expects to wait 30 minutes in line to buy them. If her wage is $16 per hour, the economic cost of buying the two tickets is:
a) $15.
b) $30.
c) $38.
d) $46.
e) None of the above is correct.

22. In the short run, when capital is fixed, marginal cost equals:
a) MP_L.
b) w (the wage rate).
c) $(w)(MP_L)$.
d) w/MP_L.
e) MP_L/w.

23. If MC > AVC:
a) AFC must be increasing with output.
b) ATC must be increasing with output.
c) AVC must be increasing with output.
d) b) and c)
e) a), b), and c)

24. Assume that capital input is drawn on the vertical axis and labor input on the horizontal axis. If machine-hours can be rented for $8/hour and labor can be hired for $32/hour, the slope of an isocost line is:
a) – 4.
b – 1/4.
c – P, where P is the price of a unit of output.
d – 4P.
e) More information is needed.

25. The firm in the above question should choose inputs such that:
a) the MRTS equals 4.
b) the MRTS equals 1/4.
c) the MRTS equals P/4.
d) the MRTS equals 4P.
e) None of the above is correct.

26. If the expansion path is a straight line through the origin, then:
a) the production function exhibits constant returns to scale.
b) the capital-labor ratio increases as output increases.
c) the capital-labor ratio does not change as output increases.
d) the production function exhibits decreasing returns to scale.
e) a) and c)

27. A sparkling water bottler finds that producing 2,000 cases of canned water and 3,000 cases bottled water in one plant is less costly than using two separate plants to produce the same total output. This production process exhibits:
a) increasing returns to scale.
b) economies of scope.
c) diminishing returns.
d) a) and b)
e) b) and c)

28. Since their introduction in the 1990s, flat-screen televisions have fallen dramatically in price. Per unit production costs have fallen as total cumulative production has grown. This is an example of:
a) economies of scope.
b) increasing returns to scale.
c) the learning curve.
d) a) and b)
e) a) and c)

29. With constant returns to scale, long-run average total cost:
a) is constant.
b) equals long run marginal cost.
c) equals short run marginal cost.
d) a) and b)
e) a) and c)

30. If the MRTS is greater than the wage-rental ratio (w/r), then to minimize cost the firm should:
a) increase K and decrease L.
b) decrease K and increase L.
c) increase both K and L.
d) decrease both K and L.
e) Either b) or d)

31. If firms in a new industry each have a learning curve with respect to their own output, then
a) the firm with the most sales in the past will have the highest average cost now.
b) the firm with the most current sales will have the highest average cost now.
c) the firm with the most sales in the past will have the lowest average cost now.
d) the firm with the most current sales will have the lowest average cost now.
e) c) and d).

32. Which of the following is true?
a) If fixed costs are positive, the AVC and ATC curves move closer to each other as output increases.
b) If there are no fixed costs, the ATC curve is a horizontal line.
c) If fixed costs are positive, the output at which ATC is minimized is less than the output at which AVC is minimized.
d) a) and b)
e) a), b), and c)

ANSWERS TO CHAPTER 7

EXERCISE ANSWERS

1. False. The opportunity cost would be the interest the collector could have earned on the current market price of the painting.

2. His economic cost is 8 + 3 + 3(20) = $71. The income forgone by not taking the grading job is ignored because it is not the highest valued use of his time.

3. Quick Corp. should stay in business. The start-up costs are now sunk. Quick is earning a normal rate of return on the forward-looking costs of production. With hindsight, entry was a bad idea, but looking forward from this point, staying in business is a good idea.

4. Since fixed cost is $2,000 at all outputs, $AFC = FC/Q = 2{,}000/Q$. For $Q = 8$, $AFC = 2{,}000/8 = \$250$. For Q = 9, AFC = 2,000/9 = $222.2. For Q = 10, AFC = $200, and for Q = 11, AFC = $181.8.

At Q = 8, ATC – AVC = 350 – 100 = $250. At Q = 9, ATC – AVC = 320 – 97.8 = $222.2. At Q = 10, ATC – AVC = 298 – 98 = $200. At Q = 11, ATC – AVC = 281.8 – 100 = $181.8. Therefore, either method of deriving AFC gives the same answer.

5. Average fixed cost, AFC = FC/Q, always declines as output increases. Since FC is, by definition, a fixed number, and since AFC equals a constant divided by Q, AFC will always fall as Q rises.

6. See Table 7A.1.

Fixed cost, by definition, is 1,125 at all output levels.
TC at Q = 13 is 1,125 + 975 = 2,100.
TC at Q = 14 is 1,125 + 1,120 = 2,245.
TC at Q = 15 is 1,125 + 1,275 = 2,400.
VC at Q = 16 is AVC · Q = 90(16) = 1,440, implying that TC = 1,125 + 1,440 = 2,565.
VC at Q = 17 is AVC · Q = 95(17) = 1,615, implying that TC = 2,740.

With this information you can now derive AVC = VC/Q, ATC = TC/Q, and MC = ΔVC/ΔQ. For example, MC from Q = 13 to Q = 14 is 1,120 – 975 = 145.

Q	FC	VC	TC	AVC	ATC	MC
13	1,125	975	2,100	75	161.5	—
14	1,125	1,120	2,245	80	160.4	145
15	1,125	1,275	2,400	85	160	155
16	1,125	1,440	2,565	90	160.3	165
17	1,125	1,615	2,740	95	161.2	175

Table 7A.1

7. See Figure 7A.1 for isocost lines depicting the information given in a), b), and c). The slope of a) is –w/r = –0.5. The slope of b) is also –0.5. The slope of c) is –30/40 = –0.75. Note that a) and b) are parallel, reflecting their identical slopes, but b) is shifted further out because the total cost of production is higher.

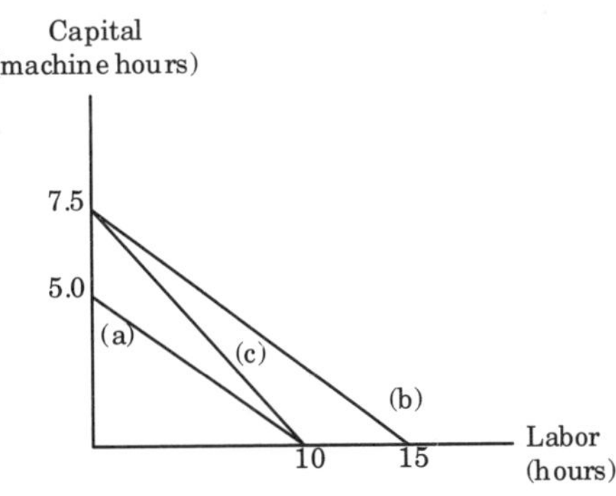

Figure 7A.1

8. a) See Figure 7A.2 (on the next page). The line (a) is 1,000 = 5L + 20K or K = 50 – 0.25L. The optimal input mix for Q_0 is labeled E_0.

b) With capital fixed at K, the firm must continue to use L* units of labor to produce Q_0. But L now costs $6 per unit. As shown in Figure 7A.2, the slope of the new isocost line (b) is steeper: 6/20 = 0.30 > 0.25 = 5/20.

c) When the firm can adjust its capital, it will shift out of the relatively more expensive labor input into capital. Its long-run cost-minimizing bundle in the new situation will be E_1 in Figure 7A.2, where the original isoquant is tangent to the lowest attainable isocost line (c), reflecting the higher wage rate. Since E_1 lies above the original isocost line, the cost of producing Q_0 has risen compared to the original situation, but it has *fallen* compared to part b). That is, $C_2 < C_1$.

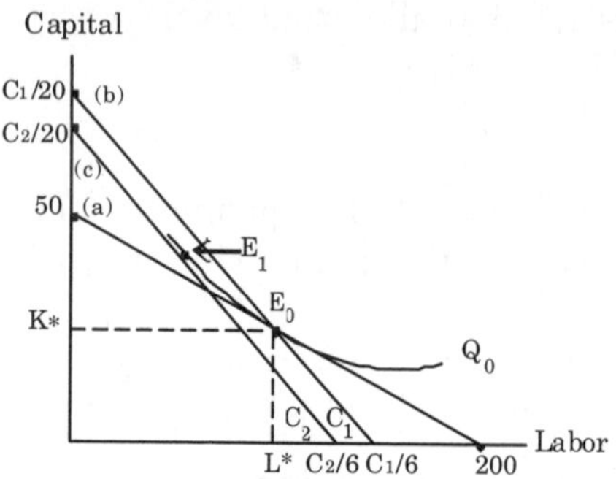

Figure 7A.2

9. If LMC > LAC and LAC is U-shaped then the firm must currently be to the right of the point of minimum long-run average cost. The firm should reduce output.

10. This long-run average cost curve is U-shaped, with a minimum at Q = 150. Therefore, there are economies of scale for Q < 150 and diseconomies of scale for Q > 150.

11. a) The estimated SCs are both greater than zero, indicating that economies of scope exist. Since the SC for reasonably large firms is greater (1.576 > 0.104), the economies of scope are greater for reasonably large firms than for very large firms.

b) Disadvantages associated with management are one source of diseconomies of scale, which can be present along with diseconomies of scope for very large firms.

12. a) Increasing returns to scale are evident, since the slope of the AC curve is negative.

b) There may be a learning curve effect. The AC curve has shifted down this year (the intercept has fallen from 1,000 to 900). We cannot know for sure whether this is due to a learning effect or technological change.

13. a) Based on this estimated LAC, the merger would reduce costs. The two banks are operating in a region of increasing returns to scale (the downward-sloping part of the U-shaped LAC).

b) At Q = 5.74, LAC = 0.61. Therefore, a firm operating at Q = 5.74 with LAC = 0.75 is not operating at minimum average cost.

PROBLEM SET ANSWERS

14. a) The economic cost of purchasing a ticket is \$10: \$6 for the ticket and \$4 that you could have earned in that half-hour of waiting in line.

b) Since you could sell the ticket for \$20 and you could work for four hours during the game, the economic cost of attending the game is \$20 + \$8(4) = \$52.

c) Yes, since the economic cost of obtaining a ticket worth \$20 is only \$10.

15. The total cost curves are given in Figure 7A.3. To make 15,000 copies per month costs [200 + 0.035(15,000)] = \$725 on the small machine and [400 + 0.02(15,000)] = \$700 on the larger machine. Therefore, they should rent the larger machine.

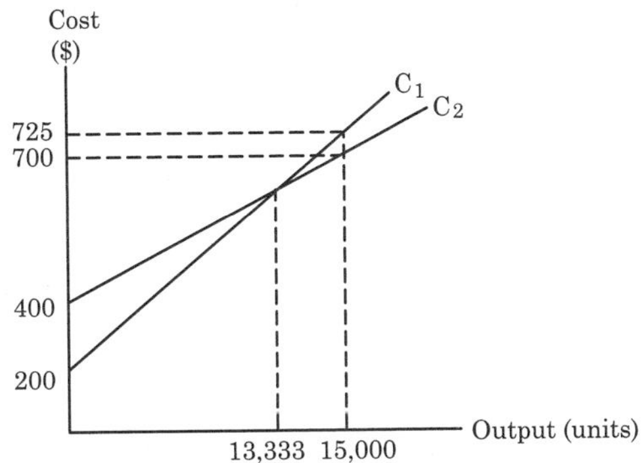

Figure 7A.3

To find the switchpoint (or breakeven point), set 200 + 0.035Q = 400 + 0.02Q and solve for Q. The switchpoint is at Q = 13,333.33. This is the smallest number of copies that would make it desirable to rent the larger machine.

16. Fixed cost equals TC – VC or 4,000. AFC(100) = 4,000/100 = 40; AFC(101) = 4,000/101 = 39.6; and AFC(102) = 39.22. AVC(100) = 3,000/100 = 30; AVC(101) = 33.66; and AVC(102) = 38.24. ATC(100) = AFC(100) + AVC(100) = 70; ATC(101) = 73.27; and ATC(102) = 77.45. Between 100 and 101, MC = C(101) – C(100) = 400; between 101 and 102, MC = 500.

17. ATC = TC/Q = 300/Q + 3 + 0.02Q; AVC = VC/Q = [3Q + 0.02Q]/Q = 3 + 0.02Q; and MC = dTC/dQ = 3 + 0.04Q.

18. a) ATC = 180,000/Q + 30 + 2Q. (Note: At Q = 0, ATC = $\frac{0}{0}$, so it is not well-defined.)

b) The minimum of the ATC curve occurs where

$$ATC{=}MC\text{: } 180{,}000/Q{+}30{+}2Q{=}30{+}4Q\text{, or}$$

Q^2 = 90,000, so Q* = 300. At Q = 300, MC = 30 + 4(300) = 1,230, so minimum ATC is 1,230.

19. a) There are economies of scale, since the long-run average total cost curve slopes down as output increases. The easiest way to see this is to note the negative sign in front of the output term (–0.2Q). You could also plot the curve, holding CUMQ constant, and see that it is not a typical U-shaped cost curve, but a straight line with a slope of –0.2.

b) Average cost decreases with cumulative output (note the negative sign in front of the CUMQ term), and therefore there is a learning curve effect.

20. See Figure 7A.4. The slope of the isocost lines changes from –2 to –2.5. Since the new isocost line must still go through the point (L = 10, K = 20), the horizontal intercept for the new isocost line is 18 workers per month, as compared with a horizontal intercept of 20 workers per month with the original isocost line. Since w is unchanged, total cost falls by 10%.

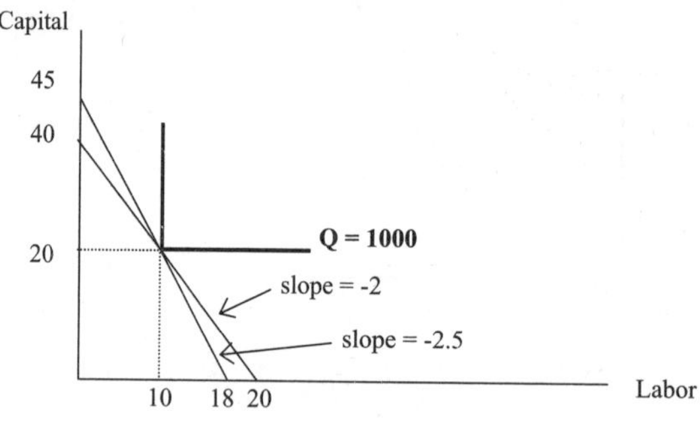

Figure 7A.4

SELF-TEST ANSWERS

21. c) To buy two tickets, Phyllis will have to spend $30 on the tickets plus half an hour waiting. With a time value of $16/hour, this half-hour has an opportunity cost of $8 for a total economic cost of $38.

22. d) Marginal cost is the cost of producing one more unit of output. The cost of a unit of labor is w. That additional unit of labor produces MP_L units of output. Marginal cost is therefore w/MP_L.

23. c) This is the only fact guaranteed by MC > AVC. Choice a) is ruled out because AFC is always decreasing as output increases. Since ATC and MC intersect to the right of minimum AVC, the ATC curve could be declining, eliminating b).

24. a) The slope of an isocost line is – w/r = – 32/8 = –4.

25. a) The firm should operate so that the MRTS equals the wage-rental ratio.

26. c) K/L is constant in this case. The expansion path does not determine returns to scale.

27. b) Economies of scope is a concept we use to compare separate production to joint production.

28. c) The learning curve pertains to cost changes as *cumulative* production grows.

29. d) Returns to scale are reflected in the shape of long-run cost curves. If there are constant returns to scale, then LAC and LMC are the same horizontal line. SMC is measured with capital fixed, so returns to scale do not tell us about SMC.

30. b) Costs are minimized when MRTS = w/r. Therefore, the firm should move from point A to point B in Figure 7A.5.

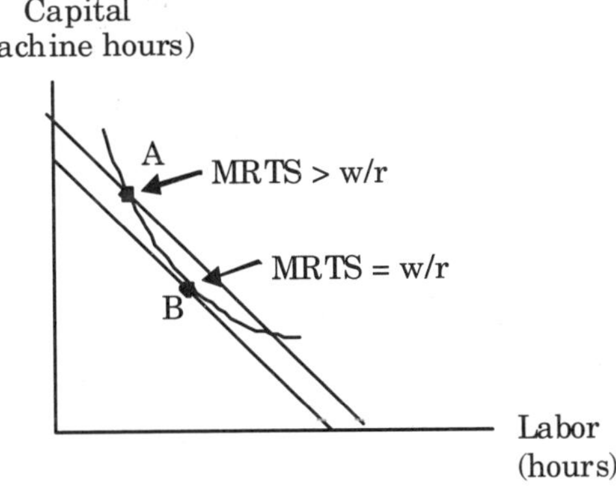

Figure 7A.5

31. c) By definition of a learning curve, average cost falls with cumulative output. Choice d) relates to scale economies, and we do not know whether or not production in this industry exhibits economies of scale.

32. a) Even if there are no fixed costs, ATC can be U-shaped if AVC is U-shaped (since the two curves would be identical), thus ruling out choice b). Choice c) is also false since AFC falls as output increases, which implies that minimum ATC occurs at a larger output level than minimum AVC.

CHAPTER 8
PROFIT MAXIMIZATION AND COMPETITIVE SUPPLY

IMPORTANT CONCEPTS

- Assumptions of Perfect Competition
- Marginal Revenue and Marginal Cost (MR and MC)
- Short-Run Profit Maximization Condition (P = MC)
- Short-Run Shutdown Condition
- Derivation of Short-Run Supply Curve
- Derivation of Long-Run Supply Curve
- Long-Run Competitive Equilibrium (P = LMC and P = LAC)
- Producer Surplus
- Economic Rent
- Constant Cost, Increasing Cost, and Decreasing Cost Industry

CHAPTER HIGHLIGHTS

This chapter analyzes profit maximization in a perfectly competitive market setting. The first necessary condition for perfect competition is price taking—no individual firm has a power to set a price different from the market price without losing most or all of its customers. Second, all firms sell a homogeneous (not differentiated) good. Finally, we require that in the long run firms can freely enter and exit the market.

We assume that the motivation for entry and exit is profit. Firms will enter an industry if they can make economic profit greater than zero and they will exit if they are losing money. Although a firm's managers may not always have profit maximization as their goal, we will take profit maximization as a reasonable assumption that applies to most firms operating in competitive industries. To find the output level that maximizes a firm's profits, one could clearly calculate revenue at each output level and subtract it from cost at each output level to find the output which maximizes the difference between total revenue and total cost. While this will work, an easier way to look at this analytically involves focusing on *marginal revenue* (the change in revenue from a one unit increase in output) and *marginal cost* (the change in cost from a 1 unit increase in output).

If the firm is operating at a point where marginal revenue is greater than marginal cost, it should clearly go ahead and produce the next unit. If the firm is operating at a point where marginal revenue is less than marginal cost, it clearly has produced at least one unit too many (the firm will make more money by lowering output). Therefore, profit is maximized by continuing to increase output as long as MR > MC. For mathematical simplicity, we say that the firm should produce up to the point where MR = MC (even though the firm is breaking even on the last unit). This is a general result. For the special case of perfect competition, the profit maximizing condition becomes P = MC. This is due to the fact that the demand curve facing an individual competitive firm is horizontal (perfectly elastic) at the level of the current market price, P. Each unit of output sold by an individual firm will bring in P dollars in revenue.

If the firm is not covering its fixed costs at the point where P = MC, but is earning enough revenue to cover its variable costs, it should stay in operation in the short run. However, if the firm is covering neither fixed nor variable costs, it should shut down in the short run. The *short-run shutdown condition* specifies that the firm should only stay in business if price is greater than minimum average variable cost. This initial analysis must be tempered by other considerations, such as maintaining some flexibility to change the amount of capital the firm uses, or taking reputation with consumers into consideration.

Given that the competitive firm produces up to the point where P = MC, the marginal cost curve is the *short-run supply curve* for the firm. There is one qualification: the firm will only be in operation for prices above minimum average variable cost, and, therefore, the short-run supply curve is only that part of marginal cost above minimum average variable cost. The short-run market supply curve is the sum of the individual firm's short-run supply curves. Anything that affects the firm's marginal cost will also shift the market supply curve.

In the long run, the firm sets output where price equals long-run marginal cost (LMC). This will guarantee profit maximization for the individual firm, but it will not guarantee a *long-run equilibrium* in the market. One of the characteristics of a perfectly competitive market is free entry and exit in the long run. If economic profits are greater than zero (if firms in the industry are earning more than a normal rate of return on their investment), then other firms will be attracted to this industry. This additional supply will drive the price down. If economic profits are less than zero, firms will want to exit the industry. This will drive up the market price. The industry will only settle into long-run equilibrium when economic profits are zero. This will happen when the market price is equal to long-run average cost (LAC). In order to have both P = LMC and P = LAC, each firm must be producing at minimum long-run average cost.

Economic rent is defined as the difference between what firms are willing to pay for an input to production, less the minimum amount necessary to buy that input. *Producer surplus* measures the difference between the market price a producer receives and the marginal cost of production. In the long run, the producer surplus earned by a firm consists of the economic rent that it enjoys from all its scarce inputs.

Although the *long-run supply curve* for the firm is the long-run marginal cost curve above minimum long-run average cost, the industry long-run supply curve is not simply the sum of the individual curves.

The shape of the industry long-run supply curve depends on the extent to which increases and decreases in industry output affect the prices that the firms must pay for their inputs. If input prices do not change when conditions change in the output market, then the long-run supply curve is a horizontal line at a price equal to minimum LAC. This is called a *constant-cost industry*. If input prices increase as output increases, known as an *increasing-cost industry*, the long-run industry supply curve is upward sloping. For a *decreasing-cost industry*, input prices fall as output increases and the long-run industry supply curve is downward sloping.

CONCEPT REVIEW AND EXERCISES

PERFECTLY COMPETITIVE MARKETS (Section 8.1)

The perfectly competitive model requires several strict assumptions. The three basic assumptions are *price taking, product homogeneity*, and *free entry and exit*:

1. *Price Taking*: Each firm passively accepts the going market price as given, and does the best they can to maximize profits. If a firm tries to set a higher price, it will lose all of its sales. Consumers will know that they can buy at a lower price from another firm.

2. *Product Homogeneity*: We assume that firms produce the identical product. Consumers see the product offered by one firm as a perfect substitute for the product offered by any other firm in the market.

3. *Free Entry and Exit*: Firms can costlessly move into a perfectly competitive market if there is a profit opportunity, and they can exit if they are incurring losses. In short-run analysis of perfect competition, we assume that the number of firms is fixed. In the long run, however, free entry and exit are a critical part of the analysis. This flow of firms into and out of the industry is what drives economic profits to zero in perfectly competitive markets in the long run.

We use these assumptions as a starting point for our analysis of market structure and firm behavior. Although these assumptions are rarely satisfied exactly as presented in an economics textbook, there are markets that exhibit many of these characteristics. We call such markets *highly competitive*: products may be almost perfect substitutes, entry may be relatively low cost, and so on. The explosion of online commerce, for example, has created highly competitive markets for certain products. Consumers can more easily search for information on prices. This means that they can more easily comparison shop and refuse to buy from one firm if it raises the price. Firms' ability to set a significantly higher price than the competition is much more limited than it was before the Internet was widely used for commercial purposes.

Exercise: ◗ ◗ ◗ ◗ ◗ ◗ ◗

1. The assumption of price-taking in perfectly competitive markets is justified when there are a large number of buyers and sellers in the market. In large cities, there are many restaurants and many radio stations. Would you describe the restaurant market and the market for radio advertising as perfectly competitive? Explain whether the other assumptions are satisfied.

PROFIT MAXIMIZATION (Section 8.2)

Economic profit equals total revenue minus total economic cost (opportunity cost). Our basic assumption about the behavior of firms is that they strive to maximize economic profit. As a general rule, a firm that does not maximize profit may not survive the competitive process.

Our assumption that firms maximize profit means simply that firms put resources to their best available use. If the managers of a firm do not use inputs efficiently, bankruptcy may occur because the firm's cost of production is higher than the market equilibrium price. If another firm recognizes that current management is inefficiently using a firm's resources, the inefficient managers may be replaced in a corporate takeover.

Exercise: ◗ ◗ ◗ ◗ ◗ ◗ ◗

2. The Cummins Engine Co. is a successful producer of diesel engines for trucks and stationary power sources. Since the 1950s, Cummins has paid architects' fees for public buildings in Columbus, Indiana, the site of its main factory and corporate headquarters. Why might this be consistent with long-run profit maximization?

MARGINAL REVENUE, MARGINAL COST, AND PROFIT MAXIMIZATION (Section 8.3)

Table 8.1 examines a firm's cost data. The firm can sell any quantity it wishes at the current market price of $170 per unit.

Output q	Revenue R($170 · q)	Total Cost TC	Profit π	Average Total Cost ATC	Average Variable Cost AVC	Marginal Cost MC
13	2,210	2,100	110	161.54	75	—
14	2,380	2,245	135	160.36	80	145
15	2,550	2,400	150	160.00	85	155
16	2,720	2,565	155	160.31	90	165
17	2,890	2,740	150	161.18	95	175

Table 8.1

You should already be familiar with the cost concepts listed in Table 8.1. The two new concepts we add in this chapter are revenue and profit. Revenue is price per unit times the quantity sold. Profit equals total revenue minus total cost. Since, by assumption, an individual competitive firm has no effect on the market price, each additional unit sold produces the same amount of additional revenue, or *marginal revenue*, to the firm: MR = ΔTR/ΔQ. The marginal revenue for the competitive firm is exactly equal to the market price: for every unit that the firm sells, the revenue it takes in is P. (Be careful: the demand curve for the *firm* is horizontal in perfect competition, but the *market* demand curve is still downward sloping.)

What is the firm's profit-maximizing output? In Table 8.1, the firm would choose to sell 16 units of output, thereby earning a maximum profit of $155. If it produced and sold another unit of output, the firm would increase revenue by $170 (the market price), but its cost would rise by $175 (its marginal cost). Therefore, increasing production from 16 to 17 units would cause profit to fall by $5.

We can also compare profits when the firm produces 15 rather than 16 units. Starting from an output of 15 units, selling one more unit of output brings in an additional $170 in revenue, but it only costs the firm an additional $165. Profit increases by $5 when the firm expands output from 15 to 16 units. Therefore, the firm should definitely expand output from 15 to 16 units. Stopping at q = 15 would not maximize total profit.

The example just discussed illustrates a general rule for the firm's short-run output choice when there are discrete output levels—produce up to the output where the marginal cost of the next unit of output exceeds the marginal revenue. In this example, marginal cost jumps between output levels. However, when output can be produced in fractional units, as is assumed in the text, the rule is simpler: *A firm maximizes profit by producing the output at which marginal revenue equals marginal cost.* Or, you can say that a firm should continue to produce *up to the point where* MR = MC. Since marginal revenue equals price for a competitive firm, we can restate the profit maximizing condition for a perfectly competitive firm as follows: *A perfectly competitive firm maximizes profit by producing the output at which price equals marginal cost.*

In other words, *given* the current demand and cost conditions, producing up to the point where P = MC is the best a firm can do. But if the firm is losing money at that point, it may be better off shutting down (we will look at this in more detail in the next section). In Table 8.1, however, the firm is earning a positive profit when it sells 16 units, so it will clearly choose to stay in business.

Exercise: ◗ ◗ ◗ ◗ ◗ ◗ ◗

3. Table 8.2 contains the same cost information as Table 8.1. Fill in the blanks and then find the profit maximizing (or loss minimizing) output level when P = $150.

Output q	Revenue R($150 · q)	Total Cost TC	Profit π	Average Total Cost ATC	Average Variable Cost AVC	Marginal Cost MC
13	______	2,100	______	161.54	75	n.a.
14	______	2,245	______	160.36	80	145
15	______	2,400	______	160.00	85	155
16	______	2,565	______	160.31	90	165
17	______	2,740	______	161.18	95	175

Table 8.2

Although the firm is losing money in the situation given in Table 8.2 (π = –$145 at the optimal output of 14), the firm loses the *least* money when it produces 14 units. If the firm were to produce no output in the short run, it would still have to pay its fixed costs of $1,125, a substantially greater loss than $145. Thus, the firm will continue to produce in the short run. However, at a market price of $150, the firm will go out of business in the long run (unless it can lower its fixed costs) because it cannot cover its opportunity costs—the resources of the firm can be used more profitably elsewhere.

Exercise: ◗ ◗ ◗ ◗ ◗ ◗ ◗

4. The seller of a breakfast cereal, Boasties, knows that selling an additional carload of product would bring an additional $43,020 in revenue. The plant manager knows that producing an additional carload would cost the firm $29,754. Would selling one additional carload raise the firm's profit from the current level of $895,000? By how much would profit rise or fall? Should the manager increase production by one carload?

5. Suppose that marginal cost is falling at a point where MC(q*) = P, as at point A in Figure 8.1. Why will the firm increase profit by producing more output (up to point B)?

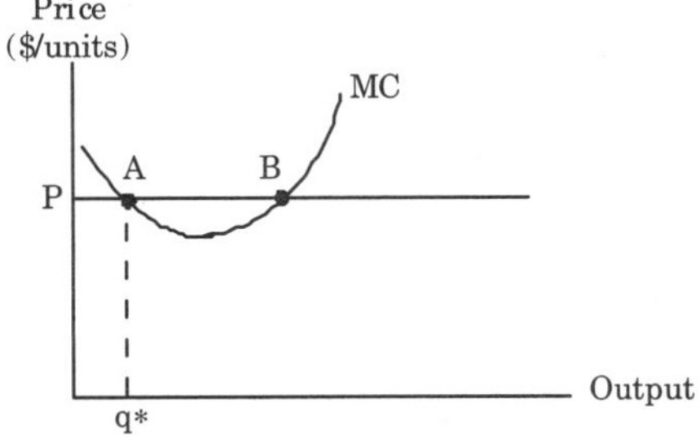

Figure 8.1

To review, when producing an additional unit of output, the firm's profit will change by $\Delta\pi/\Delta q = MR - MC$. If MR > MC, the firm can increase profit by expanding output. If MR < MC, the firm can increase profit by decreasing output. Only if MR = MC is the firm maximizing profit at its current output. Thus, a profit-maximizing firm should choose q so that MR = MC. A profit-maximizing competitive firm should choose q so that P = MC, since MR = P.

CHOOSING OUTPUT IN THE SHORT RUN (Section 8.4)

To establish formally whether a competitive firm wishes to produce a positive amount, consider a competitive firm with the ATC, AVC, and MC curves displayed in Figure 8.2. If price equals P_1, the firm sets MC = P_1 by producing q_1. Profit can be written $\pi(q_1) = [P_1 - ATC(q_1)]q_1$. Since $P_1 > ATC(q_1)$, $\pi(q_1) > 0$. Thus, the firm does better to sell q_1 than to sell zero. To generalize this result for all prices, note that since the firm produces on the upward-sloping portion of its MC curve, if P > Minimum ATC then $\pi(q) > 0$ at the profit-maximizing output. So, we only need to check if P > Minimum ATC to see if the firm will produce in the long run.

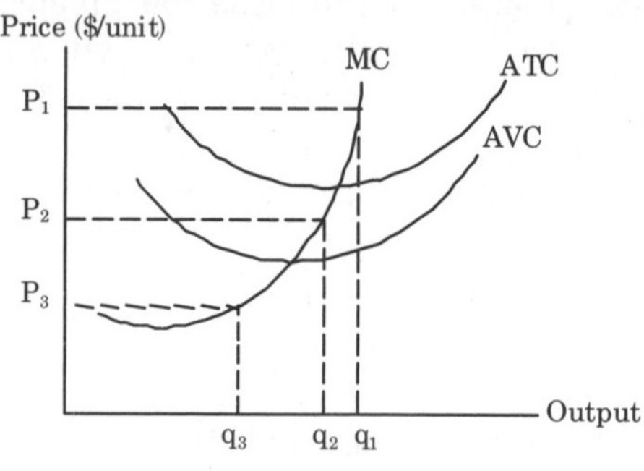

Figure 8.2

Suppose, however, that price equals P_2 in Figure 8.2. Then, the firm sets MC = P_2 by producing q_2. Since $P_2 < ATC(q_2)$, $\pi(q_2) = [P_2 - ATC(q_2)]q_2 < 0$. Should the firm produce q_2 or zero? To answer this, we need to make another comparison. Rewriting profit, we find $\pi(q_2) = [P_2 - AVC(q_2)]q_2 - FC$. Since $P_2 > AVC(q_2)$, the firm loses less than its fixed costs when it operates at q_2. But if the firm were to sell zero output, it would lose *all* its fixed costs. Thus, at P_2, the firm does best to continue to operate. Since, in the short run, fixed costs are unavoidable, the firm should ignore them when deciding whether to produce. Hence, we need only *check if* P > Minimum AVC to see if the firm will produce in the short run. This is the firm's *short-run shutdown condition.* Managers must, however, take other factors into consideration, such as maintaining flexibility, loss of reputation with consumers, and forecast of how quickly conditions might change.

Finally, suppose that price equals P_3 in Figure 8.2. Then, the firm sets MC = P_3 by producing q_3. Here, $AVC(q_3) > P_3$. Since $\pi(q_3) = [P_3 - AVC(q_3)]q_3 - FC$, the loss is greater than the firm's fixed costs (i.e., not only can the firm not afford to pay its fixed costs, but it can't even earn enough to pay for its raw materials and workers!). The firm could produce zero and lose only its fixed costs, so it would do better to shut down. By producing zero, the firm limits its losses to its fixed costs.

Exercise: ◗ ◗ ◗ ◗ ◗ ◗ ◗

6. Your coffee mug company is currently producing at an output level of 200 units per month. Fixed costs are $500 per month. At the current output level, you know that marginal cost is $10 and equal to average total cost. At an output level of 150, you have determined that marginal cost would be $6 and equal to average variable cost. The market price for your coffee mugs is $8. If your goal is profit maximization, should you continue at q = 200, increase q above 200, or reduce q below 200? Would you do better to shut down?

THE COMPETITIVE FIRM'S SHORT-RUN SUPPLY CURVE (Section 8.5)

A *firm's short-run supply curve* tells us the quantity of output that will be produced at each price. We have seen that the competitive firm will supply a quantity such that P = MC, as long as P > Minimum AVC in the short run. Thus, the short-run supply curve is the portion of the marginal cost curve above the minimum AVC. Suppose that Minimum AVC = 10 and MC = 2q, as shown in Figure 8.3. Then the supply curve is that part of MC above P = 10. The equation of the firm's supply curve is written as q = P/2 for all P ≥ 10.

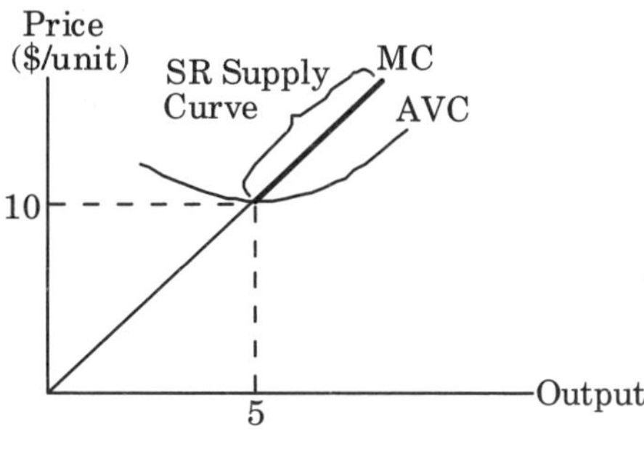

Figure 8.3

Input price changes cause a shift in the MC and AVC curves, and, hence, a shift in the short-run supply curve. The ATC curve also shifts as a result of an input price change.

THE SHORT-RUN MARKET SUPPLY CURVE (Section 8.6)

The *industry short-run supply curve* is simply the horizontal sum of the individual firm short-run supply curves. The next exercise shows how to find the market supply curve.

Exercise: ▶ ▶ ▶ ▶ ▶ ▶ ▶

7. Suppose that there are eight firms in an industry. For five firms, MC = 5q and Minimum AVC = 15. The other three firms have MC = 4q and Minimum AVC = 20. What is the equation for market supply curve in the short run? (Hint: Write quantity supplied as a function of price.) Carefully draw the supply curve.

A downward-sloping demand curve indicates that a consumer values the first units of a product more highly than the last units purchased. Buying all units at the market price thus yields consumer surplus or gains from trade for the consumer. An upward sloping supply curve reveals a parallel concept for a firm—*producer surplus*. Short-run producer surplus for an individual firm is the excess of revenues over variable costs, which can be measured using either the marginal cost curve or the average variable cost curve. For example, in Figure 8.4, the firm will maximize profit by setting an output of q_1 if price is P_1. Producer surplus is the sum over all units between zero and q_1 of the difference between the price the firm actually receives for the good (P_1) and the minimum price the firm would have been willing to receive (given by MC at each q). The shaded area in Figure 8.4 represents producer surplus. Or, you can think of producer surplus as the profit over variable costs: PS = Total Revenue – Variable Cost. (Note that to calculate profit, as opposed to producer surplus, you would want to subtract fixed costs as well.) For the industry as a whole, short-run producer surplus is the area below the market price and above the market supply curve (which is derived from the marginal cost curves of the individual firms).

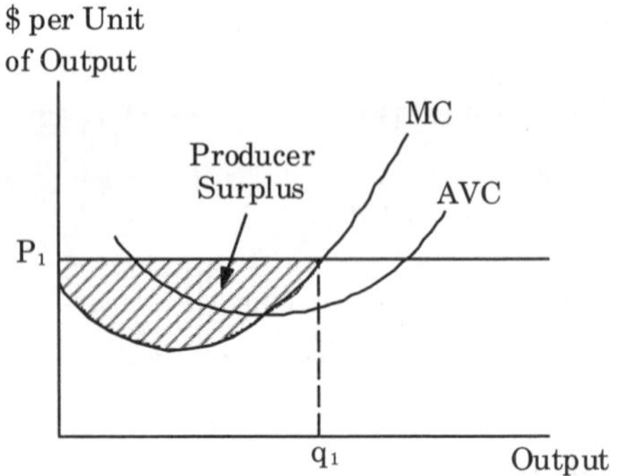

Figure 8.4

Exercise: ◗ ◗ ◗ ◗ ◗ ◗ ◗

8. The Nick and Nora Company has the short-run supply curve in Figure 8.5. If P = 40, how much short-run producer surplus does the firm earn?

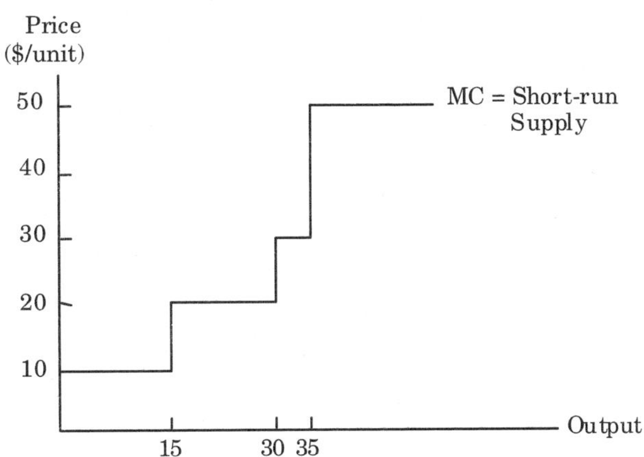

Figure 8.5

Long-run producer surplus equals the excess of revenue over long-run opportunity cost. If we use the area under MC as the measure of opportunity cost, we must subtract from it any area where MC > P, such as area B in Figure 8.6. In Figure 8.6, long-run producer surplus is A – B.

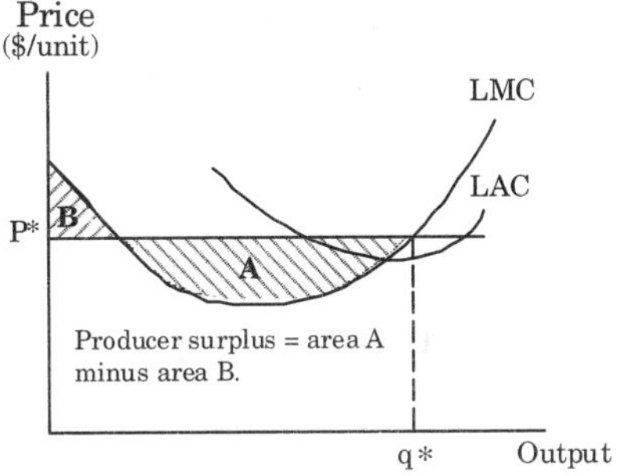

Figure 8.6

CHOOSING OUTPUT IN THE LONG RUN (Section 8.7)

In the long run, a firm chooses to produce an output such that long-run marginal cost equals price, as long as profit is greater than or equal to zero. Consequently, price must be at least as high as minimum average total cost for the firm to produce in the long run.

In the long run, firms that are losing money leave the industry. As firms exit, market supply decreases, driving the price up to the point where profits are zero. If firms earn positive profit, entry will occur in the long run. Entry will stop when profits have fallen back to zero. As a result, in long-run equilibrium, firms earn zero economic profit.

There are two conditions for long-run equilibrium: 1) P = LMC guarantees individual firm profit maximization; and 2) P = LAC guarantees no incentive for entry and exit (zero economic profit). Note that individual firms are not *trying* to earn zero economic profit (a normal rate of return). They are trying to earn as high a profit as possible. It is the free entry and exit of firms that drives economic profit to zero (P = LAC) in long-run equilibrium. Putting the two conditions together, P = LMC and P = LAC, we conclude that *firm output will be set at the point where* P = Minimum LAC *in long-run equilibrium.*

In the long run no costs need be incurred if the firm shuts down—all costs are variable because all input choices can be changed. As a result, a firm must either break even or earn a positive profit to stay in business. Requiring $\pi(q) \geq 0$ means that $[P - LAC]q \geq 0$ must hold. As with the short-run supply curve, the quantity chosen must be on the upward-sloping portion of the supply curve. Together, these two conditions imply that P ≥ Minimum LAC on the supply curve. The *firm's long-run supply curve* is the rising portion of a firm's MC curve above Minimum LAC.

Why do we only require $\pi(q) \geq 0$ and not $\pi(q) > 0$? Why would a business be content with zero profit? Recall that economic profit covers all opportunity costs. This means that *zero economic profit includes a normal return on investment.* (In fact, you can substitute the phrase "earning a normal rate of return" whenever you think about zero economic profit if it makes it less confusing.) Zero economic profit may be the best the firm can do in a highly competitive industry. The firm can do no better by exiting this industry and entering another competitive industry.

Exercise: ◗ ◗ ◗ ◗ ◗ ◗ ◗

9. Suppose license fees for building contractors double in Michigan. A license fee must be paid to the state each year before the contractor is permitted to work. Assuming the market is perfectly competitive, what will be the effect of the increased license fee on the number of firms, the market price and output, and economic profits?

ECONOMIC RENT

From a firm's perspective, *economic rent* is the difference between what a firm is willing to pay for an input and the minimum amount necessary to buy the input. Economic rent for an industry is another name for long-run producer surplus. Suppose, for example, that you owned a stand of mesquite bushes that earned a producer surplus of \$100 per year in long-run equilibrium. You would be willing to sell the stand if you could invest the proceeds and obtain \$100 per year in interest payments. Thus, the \$100 surplus you obtain for supplying the mesquite is merely compensation for the opportunity cost of not selling the stand (the next best use of the resources you have invested in the mesquite business). The producer surplus has been capitalized into the value of the stand of mesquite.

THE INDUSTRY'S LONG-RUN SUPPLY CURVE (Section 8.8)

The slope of the *industry long-run supply curve* depends on how costs for *all* firms change with entry. If input costs do not change with the entry of new firms, the long-run industry supply curve will be horizontal. This is the definition of a *constant-cost industry* and it is a reasonable assumption if the industry uses no specialized inputs. However, if input prices rise with industry output, the long-run supply curve will slope upward (an *increasing-cost industry*). Conversely, if input prices fall with increases in output, the long-run supply curve will slope downward and the industry is called *decreasing-cost*.

Start with the assumption that the industry is constant-cost. Suppose current producers are initially earning positive profits, as in Figure 8.7a at P_2. This means that the industry is not in long-run equilibrium. Entrepreneurs will see that they could enter the industry and also earn positive profits. Entry will shift the short-run supply curve to S_2 in Figure 8.7b. Entry will continue to occur over time until long-run equilibrium is reached at a price of P_1. At P_1, economic profits are zero and there is no incentive for additional entry into the industry. The long-run industry supply curve is horizontal, as shown in Figure 8.7b. Any price above P_1, the price that is equal to minimum long-run average cost, will attract entry; similarly, any price below P_1 will cause firms to exit. But this entry and exit will not change the AC curve, so long-run supply will always settle back to a price of P_1.

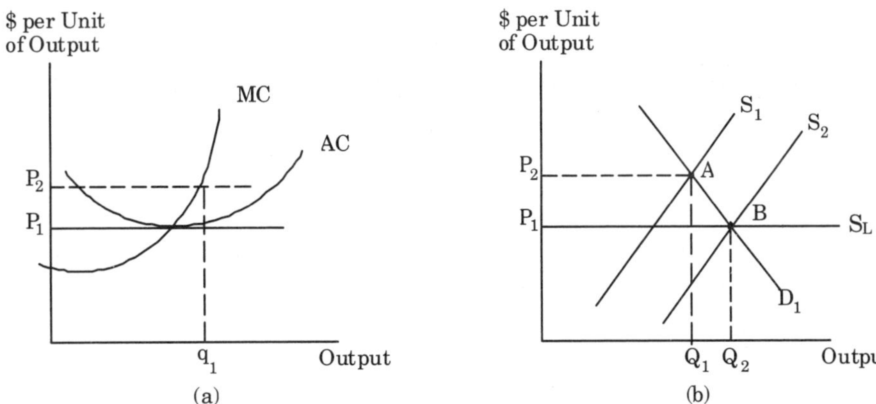

Figure 8.7

Exercise: ▶ ▶ ▶ ▶ ▶ ▶ ▶

10. In a constant-cost industry, what is the long-run effect of a shift in demand to the right? Will the price rise, fall, or remain unchanged in the long run compared to the previous equilibrium? What is the effect on the long-run equilibrium quantity?

If an industry uses specialized inputs that are in short supply, then entry of new firms (or expansion of output by existing firms) will raise input prices. Even if each firm's production function exhibits constant returns to scale, upward-sloping supply curves for inputs can cause increasing costs in the industry. In the case of an increasing-cost industry, a shift in the market demand curve to the right causes entry, but as this entry occurs the demand for inputs increases, and that in turn will raise input prices. Each firm's cost curves will then shift up in response to higher input prices. At the new equilibrium, profits are again zero for all the firms, but at a higher price than before. Consequently, the long-run industry supply curve slopes upward.

Exercise: ◗◗◗◗◗◗◗

11. In an increasing-cost industry, how will the long-run equilibrium price change when the demand curve shifts to the right? To the left?

PROBLEM SET

12. A firm has short-run total costs given by:

$$C(q) = 100 + 2q + q^2,$$

with marginal cost MC = 2 + 2q.

a) Find average total cost and average variable cost as a function of the level of output.
b) If P = 25, how much will the firm produce in the short run?
c) If P = 20, how much will the firm produce in the short run?
d) Assuming the firm has the same cost curves in the long run for $q > 0$ and $C(0) = 0$, how much will it produce in the long run?

13. A firm has marginal costs given by MC = 10 + q and average variable costs AVC = 10 + q/2. If fixed costs are 5,000 and the market price is 100, find the firm's maximum profit. Will the firm continue to operate in the short run? In the long run? Explain.

14. Suppose a competitive firm has long run total costs $C(q) = 300 + 5q + 3q^2$ for $q > 0$ and $C(0) = 0$. Marginal costs are MC = 5 + 6q. The minimum of average total cost is \$65 at q = 10. Now a tax is imposed on the firm—for each unit of output produced, it must pay \$15 in taxes. Derive the new MC curve. What is minimum average total cost? At what output does this occur? What was the firm's original supply curve? What is the firm's new supply curve?

15. A corn syrup refinery's total variable cost curve is given in Figure 8.8. Explain why there is a range of prices such that the firm produces Q* units of output.

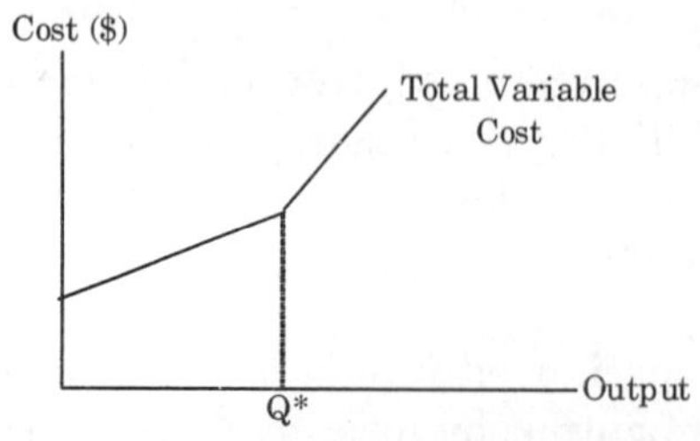

Figure 8.8

16. *[Calculus] An industry is composed of identical firms with total costs $C(q_i) = 2q_i^2 + 6q_i + 18$ for $q_i > 0$ and $C(0) = 0$, where q_i is firm i's output. Marginal cost for each firm is $MC(q_i) = 4q_i + 6$.

a) Draw the AFC, AVC, and MC curves for a single firm.

b) Suppose there are currently 100 firms in the industry. What is the short-run supply curve for the industry (expressing quantity as a function of price)?

c) What is the long run supply curve with free entry? (Assume a constant-cost industry.)

d) Suppose the demand curve for the industry is $Q_D - 660 - 20P$, where P is the market price. What is the long-run equilibrium price and output?

e) Suppose the demand curve shifts to $Q_D = 840 - 20P$. What happens to price, output, and profit in the short run?

f) What happens to price, output, and profit in the long run?

17. *[Calculus] Suppose that a widget producer's total cost function is $C(q) = 500 + 7q + 0.04q^2$ for $q > 0$ and $C(0) = 0$, where C is total cost in dollars and q is the number of cases of widgets produced. What are the corresponding ATC, AVC, and MC functions? If this industry is characterized by free entry, what is the long-run market equilibrium price?

SELF-TEST

18. The price elasticity of the demand curve faced by a perfectly competitive firm is:

a) 0.

b) –1.

c) $-\infty$.

d) the price elasticity of the market demand curve.

e) None of the above.

19. The Smith Company produces widgets. Smith's average variable cost at its current output level is $30 per unit. Its current average total cost per unit is $60 per unit. If the market price is $45:

a) it should produce a quantity to minimize marginal cost.

b) it should shut down immediately.

c) it should stay in business in the short run.

d) it should produce a quantity to minimize average variable cost.

e) a) and c)

20. A profit maximizing competitive firm making positive economic profits will produce in the short run up to the point at which:

a) total revenue is maximized.

b) marginal cost is minimized.

c) marginal revenue is maximized.

d) average revenue equals average total cost.

e) marginal revenue equals marginal cost.

21. A competitive firm earning zero profit should:
a) exit the industry and find a more lucrative use for the resources employed.
b) expand production to try to earn a positive profit.
c) continue doing what it is doing.
d) raise its price.
e) b) or d)

22. In a constant-cost industry, the elasticity of long-run industry supply equals:
a) $+\infty$.
b) 1.
c) 0.
d) the elasticity of long-run firm supply.
e) More information is needed.

23. If MC = 50 + 6q and AVC = 50 + 3q, and if P = 110, what should the perfectly competitive firm produce in the short run?
a) 0
b) 10
c) 20
d) 30
e) None of the above is correct.

24. If MC = 50 + 6q and ATC = 50 + 3q + 675/q, and if the current price is P = 140, the firm should produce ____ in the short run and ____ in the long run.
a) 0 and 0
b) 15 and 15
c) 25 and 0
d) 15 and 0
e) None of the above is correct.

25. The shirt industry consists of firms with U-shaped average total cost curves and is in long-run competitive equilibrium. Assume a constant cost industry. If Congress imposes a per-unit tax on suppliers for each shirt produced, then which of the following is true? (Hint: Does the per-unit tax shift MC? Does the per-unit tax change the quantity at which average total cost is minimized?)
a) The number of firms will drop, but total output will stay the same.
b) The number of firms will drop, but output per firm will stay the same.
c) The number of firms will stay the same, but total output will drop.
d) Total output will drop, but output per firm may rise or fall.
e) None of the above is correct.

26. If the managers of a competitive firm do not maximize their profit:
a) the stockholders will replace them.
b) the firm may be bought in a takeover.
c) the firm will be unable to attract capital to expand.
d) All of the above are possible consequences.
e) None of the above is correct.

27. If price equals marginal revenue for a firm:
a) it is maximizing profit.
b) it faces a horizontal demand curve.
c) it should produce zero.
d) it should produce as much as possible.
e) a) and b)

The next two questions refer to a firm in a constant-cost industry with ATC(q) = 2,000/q + 100 + 5q and MC(q) = 100 + 10q.

28. The long-run equilibrium price equals:
a) $100.
b) $200.
c) $300.
d) $500.
e) None of the above is correct.

29. Demand for industry output has just increased. If the market price initially rises to $600, each firm in the long run will produce:
a) 20 units.
b) 50 units.
c) 88.7 units.
d) 100 units.
e) More information is needed.

ANSWERS TO CHAPTER 8

EXERCISE ANSWERS

1. Neither market satisfies all of the conditions for perfect competition. The restaurant market does not exhibit product homogeneity—the various firms offer different types of food, occupy different locations, and offer different degrees of comfort and elegance. Advertisers would find radio stations to differ in the types of listeners they attract, so the product is also not homogeneous. Since a broadcaster needs to obtain a license from the Federal Communications Commission, the free entry condition is also not satisfied.

2. One reason might be to enhance the town's atmosphere. The company might then find it easier to recruit executives. In general, long-run profit maximization may well be consistent with charitable contributions and other activities that do not generate short-run revenues for the firm, if they improve the firm's reputation and lead to increased revenues in the long run.

3. The total revenue, total cost, and profit columns for Table 8.2 are:

Output	Revenue	Total Cost	Profit
13	1,950	2,100	–150
14	2,100	2,245	–145
15	2,250	2,400	–150
16	2,400	2,565	–165
17	2,550	2,740	–190

The profit maximizing output level is q = 14. If it expands output by one unit to 15 units, it will take in an additional $150 in revenue, but it will pay an additional $155 in production costs. So, expanding output to 15 units will cause the firm to lose an extra $5 in profits. Likewise, if it reduces its output by one unit to 13, it saves $145 in costs, but it gives up $150 in revenue. Thus, profit would fall by $5 compared with producing 14 units of output. Although profits are negative (–$145), it is clear that losses will be minimized at q = 14.

4. Yes, the firm gains by selling an extra carload; profit grows by $43,020 – $29,754 = $13,266. The firm should increase production.

5. Suppose the firm expands output from q^* by a small amount. The area under the MC curve is the total cost of the output increase. The area under the demand curve (horizontal at P) represents the revenue gained by the output increase. Since MC < P for a small increase in output above q, the firm gains by expanding output to point B where P = MC and MC is upward sloping.

6. See Figure 8A.1. Currently you are producing where MC = 10 and P = 8. You should reduce output to the point where P = MC. Without more information, we cannot calculate the profit maximizing output. But we do know that (1) the optimal q lies somewhere between $q = 150$ and $q = 200$, and (2) you should not shut down in the short run since you are covering variable costs.

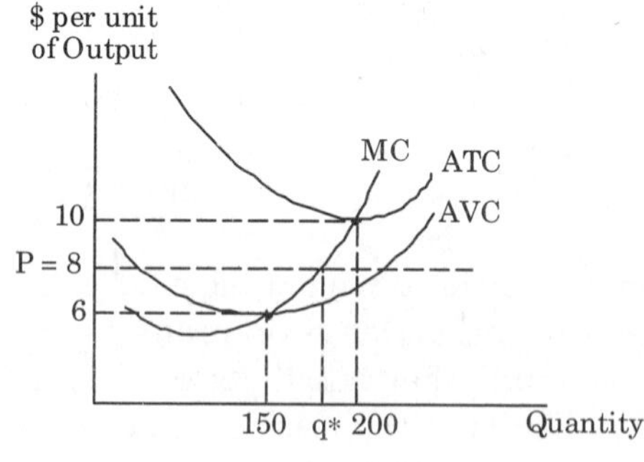

Figure 8A.1

7. For the first five firms, MC = $5q_i$ = P implies q_i = P/5. These five firms have supply curves equal to:

q_i = P/5 if P > 15 and q_i = 0 if P < 15 (since Minimum AVC = 15).

For the other three firms, MC = $4q_j$ = P implies q_j = P/4. These three firms have supply curves:

$$q_j = P/4 \text{ if } P \geq 20 \text{ and } q_j = 0 \text{ if } P < 20 \text{ (since Minimum AVC = 20).}$$

The short-run market supply curve is just the horizontal sum of the eight individual firm supply curves. Therefore, the short-run market supply curve (shown in Figure 8A.2) is:

$$Q = \begin{cases} 0 & \text{if } P < 15 \\ P & \text{if } 15 < P < 20 \quad \text{since } P = 5(P/5) \\ 7P/4 & \text{if } P > 20 \quad \text{since } 7P/4 = 5(P/5) + 3(P/4) \end{cases}$$

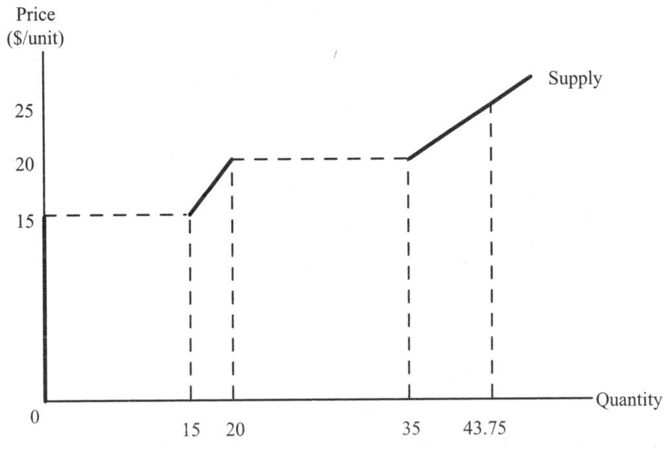

Figure 8A.2

8. At P = 40, the firm produces 35 units. The shaded area in Figure 8A.3 equals total surplus. The first 15 units cost $10 each, so the surplus on these units is (30)15 = $450. The next 15 units cost $20 each, so the surplus on these units is (20)15 = $300. The last 5 units cost $30 each, so the surplus is (10)5 = $50. Total surplus is, therefore, $800.

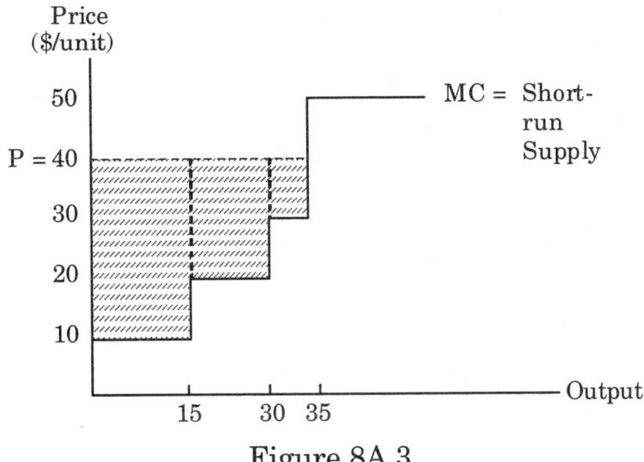

Figure 8A.3

9. The increase in license fees is an increase in fixed costs. This increase will cause the LAC curve to shift up, as shown in Figure 8A.4a. Firms will exit, the short-run market supply curve in Figure 8A.4b will shift to the left, and there will be fewer firms, each producing larger individual output, but together producing a smaller *aggregate* output. This process will continue until the price rises to P_1 = Minimum LAC_1 and economic profits eventually return to zero.

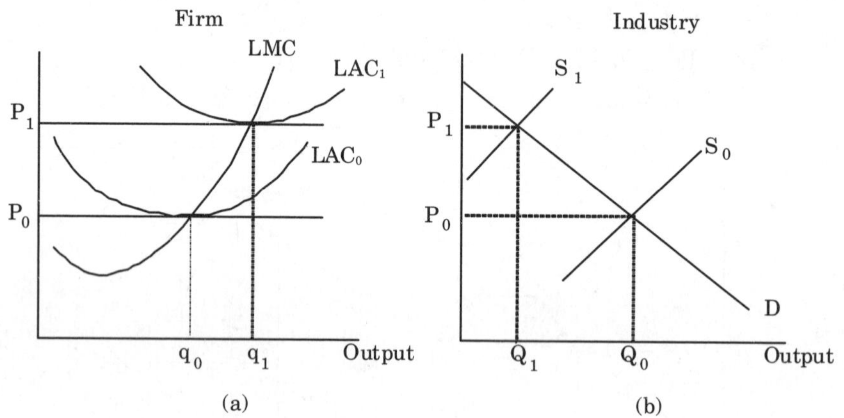

Figure 8A.4

10. In a constant-cost industry, the long-run industry supply curve is flat. If demand shifts to the right, the intersection of the demand curve with the long-run industry supply curve will be at the same price as before the demand shift (the point of minimum ATC for all firms). The quantity sold will increase as will the number of firms, but although price will rise in the short run, it will return to its original level in the long run.

11. With an increasing-cost industry, the long-run supply curve is upward sloping. The shift of the demand curve to the right will increase output and price (see Figure 8A.5a). A shift of the demand curve to the left will decrease price and output (see Figure 8A.5b).

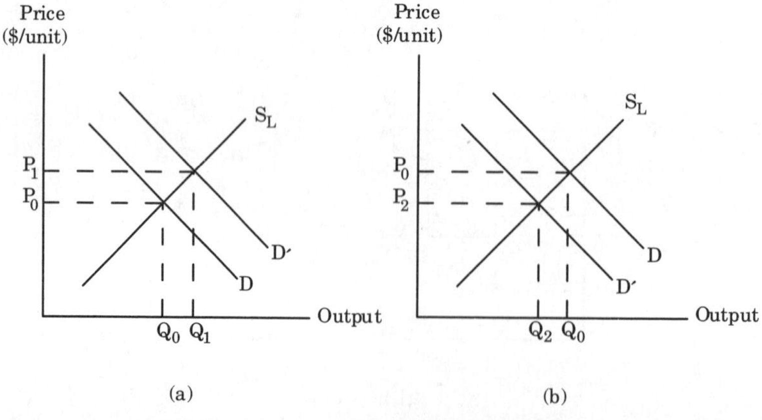

Figure 8A.5

PROBLEM SET ANSWERS

12. a) ATC = C(q)/q = 100/q + 2 + q; AVC = VC/q = $(2q + q^2)/q$ = 2 + q.

b) MC = P implies 2 + 2q = 25, or q = 23/2 = 11.5. The minimum of AVC occurs at q = 0 (graph MC and AVC to see this), so there is no doubt that the firm will stay open, and produce 11.5 units.

c) If P = 20, MC = P implies 2 + 2q = 20, so q = 18/2 = 9.

d) For the long run, P ≥ Minimum ATC is also a necessary condition. ATC is minimized where ATC = MC, or $100/q^* + 2 + q^* = 2 + 2q^*$ or $q^* = 10$. Thus, Minimum ATC = ATC(10) = 100/10 + 2 + 10 = 22. In the long run, the firm will produce 10 if P = 22 and it will not produce anything if P < 22.

13. In the short run, MC > AVC for all q > 0. At P =100, setting MC = 100 yields 10 + q = 100 or q = 90. Maximum profit is $\pi(q)$ = TR – TC = 100(90) – (10 + 90/2)90 – 5,000 = – \$950.

In the short run, the \$950 loss from operating is less than the \$5000 loss from staying open and having to pay fixed costs without any revenues coming into the business. Therefore, the firm will not shut down. In the long run, the firm will go out of business.

14. After the tax is imposed, the new total cost is given by the original total cost plus the taxes paid. Define C´(q) = C(q) + 15q = 300 + 20q + 3q2. MC´ = 20 + 6q and ATC´= 300/q + 20 + 3q. The quantity at which ATC´ is minimized is found by setting MC´ = ATC´. We then obtain 20 + 6q = 300/q + 20 + 3q or q = 10. (Note that the shift in costs due to the tax does not change the firm's efficient scale.) With the tax, the minimum of ATC´= 30 + 20 + 3(10) = 80.
The long-run supply curve before the tax is found by taking the MC curve above minimum ATC. Since MC = 5 + 6q and Minimum ATC = 65, we find the supply curve by setting $5 + 6q = P$ and rewriting it as q = (P – 5)/6. Truncating the MC curve below Minimum ATC means that the supply curve is q_S = (P – 5)/6 if P ≥ 65, and q_S = 0 if P < 65.

Setting MC´ = P, or 20 + 6q = P yields a long-run supply curve after the tax of q_S = (P – 20)/6 if P ≥ 80 and q_S = 0 if P < 80.

15. Figure 8A.6 displays the marginal cost curve for this refinery. The kink in the variable cost curve means that there is a jump in the marginal cost curve. For any price between P_0 and P_1, the firm will produce Q* units in order to satisfy MC(Q) = P.

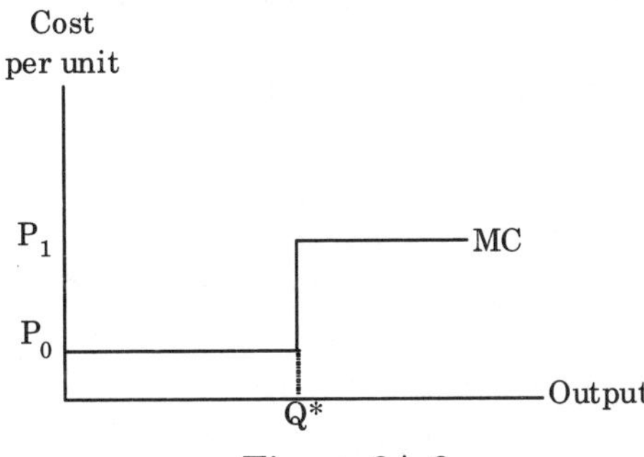

Figure 8A.6

16. a) AVC = $2q_i + 6$ and MC = $\partial C(q_i)/\partial q_i = 4q_i + 6$. MC > AVC for all $q_i > 0$. AFC = $18/q_i$. See Figure 8A.7. The U-shaped ATC curve indicates that first we have increasing returns to scale, then constant returns to scale at the point of minimum ATC, and then decreasing returns to scale.

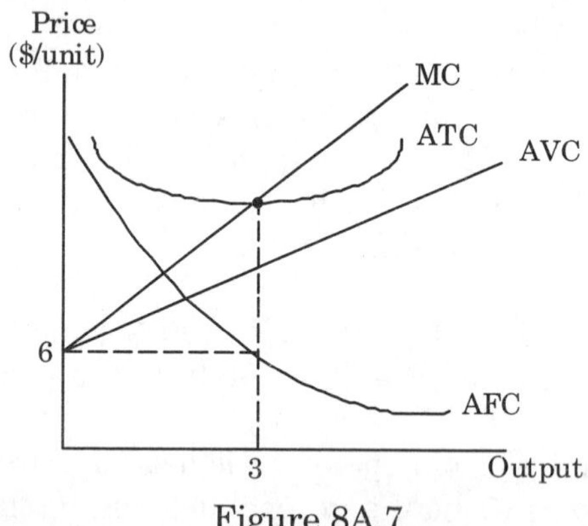

Figure 8A.7

b) For each firm, MC = P implies $4q_i + 6 = P$, or $q_i = (P - 6)/4$. This is for all P > 6 since Minimum AVC occurs at $q_i = 0$. The market supply curve in the short run (with 100 firms) is $Q_S = 100[(P - 6)/4] = 25(P - 6) = 25P - 150$.

c) The minimum of ATC can be found by equating ATC and MC: $2q_i + 6 + 18/q_i = 4q_i + 6$ implies $q_i^* = 3$ and ATC(3) = MC(3) = 18. The long run equilibrium price is thus \$18. The long-run supply curve is horizontal at P = \$18 if this is a constant-cost industry.

d) The long-run equilibrium price of \$18 yields demand of

$$Q_D = 660 - 20P = 660 - 20(18) = 300.$$

Since each firm produces 3 units when P = 18, 100 firms will be active in the industry.

e) After the demand curve shifts, we can find the short-run equilibrium price and output by equating Q_D and Q_S: $840 - 20P = 25P - 150$, or $P^* = \$22$. If $P^* = \$22$, $Q^* = 400$. Each firm produces $q_i^* = 4$. Profit for each firm is

$$\pi(4) = 22(4) - [2(4)^2 + 6(4) + 18] = 88 - 74 = \$14.$$

Total industry profit equals 100(14) = \$1,400.

f) In the long run $P^* = \$18$ once again (price will increase in the short run, but price in the long run must fall back to minimum long-run average cost) and each firm produces 3 units. Market demand is $Q_D = 840 - 20(18) = 480$. Profit is zero for all firms ($0 = 18(3) - [2(3)^2 + 6(3) + 18]$) and 160 (= 480/3) firms are active in the industry.

17. ATC(q) = 500/q + 7 + 0.04q. AVC(q) = 7 + 0.04q and MC(q) = 7 + 0.08q (differentiate total cost with respect to q). The point at which ATC is minimized can be found by finding the quantity at which MC and ATC are equal:

$$7 + 0.08q = 500/q + 7 + 0.04q \text{ yields } q^* = \sqrt{12{,}500}$$

or $q^* = 111.80$. One can also find Minimum ATC by taking the derivative of ATC and setting it equal to zero: $-500q^{-2} + 0.04 = 0$ implies $q^* = 111.80$. With free entry, the market equilibrium price will be equal to Minimum ATC or \$15.94.

SELF-TEST ANSWERS

18. c) Each perfectly competitive firm takes the market price as given. This implies that each firm faces a horizontal demand curve, even though the market demand curve is downward sloping. A horizontal demand curve has an elasticity of $-\infty$.

19. c) In the current situation, Smith is covering all of its variable costs, but only part of its fixed costs. If it shut down immediately, it would have zero revenue and be unable to cover any of its fixed costs. Smith should stay open in the short run, but work to reduce its fixed costs.

20. e) The firm should produce up to the point where MR = MC. (It also happens to be true for perfect competition that P = MR, so you can state the profit maximization condition as "produce up to the point where P = MC." But the more general condition, MR = MC, is also true.)

21. c) Choice d) is impossible for a perfect competitor, and b) won't work if it is maximizing profits already (as we assume). Since it is covering its opportunity costs, it should stay in business.

22. a) The supply curve is horizontal, so $E_S = \infty$.

23. b) For the short run, set MC = P to find q*. In this case, 50 + 6q = 110 implies q* = 10. The firm stay open in the short run if P > AVC at q*. At q* = 10, AVC = 80 which is less than the price of 110. The firm should stay open (in other words, q* is in fact 10 and not 0).

24. b) Set P = MC to find the short-run profit maximizing output of q* = 15. In the long run, price will settle at minimum long-run average cost. By setting ATC = MC you can find the quantity that minimizes long-run average cost, which turns out to be q* = 15. (P = 140 is the long-run equilibrium price.)

25. b) A per-unit tax shifts up both MC and ATC, but it does not shift the quantity at which ATC is minimized. (To see this within the context of a specific numerical example, consider the MC and ATC equations of the problem above, where MC = 50 + 6q and ATC = 50 + 3q + 675/q. Suppose the tax adds 10 to both MC and ATC. In solving for the new minimum ATC you set MC = ATC or 60 + 6q = 60 + 3q + 675/q. The "60" drops out and ATC is still minimized at q = 15.) The shifts in MC and ATC will therefore not change the long-run profit maximizing output level per firm, but there will be a higher price in the long run, lower industry output, and fewer firms.

26. d) Although managers can follow goals other than profit maximization, their ability to do so is limited in the long run. Shareholders keep a careful eye on firm performance and can replace managers if the firm does poorly for too long a period. The firm may become a takeover target. Or, the firm will be unable to attract new investors. Any or all of these are possibilities.

27. b) Only if demand is horizontal will P equal MR. Choice (a) is not true because we don't know if the firm has set P = MC. For the same reason, we don't know if (c) is true. In general, the firm should not simply "produce" as much as possible (choice (d)), but rather should produce the profit-maximizing output.

28. c) Find minimum ATC by setting ATC = MC; this yields q = 20. Plug q = 20 into ATC to find the long-run equilibrium price of $300.

29. a) The long-run equilibrium will again have each firm producing at minimum ATC. Each firm produces 20 units, as in Question 28.

CHAPTER 9
THE ANALYSIS OF COMPETITIVE MARKETS

IMPORTANT CONCEPTS

- Welfare Effect
- Economic Efficiency
- Price Controls
- Deadweight Loss
- Minimum Prices
- Price Supports
- Production Quotas
- Acreage Limitations
- Tariffs
- Quotas
- Taxes
- Subsidies
- Pass-Through Fraction of a Tax

CHAPTER HIGHLIGHTS

Using the tools of demand and supply, and armed with a basic understanding of competitive markets, we can analyze how markets react to a variety of government policies. Supply-demand analysis can be used not only to make predictions about how the equilibrium price and quantity will change, but also to assess who wins and who loses from a particular policy and whether society gains or loses as a whole. Society's gain or loss as a whole is called the *welfare effect* of a policy. The change in aggregate welfare of consumers and producers reflects the *economic efficiency* of the market. While economists can measure changes in economic efficiency and use that as a yardstick to judge whether a policy is good or bad, it is important to realize that economic efficiency may not be the goal of policymakers. Other objectives, such as income stability for farmers (as in the case of agricultural price supports) or a redistribution of income from landlords to tenants (as in the case of rent control laws) may be more important.

If, for example, the government institutes a *price ceiling* (a price set below the market equilibrium price), there will be a loss in consumer surplus by those consumers who can no longer buy the good.

On the other hand, there will be a gain in consumer surplus for those consumers who are purchasing the good at the new lower price. On the producer side, there will be an unambiguous loss in producer surplus because (1) some producers will leave the market, and (2) those who are still selling are being forced to accept a lower price. The net result is a *deadweight loss* in total surplus (consumer plus producer surplus). There will be a similar deadweight loss from a government policy which sets a *price minimum* (where the price is held above the equilibrium price). In general, a deadweight loss is created whenever the price is regulated away from the competitive market equilibrium price and the quantity traded on the market is different from the competitive market equilibrium quantity.

In agricultural markets, the government's minimum price programs are called *price support* programs. Under a system of price supports, the government promises to buy the excess supply created by the price that is set above the equilibrium price. Producers will clearly gain from this policy, and consumers will lose. The government often ends up spending a great deal of money buying the excess supply, and the net welfare loss (deadweight loss) can be quite large. To get around this, the government sometimes combines price supports with a method of reducing supply. Two common methods are imposing *production quotas* or instituting an *acreage limitation program*, whereby farmers are given a financial incentive to leave some of their acreage idle.

The tools of demand and supply can also be used to analyze the effects of *tariff* or *quota* policies, designed (at least in part) to limit foreign competition. In the case of an import quota, supply is reduced by directly limiting the quantity of imports. In the case of a tariff, supply is reduced in essence by taxing imports. The price rises and the supply of imports is reduced. In both cases, there will be a deadweight loss to society. The policies differ in that the domestic government collects revenue from a tariff, while a quota funnels that same money to foreign producers in the form of higher profits.

Taxes and *subsidies* are another form of government intervention in markets. In the case of a specific tax (i.e., a tax of a certain amount of money per unit sold) the price the consumer pays exceeds the net price the seller receives by the amount of the tax. Although a tax results in a deadweight loss, the focus of the analysis in this chapter is on the question of whether consumers or producers bear the burden of the tax. We measure the burden of the tax by the *"pass-through" fraction* that is based on the elasticities of demand and supply. A tax falls mostly on the buyer if the demand elasticity is small relative to the supply elasticity. If the opposite condition holds, then the burden of the tax will fall mostly on the seller. A subsidy can be seen as a negative tax and is analyzed in much the same way.

CONCEPT REVIEW AND EXERCISES

EVALUATING THE GAINS AND LOSSES FROM GOVERNMENT POLICIES—CONSUMER AND PRODUCER SURPLUS (Section 9.1)

In a competitive market equilibrium, the area between the demand curve and the market price is consumer surplus and the area between the supply curve and the market price is producer surplus. Total surplus is the sum of consumer and producer surplus.

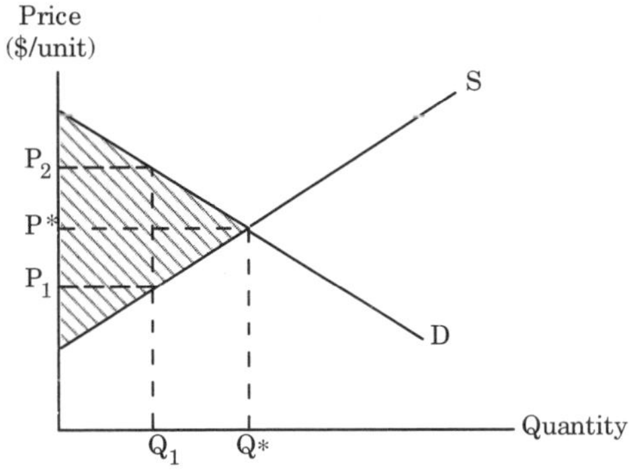

Figure 9.1

Figure 9.1 displays total surplus in a competitive equilibrium but with a slightly different interpretation. Suppose Q_1 units of output are currently being sold. To produce one more unit, a producer needs to receive at least P_1 (the price on the supply curve at that quantity). A consumer obtaining an additional unit is willing to pay P_2 (the price on the demand curve at that quantity). If P^* is the actual price for that unit, then the consumer's gain is $P_2 - P^*$ and the producer's gain is $P^* - P_1$. The *aggregate* gain to both the producer and consumer is $P_2 - P_1$ (regardless of the level of P^*). Adding up the total gain to producers and consumers for all units sold up to Q^* gives us the total gains from trade (which is equal to the sum of consumer and producer surplus) in the market. This is equal to the shaded area in Figure 9.1. *Efficiency* means that the sum of consumer and producer surplus is maximized. Goods are allocated efficiently only in a competitive equilibrium. In the absence of market failure (which can happen, for example, if consumers lack adequate information about the product to make utility-maximizing choices), an unregulated market equilibrium occurs at the efficient price and output.

Stated differently, the equilibrium quantity Q^* maximizes the sum of consumer and producer surplus. At any price other than the equilibrium price, the quantity produced and consumed is less than Q^* because either producers are unwilling to sell or consumers are unwilling to buy a larger quantity. A price different from P^* is *inefficient* because the aggregate gains from trade are less than the maximum possible amount.

Exercise: ▶ ▶ ▶ ▶ ▶ ▶ ▶

1. The demand for milk in the United States is given by $Q_D = 152 - 20P$ and the U.S. supply of milk is $Q_S = -4 + 188P$, where Q is measured in billions of gallons per year, and P is measured in dollars per gallon.
   a) Calculate the competitive market equilibrium price and quantity and total surplus at that price. Illustrate your answer.
   b) Show that total surplus at a price of $1.00 per gallon is less than total surplus at the equilibrium price.

A *price ceiling* is a legal maximum on the price per unit that a producer can receive. The price ceiling is called "binding" if it is below the equilibrium price, as in Figure 9.2 where P_{max} is the ceiling price. The quantity purchased equals the quantity producers are willing to supply at the ceiling price (Q_1). To calculate the *deadweight loss* of the price ceiling, compare total surplus at a price of P_0 (the unregulated, competitive equilibrium price) with total surplus at the regulated price P_{max}. Consumer surplus at P_0 and Q_0 is area B + D. Producer surplus at P_0 and Q_0 is area A + C + E. With a price ceiling, consumer surplus becomes area A + D. Those consumers who can no longer buy the good lose area B, while those who bought Q_1 before at P_0 and buy Q_1 now at P_{max} gain area A. A price ceiling results in a producer surplus of only area E. Producers lose area A to consumers and area C due to a drop in production. Compared to the competitive equilibrium, consumers and producers together lose areas B and C. Area A is a transfer of surplus from producers to consumers and is not counted as part of deadweight loss. Therefore, the *deadweight loss* of the price ceiling is measured by area B + C.

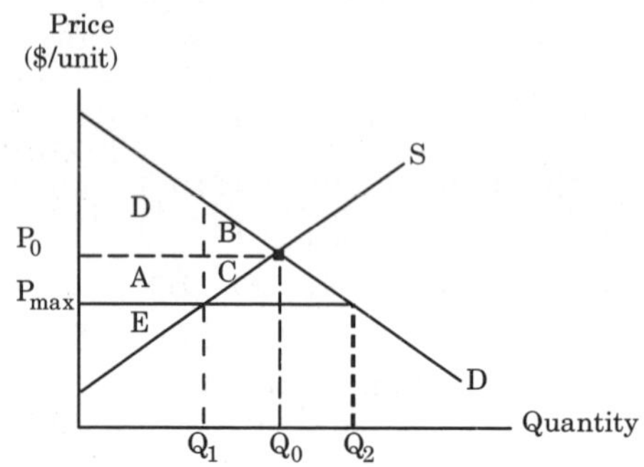

Figure 9.2

Exercise: ▶ ▶ ▶ ▶ ▶ ▶ ▶

2. Draw a figure like the one in Figure 9.2, but with a relatively inelastic supply curve. Can you tell from your drawing whether consumers gain or lose on net from the imposition of a price ceiling? Does your answer make intuitive sense?

An additional factor may increase the deadweight loss associated with a price ceiling. At P_{max} in Figure 9.2, consumers wish to buy Q_2 units. Since only Q_1 units are produced, how do we know *which* consumers buy the good, and how many units each consumer buys?

At the free-market equilibrium price P_0, all consumers with reservation prices greater than or equal to P_0 buy as much as they wish at that price. But at the ceiling price, some type of rationing must occur. Our calculation of deadweight loss assumes that those who value the good the most get to buy it. If this is not the case, the calculation of the losses from the price ceiling will understate the deadweight loss. For example, suppose some consumers can buy as much as they wish at the ceiling price. Then, their valuations for their last units purchased are less than the valuations of other consumers who cannot buy as much as they wish. In such a case, besides the inefficiency of too little production, what is produced is also inefficiently distributed.

MINIMUM PRICES (Section 9.3)

The government will at times determine that the equilibrium price is too low, and sets a *price minimum* above the market equilibrium. (This is often referred to as a price floor.) Examples are federally imposed minimum wage laws and locally regulated taxi fares in many cities. A minimum price regulation that raises the price above the equilibrium level causes excess supply in the market. Consumers always lose because they buy a smaller quantity at a higher price. Sellers may gain or lose, depending on the cost of producing output that cannot be sold at the minimum price.

Exercise: ▶ ▶ ▶ ▶ ▶ ▶ ▶

3. a) Draw a figure analogous to Figure 9.2, but depicting the deadweight loss due to a price minimum rather than a price ceiling.

b) Return to the demand and supply equations for milk given in Exercise 1:

$$Q_D = 152 - 20P \text{ and } Q_S = -4 + 188P.$$

Calculate the deadweight loss resulting from a price minimum set at P = \$1.00.

PRICE SUPPORTS AND PRODUCTION QUOTAS (Section 9.4)

Price supports are a major element of U.S. agricultural policy. The Federal government uses price supports to raise prices and increase farmers' incomes. A number of different policies are used. For some crops, the government sets a support price and buys whatever output it needs to keep the market price at this level. In this case, the farmers produce in excess of what private citizens demand, and the government purchases the excess supply. Such a program may be very costly because the government pays farmers to produce output that no one consumes. Figure 9.3 shows the cost to the government when a support price of P_S is set. Consumers demand Q_1, but producers will supply Q_2. In order to keep the price at P_S, the government must buy $Q_g = Q_2 - Q_1$. If it didn't, the price would fall back to the equilibrium price, P_0. This demand by the government, Q_g, is added to the consumers' demand curve. The government pays $P_S(Q_2 - Q_1)$ for this excess supply. This cost to the government is the shaded area in Figure 9.3.

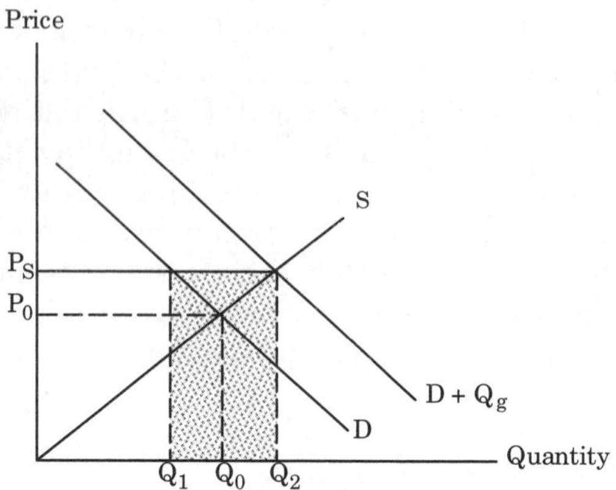

Figure 9.3

Figure 9.4 (on the next page) shows a change in the supply curve from S_0 to S_1 when the government gives producers a financial incentive to reduce output from Q_0 to Q_1. Note that for prices below P′, the producers would choose on their own to produce less than Q_1. It is only when the market price rises above P′ that producers would want to set $Q > Q_1$. Limiting production to Q_1 causes the supply curve to become completely inelastic at Q_1. Producer surplus at P_0 was E + C + F. Producer surplus at P_S but *without* acreage limitations would be E + C + F + A + B + D (recall that producer surplus is always the area between price and the supply curve out to the quantity sold, which is Q_2 in this case). Producer surplus at P_s and a quantity of Q_1 (i.e., *with* the acreage limitation) would be A + E + F. Therefore, the (minimum) cost to the government to induce farmers to produce only Q_1 at P_S is C + B + D. For both price supports and production quotas, the cost of the programs exceeds the cost of simply paying cash directly to farmers.

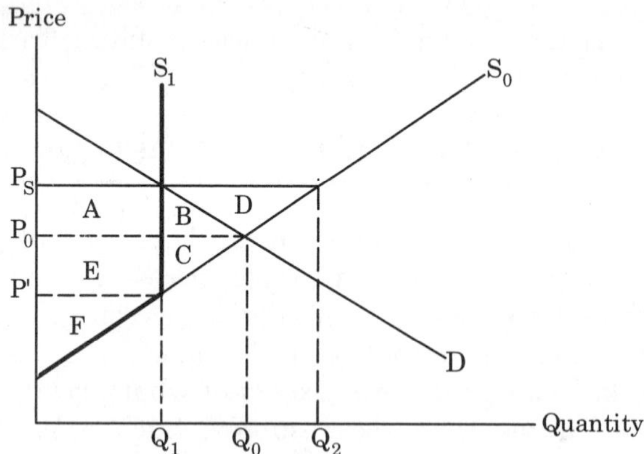

Figure 9.4

Exercise: ◗ ◗ ◗ ◗ ◗ ◗ ◗

4. Let's continue with the milk products example:

$$Q_D = 152 - 20P \text{ and } Q_S = -4 + 188P.$$

a) How much will it cost the government to buy the excess supply if a price support is set at $P_S = \$1.25$?

b) How much would the government have to pay the milk producers to entice them to restrict their production to Q = 127?

c) The Food and Drug Administration has approved a bovine growth hormone that can boost milk production by as much as 30 percent per cow with little added cost. Holding the milk support price constant, discuss the effect that the introduction of this growth hormone will have on the cost of the government's policies in parts a) and b).

IMPORT QUOTAS AND TARIFFS (Section 9.5)

When imports are added to the market, changes in the quantity consumed need not equal changes in the quantity produced domestically. For simplicity, consider the case of a horizontal import supply curve–this will occur if the world price is unaffected by domestic demand and supply changes. Thus, the country can import as much as it wants at the world price. In Figure 9.5a (on the next page), the world supply curve is shifted up to S'_w, to reflect a tariff of \$t per unit. The domestic price rises from P_w to P'_w, where $t = P'_w - P_w$. The triangle A is part of the deadweight loss created by the tariff, since the equilibrium quantity falls from Q_0 to Q_1. In other words, A is the loss to the domestic society from too little consumption.

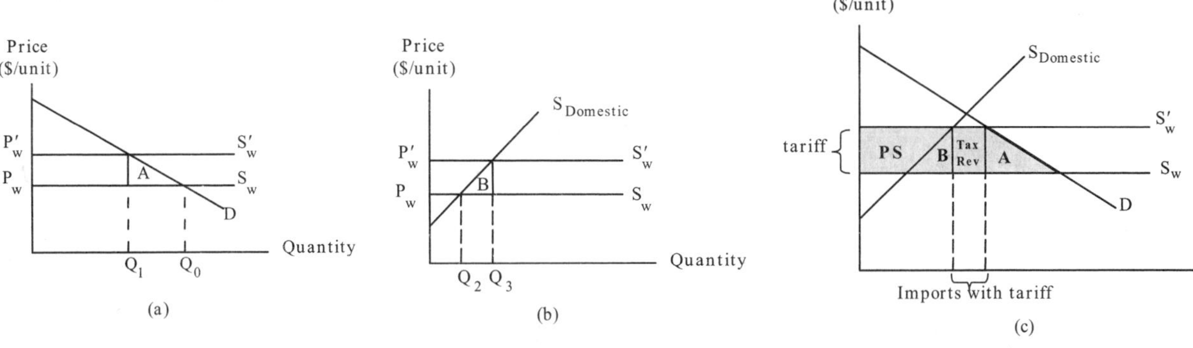

Figure 9.5

The tariff has another effect—the increase in the equilibrium price increases the equilibrium quantity supplied by domestic firms. In Figure 9.5b, the triangle B is the deadweight loss from domestic overproduction. This deadweight loss arises because domestic firms are less efficient at supplying the extra output. (Recall that the supply curve is derived from the marginal cost curve.

Area B is a deadweight loss because domestic producers use up more resources increasing supply from Q_2 to Q_3 than foreign firms would.) Therefore, the aggregate deadweight loss from the tariff is the sum of the areas of triangles A and B.

Figure 9.5c shows the same deadweight loss in a different way. The loss in consumer surplus from the tariff is the shaded area. Offsetting part of that loss is the increase in produce surplus (labeled **PS** in Figure 9.5c) and the increase in revenues collected by the government from the tariff (**Tax Rev** in Figure 9.5c). The *net* loss in total surplus is therefore areas **A** and **B**.

Tariffs are one tool used by the government to protect domestic industries and/or punish foreign industries or governments. Quotas, another frequently used policy tool, are quantity limits on imports. Consider a quota designed to yield the same outcome as a tariff. If the quantities produced and imported are the same as under the tariff, the gains to domestic producers and the losses to consumers will be identical with a quota. However, the outcome is worse for the nation as a whole when quotas are used, since foreign producers get to keep any windfall profits that come with a rise in the price due to the restriction on supply created by a quota. This increases the deadweight loss in Figure 9.5c to **A** + **B** + **Tax Rev**.

Exercise: ◗ ◗ ◗ ◗ ◗ ◗ ◗

5. The world producer price for baseballs is \$24 per dozen, and almost all of them are produced outside the United States. Suppose the U.S. demand curve is $Q_D = 100{,}000 - 2{,}000P$, where P is price per dozen, and Q is measured in dozens. The U.S. domestic supply curve is $Q_S = -10{,}000 + 1{,}000P$.

a) Before a tariff is imposed, what is the U.S. equilibrium price? Domestic consumption? Domestic production? Imports?

b) Congress has decided to help the baseball manufacturing industry by imposing a tariff of \$6 per dozen. What are the new equilibrium price, domestic consumption, domestic production, and imports?

c) What are the losses to U.S. consumers, gains to U.S. producers, and deadweight loss? (Hint: The area of a trapezoid is (height)(base1 + base2)/2 where base1 and base2 are the parallel sides of the trapezoid.)

d) What quota level would have the equivalent affect on price as the \$6 tariff?

e) What is the deadweight loss from the quota?

THE IMPACT OF A TAX OR SUBSIDY (Section 9.6)

Taxes and subsidies also affect the efficiency of competitive markets. We will consider a "specific tax," which is a fixed dollar amount per unit sold. Figure 9.6a displays the original market equilibrium before the assessment of the tax.

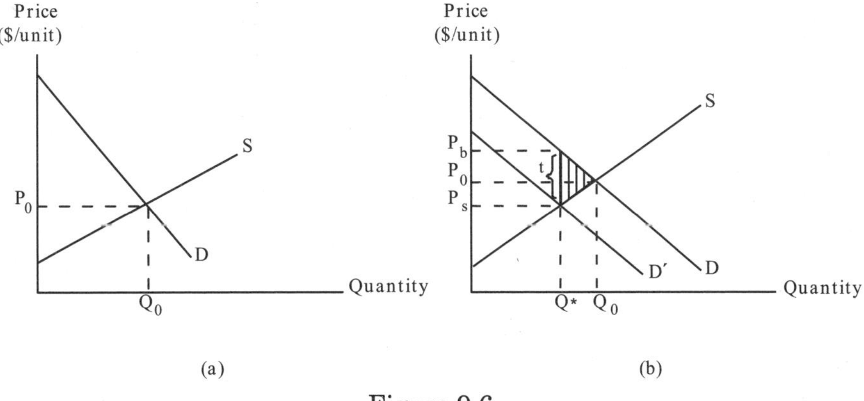

Figure 9.6

Let the market demand curve be $Q_D = a - bP$, where price is measured in dollars. Let the market supply curve be $Q_S = c + dP$. What happens to the equilibrium price and quantity with a tax of \$t per unit? There are now two "market prices," the one paid by consumers, and the one received by sellers. The price paid by the buyers is P_b and P_s is the price obtained by the sellers. Then, $P_b - P_s = t$, the amount of the tax. The price the buyer pays is $P_b = P_s + t$. (With no tax, these two prices are equal.) The government collects tax revenue equal to t times the quantity sold after the tax is imposed. Rewrite the demand curve as a function of P_s and t (rather than P_b):

$$Q_D(P_b) = a - b(P_s + t) = a - bt - bP_s.$$

Figure 9.6b displays the after-tax equilibrium. The curve D′ tells us the quantity demanded for each price received by sellers. Q* is the quantity at which the curve D′ intersects the supply curve. Note that P_b is higher than P_0, the original equilibrium price, and P_s is lower than P_0. The tax hurts both consumers and producers, which is not surprising because the government is collecting revenue equal to $(P_b - P_s)Q^*$, the tax per unit times the number of units sold. However, the government's gain in revenue is less than the loss of surplus by consumers and firms, so a tax creates inefficiency. The shaded area in Figure 9.6b is the deadweight loss of the tax. It arises because fewer units are sold (compared to the competitive equilibrium without taxes) when the tax is levied.

Exercise: ◗ ◗ ◗ ◗ ◗ ◗ ◗

6. A per-unit tax imposed on suppliers will shift the supply curve up by the amount of the tax. Illustrate the deadweight loss from the tax.

7. If the supply curve is perfectly inelastic and a per-unit tax is imposed on consumers, will there be deadweight loss to society? Why or why not?

8. Suppose $Q_D = 100 - 2P$, and $Q_S = -50 + 3P$.

a) What is the original market equilibrium price and quantity?

b) The government imposes a tax of \$1 per unit. Compute the after-tax equilibrium. What are the new equilibrium price and quantity? How much revenue does the government collect?

c) What is the deadweight loss?

d) Rather than using $Q_D(P_b) = a - b(P_s + t)$, shift the supply curve instead, so that $Q_s(P_s) = c + d(P_b - t)$. Show that the after-tax equilibrium is identical, whether you shift the demand curve or the supply curve.

e) What does this tell us about the effect of a tax paid by the buyers versus a tax paid by sellers?

A tax raises the price to buyers and lowers the price for sellers as long as the demand curve slopes downward and the supply curve slopes upward. The relative burden of the tax depends on the elasticities of supply and demand. The fraction of the tax borne by consumers is called the *pass-through fraction*. It equals $E_S/(E_S - E_D)$, where E_S and E_D are the price elasticities of supply and demand. In general, the more elastic side of the market bears less of the tax. With a horizontal supply curve, $E_S = \infty$ and the pass-through fraction equals 1. Therefore, all of the tax is paid by consumers, and the price received by sellers is unaffected by the tax. Thus, for a constant-cost industry, the long-run effect of the tax is to decrease the quantity sold, with no change in the price obtained by sellers. If a good has a vertical supply curve, $E_S = 0$, and the pass-through fraction equals 0. In this case, the quantity sold does not change, so there is no deadweight loss, and the price for sellers falls by the full amount of the tax.

PROBLEM SET

9. The market for college hockey players is characterized by the following supply and demand curves, where Q is the number of athletes and P is the weekly wage in excess of their scholarship payments:

$$Q_D = 1{,}600 - 20P,$$

$$Q_S = -900 + 30P.$$

a) Suppose there is a completely free market. What is the equilibrium weekly wage? How many athletes are hired?

b) Now suppose that the National Collegiate Athletic Association (NCAA) steps in and decides to crack down on payments to players. The NCAA is bothered not by the existence of these payments, but by their level, so the NCAA restricts players to be paid no more than \$35/week above the scholarship payment. How many athletes are now hired?

c) What is the change in producer surplus (i.e., the players' surplus) as a result of the price control?

d) How much do schools now spend on players in comparison to the free market equilibrium?

e) What is the deadweight loss of the price ceiling?

10. Suppose a price ceiling is imposed on a good and the rationing system requires consumers to wait in line to buy the good. How would this affect the deadweight loss associated with the price ceiling?

11. After a late-winter freeze in Florida, the supply curve for early-season blueberries was estimated as:

$$Q_S = -500 + 5{,}000P,$$

where P is measured in dollars and Q is measured in pints. The demand curve for blueberries is:

$$Q_D = 19{,}000 - 1{,}500P.$$

a) Before the freeze, the equilibrium price was \$0.50 per pint. Find the equilibrium price and quantity after the freeze.

b) There is a price ceiling in place of \$1.00 per pint. If there is no illegal trading, how many pints of blueberries will be sold?

c) If this many blueberries were sold, what would be the market-clearing price?

d) Suppose that sellers of blueberries must spend \$0.50 per pint to pick blueberries. The sellers try to evade the price ceiling by selling only U-pick blueberries. Consumers value U-pick pints of blueberries at \$0.50 per pint less than picked blueberries because of the opportunity cost of picking time. If all blueberries sold are U-pick blueberries, how many pints of blueberries are sold?

e) What is the equilibrium price of U-pick blueberries?

f) Is the outcome in d) more efficient than the outcome in b)?

12. A college allocated championship football tickets to student season ticket holders by having the students wait in line after obtaining priority numbers. The college could charge no more than \$75 per ticket. Resale of tickets was forbidden.

a) What was the efficiency loss of this allocation system?

b) Would running a lottery for championship game tickets among student season ticket holders be a more or less efficient allocation method?

c) Which allocation system would students prefer?

13. The supply and demand curves for wickets are:

$$Q_S = -800 + 15P \text{ and } Q_D = 3200 - 25P.$$

a) What is the market equilibrium price and quantity?

b) Now suppose a tax of \$20 per unit is imposed on consumers. What are the new equilibrium buyer's price, seller's price, and quantity? What is tax revenue? Graph your answer.

c) Calculate the losses in consumer surplus and producer surplus. What is the deadweight loss from the tax? (Recall that the area of a triangle is 1/2 (base)(height); the area of a trapezoid is (height)(average of the bases).)

d) Explain how the price changes for buyers and sellers relate to the supply and demand elasticities.

14. A city council is considering adopting a rent-control policy. They are concerned about the amount of excess demand for rent-controlled apartments that they know will arise. *Holding all else constant*, will the amount of excess demand be lower if demand is less elastic or more elastic? Will the amount of excess demand be lower if supply is less elastic or more elastic? Illustrate your answer.

SELF-TEST

15. Price ceilings are inefficient because:
a) both producers and consumers lose.
b) producers lose, consumers may gain or lose, but a loss occurs on net.
c) producers lose, consumers gain, but a loss occurs on net.
d) producers and consumers may gain or lose, but a loss occurs on net.
e) None of the above is correct.

16. Minimum price regulations are inefficient because:
a) both consumers and producers lose.
b) consumers lose, producers gain, but a loss occurs on net.
c) consumers lose, producers may gain or lose, but a loss occurs on net.
d) consumers and producers may gain or lose, but a loss occurs on net.
e) None of the above is correct.

17. If the demand for baseballs is more elastic than supply, a tax of $3 per baseball will increase the consumer price by:
a) $3.
b) more than $1.50, but less than $3.
c) $1.50.
d) less than $1.50.
e) $0 (the price to consumers will not change).

18. If the supply of basketballs is perfectly elastic, a tax of $3 per basketball will increase the consumer price by:
a) $3.
b) more than $1.50, but less than $3.
c) $1.50.
d) less than $1.50.
e) $0 (the price to consumers will not change).

19. A quota on imports may be preferred to a tariff by some foreign producers because:
a) the tariff raises no revenue.
b) some foreign producers receive a lower price with a quota.
c) some foreign producers receive a higher price with a quota.
d) domestic producers prefer a quota
e) None of the above is correct: foreign producers always prefer a tariff to a quota.

The next three questions refer to the alfalfa market described in Figure 9.7. The government is attempting to support the market price.

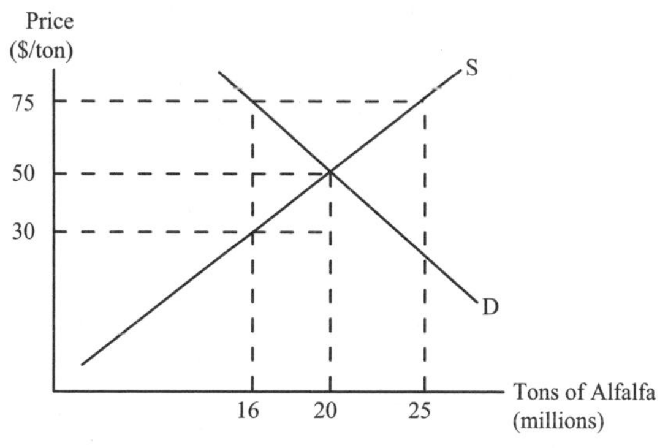

Figure 9.7

20. If the government purchases enough alfalfa to raise the price from $50/ton to $75/ton, the cost of the program will be:
a) $100 million.
b) $225 million.
c) $315 million.
d) $675 million.
e) None of the above is correct.

21. If the government raises the price to $75/ton, producer surplus will increase by:
a) $400 million.
b) $500 million.
c) $562.5 million.
d) $1,875 million.
e) None of the above is correct.

22. Suppose the government decides to support a price of $75/ton by paying producers *not* to produce the excess supply of alfalfa (which is 25 – 16 = 9 million tons). The minimum cost of this program will be:
a) $157.5 million.
b) $202.5 million.
c) $315 million.
d) $1,875 million.
e) None of the above is correct.

23. The U.S. supply and demand curves for soybeans are given by:

D: Q = 1400 – 4P S: Q = 4P

where Q is tons of soybeans per year and P is the price per ton, in dollars. The competitive world price is $75 per ton and the U.S. is a price-taker on the world market. There are currently no barriers to trade. The U.S. government is thinking of closing its borders to soybean trade. In order to eliminate soybean imports completely, the U.S. would have to impose a tariff of

a) $350 per ton.
b) $175 per ton.
c) $100 per ton.
d) $75 per ton.
e) $0 per ton—the U.S. market is already in equilibrium.

24. Minimum wage increases:

a) increase total wage payments to unskilled labor if the demand for unskilled labor is inelastic.
b) increase total wage payments to unskilled labor if the demand for unskilled labor is elastic.
c) might encourage low-wage workers to obtain more skills in order to find jobs.
d) a) and c)
e) b) and c)

25. In competitive markets, when a government imposes a tax,

a) the price of the good rises by a larger fraction of the tax if demand is more elastic than supply.
b) the price of the good rises by a larger fraction of the tax if demand is less elastic than supply.
c) the prices of complementary goods rise.
d) the prices of substitute goods fall.
e) a) and d)

ANSWERS TO CHAPTER 9

EXERCISE ANSWERS

1. a) See Figure 9A.1a (on the next page). Market equilibrium price and quantity are found by equating demand and supply:

$$152 - 20P = -4 + 188P, \ or$$
$$P^* = 0.75$$

Substituting P* = 0.75 into the demand or supply curve yields $Q^* = 137$. Then,

$$CS^* = 0.5(137)\,(7.6 - 0.75) = \$469.225$$

$$\text{and } PS^* = 0.5(137)\,(0.75 - 0.02) = \$50.005.$$

Total surplus is $CS^* + PS^* = \$519.23$ (all surplus units are in billions of dollars per year).

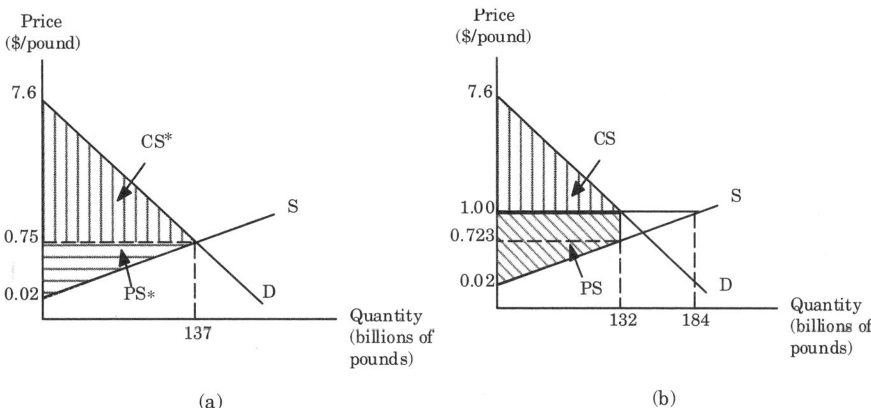

Figure 9A.1

b) Producers will want to sell $Q = 184$ at $P = \$1.00$, but only 132 units will be demanded. You can see the answer graphically by comparing the shaded area (total surplus) in Figure 9A.1b to the analogous area in Figure 9A.1a. Total surplus is clearly smaller with P = \$1.00. You can verify this by calculating these areas:

$$CS = 0.5(132)(7.6 - 1) = \$435.6,$$

and $$PS = 0.5(132)(0.723 - 0.02) + 132(1 - 0.723) = \$82.96.$$

Therefore, total surplus is \$518.56. This is less than \$519.23 from part a), although not by much in this particular case.

2. See Figure 9A.2. Consumers gain area A and lose area B (the small triangle), so they gain on net when supply is relatively inelastic. This makes intuitive sense because an inelastic supply curve implies that quantity supplied is relatively insensitive to price changes. When P_{max} is imposed, very few consumers have to leave the market, since production barely falls, and all of those that stay pay a lower price. Consumer surplus goes up on net.

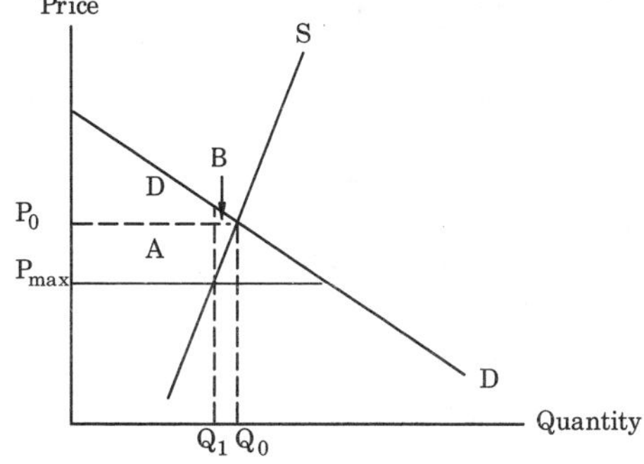

Figure 9A.2

3. a) See Figure 9A.3 (on the next page). Note that at P_{min} only Q_1 units are actually sold, because that is all that consumers will demand at such a high price.

Consumer surplus at P_0 = A + B + D.
Producer surplus at P_0 = E + C.

Consumer surplus at P_{min} = D.
Producer surplus at P_{min} = A + E.

Therefore, consumers lose A + B and producers lose C and gain A. Area A is a transfer of surplus and is not counted in deadweight loss. This leaves a deadweight loss of B + C.

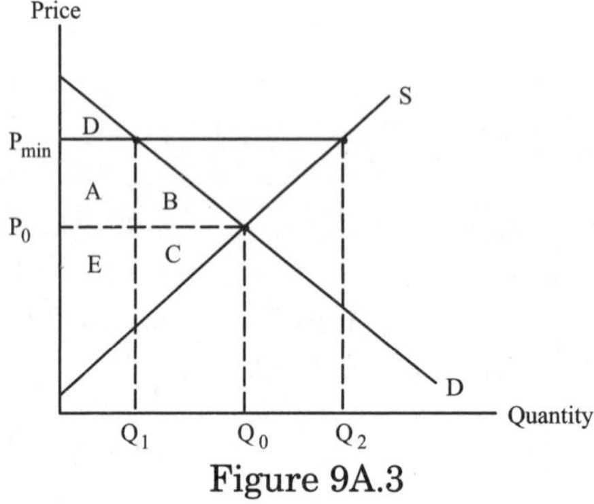

Figure 9A.3

b) Referring back to Figure 9A.3, we have to calculate the two triangles B + C to find deadweight loss.

In this numerical example $P_0 = 0.75$, $Q_0 = 137$ (from Exercise 1a), $P_{min} = \$1.00$, and $Q_1 = 132$ (plugging P = 1.00 into the demand equation). It follows that,

$$\text{Area B} = 0.5(137 - 132)\ (1 - 0.75) = \$0.625.$$

We need one more point to find area C: plug $Q_1 = 132$ into the supply equation to find the minimum price producers would have been willing to accept for Q_1. The answer is P = 0.723 (approximately). Therefore,

$$\text{Area C} = 0.5(137 - 132)\ (0.75 - 0.723) = \$0.0675.$$

Total deadweight loss is B + C = \$0.6925.

4. a) At $P_S = 1.25$, $Q_D = 152 - 20(1.25) = 127$ and $Q_S = -4 + 188(1.25) = 231$. Excess supply is $Q_S - Q_D = 231 - 127 = 104$. The government will pay 1.25(104) = \$130 billion per year, given the units stated in Exercise 1.

b) See Figure 9A.4 (on the next page). Equilibrium in this market is at P* = 0.75 and Q* = 137 (setting $Q_D = Q_S$). Substituting Q_S = 127 into the supply equation we find P = 0.70. The cost to the government is B + C + D:

B = 0.5(137 – 127)(1.25 – 0.75) = $2.5
C = 0.5(137 – 127)(0.75 – 0.70) = $.25
D = 0.5(231 – 137)(1.25 – 0.75) + 0.5(137 – 127)(1.25 – 0.75) = $26.

Therefore B + C + D = $28.75.

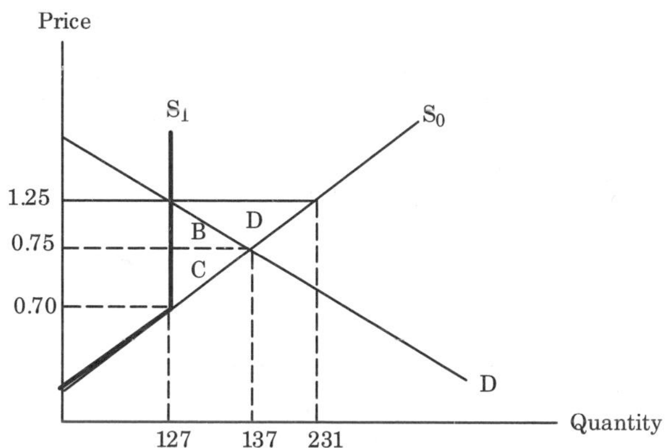

Figure 9A.4

c) The bovine growth hormone will increase productivity and shift the S_0 supply curve to the right, since more milk can be supplied at any given price. This will increase the cost of operating either a price support program or a production quota program (where producers are paid to limit production).

5. a) Without a tariff, the domestic equilibrium price is the world price of $24. The domestic consumption equilibrium is Q_D = 100,000 – 2,000(24) = 52,000. Domestic supply is Q_S = – 10,000 + 1,000(24) = 14,000. Imports are equal to 52,000 – 14,000 = 38,000.

b) The new equilibrium price after the tariff is 24 + 6 = $30. Domestic demand is

$$Q_D = 100{,}000 - 2{,}000(30) = 40{,}000,$$

and domestic supply is

$$Q_S = -10{,}000 + 1{,}000(30) = 20{,}000.$$

Imports therefore fall to 20,000.

c) In Figure 9A.5 (on the next page), the loss in consumer surplus is the area of the trapezoid **acdh** = $6(40,000 + 52,000)/2 = $276,000. The gain in producer surplus is the area of the trapezoid **abgh** = $6(20,000 + 14,000)/2 = $102,000. Revenue earned by the government from the tariff equals the tariff times after-tariff imports, or $6(40,000 – 20,000) = $120,000 (denoted by rectangle **bcef**). The deadweight loss (denoted by the two triangles **bgf** and **cde**) therefore equals $276,000 – $102,000 – $120,000, or $54,000. (Note that you can always split the area of a trapezoid into a rectangle and a triangle and calculate those areas instead, if you find that simpler.)

d) If the quota is set at 20,000 (the difference between 40,000 and 20,000 in Figure 9A.5) then price will rise from \$24 to \$30.

e) The deadweight loss includes areas **bgf** + **cde**, as before, but now it also includes area **bfec**, or the \$120,000 that was tariff revenue in part c). Deadweight loss is therefore equal to 18,000 + 36,000 + 120,000 = \$174,000. (You can get the same answer by using the answer from part c), which was \$54,000 and adding \$120,000.

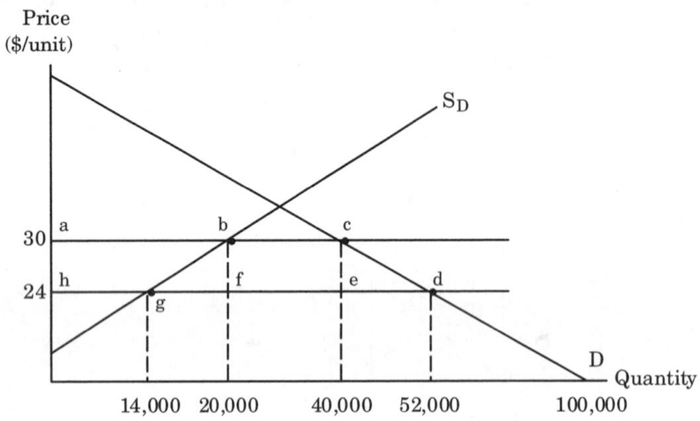

Figure 9A.5

6. In Figure 9A.6, the change in consumer surplus is the area **abce** and the change in producer surplus is the area **ecgf**. Since the government collects tax revenue equal to the area **abgf**, the deadweight loss equals the area of the triangle **bcg**. Without the tax, Q_0 units are traded, while after the tax, only Q^* units are traded. Thus, the gains from trade that are lost equal the area between the demand and supply curves between these two output levels, or the area **bcg.**

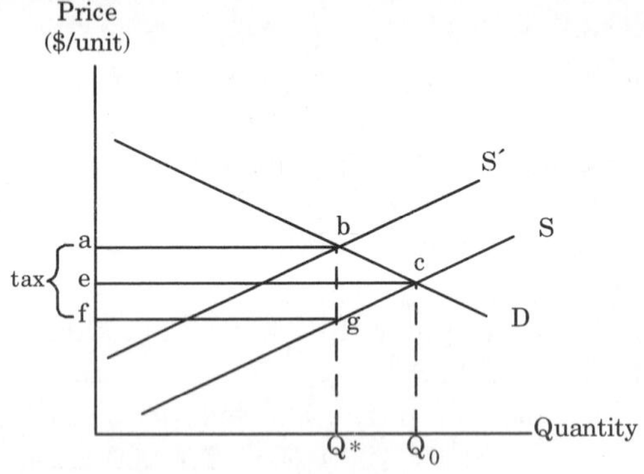

Figure 9A.6

7. No. If supply is perfectly inelastic there will be no reduction in the number of units traded when the tax is imposed and therefore no deadweight loss.

8. a) Setting $Q_D = Q_S$, the original equilibrium is the solution to 100 – 2P = –50 + 3P or P_0 = \$30 and Q_0 = 40.

b) After a \$1 tax is imposed, we can solve for the price received by sellers by using the equation $Q_D(P_b) = a - b(P_s + t)$.

Thus, $100 - 2(P_S + 1) = -50 + 3P_S$ or $P_S = 148/5 = \$29.60$. The price paid by buyers is $29.60 + 1 = \$30.60$. The new quantity is $Q^* = 38.8$.

The government collects \$1(38.8) = \$38.80.

c) Deadweight loss is the shaded triangle in Figure 9A.7 (on the next page), with a base of \$1 (the tax) and a height of $Q_0 - Q^*\,(40 - 38.8 = 1.2)$. Thus, deadweight loss equals 0.5(1)(1.2) = \$0.60.

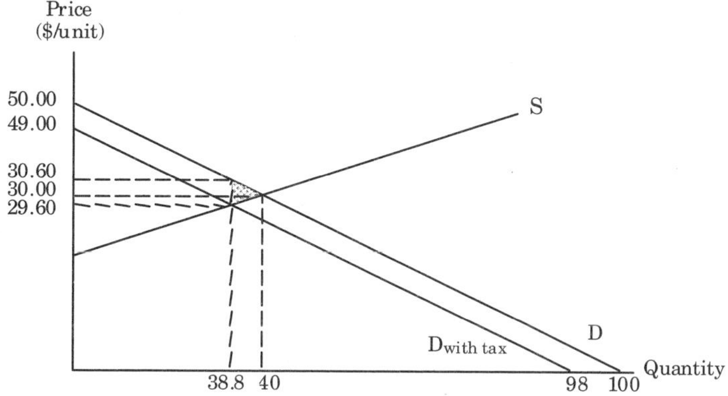

Figure 9A.7

d) $Q_S = c + dP_b - dt = -50 + 3P_b - 3(\$1) = -53 + 3P_b$. Setting demand and supply equal gives, $100 - 2P_b = -53 + 3P_b$, or $P_b = 30.6$. Thus, $P_b^* = \$30.60$ and $Q^* = 38.8$, which is the same market equilibrium as in part (b).

e) Whether the tax is placed on the buyers or the sellers does not affect the market equilibrium.

PROBLEM SET ANSWERS

9. a) Setting $Q_D = Q_S$ yields 1600 – 20P = –900 + 30P or $P^* = \$50$ and $Q^* = 600$.

b) If $P_{max} = \$35$, $Q_S = -900 + 30(35) = 150$. (Since $P_{max} < P^*$, there will be excess demand at this price, so the quantity supplied is the quantity traded, and 150 athletes will be hired.)

c) In Figure 9A.8, the change in producer surplus is the area of the trapezoid **bcef**. This area equals (\$50 – \$35)(150 + 600)/2 = \$5,625.

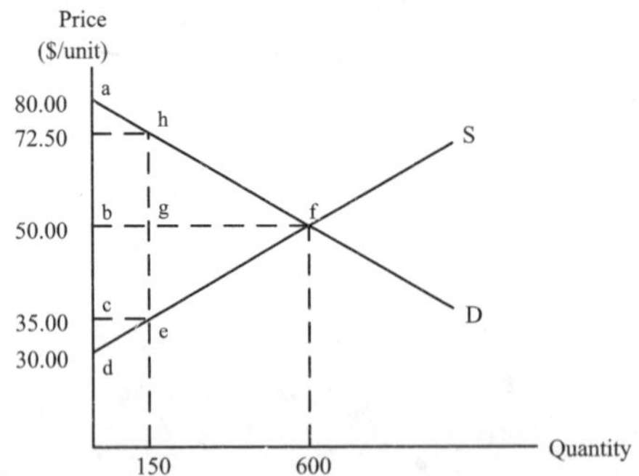

Figure 9A.8

d) The schools now spend \$35(150) = \$5,250 per week on players, compared to \$50(600) = \$30,000 before.

e) Deadweight loss is the area of the triangle **hef**. At Q = 150, the price on the demand curve is \$72.50 (since 1,600 – 20(72.5)=150). The area equals

$$1/2(\$72.5 - \$35)(600 - 150) = \$8,437.5$$

10. In Figure 9A.9, a price ceiling of P_0 is imposed on the market and Q_0 units are supplied. The market-clearing price for Q_0 units is P_1, so consumers whose willingness to pay is equal to or greater than P_1 are willing to spend at least $P_1 - P_0$ per unit in waiting time (converting the hours to their dollar opportunity cost). Since this cost is not a payment to anyone else, it should be added to the usual deadweight loss triangle to reflect the true deadweight loss to society. The shaded rectangle is a lower bound on this cost of waiting in line.

If consumers do not have accurate information about the demand curve, they may not be able to calculate P_1 accurately. In this case, they may spend up to the difference between their full willingness to pay and P_0 in waiting time. In this case, the triangle above the shaded rectangle would also be part of the deadweight loss.

Since willingness to wait in line depends on a consumer's opportunity cost of time, it is also possible that some successful buyers value the good at less than P_1, while some consumers who value the good at more than P_1 do not end up consuming the good (this would also occur if the Q_0 units sold were randomly rationed to consumers). If this occurs, deadweight loss is even greater.

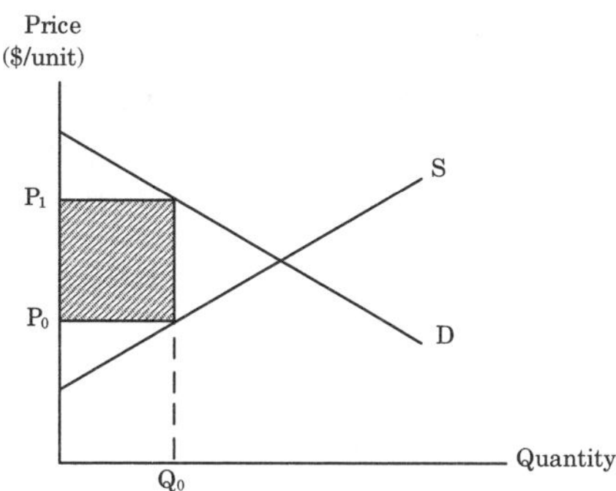

Figure 9A.9

11. a) Equate supply and demand, or – 500 + 5,000P = 19,000 – 1,500P, or $P^* = \$3$ and $Q^* = 14{,}500$.

b) At P = \$1, Q = –500 + 5,000(1) = 4,500 pints of blueberries are sold.

c) If $Q_D = 4{,}500$, P = 14,500/1,500 or \$9.67. Thus, the market-clearing price for 4,500 pints would be \$9.67.

d) Rewrite the supply curve as P = 0.10 + 0.0002Qs. Then, since sellers save \$0.50 per pint in U-pick sales, the U-pick supply curve becomes:

$$P + 0.50 = 0.10 + 0.0002Q_S, \text{ or}$$

$$P = -0.40 + 0.0002Q_S$$

With the price ceiling, P = \$1.00, so $Q_S = 7{,}000$.

e) The U-pick demand curve is $Q_D = 19{,}000 - 1{,}500(P + 0.50) = 18{,}250 - 1{,}500P$. The U-pick supply curve is:

$$P = -0.40 + 0.0002Q_S, \text{ or}$$

$$Q_S = 2{,}000 + 5{,}000P.$$

Equating Q_S and Q_D for U-pick blueberries: 2,000 + 5,000P = 18,250 – 1,500P, so P = \$2.50.

f) More U-pick berries are sold, so the outcome is closer to the equilibrium outcome. Since buyers and sellers both value picking at \$0.50 per pint, there is no inefficiency in switching to U-pick to evade the price ceiling. Hence, U-pick is more efficient, given the price ceiling.

12. a) The efficiency loss of the allocation system comes from the waiting, which costs the students buying tickets their time but provides no revenue or benefit to anyone.

b) The lottery eliminates the waiting cost but adds administrative costs. Of course, handing out priority numbers also has some administrative costs, but the lottery system is probably more efficient overall.

c) Only the students with the lowest value of time or the highest reservation prices for the tickets might prefer waiting in line to a lottery.

13. a) Equating Q_D and Q_S, we have –800 + 15P = 3200 – 25P, or P* = \$100 and Q* = 700.

b) The demand curve shifts down by \$20, as shown in Figure 9A.10a. Solve for the price received by buyers and sellers by using the equation $P_B = P_S + 20$. At the new equilibrium, $-800 + 15P_S = 3200 - 25(P_S + 20)$, or P_S = \$87.50, P_B = \$107.50, and Q^T = 512.50. Tax revenue is (512.50) (20) = 10,250.

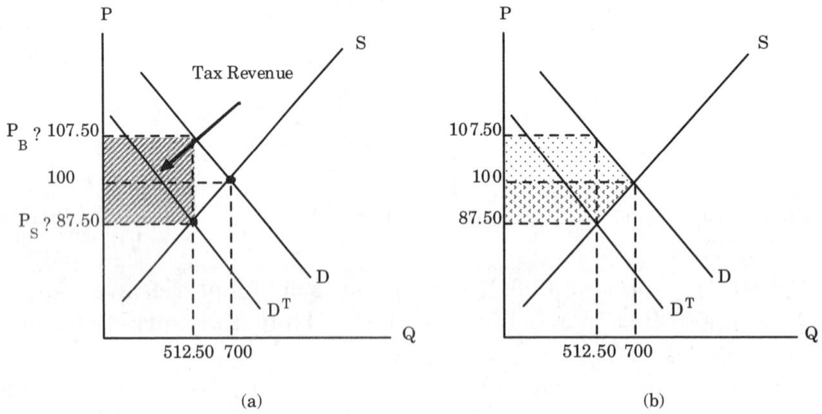

Figure 9A.10

c) Lost consumer surplus is the lightly shaded area in Figure 9A.10b. Mathematically, it can be found by using the formula for the area of a trapezoid: $\left[(107.50-100)\cdot\left(\frac{512.50+700}{2}\right)\right] = \$4{,}546.88$. Lost producer surplus, the darker shaded area, can be found similarly: $\left[(100-87.50)\cdot\left(\frac{512.50+700}{2}\right)\right] = \$7{,}578.13$.

Deadweight loss equals the loss in consumer surplus plus producer surplus minus the tax revenue: (4,546.88 + 7,578.13) – 10,250 = \$1,875.01.

d) At the original equilibrium price, demand is more elastic than supply, so the change in the price received by the sellers is greater than the change in the price paid by the buyers.

14. In Figure 9A.11, the price ceiling is set at P_1. The amount of excess demand created by the price ceiling is smallest when supply and demand are relatively less elastic at prevailing prices and quantities. Figure 9A.11a shows that, holding all else constant, excess demand is smaller when demand is less elastic (rotating demand through the original equilibrium price at P*). Figure 9A.11b shows the similar effect, but on the supply side.

(XSD = excess demand)

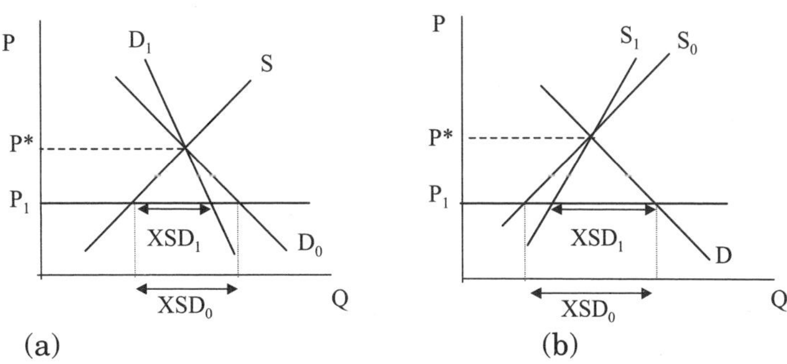

Figure 9A.11

SELF-TEST ANSWERS

15. b) Consumers gain from a lower price, but lose because they are able to buy less. Producers clearly lose from the regulated price. There is always a welfare loss from price ceilings (assuming that the price ceiling is binding).

16. c) Producers gain from a higher price, but lose because they sell less. Consumers clearly lose when price is regulated above the equilibrium price. There is always a welfare loss from minimum price regulations (assuming that it is binding).

17. d) When supply is less elastic than demand, the burden of the tax is borne by suppliers. This means that consumers will see an increase in price of less than half the tax.

18. a) All of the tax is passed on to consumers with perfectly elastic supply.

19. c) Some foreign producers (those with quota rights) are able to sell the good at the higher domestic price with a quota.

20. d) The government pays \$75/ton for the surplus of $25 - 16 = 9$ million tons: $75(9) = \$675$.

21. c) Producer surplus increases by the area of the trapezoid between P = \$50 and P = \$75, and Q = 20 and Q = 25 million: $\$25(20 + 25)/2 = \$562.5$ million.

22. b) To idle acreage, producers must be paid at least the shaded area in Figure 9A.12: 0.5(25 – 16) (75 – 30) = $202.5 million.

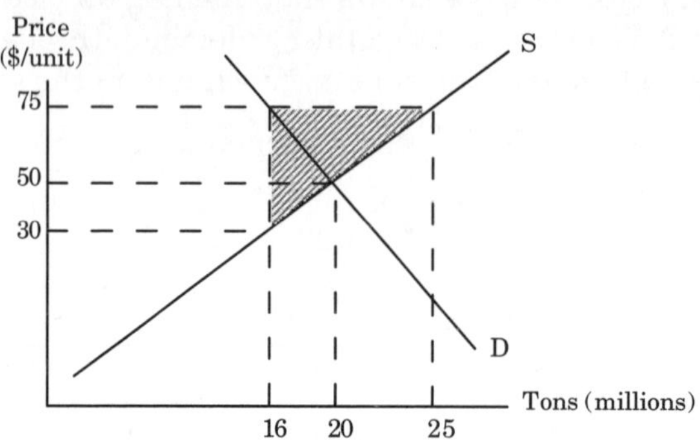

Figure 9A.12

23. c) The domestic equilibrium price, which the U.S. would only reach by closing its borders to all trade, is found by setting U.S. demand equal to U.S. supply, which yields Q = 700 and P = 175. A tariff of $100 would raise the domestic price from the current price of $75 to $175, at which point no soybeans will be imported.

24. d) A price increase (in this case, a wage increase) raises total revenue if demand is inelastic, so a) is true. An increase in the minimum wage will certainly raise unemployment by some amount. If unemployment rises substantially for unskilled labor, some workers may seek to increase their skills, so c) is true as well.

25. b) The fraction of a tax that is passed on to consumers is $E_S/(E_S - E_D)$.

CHAPTER 10
MARKET POWER: MONOPOLY AND MONOPSONY

IMPORTANT CONCEPTS

- Meaning of Monopoly
- Barriers to Entry
- Marginal Revenue for Monopolist
- Rule of Thumb for Pricing
- Multiplant Monopoly
- Monopoly Power
- Lerner Index
- Monopoly Deadweight Loss
- Price Regulation
- Natural Monopoly
- Monopsony
    - Marginal Expenditure
    - Marginal Value
- Antitrust Laws

CHAPTER HIGHLIGHTS

While most markets look about the same on the consumer side, they can look incredibly different on the producer side. A *monopoly* is a market that has only one seller, but many buyers. The monopolist, as the sole seller, faces the entire market demand curve when deciding what price to set or what quantity to sell in order to maximize profits. Unlike the individual competitive firm, which faces a perfectly horizontal demand curve, the monopolist faces a downward sloping demand curve.

The change in revenue that results from a unit change in output is called *marginal revenue*. Under perfect competition, marginal revenue is equal to the market price. When the demand curve is downward sloping, this is no longer true. Marginal revenue is less than price for the monopolist. To maximize profits, the monopolist should set output at the point where marginal revenue is equal to marginal cost. This will lead to an output level less than the competitive output and a price higher than the competitive price. Using the condition that marginal revenue should equal

marginal cost at the profit-maximizing point, we can derive the *rule of thumb for pricing*: $(P - MC)/P = -1/E_d$, where E_d is the elasticity of demand.
Or, this expression can be rearranged to directly show the markup of price over marginal cost: $P = MC/[1 + (1/E_d)]$.

For a *multiplant monopolist*, production is allocated across plants such that marginal cost in each plant is the same. Then, total output is chosen such that marginal revenue is set equal to the common marginal cost.

The model of pure monopoly is easy to work with, but it does not reflect many actual markets. More often we find markets where *monopoly power* rather than a pure monopoly exists. In these markets, there may be several firms, each with the ability to charge a price greater than marginal cost. Each of these firms faces a downward sloping demand curve. The less elastic a firm's demand curve, the more monopoly power the firm has. The elasticity of a firm's demand curve depends on the elasticity of the market demand curve, the number of firms in the market, and the nature of interaction among the firms (i.e., whether firms compete aggressively or cooperate). To measure the degree of monopoly power we use the *Lerner index*: $L = (P - MC)/P$. For a perfectly competitive firm $L = 0$ (since price equals marginal cost at the profit-maximizing output level). As we move to industries where monopoly power exists, the value of the Lerner index will grow. The Lerner index always has a value between zero and one.

Total surplus in a market is reduced when the market is monopolized. Comparing consumer and producer surplus under perfect competition with consumer and producer surplus under monopoly, we find that there is a net loss in surplus. In other words, there is a *deadweight loss* from monopoly power. This inefficiency results because output is lower under monopoly than it would be under competition. *Price regulation* can reduce or sometimes eliminate this deadweight loss. In the case of a *natural monopoly*, where average cost is declining everywhere, the regulator will try to set the price where average cost and average revenue (the demand curve) intersect.

A *monopsony* is a market with many sellers, but only one buyer. Sources of monopsony power are the elasticity of market supply, the number of buyers in the market, and how those buyers interact. In a competitive market, the marginal expenditure (the price paid on the last unit) is equal to the market price. When dealing with monopsony we call the demand curve the *marginal value* curve and distinguish it from the *marginal expenditure* curve. In a market with just one buyer, the supply curve reflects average expenditure and the marginal expenditure curve lies above the supply curve. In order to buy an extra unit, the monopsonist must pay a higher price on all units purchased. The monopsonist maximizes profits by purchasing up to the point where marginal expenditure is equal to marginal value. A deadweight loss arises from monopsony power because the monopsonist pays a lower price for the product and less is sold than would be if the buyer's market were competitive.

Antitrust laws are designed to promote competition in the economy and limit the deadweight loss from monopoly and monopsony power. Section 1 of the Sherman Act (passed in 1890) prohibits conspiracies in restraint of trade. Section 2 of the Sherman Act prohibits attempts to monopolize a market.

Other laws, such as the Clayton Act (1914) and the Robinson-Patman Act (1936), prohibit predatory pricing, mergers which may tend to create a monopoly, and price discrimination.

CONCEPT REVIEW AND EXERCISES

MONOPOLY (Section 10.1)

While perfect competition is a good assumption in some markets, it is obviously inappropriate in others. In this chapter we look at *imperfect competition*, the study of markets where buyers or sellers do not take prices as given. For example, the local electric utility will not lose all its sales if it raises its price by a small amount. The utility is not a passive price taker, since it does not face a horizontal demand curve for its output.

A pure *monopolist* is the only seller in its market. Although the monopolist can select any price it wants, there is no guarantee that consumers will demand anything at that price. As a monopolist raises price, the quantity sold will fall (unless demand is perfectly inelastic). A monopolist may choose either price or quantity, but not both. As a simple (non-price discriminating) monopolist, if it chooses to sell a larger quantity it must charge a lower price on *all* its output.

A monopolist will maximize profit by producing up to the point where marginal revenue equals marginal cost. The logic behind the monopolist's profit maximizing output choice is the same as that used by a perfectly competitive firm. Under perfect competition, however, marginal revenue equals price. For the monopolist facing a downward sloping demand curve, we will see that this is no longer true.

Consider the monopolist with the demand curve information given in Table 10.1.

Output Q	Price P	Revenue $R = P \cdot Q$	Marginal Revenue MR = ΔR/ΔQ
1	10	10	———
2	8	16	6
3	6	18	2
4	4	16	–2
5	2	10	–6

Table 10.1

The output column lists various quantities, and the price column lists the prices at which these quantities can be sold. The revenue column gives the total revenue for the monopolist for each of its output levels, and the marginal revenue column lists the additional revenue from selling one more unit.

Consider what happens to marginal revenue when the monopolist lowers the price. Figure 10.1 (on the next page) graphs the demand curve given the information in Table 10.1.

In Figure 10.1, we distinguish between two components of the monopolist's marginal revenue. The first is the price received for the incremental unit sold; the second is the revenue lost from the lower price now charged on all the other units. For example, suppose the monopolist's price is \$8 initially. It sells 2 units, so its revenue equals \$16. When it lowers its price to \$6, its sales increase by 1 unit, and its revenue from selling the additional unit is \$6. However, its revenue from the first two units has fallen to \$12 (since it must sell all three units at the new price of \$6). Thus, marginal revenue from selling the third unit is MR = \$6 – (\$16 – \$12) = \$2. Total revenue has therefore increased from \$16 to \$18 when price is reduced from \$8 to \$6. Whenever the demand curve slopes downward, marginal revenue will be less than price (in this case \$2 < \$6) because of this second component of MR. The revenue lost from having to lower the price on all units, not just the last unit sold, creates a difference between the price charged and the marginal revenue earned.

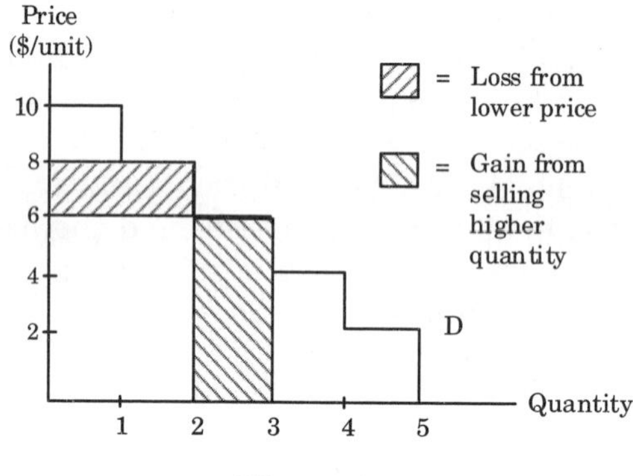

Figure 10.1

Exercise:

1. For the firm with the demand curve displayed in Figure 10.1, what is the marginal revenue from increasing sales from 3 units to 4 units?

Now suppose that the firm can sell fractional units of output. Symbolically, we can write marginal revenue as $MR = P + (\Delta P/\Delta Q)Q$, where $\Delta P/\Delta Q$ is the slope of the demand curve when quantity appears on the horizontal axis. P is the price received for the last unit sold; $(\Delta P/\Delta Q)Q$ is the revenue lost from the lower price now charged on all other units. Using a general linear demand curve written as $P(Q) = a - bQ$, we get $MR = P(Q) + (\Delta P/\Delta Q)Q = P(Q) - bQ$, since $\Delta P/\Delta Q = -b$. Thus, $MR = (a - bQ) - bQ = a - 2bQ$. This is a general rule that you can use for linear demand curves; *the marginal revenue curve has the same vertical intercept as the demand curve and twice the slope of the demand curve.* (Remember that this relationship between demand and marginal revenue holds only if we write price as a function of output.)

For example, if P = 100 – 2Q then MR = 100 – 4Q. Figure 10.2 (on the next page) displays the demand curve and the marginal revenue curve for this example.

Graphically, the marginal revenue curve has the same vertical intercept as the demand curve and a horizontal intercept at one half the horizontal intercept of the demand curve. (Since the MR curve has *twice* the slope of the demand curve it reaches the horizontal axis *twice* as fast.)

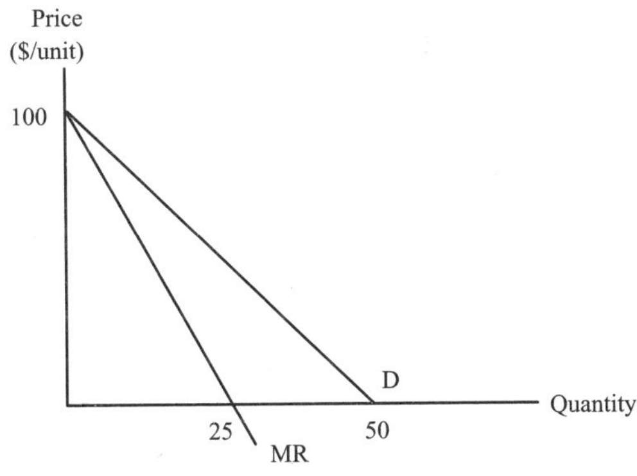

Figure 10.2

Exercise: ▶ ▶ ▶ ▶ ▶ ▶ ▶

2. A monopolist faces a demand curve Q = 75 – P/4. Find the equation of the marginal revenue curve.

We can now examine a monopolist's profit maximizing output choice. Consider the monopolist with the demand and cost data listed in Table 10.2.

Output Q	Price P	Total Revenue R	Marginal Revenue MR	Total Cost TC	Marginal Cost MC	Profit p
18	146	2,628	——	1,080	——	1,548
19	143	2,717	89	1,125	45	1,592
20	140	2,800	83	1,200	75	1,600
21	137	2,877	77	1,285	85	1,592
22	134	2,948	71	1,383	98	1,565

Table 10.2

This monopolist earns the highest possible profit by selling 20 units of output. Reducing output to 19 units lowers revenue by $83 (the marginal revenue from the 20th unit sold) but only lowers total costs by $75 (the marginal cost of the 20th unit sold). Since marginal revenue from this last unit exceeds its marginal cost, the firm gains $8 in profit by producing 20 units instead of 19 units. Now, consider increasing output from 20 units to 21 units. The output increase would raise revenue by $77 (the marginal revenue from the 21st unit), but it would increase cost by $85 (the marginal cost of the 21st unit). Thus, the firm gains $8 in profit by selling 20 units instead of 21 units. The profit maximizing output is therefore Q = 20.

In general, since profit is simply revenue minus total cost, we can write the change in profit caused by a change in output as $\Delta\pi = \Delta R - \Delta C$. Dividing by ΔQ, the change in output, we find $\Delta\pi/\Delta Q = \Delta R/\Delta Q - \Delta C/\Delta Q = MR - MC$. Thus, the change in profit from an increase in output of one unit equals marginal revenue minus marginal cost. Starting from Q = 0 the monopolist will increase profit ($\Delta\pi/\Delta Q > 0$) as long as MR > MC. The monopolist should stop increasing Q when MR = MC. *A monopolist maximizes profit by choosing output such that marginal revenue equals marginal cost, or MR = MC.* (Note: While it may seem more natural for a monopolist to set price, we can also view the monopolist as choosing a quantity to sell and letting consumers determine the market price according to their willingness to pay for that quantity. Setting up the problem as choosing quantity makes comparisons with competitive markets easier.)

The rule that MC = P for perfect competitors is simply a special case of MR = MC. For a competitive firm that cannot affect the market price by selling additional units $\Delta P/\Delta q = 0$, and MR = P. A competitive firm takes *price* as given; a monopolist takes its *entire demand curve* as given when choosing output.

Recall that MC does not capture fixed costs. If fixed costs are very high it might be more profitable to shut down. Therefore, after finding the profit-maximizing output using MR = MC, always check that profit is positive at that output level.

Notice that we have not referred to a supply curve for the monopolist. A monopolist, in fact, has no supply curve. A monopolist chooses the quantity to supply based on both MC and MR, which is in turn derived from the demand curve. In response to a shift in the demand curve, the monopolist will use the new MR curve and its MC curve to choose a point on the new demand curve. Clearly the monopolist has a way of choosing supply given demand and marginal cost, but there is no set supply curve.

Exercise:

3.

a) A monopolist with the demand curve P = 300 – 4Q has constant average variable cost equal to 100 and fixed costs equal to 50. What is the profit-maximizing price and output?

b) If fixed costs were instead equal to 2,600, what is the profit-maximizing price and output?

c) If AVC = 200 and FC = 50, what is the profit-maximizing output?

By expressing marginal revenue in a different way we can relate it directly to the market demand elasticity: MR = P + (ΔP/ΔQ)Q = P[1 + (Q/P)(ΔP/ΔQ)]. The second term in brackets is the inverse of the elasticity of demand, since E_d = (P/Q)ΔQ/ΔP. Thus, we can write MR = P[1 + 1/E_d]. Observe that if $E_d > -1$, MR < 0. That is, if demand is inelastic then marginal revenue is negative. An immediate implication is that a monopolist never chooses to produce an output level that would put it on the inelastic portion of the demand curve.

Exercise: ▶ ▶ ▶ ▶ ▶ ▶ ▶

4. A plastics monopolist faces the demand curve P = 180 – Q, where Q is measured in thousands of pounds per year and P is measured in dollars per pound. Marginal cost is constant at MC = $60 per pound.

a) Find the monopolist's profit-maximizing price and quantity. What is the elasticity of demand at the profit-maximizing price?

b) Suppose MC = 0. Find the monopolist's profit maximizing price and quantity and the price elasticity at that point.

Since MR = MC at the monopolist's profit maximizing output level, we can use the formula MR = P[1 + 1/E_d] to get:

$$\frac{P - MC}{P} = -\frac{1}{E_d}.$$

This *rule of thumb for pricing* says that the difference between price and marginal cost as a fraction of price (the markup) is equal to minus the inverse of the elasticity of demand. Alternatively, we can write:

$$P = \frac{MC}{1 + 1/E_d}.$$

For example if $E_d = -2$ and MC = 5, then price should be $5/(1 – 1/2) = $10 per unit. This "markup equation" shows that the monopolist charges a markup of price over marginal cost that varies inversely with the elasticity of demand.

THE EFFECT OF A TAX

In Chapter 9 we analyzed who bears the burden of a tax on a commodity in competitive markets using supply and demand curves . Since a monopolist does not have a supply curve, our analysis of the effect of a tax on a monopolist is different. To make an easy comparison of tax incidence between competition and monopoly, we will consider a constant-cost industry with a horizontal long-run supply curve. Then, what we call the long-run supply curve for the competitive market becomes the (horizontal) marginal cost curve for the monopolist.

While we can analyze a tax placed either on consumers or firms, it is easier to shift the marginal cost curve rather than the demand curve. We therefore restrict the analysis to a tax on supply. Under perfect competition, the tax causes an upward shift of the supply curve. Given our assumption of a horizontal long-run supply curve, the consumers would bear the entire tax. Under monopoly, when we shift the marginal cost curve up by the amount of the tax, the effect on price is not immediately seen. We must look for the intersection of the new MC curve (including the tax) and the MR curve, find the new profit-maximizing output, and then find the price consumers are willing to pay for that output level. In Figure 10.3 (on the next page), the quantity sold before the tax is Q_0, and the after-tax quantity sold is Q*. By what amount did the price change? Figure 10.3 shows that the price has gone up by less than the full amount of the tax. The monopolist has absorbed part of the increase in cost.

To understand why price rises by less than the tax, remember that the monopolist sets MR = MC in order to maximize profits. If MC rises due to the tax, then the level of MR must rise to equal the new MC. But MR is twice as steep as the demand curve, so for a given increase in MR, price will rise by half that amount. This means that *with linear demand the price increase to consumers in monopoly is one-half the amount of the tax*. The difference between the old and new prices can be found from the following rule: the slope of MR times the change in quantity (equal to $Q^* - Q_0$) equals the amount of the tax.

This apparently surprising result makes sense when you consider the monopolist's problem. The monopolist was pricing high enough to maximize profit before the tax. As a result, there is a limit to how much consumers will pay after the tax is put in place. The particular numerical result that the monopolist can only pass on half of the tax depends critically on the linearity of the demand curve. Price can rise by more than the amount of the tax with a nonlinear demand curve.

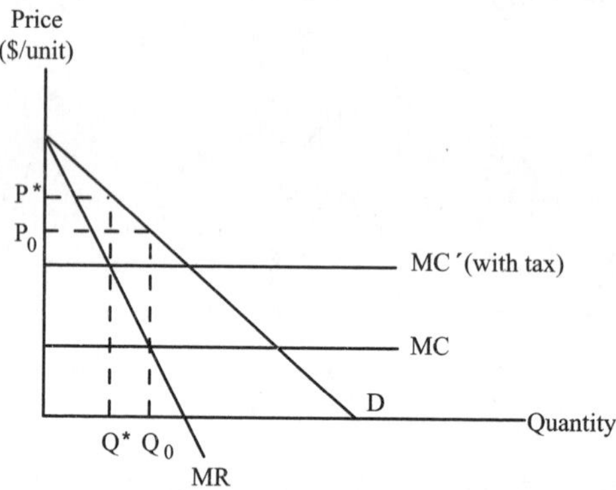

Figure 10.3

Exercise: ▶ ▶ ▶ ▶ ▶ ▶ ▶

5. a) The demand for widgets is $Q_D(P) = 1{,}000 - 50P$. The long run marginal and average total cost is $10 per unit. What is the equilibrium price and quantity under competition and under monopoly?

b) Now suppose a tax of $2 per unit is imposed (shifting the marginal cost curve). What is the new equilibrium price and quantity under competition? Under monopoly?

c) How much of the tax increase was passed on to consumers under competition? Under monopoly?

6. *[Mathematical] Analyze the effect of a tax per unit of output on the monopolist in Exercise 5 by shifting the demand curve rather than the marginal cost curve. Remember to derive the new marginal revenue curve after shifting the demand curve. Graph your answer.

*THE MULTIPLANT FIRM

A monopolist with several plants uses the same principles to maximize profits as a single-plant monopolist. The two problems for the firm to solve are determining the optimal output level for the firm as a whole and determining how much of that output to produce at each plant. If the marginal cost of production in one plant is greater than the marginal cost in another plant, the firm should move some production to the lower-cost plant to reduce total production costs. A monopolist with several plants minimizes its cost of production for a given total output level when it allocates production across plants such that marginal cost in each plant is the same. Therefore, to maximize profit, it should choose its total output level such that its marginal revenue is equal to the common marginal cost.

Exercise: ▶ ▶ ▶ ▶ ▶ ▶ ▶

***7.** Jones Industries is a monopolist in the Podunk lacrosse ball market. Lacrosse is very popular, and there is little else to do. Jones has two factories, one with $MC_1 = 0.005Q_1$ and one with $MC_2 = 6$. The fixed costs of operating each plant are zero. Jones is currently producing 1,400 units in plant 1 and 800 units in plant 2. What could Jones Industries do to save on production costs while maintaining the *same* total output?

In Exercise 7 we assumed that output was fixed at 2,200. What if the monopolist is not sure that 2,200 is the profit maximizing output level? The monopolist can solve this problem in two steps: first, choose the output in each plant such that marginal cost is equal in each plant; and second, choose total output such that marginal revenue equals marginal cost.

Exercise: ▶ ▶ ▶ ▶ ▶ ▶ ▶

***8.** Jones Industries faces the demand curve $Q_D = 6{,}000 - 20P$. The marginal cost for each factory is the same as above (Exercise 7). How many lacrosse balls should Jones produce? How should this production be divided between each of its plants?

MONOPOLY POWER (Section 10.2)

A firm may face a downward-sloping demand curve for its product even if other firms compete in the market. As long as its demand curve is not perfectly elastic, the firm should produce where marginal revenue equals marginal cost. Such a firm is exercising *monopoly power*, even though it is not a pure monopoly. Monopoly power (or market power) is the ability to markup price over marginal cost without attracting entry. One measure of monopoly power is the *Lerner index*, $L=(P-MC)/P$, where P is the price charged by the firm. The higher the markup of price over marginal cost, the higher L, and the more monopoly power the firm has. Recall that $MR=P[1+1/E_d]$ implies that we can write $MR=MC$ as $P=MC/[1+1/E_d]$.

Rewriting this equation as $P+P/E_d=MC$, we get $L=-1/E_d$, where E_d is the price elasticity of demand for the firm's product. This measure describes the divergence of the monopoly from the competitive outcome. Since L increases as E_d falls, a monopolist charges a higher markup when faced with a less elastic demand curve, all else being equal. (Assuming linear demand, the monopolist will always choose an output level on the elastic portion of the demand curve.)

It is important to recognize that a firm with monopoly power will not necessarily have a large profit, either in absolute or relative terms. In general, the higher fixed costs are the lower the firm's profit. Suppose, for example, that two firms with identical marginal cost and facing the same demand curve charge the same markup over marginal cost. The firm with a high fixed cost will have a lower profit than the firm with a low fixed cost.

Exercise: ▶ ▶ ▶ ▶ ▶ ▶ ▶

9. If a firm is pricing to maximize profit and has a price-cost margin of 45 percent, what is the elasticity of demand at that price?

THE SOCIAL COSTS OF MONOPOLY POWER (Section 10.4)

Using Figure 10.4, we can compare total surplus at the monopolist's output (where MR = MC) and at the competitive output (where P* = MC). The horizontal MC curve keeps the analysis simple, but still illustrates the basic idea. Equilibrium output under perfect competition is Q* where the demand curve intersects the supply curve (which is identical to the monopolist's marginal cost curve). Output under a monopoly market structure is Q_1. The monopolist could supply $Q^* - Q_1$ additional units of output, but that would require a lower price on the first Q_1 units sold. In moving from perfect competition to monopoly, consumers lose surplus shown by areas A (the rectangle) and B (the triangle). With horizontal MC, producer surplus under competition is zero. Producer surplus under monopoly is area A. Therefore, area A is that part of consumer surplus transferred to the monopolist. Area B is the deadweight loss (the net loss in total surplus). Thus, the social cost of monopoly power, relative to the ideal of a perfectly competitive market, arises because the consumer surplus lost due to the high price and output restriction is greater than the producer surplus gained from charging a higher price.

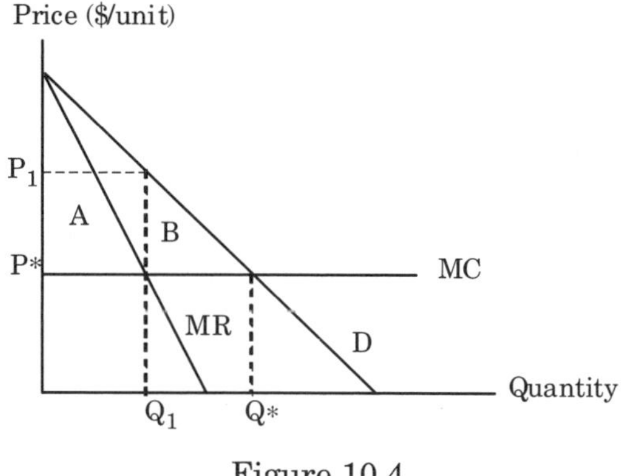

Figure 10.4

This calculation of deadweight loss may understate the true social losses due to monopoly because the monopolist may expend some fraction of its monopoly profit to acquire or defend its monopoly position. Such expenditures (lobbying Congress for protection from imports, for example) are considered wasteful or unproductive because they serve only to maintain the monopolist's market power. Therefore, some economists argue that in addition to the deadweight loss triangle (B), we should add the monopolist's profits (A) to find total monopoly deadweight loss.

Exercise: ◗ ◗ ◗ ◗ ◗ ◗ ◗

10. The plastics monopolist in Exercise 4 faced a demand curve of $P = 180 - Q$ and a constant marginal cost of $60 per unit.

a) Calculate and illustrate the deadweight loss due to monopoly.

b) Suppose the marginal cost of production is given by $MC = 60 + 2Q$. Illustrate and explain the deadweight loss from monopoly in this case of upward sloping marginal cost. Calculate deadweight loss.

PRICE REGULATION

How can the social loss of monopoly be avoided? One solution would be to split the monopoly firm into a number of different firms—this is possible, for example, when the monopoly has many independent factories. Another solution is to constrain the monopolist by regulating the maximum price it can charge. If the firm in Figure 10.5 (on the next page) could charge an unregulated monopoly price it would set P_m and sell Q_m units. Suppose that the firm cannot charge more than P_1. The demand curve becomes kinked (the heavy line). The marginal revenue becomes discontinuous (the gray dotted line). Marginal revenue now equals P_1 up to Q_1 and equals the original value of marginal revenue for Q > Q_1. Before we continue with this discussion, the next exercise examines why MR drops at the kink in the demand curve.

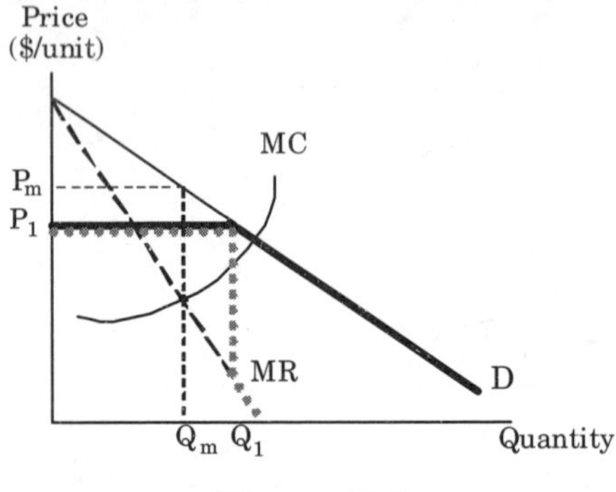

Figure 10.5

Exercise: ◗ ◗ ◗ ◗ ◗ ◗ ◗

11. In Figure 10.6, the demand curve kinks at Q^* and is steeper to the right of Q^* than to the left. What happens to MR at Q^*? (Hint: Think of the definition of MR.)

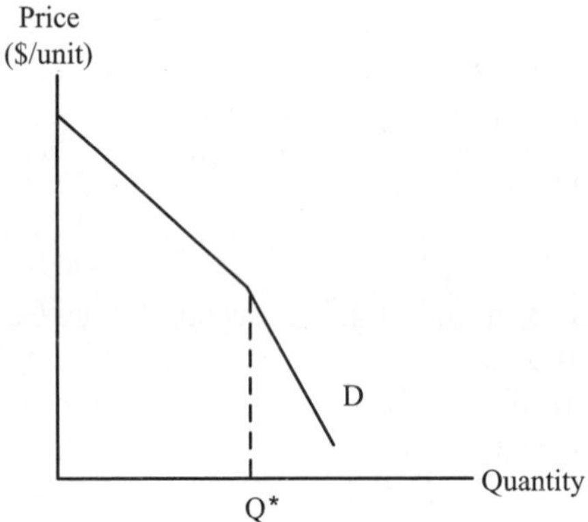

Figure 10.6

Now look back at Figure 10.5. Since price and marginal revenue exceed marginal cost for all Q less than Q_1, and marginal cost is greater than marginal revenue for all Q greater than Q_1, the firm will maximize profit by producing Q_1. Thus, price regulation has increased output from Q_m to Q_1 and lowered price from P_m to P_1. Therefore, regulating the maximum price a monopolist may charge is one way to reduce deadweight loss from monopoly.

Exercise: ◗ ◗ ◗ ◗ ◗ ◗ ◗

12. Assume a linear demand curve and upward sloping marginal cost curve. Show that there is always a price ceiling below the monopoly price that leads to an increase in output.

13. What ceiling price will result in the greatest reduction in deadweight loss in Figure 10.5? Why will a price ceiling below that be inefficient?

Figure 10.7 depicts a *natural monopoly* (for example, a local public utility), where average total cost is declining at all output levels and is therefore greater than marginal cost. In this case, setting a ceiling price, P_c, where MC and demand intersect, would result in losses for the firm. A solution with zero deadweight loss may not be feasible. Thus, in Figure 10.7, a price ceiling of P_c would cause the monopolist to go out of business in the long run (since P < AC at Q_c). One possible solution might be to pay the monopolist a subsidy. This idea unfortunately leads to other problems since raising the money for the subsidy may also create inefficiencies. A second-best solution is to set a ceiling price of P_r, the lowest price consistent with a profit greater than or equal to zero for the monopolist. This is the same as saying that the *price ceiling should be set where the demand curve intersects the average total cost curve*. When P = ATC, economic profit is zero.

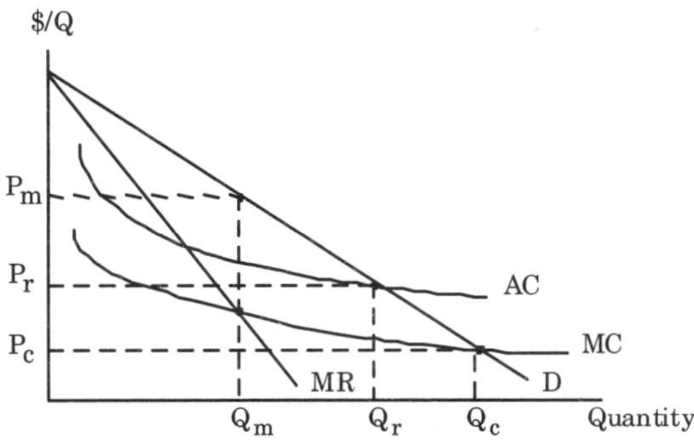

Figure 10.7

In practice, *rate-of-return regulation* sets the price ceiling by determining a "fair" or "competitive" rate of return for the firm's capital and then setting a price that will generate that rate of return.

Exercise:

14. A local regulated public utility faces the demand curve P = 100 – 0.5Q. Average cost is AC = 70 – 0.25Q and marginal cost is MC = 60 – 0.25Q. What price would you try to set if your goal were to maximize consumer surplus while allowing the firm to break even (earn zero economic profit)? Why can't the regulator reach the competitive price?

MONOPSONY (Section 10.5)

A *monopsony* is a market with a single buyer. Much of what you have already learned in order to analyze monopolized markets will apply for markets where monopsony exists. Just as a monopolist faces the entire market demand curve, a monopsonist faces the entire market supply curve. The supply curve is a constraint for the monopsonist in its price-quantity choice, just as the demand curve is a constraint for a monopolist.

The price on the supply curve indicates average expenditure. *Marginal expenditure*, the additional cost of buying one more unit, exceeds price if the supply curve slopes upward. To purchase a larger quantity requires paying a higher price for all units. Only if the supply curve is horizontal does marginal expenditure equal price. Let V(Q) be the benefit to the firm of buying Q units of the input. (You can think of V(Q) as the profit earned from using Q units of the input.) The marginal benefit from the last unit is the *marginal value* or MV(Q).

The monopsonist maximizes its profit by buying the quantity of the good where its marginal expenditure equals its marginal valuation. Notice in Figure 10.8 the difference between the monopsonist's profit-maximizing quantity choice, Q_m, and the competitive equilibrium quantity Q_c. (Recall that the market supply curve is the monopsonist's average expenditure curve, AE.) The deadweight loss due to monopsony equals the area of the triangles B and C, where A (the rectangle) and B are the loss in producer surplus and A is a gain to the monopsonist relative to the competitive outcome. The social cost of monopsony power arises because sellers of goods lose more producer surplus than the monopsonist gains by paying a lower price.

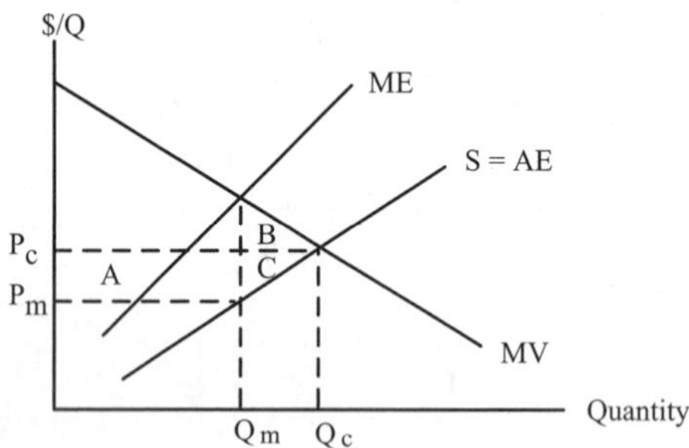

Figure 10.8

Even though a firm may not be a pure monopsonist, it may have monopsony power if there are only a few other buyers present in the market. Monopsony power depends on the elasticity of market supply, the number of buyers, and the interaction among the buyers.

Exercise: ◗ ◗ ◗ ◗ ◗ ◗ ◗

15. Suppose a monopsonist faces a horizontal supply curve and has a downward sloping marginal value curve. What is the gain from behaving as a monopsonist instead of as a competitive buyer? (Hint: What is the marginal expenditure curve in this case?)

LIMITING MARKET POWER: THE ANTITRUST LAWS (Section 10.7)

Antitrust laws are designed to restrain monopoly power and anticompetitive practices. These laws are aimed at both structure (the number of firms in an industry) and conduct (primarily pricing behavior). The main piece of antitrust legislation in the United States is the Sherman Act (1890), which is enforced by the Antitrust Division of the Department of Justice. Section 1 prohibits price fixing. Section 2 makes it illegal to monopolize a market. Notice that "monopolizing" is illegal rather than "monopoly." This has created a tension in legal decisions over the years: is it acceptable to have a monopoly as long as you don't aggressively pursue it?

The Clayton Act (1914) created the Federal Trade Commission, which is an administrative body that enforces the Clayton Act and its amendments. For example, the Clayton Act prohibits exclusive dealing contracts and makes merger illegal where the effect may be to "substantially lessen competition or tend to create a monopoly." The Federal Trade Commission also enforces laws against deceptive advertising and labeling, and many other anticompetitive practices.

Exercise: ▶ ▶ ▶ ▶ ▶ ▶ ▶

16. Explicit price fixing is "per se" illegal under the Sherman Act, meaning that firms cannot argue that the benefits to society outweigh the costs. In monopolization cases, however, the courts are willing to listen to arguments on both sides. Discuss why the deadweight loss from price fixing is more evident than the deadweight loss from monopolization.

PROBLEM SET

17. A monopolist is currently selling 400 units of output at a price of \$20 per unit. The elasticity of demand is –2. Would this firm wish to sell an additional unit for \$19.50 if it could do so without cutting the price charged for the first 400 units sold? Would a perfect competitor ever wish to sell an additional unit at a lower price? Why or why not?

18. Draw a graph with linear demand and marginal curves and a horizontal MC curve. Find the monopolist's profit-maximizing price (P^*) and output (Q^*). Now change the demand curve by rotating it clockwise (making it steeper) through the point (Q^*, P^*). What is the new profit-maximizing price and quantity? Is price higher or lower? Relate your answer to the fact that a monopolist does not have a supply curve.

19. A monopolist has the total cost function $C = 3Q^2$ and marginal cost is $MC = 6Q$. It faces the demand curve $P = 1{,}200 - Q$.

a) What is the profit-maximizing price and output? What is total profit?

b) What will the monopolist do if it faces a lump-sum tax of \$50,000? Of \$100,000?

c) What price ceiling would maximize total surplus (consumer surplus plus producer surplus)?

d) What will the monopolist do if it must pay a tax of \$40 per unit sold? What are its profits now?

20. Tinytown is a small community in which residents are fairly homogeneous and fairly wealthy. Tinytown Power is a natural monopoly, due to the high fixed costs associated with maintaining the generation facility and distribution grid. The Tinytown Utilities Commission (TUC), whose primary objective is to maximize consumer surplus, regulates Tinytown Power's operations. The TUC would also like to limit any deadweight loss, as long as this does not interfere with their primary goal. Traditionally, the TUC has required Tinytown Power to set price equal to average cost.

a) It would be easy for Tinytown Power to charge each consumer a fixed fee, in addition to the per-unit price, every billing period. Given that all consumers can easily afford to pay such fixed fees, is P = ATC the best the TUC can do? If so, why? If not, why, and how close can they get to the fully efficient outcome (no deadweight loss)? Use a graph to illustrate your answer.

b) When the TUC first considers this proposal to levy a fixed fee and a lower per-unit fee, the members are under the impression that the fee would be about 10% of the median electricity bill. With the reduction in the per-unit fee, no consumer's bill will increase by more than 10%. Do you think it is likely that the commission will adopt the new pricing system?

c) After exploring the new pricing proposal further, the TUC learns that the fee would be 80% of the median electricity bill, that 60% of consumers will pay more under the new plan, and that some consumers' bills will increase by over 100%. Do you think it is likely that the TUC will still adopt the new pricing system?

21. The market for anvils has a demand curve given by $Q_D = 1400 - 50P$. The firms in the industry produce anvils with constant long-run average total cost (equal to marginal cost) of $8 per unit.

a) If the suppliers in the anvil market are perfect competitors, what is the equilibrium price of anvils and how many are produced?

b) If a tax of $12 per anvil is introduced, what are the new equilibrium price paid by buyers and the new price received by sellers? How many anvils are now produced?

c) The Anderson Anvil Company succeeds in buying up all the anvil producers and monopolizing the industry. Cost conditions are the same as under perfect competition without any tax. What is the equilibrium price charged by Anderson and how many anvils are sold?

d) If a tax of $12 per unit is now introduced, what happens to the monopoly price and output?

22. Two firms are monopoly sellers of custom kitchen cabinets in different cities. The firms have identical horizontal marginal cost curves (MC = LAC). The demand curve is linear in each market. The demand curve for Firm 1 intersects the price axis at a higher price than the demand curve for Firm 2, and Firm 1's demand curve intersects the quantity axis at a smaller quantity than Firm 2's demand curve. Which monopolist will charge a higher price?

SELF-TEST

23. Your consulting firm has estimated that the price elasticity of demand is –0.6 for your client's product. Your client is Grand Canyon Adventures, the only company licensed to guide tourists through the Grand Canyon. No unguided walks are allowed. You recommend that your client could increase profits by:

a) increasing output (the number of tours offered per week).
b) lowering price.
c) decreasing output.
d) choosing the output level where marginal cost equals price.
e) choosing the output level where average cost equals price.

24. Why will a monopolist never choose a quantity that is on the inelastic portion of the demand curve?

a) P > MC in such a case.
b) MR > MC in such a case.
c) MR < 0 in such a case.
d) P < ATC in such a case.
e) A monopolist will often produce a quantity where demand is inelastic.

25. Lerner's index of monopoly power is L = (P – MC)/P. This implies that:

a) L = 0 for a perfectly competitive firm.
b) the larger L is the smaller the degree of monopoly power.
c) L always has a value between zero and one.
d) the larger L is the higher profits are.
e) a) and c)

26. If marginal cost is $40 and the elasticity of demand is –5, a profit-maximizing monopolist will charge a price of:

a) $200.
b) $80.
c) $73.33.
d) $50.
e) None of the above is correct.

27. Which of the following activities are illegal under U.S. antitrust laws?

a) Conspiring among competitors to fix prices
b) Merging firms together where the effect is to create a monopoly
c) Having a patent with exclusive rights to produce a good
d) a) and b) only
e) a), b), and c)

28. For a natural monopoly, the optimal policy for a regulator to set is a price such that:

a) P = MC.
b) P = AVC.
c) P = ATC, but P > MC.
d) P < MC, but P > ATC.
e) None of the above is correct.

The next four questions refer to the Zwift Corporation, which has a monopoly in the Zouvenier market in Zuburbia. Zwift has a constant average variable cost of $5 per unit and no fixed costs. It faces the demand curve P = 85 – 2Q, where P is measured in dollars.

29. Zwift should produce an output of:
a) 42.5 units.
b) 40 units.
c) 20 units.
d) 10 units.
e) None of the above is correct.

30. It should charge a price per unit of:
a) $45.
b) $5.
c) $85.
d) $10.
e) None of the above is correct.

31. At the profit-maximizing output, it will earn profits of:
a) $1,700.
b) $1,600.
c) $800.
d) $400.
e) None of the above is correct.

32. The deadweight loss from Zwift's monopoly is:
a) $400.
b) $800.
c) $900.
d) $1,600.
e) $1,806.25.

33. A profit-maximizing monopolist with a constant marginal cost of $20 per unit faces the demand curve P = 60 – 2Q. A sales tax of $4 per unit will increase the monopolist's price by:
a) $1.
b) $2.
c) $4.
d) $8.
e) $20.

34. Deadweight loss due to monopoly power is:
a) equal to the value of monopoly profits.
b) equal to the transfer of surplus from consumers to the monopolist when the monopolist raises price above marginal cost.
c) created by the monopolist's restriction of output below the competitive level.
d) affected in the short-run by changes in lump-sum taxes.
e) c) and d).

ANSWERS TO CHAPTER 10

EXERCISE ANSWERS

1. Total revenue from selling 3 units is \$6(3) = \$18. Total revenue from selling 4 units is \$4(4) = \$16. Thus, marginal revenue is –\$2. The last unit sold brings the firm \$4, but the firm must also sell the other 3 units at \$4 each, which is a loss of \$2 on each of those 3 units (price has to fall from \$6 to \$4 to increase total sales from 3 to 4 units). So marginal revenue can be written \$4 – \$2(3) = –\$2.

2. The market demand curve is usually written with quantity on the left-hand side. To find the marginal revenue curve, we must first rewrite the demand curve with price on the left-hand side (the inverse demand curve). Rewriting the market demand curve, $Q = 75 - P/4$, as $P = 300 - 4Q$, yields a marginal revenue equation of $MR = 300 - 8Q$ (the marginal revenue curve has the same intercept and twice the slope of the inverse demand curve).

3. a) Since average variable cost is constant, marginal cost equals average variable cost, so MC = 100. To maximize profit, a monopolist sets MR = MC. Thus, the profit-maximizing quantity is the solution to $300 - 8Q = 100$, or $Q^* = 25$. Plugging Q^* back into the inverse demand curve, we find $P^* = 300 - 4Q^* = 300 - 4(25) = \$200$.

   We must check that profit is positive, otherwise the monopolist would do better to shut down. We can write profit as $\pi = [P - AVC]Q - FC$. Since fixed cost equals 50, profit is:

   $$\pi = [200 - 100]25 - 50 = 2{,}500 - 50 = \$2{,}450.$$

   The monopolist is earning a positive profit and sells 25 units.

   b) If fixed costs equal \$2,600, MR = MC will be no different than above (Q^* = 25), but profit is:

   $$\pi = [200 - 100]25 - 2{,}600 = 2{,}500 - 2{,}600 = -\$100.$$

   The monopolist is losing money and prefers to go out of business. Even monopoly power may not be enough to keep a firm profitable with high fixed costs relative to the size of the market.

   c) MR = MC is $300 - 8Q = 200$ or $Q^* = 12.5$ and $P^* = 300 - 4(12.5) = \$250$. Profits are $(250 - 200)12.5 - 50 = \$575$. The monopolist will stay open and produce 12.5 units.

4. a) Set MR = MC, or $180 - 2Q = 60$ to find $Q^* = 60$ and $P^* = 180 - 60 = 120$. The point elasticity of demand at $P^* = 120$ is $E_d = -bP/Q = -1(120/60) = -2$. As is always true with linear demand, the monopolist produces in the elastic portion of the demand curve.

   b) Set MR = MC, or $180 - 2Q = 0$ to find $Q^* = 90$ and $P^* = 180 - 90 = 90$. The point elasticity at $P^* = 90$ is $E_d = -bP/Q = -1(90/90) = -1$. *Only* when MC = 0 does the monopolist produce at the midpoint on the demand curve, which is always the point of unit elasticity.

5. a) MC = ATC = 10, so the competitive equilibrium price must be \$10, and equilibrium output equals Q_D = 1,000 – 50(10) = 500. This is illustrated in Figure 10A.1a (on the next page).

Under monopoly, the profit-maximizing output is the solution to MR = MC. First, derive the inverse demand curve P = 20 – Q/50. Marginal revenue is MR = 20 – Q/25 (which is twice as steep as the inverse demand function). Setting MR = MC, we get 20 – Q/25 = 10, so Q^* = 250. At this output, P^* = 20 – 250/50 = 15. See Figure 10A.1b.

b) With the tax of \$2 per unit and a competitive market, the price to buyers rises to \$12, and the price for sellers remains unchanged at \$10. The equilibrium quantity falls to Q_D = 1,000 – 50(12) = 400, as shown in Figure 10A.1a.

For the monopolist, the easiest approach is to shift the marginal cost curve to include the \$2 tax. Now set MR = MC′ to obtain 20 – Q/25 = 12, or Q′ = 200. The price to buyers is now P′ = 20 – 200/50 = \$16.

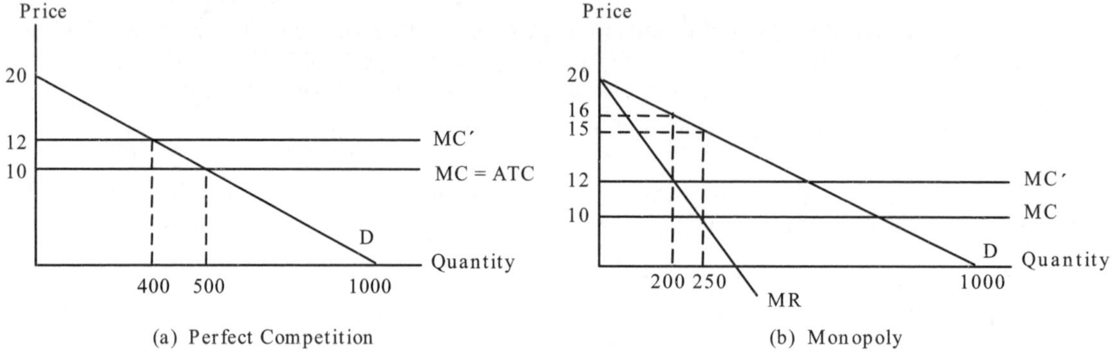

(a) Perfect Competition (b) Monopoly

Figure 10A.1

c) The price to the seller is therefore \$16 – \$2 or \$14. The price to buyers rose by \$1 (one-half the tax) and the price to sellers fell by \$1 (one-half the tax). In contrast, with competition the buyers paid all of the tax. See Figure 10A.1b.

6. The original demand curve was $P(Q) = 20 - Q/50$. To shift the demand curve, we can write $P_b - t = P'(Q)$ where P_b is the buyer's price and $P'(Q)$ is the demand curve facing the monopolist after the tax is imposed. In this case, $P'(Q) = 20 - Q/50 - 2 = 18 - Q/50$. Marginal revenue has now shifted: $MR' = 18 - Q/25$. Setting $MR' = MC$ we obtain, $18 - Q/25 = 10$, or $Q' = 200$. Then using the formula for $P'(Q)$, we obtain $P = 18 - 200/50 = \$14$, which is the same seller's price as we found by shifting the marginal cost curve. See Figure 10A.2.

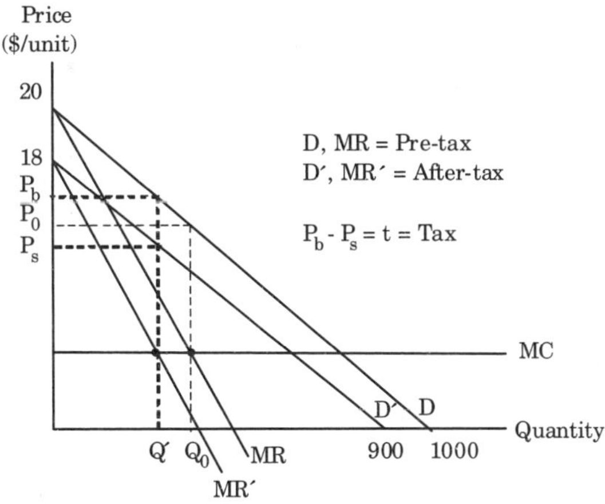

Figure 10A.2

7. Total output is $Q_1 + Q_2 = 1{,}400 + 800 = 2{,}200$. The two marginal cost curves are drawn in Figure 10A.3. We see that $MC_1(1{,}400) = 7$. The firm should use plant 1 up to the point where $MC_1(Q_1^*) = 6$, and then produce the excess in plant 2. This minimizes the total cost of production. $MC_1 = 6$ if $Q_1 = 1{,}200$, so the firm should set $Q_1 = 1{,}200$ and $Q_2 = 1{,}000$. (Note: Since this lowers its costs of production, it may now wish to increase output.)

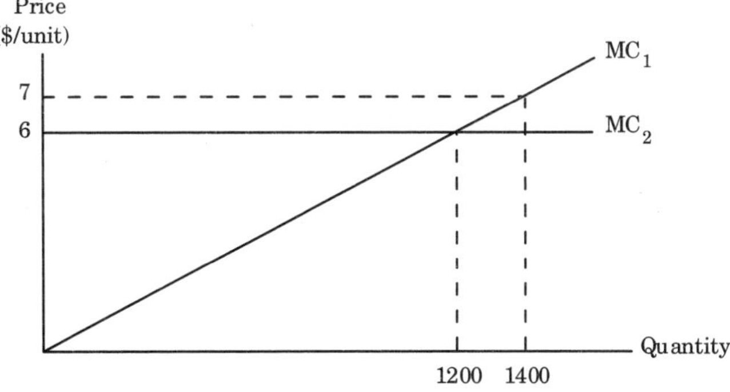

Figure 10A.3

8. P = 300 – Q/20, so MR = 300 – Q/10. Marginal cost can be derived as follows: use plant 1 until $MC_1 = 6$, then use plant 2 for any additional production. This means that:

$$MC = \begin{cases} 0.005Q < 1{,}200 \\ 6 \text{ if } Q \geq 1{,}200 \end{cases}$$

One way to solve this problem is to try MR = 6, and see if the resulting solution has output greater than 1,200 (if so, that is the solution, since marginal cost is less than 6 for smaller outputs). Trying this, we obtain 300 – Q/10 = 6, or $Q^* = 2{,}940$. $Q_1^* = 6/0.005 = 1{,}200$ and $Q_2^* = 2{,}940 - 1{,}200 = 1{,}740$. Then, $P^* = 300 - (2{,}940/20) = \$153$.

9. The rule of thumb is that the price-cost margin equals minus the inverse elasticity of demand, so a margin of 45 percent means that $0.45 = -1/E_d$ or $E_d = -2.22$.

10. a) First find the competitive price and output: $P^* = MC = 60$ and 60 = 180 – Q, or $Q^* = 120$. Then find the monopoly solution: MR = MC, or 180 – 2Q = 60, or $Q^M = 60$. Therefore $P^* = 180 - 60$ or $P^M = 120$. Deadweight loss is the area of the shaded triangle in Figure 10A.4a (on the next page), or 0.5(120 – 60)(120 – 60) = 1,800.

b) Under competition: P = MC or 180 – Q = 60 + 2Q, or $Q^* = 40$ and $P^* = 180 - 40 = \$140$. Under monopoly: MR = MC or 180 – 2Q = 60 + 2Q, or $Q^M = 30$ and $P^M = 180 - 30 =$ \$150. The shaded area in Figure 10A.4b is deadweight loss: DWL = 0.5(40 – 30)(150 – 120) = \$150. The reason why this area is DWL is as follows: CS under competition is area **acf**. CS under monopoly is area **abh**. Therefore the loss in CS due to monopoly is **bcfh**. PS under competition is **cjf**. PS under monopoly is **bjeh**. There is a transfer from consumers to producers of **bcgh**. The rest of what used to be either CS or PS (the shaded area in Figure 10A.4b) is DWL.

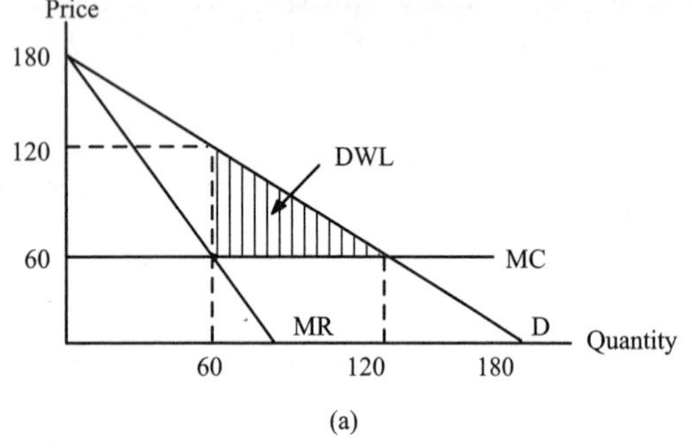

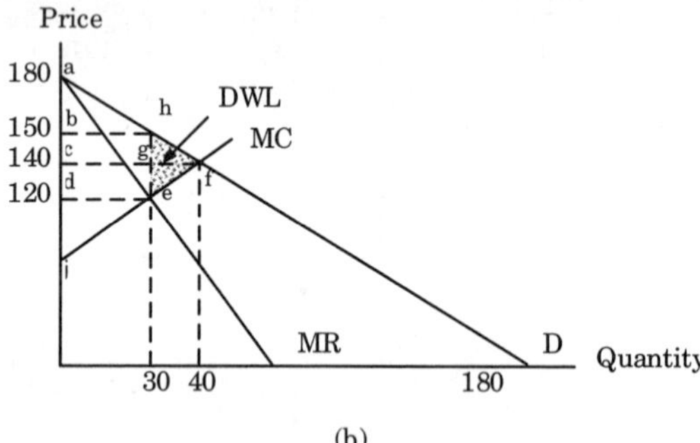

Figure 10A.4

11. See Figure 10A.5. Remember that the definition of marginal revenue is $MR(Q) = P(Q) + [\Delta P/\Delta Q]Q$. At Q^*, the slope of the inverse demand curve becomes more negative, so MR drops down. We can also see this by running both demand-curve segments back to the price axis and constructing the marginal revenue segments. The MR curve is given by MR_1 when D_1 is the relevant segment and by MR_2 when D_2 is the relevant segment.

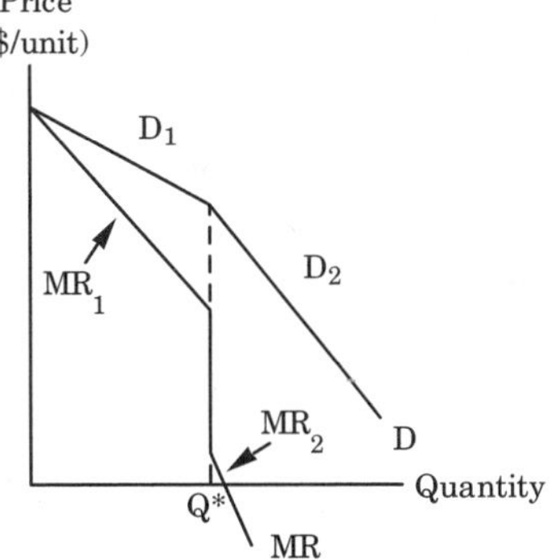

Figure 10A.5

12. See Figure 10A.6. A ceiling price (P_C) below P_m means that the monopolist can never charge P_m, so price must fall. What output will be produced? Recall that $MR = P_C$ for all Q less than the quantity demanded at P_C. Either the firm will find it best to produce the quantity demanded at $\bar{P}$ (as with P_{C1}) or it will find it best to produce the quantity such that $MC = P_C$ (as with P_{C2}). Too low a ceiling price, such as P_{C2} in Figure 10A.6, might even lead to an output less than Q_m. Note that setting P_C just slightly less than P_m will always induce the monopolist to produce more than Q_m.

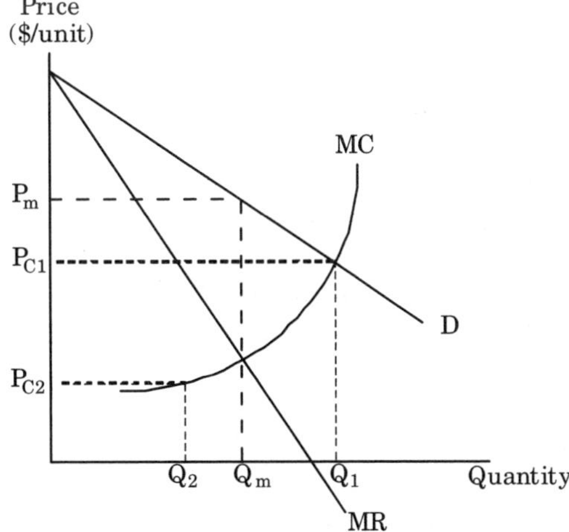

Figure 10A.6

13. The maximum output a ceiling price can induce a monopolist to produce is given by the price at which P = MC. For any lower output, P > MC, and some deadweight loss results. Deadweight loss is zero in this case, as long as the price ceiling doesn't force the firm to shut down.

14. The best (lowest) price for consumers that will earn zero economic profit for the firm is P = AC: Solve 100 – 0.5Q = 70 – 0.25Q to find $Q^* = 120$. Plugging Q^* into the demand equation yields $P^* = 100 - 0.5(120) = 40$. Therefore, you should set $P^* = \$40$. The MC curve lies below the AC curve at every output level, so setting P = MC (the competitive price) would make Q = 160 and P = 20. However, when Q = 160, ATC = 30, which exceeds the price; the firm would lose money at this output level.

15. See Figure 10A.7. Note that the ME curve is identical to the supply curve in this case. With a horizontal supply curve, the price is the same as with a competitive market. There is no gain to the monopsonist.

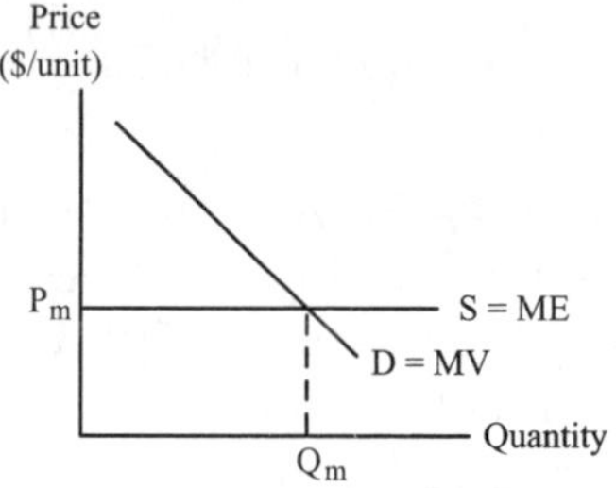

Figure 10A.7

16. There is a clear deadweight loss from price fixing without any efficiency gains. This follows from the fact that colluding firms are not actually merging to realize cost savings. They are only raising the price above the competitive level. Monopolies can be efficient if, for example, there are large economies of scale in production or if some market power helps finance innovation.

PROBLEM SET ANSWERS

17. The rule of thumb states that $(P - MC)/P = -1/E_d$. This implies that the price-cost margin is 50 percent if the demand elasticity is –2. Marginal cost must therefore be \$10 (given that P = \$20). If the firm could sell more output at \$19.50 per unit without lowering the price on units already sold, the monopolist would be better off. This possibility of capturing additional consumer surplus is what inspires attempts at price discrimination (the subject of Chapter 11).

A perfect competitor chooses output such that P = MC and is selling as much as it wishes at the going price. As a consequence, the competitive firm has no desire to sell additional output at a lower price.

18. The monopolist will prefer to decrease output. See Figure 10A.8, where the monopolist originally charges P^* and sells Q^*. When the demand curve is rotated to D', the MR curve shifts to MR'. The intersection of MR' and MC gives the new output choice of Q'. Price is higher and quantity is lower, even though we rotated the demand curve through the original profit maximizing point. This shows why the monopolist does not have a supply curve, which can be drawn independent of the demand curve.

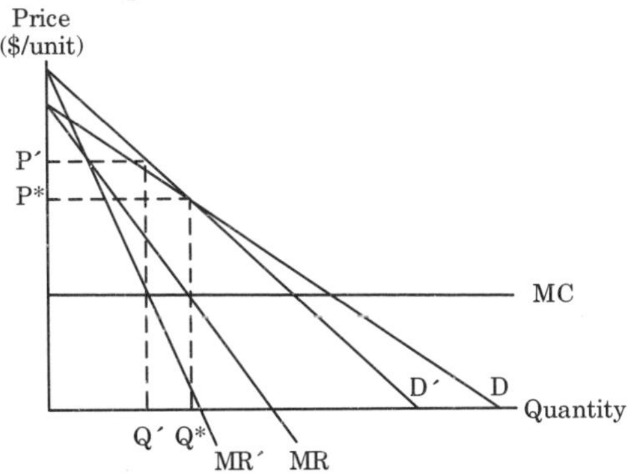

Figure 10A.8

19. a) Since the demand curve is $P = 1{,}200 - Q$, the marginal revenue curve is $MR = 1{,}200 - 2Q$. Solving for the quantity which equates MR and MC, we get $1{,}200 - 2Q = 6Q$ or $Q^* = 150$ and $P^* = 1{,}200 - 150 = \$1{,}050$.

Profit is $\pi(150) = 1{,}050(150) - 3(150)^2 = 157{,}500 - 67{,}500 = \$90{,}000$.

b) With a lump-sum tax of \$50,000, the monopolist's profit after taxes is \$40,000, so it will stay in business. Since the lump-sum tax is a fixed cost, the firm will still sell 150 units (MR and MC are unchanged). With a lump-sum tax of \$100,000, profit after tax will be –\$10,000, so the firm will be better off to shut down in the long run.

c) The best price ceiling is that at which the quantity sold is maximized. This is the same as the competitive price. The quantity sold under a price ceiling (below the monopolist's optimal price) is the minimum of the quantity demanded at that price and the quantity at which marginal cost equals price. Equating price and marginal cost to find the intersection of MC and the demand curve, we get $1{,}200 - Q = 6Q$ or $Q_c = 171.43$ and $P_c = \$1{,}028.57$.

d) It is easiest to shift the marginal cost curve to find the new profit-maximizing output. With a tax of \$40 per unit, $MC'(Q) = 6Q + 40$. Equating MC' and MR, we get $1{,}200 - 2Q = 40 + 6Q$ or $Q' = 145$, and $P' = \$1{,}055$. Subtracting the tax from the buyer's price, we get $P_s' = \$1{,}015$. The firm's profit is now $\pi'(145) = 1{,}015(145) - 3(145)^2 = \$84{,}100$. Therefore, the consumer bears \$5 of the \$40 tax, compared to part a), and the monopolist absorbs \$35.

20. a) $P = ATC$ is not the best the commission can do. They could set P = MC and set the fixed fee just high enough to give zero profits. This converts the deadweight loss to consumer surplus. Figure 10A.9 illustrates this for the simple cost function $C(q) = F + cq$ where F is the fixed cost and c is the constant marginal cost. Area A equals the fixed cost. If there were n residents, the fixed fee would be A/n. The price would be $c per unit. This would transform the deadweight loss when P = ATC (area B) into consumer surplus.

b) There are winners and losers from the change to the new pricing system. Figure 10A.9 reveals that aggregate consumer surplus increases. Since no one is hurt severely by the change, the commission is likely to adopt the new pricing system.

c) Now, not only do some of the losers lose a lot, but most people lose from the change. Since the consumers with the smallest electricity consumption tend to be poorer, the commission might not want to impose this burden on them. Furthermore, since a majority of consumers lose, the TUC will find considerable political support for sticking with the old pricing system, even if the new pricing system yields more total surplus.

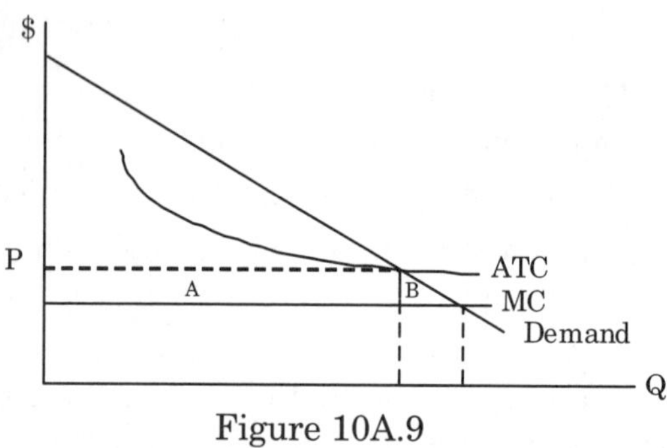

Figure 10A.9

21. a) In equilibrium, price equals marginal cost or $8 per unit. Thus, the quantity produced would be 1400 – 50(8) = 1000 anvils.

b) Now buyers pay MC plus the tax. So buyers pay $20 per unit and sellers receive $8 per unit. Production will be 1400 – 50(20) = 400 anvils.

c) For the monopoly output, set MR = MC. From Q = 1400 – 50P, we find P = 28 – Q/50. Since the MR curve is twice as steep as the inverse demand curve, MR = 28 – Q/25. Equating MR and MC, we obtain: 28 – Q/25 = 8, or $Q^* = 500$. Substituting into the inverse demand curve, we find $P^* = \$18$ per unit.

d) Here, MR = (MC + tax). Hence, MR = 28 – Q/25 = 8 + 12. So $Q' = 200$ and $P' = \$24$ per unit. Note that the price change differs between monopoly and perfect competition.

22. See Figure 10A.10 (on the next page). With linear demand, the marginal revenue curve is twice as steep with the same intercept. Thus, MR = MC at a quantity which is half the quantity at which D = MC, and the monopoly price is halfway between the vertical intercept and MC. Since D_1 has a higher intercept than D_2, Firm 1 charges a higher price.

You can also show this using algebra: If P = a – bQ, then MR = a – 2bQ. Let MC = c (a constant). Setting MR = MC implies b = (a + c)/2. Since $a_1 > a_2$, then $P_1 > P_2$.

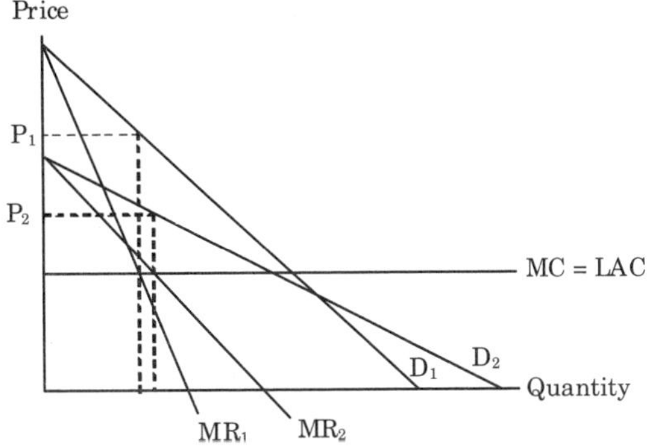

Figure 10A.10

SELF-TEST ANSWERS

23. c) A monopolist should produce in the elastic portion of the demand curve. Their price is too low and their quantity is too high.

24. c) If demand is inelastic, marginal revenue is negative. Recall that MR = P(1 + 1/E_d). If $-1 < E_d < 0$, then MR < 0.

25. e) Recall that P = MC for a competitive firm, so L = 0 in that case. In general, 0 < L < 1.

26. d) From the monopoly markup rule, P = MC/(1 + 1/E_d). Thus, P = 40/[1 + 1/(–5)] = 40/[4/5] = $50.

27. d) Patents are legal monopolies granted to inventors by the U.S. government. Price fixing conspiracies and mergers to monopoly are illegal under Sections 1 and 2 of the Sherman Act, respectively.

28. c) With declining ATC at all quantities, P = MC would result in losses for the firm. P = ATC is the regulated price ceiling with the smallest deadweight loss that still allows the firm to earn a normal rate of return (economic profit of zero).

29. c) MR = 85 – 4Q. At MR = MC, 85 – 4Q = 5, or $Q^* = 20$.

30. a) At $Q^* = 20$, $P^* = 85 - 2(20) = \$45$.

31. c) With zero fixed costs, ATC = AVC, and profit equals TR – TC = 45(20) – 5(20) = $800.

32. a) The competitive price and output would be $P^* = MC = 5$ and therefore 5 = 85 – 2Q or $Q^* = 40$. Deadweight loss is then the area of the triangle bordered by the competitive and monopoly outcomes: 0.5(40 – 20)(45 – 5) = $400.

33. b) First find the original monopoly price: MR = MC implies $60 - 4Q = 20$ or $Q^* = 10$, which means $P^* = 60 - 2(10) = \$40$. After the tax, MR = MC′ implies $60 - 4Q = 24$ or $Q' = 9$, which yields an after-tax price of $P' = 60 - 2(9) = \$42$. The price went up by \$2.

34. c) This is the definition of deadweight loss. (Note that the lump-sum tax in choice d) will not change the profit-maximizing output, since it does not change marginal cost; therefore, deadweight loss will be unaffected.)

CHAPTER 11
PRICING WITH MARKET POWER

IMPORTANT CONCEPTS

- Definition of Price Discrimination
- First-degree Price Discrimination
- Second-degree Price Discrimination
- Third-degree Price Discrimination
- Intertemporal Price Discrimination
- Peak-Load Pricing
- Two-Part Tariffs
    - Entry Fee
    - Usage Fee
- Bundling
- Tying
- Advertising
    - Full Marginal Cost of Advertising

CHAPTER HIGHLIGHTS

A firm with monopoly power does not always have to charge the same price to all customers. Charging different customers different prices for the identical good is called *price discrimination.* This is a common pricing strategy used to capture consumer surplus and transfer it to the producer. There are three basic types of price discrimination covered in this chapter. *First-degree price discrimination* (also known as perfect price discrimination) involves charging each customer the maximum price they are willing to pay for each unit purchased. The firm continues selling as long as it can charge a unit price greater than marginal cost. This is the best the firm can possibly do: by charging each customer his or her reservation price (the maximum they are willing and able to pay), the firm captures *all* consumer surplus. Carrying out this type of price discrimination is difficult in practice because it relies on having a tremendous amount of information about consumers' willingness to pay.

In *second-degree price discrimination* (also known as block pricing), customers are charged a different price depending on how much they buy. This type of pricing may or may not actually be discriminatory. If it costs less to sell items in bulk, for example, then charging lower prices for bulk purchases is not price discrimination.

If the market contains several types of customers (e.g., business and leisure travelers), the firm should set profit maximizing output such that marginal revenue is equal across groups of consumers and equal to marginal cost. By pricing to satisfy these two requirements, the firm will set the higher price in the market segment(s) with less elastic demand. Market segmentation will be profitable only if arbitrage across consumer groups is preventable.

There are several other types of "non-uniform pricing" discussed in this chapter:

1. *Intertemporal Price Discrimination*: Consumers self-select into market segments by being charged different prices at different points in time.

2. *Peak-load Pricing*: The firm charges a higher price during the peak periods (which might be a day of the week, a particular time of day, or even a season of the year). Peak-load pricing differs from third-degree price discrimination because the marginal cost of serving customers differs between peak and off-peak periods.

3. *Two-part Tariff*: Consumers pay an up-front fixed fee (the *entry fee*) for the right to consume the good and then they pay an additional per-unit price (the *usage fee*) for each unit of the product they buy.

4. *Bundling*: Sometimes firms sell two products packaged together as a bundle. This will be profitable if consumers have heterogeneous demands (different reservation prices for the two products being bundled) and if the firm cannot practice price discrimination (i.e., cannot charge different prices to different customers). *Mixed bundling* entails offering consumers the choice of buying the goods separately or as a bundle.

5. *Tying*: This is a general term used to describe situations in which customers can buy one product from a company only if they buy a second product from the same company. A common form of tying is to require customers who buy a durable good (a computer or a printer, for example) to also buy certain supplies from the same firm (special software or print cartridges).

The chapter ends with a discussion of how a firm with market power should set the optimal amount of *advertising*. Increased advertising causes the demand curve to shift out and leads to increased output, but increased output leads to increased production costs. These benefits and costs of increasing advertising need to be balanced to find the profit-maximizing advertising expenditure.

CONCEPT REVIEW AND EXERCISES

CAPTURING CONSUMER SURPLUS (Section 11.1)

A firm with market power may find it more profitable to charge different prices to different customers even though it costs the same amount to produce for each customer. By practicing *price discrimination*, the firm can capture additional consumer surplus.

Let's look at this motivation for price discrimination more closely. A single-price monopolist trying to expand output by offering a lower price to one customer will have to simultaneously offer the same lower price to all customers. Figure 11.1 shows the tradeoff for a single-price monopolist who lowers the price from P_0 to P_1. Total revenue falls by the area **abed** (the "old" customers who used to pay P_0 that are now paying P_1) and it rises by the area **efgc** (the additional units bought by new customers). A price discriminating monopolist can do better by eliminating the tradeoff: charge P_1 to attract new customers, but continue to charge P_0 to old customers. In this case, revenue will increase by **efgc**.

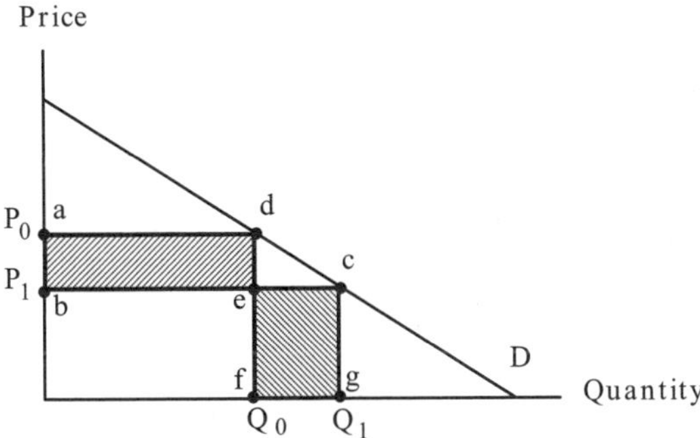

Figure 11.1

If price discrimination gives such a boost to profits, why don't all firms practice it? The answer to this question lies in realizing that certain conditions must hold for a firm to be able to price discriminate. There are three essential conditions: (1) the firm must possess some monopoly power, (2) willingness to pay for the good must vary across consumers, and (3) the firm must be able to prevent or limit resale (arbitrage). If condition (1) does not hold, there can only be one market price and price discrimination will not be possible. A competitive firm cannot effectively price discriminate because its customers will find another firm willing to sell to all customers at the market price. If condition (2) does not hold, the firm might be able to price discriminate, but it will not find it profitable. Finally, condition (3) ensures that consumers will not be able to trade with each other and undermine the firm's pricing policy.

PRICE DISCRIMINATION (Section 11.2)

FIRST-DEGREE PRICE DISCRIMINATION

Perfect, or *first-degree price discrimination*, is the ultimate form of price discrimination. Here, the firm charges *each* customer the maximum price he or she is willing to pay. In Figure 11.2 (on the next page) think of the consumers as lined up along the horizontal axis, where each consumer would like one unit of the good.

The first consumer has the highest reservation price, the second consumer has the second-highest reservation price, and so on. The dots along the demand curve in Figure 11.2 represent the different prices charged to each consumer for each unit of the good. The firm continues to expand production as long as it can charge a price for each unit greater than the marginal cost of production for that unit. Therefore, the firm practicing first-degree price discrimination will maximize profits by setting an output level of Q* in Figure 11.2 and charging an entire series of prices represented (roughly) by the dots on the demand curve.

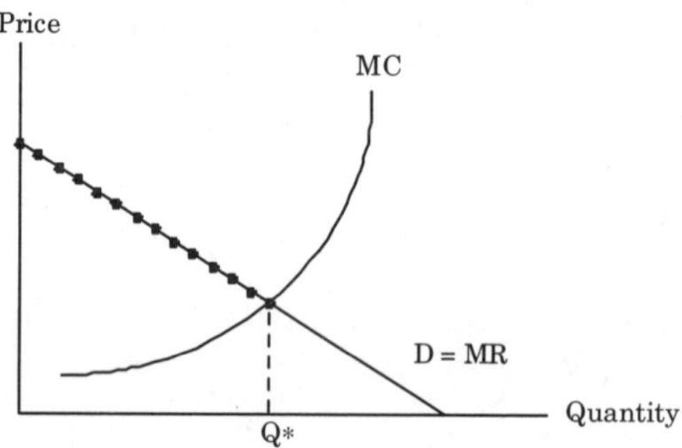

Figure 11.2

This practice of charging each consumer their reservation price has some interesting implications. First, the additional (marginal) revenue earned by selling one more unit is exactly equal to the price charged for that unit. This implies that the marginal revenue curve for a perfectly price-discriminating monopolist is equal to the demand curve. (The profit maximizing output is found, as always, by setting MR = MC.) Second, this form of price discrimination extracts *all* consumer surplus from consumers: each consumer is charged the maximum amount they are willing to pay. Third, first-degree price discrimination yields the competitive (efficient) output level. There is no deadweight loss. If you think of the MC curve in Figure 11.2 as the supply curve for a competitive industry, Q* is exactly equal to the competitive output. Therefore, although first-degree price discrimination leads to a highly unequal distribution of gains from trade (the firm has everything and consumers have nothing), it is socially efficient.

Exercise: ◗ ◗ ◗ ◗ ◗ ◗ ◗

1. Will any consumers be made worse off under first-degree price discrimination than they would be with the standard single monopoly price? In Figure 11.3, indicate which consumers gain and which consumers lose.

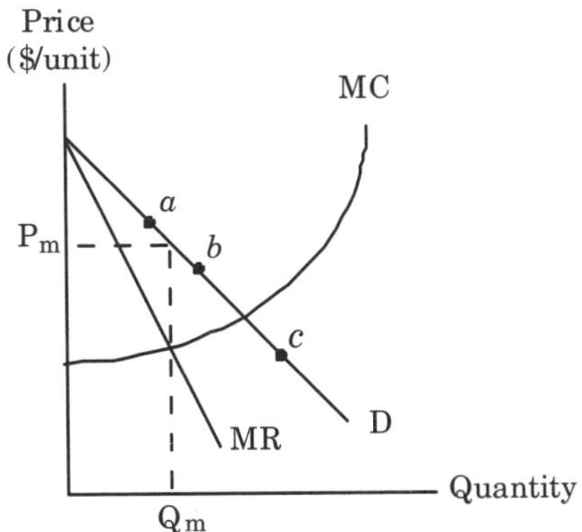

Figure 11.3

SECOND-DEGREE PRICE DISCRIMINATION

If the firm discriminates according to the quantity purchased by each consumer, it is practicing *second-degree price discrimination*. A simple diagram of second-degree price discrimination is shown in Figure 11.4. There is no longer one price, but a price schedule. Compared to charging one price of P_0 for all Q_0 units, consumer surplus is reduced, but it is not reduced to zero. The shaded area in Figure 11.4 shows the consumer surplus retained by those consumers who buy the good. In electricity markets, second-degree price discrimination is called declining-block pricing.

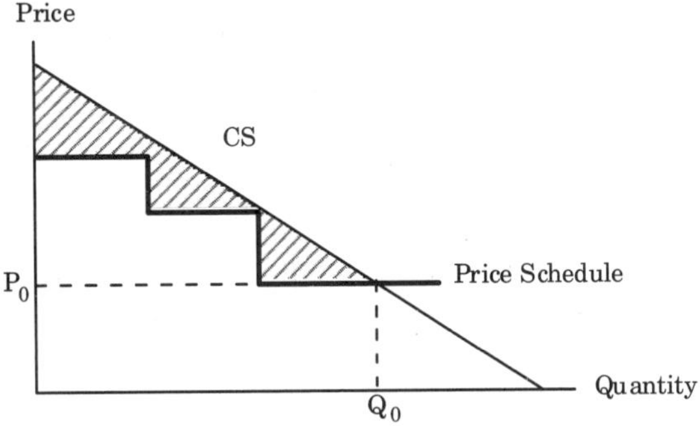

Figure 11.4

One note of caution before continuing: Offering quantity discounts can be called price discrimination if the price discounts are not based on cost differences. If it costs different amounts to serve different customers then charging different prices is not discriminatory.

Exercise: ◗ ◗ ◗ ◗ ◗ ◗ ◗

2. Figure 11.5 depicts demand curves for four individuals. What quantity will each consumer purchase? Explain.

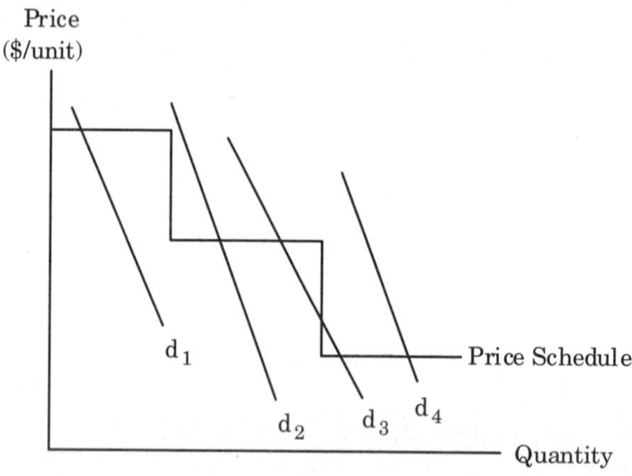

Figure 11.5

THIRD-DEGREE PRICE DISCRIMINATION

For some goods it is possible to identify separate markets, where consumers in these markets differ in their willingness to pay for the good. Consider, for example, discounts for airfares if the traveler stays over a Saturday night. This discount might attract consumers who would otherwise not take the trip. This is an example of *third-degree price discrimination*. Other examples are movie tickets (discounts for children and senior citizens) and college football tickets (discounts for college students, staff, and alumni). In carrying out this type of price discrimination the monopolist segments the market and charges a different price in each market segment. If the firm can successfully separate the market into two (or more) market segments, higher profits can be made by charging prices to reflect the elasticity of demand in each market.

Exercise: ◗ ◗ ◗ ◗ ◗ ◗ ◗

3. a) Numerous restaurants offer discounts for customers who eat dinner between 4 and 6 PM (often called "early bird" specials). Can you explain why this is a form of third-degree price discrimination and how the market is being segmented? Who is most likely to take advantage of these specials?

b) In your answer to part a) you should have discussed senior citizens as part of the target market for the discounts. Why do other types of stores not offer (or not commonly offer) lower prices to the elderly?

In order to formally analyze the optimal pricing strategy for a monopolist practicing third-degree price discrimination, consider the two decisions the firm must make: first, given total output, how should that output be divided across market segments, and second, what is the profit maximizing level of total output? Suppose we start by fixing a level of total output. The firm faces two distinct demand curves corresponding to each market segment, and each demand curve will have its own marginal revenue curve. In this case, the firm should divide sales across the two market segments such that $MR_1 = MR_2$. If instead $MR_1 > MR_2$, then the firm could earn more revenue by selling more in the first market and less in the second market, keeping total output the same. Similarly, if $MR_1 < MR_2$, we should reallocate output to the second market. Therefore, we must have $MR_1 = MR_2$ at the profit-maximizing point.

How do we go about choosing the level of total output? To do that we rely on our familiar condition of MR = MC. Putting these two requirements together we find that prices and output must be set so that:

$$MR_1 = MR_2 = MC.$$

Since $MR_1 = P_1(1 + 1/E_1)$ and $MR_2 = P_2(1 + 1/E_2)$, where E_i is the demand elasticity in market i, then:

$$P_1/P_2 = (1 + 1/E_2)/(1 + 1/E_1).$$

Thus, *price is set higher in the market with less elastic demand.*

Note that if MC is constant (e.g., MC = 5), you can treat the problem as if it were two separate monopoly markets. Set MR_1 = MC and MR_2 = MC and solve each equation separately to find the price and output in each market segment.

Exercise: ▶ ▶ ▶ ▶ ▶ ▶ ▶

4. Suppose the Eau d' Stars Corp. sells "Lassie" brand perfume at $3 per bottle and sells "Marilyn" brand perfume at $27 per bottle. Both perfumes are based on identical formulas with identical costs, although customers do not know this. If Eau is maximizing profit, what can you say about the relative elasticities of demand? If marginal cost is $1 for both perfumes, what are the price elasticities?

5. Consider the pricing of first-class and coach airline tickets on a route where the airline has a monopoly in air travel. Take a simple example: Let MC = 100, and let the demand for first-class tickets be P = 1,000 – 5Q, while the demand for coach tickets is P = 500 – Q.

a) Find the monopoly price for first-class tickets and coach tickets.

b) What is the demand elasticity for each market segment at the profit-maximizing prices you found in part a)? Do these values make sense?

INTERTEMPORAL PRICE DISCRIMINATION AND PEAK-LOAD PRICING (Section 11.3)

One profitable way to segment certain markets is to offer the good at different prices at different times. The consumers will segment themselves depending on when they want to use the good and what price they are willing to pay. Suppose a firm with a new product believes that some customers will pay a higher price now even if they know that they could wait and get a lower price later. These consumers, presumably, derive some benefit from being "first" to possess the good. If customers with a desire to be first have a demand curve that is relatively less elastic than customers who are willing to wait, the firm can practice *intertemporal price discrimination* (a form of third-degree discrimination). To maximize profits, the firm should introduce the good at a high price and then lower the price later to sell to customers who were unwilling to pay the high price. Examples are automobiles (where prices tend to decline over the model year) and high-fashion clothing (where prices drop at the end of the season).

Demand for some goods follows a "peak" (strong) and "off peak" (weak) pattern. Electricity demand, for example, is highest at night. Business air travel demand is lowest in the middle of the day on weekdays and on weekends. Marginal cost is also higher in peak than in non-peak periods because capacity is strained to the limit when operating during a peak demand period. *Peak-load pricing* involves charging a higher price for the peak period. However, peak-load pricing is *not* a form of pure price discrimination because marginal costs differ by time of service. If marginal cost is higher at peak times then prices should be higher during the peak times.

Peak-load pricing therefore resembles intertemporal price discrimination, but it has a cost justification. A monopoly practicing peak-load pricing sets its marginal revenue equal to marginal cost within each time block, just as a monopolist selling many products would do. If you think of the service delivered at different times as different goods, the analysis of peak-load pricing will be easier.

Exercise: ◗ ◗ ◗ ◗ ◗ ◗ ◗

6. A regulated electric utility company faces off-peak demand and peak demand. The regulator wants to set prices so that the utility breaks even. The market demands and cost curves are shown in Figure 11.6.

a) Suppose the regulator set one price to be charged both off-peak and peak. The price is set so that the utility breaks even in off-peak periods. Indicate this price on Figure 11.6. Will the utility make profits or losses in peak periods? (continued)

b) If the regulator wanted to set a separate price during peak periods so that it would break even, what price would that be?

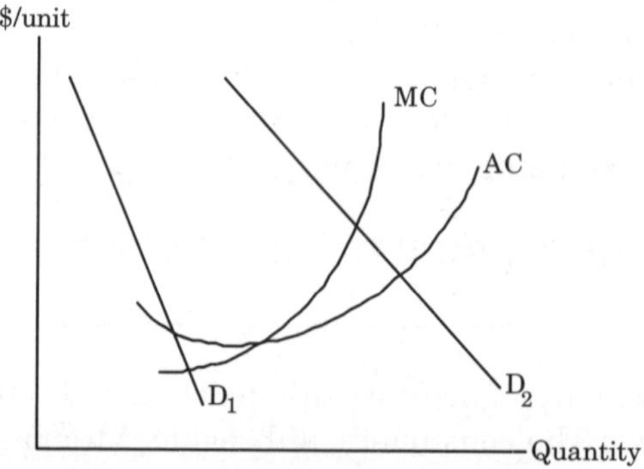

Figure 11.6

THE TWO-PART TARIFF (Section 11.4)

One special form of quantity discounting is the *two-part tariff*, which involves two separate charges to consume a single product. Customers are charged one fee for the right to the good (an *entry fee*) and another fee for every unit purchased (a *usage fee*). Telephone companies often have a fixed monthly charge for simply keeping the line open, whether you make a call or not, and a per-call charge for local calls. (There may also be a cost-based justification for this practice, but we focus on the discrimination motive.)

Consider the case of identical consumers within the context of a simple example. The demand for country club visits by each consumer is given by $P = 100 - Q$, where Q is the number of visits per year and P is the price per visit. Let marginal cost be a constant of \$10 per visit. If the country club has monopoly power and chooses to act as a single-price monopolist, it could set the price per visit (the usage fee) as shown in Figure 11.7 (on the next page): MR = MC implies $100 - 2Q = 10$ or $Q_m = 45$ and $P_m = 100 - 45 = \$55$. Profits will be 55(45) – 10(45) = \$2,025, which is the rectangle **bced** in Figure 11.7.

The country club would be better off with two-part tariff pricing. Suppose it charged an annual membership fee, T, equal to consumer surplus at Q=45 and P=55 (the shaded triangle **abd**) *plus* \$55 per visit. Profit would increase by $T = 1/2(45)(45) = \$1{,}012.50$, bringing total profits to \$3,037.50. Although this change in pricing strategy increases profits, the country club could do even better. The best strategy is to charge a price per visit equal to MC, which is \$10, and set an annual membership fee equal to the consumer surplus at P = 10 (the triangle **acf**). Then profits would increase to [(10(90) – 10(90)) + 0.5 (90)(100 – 10)] = \$4,050.

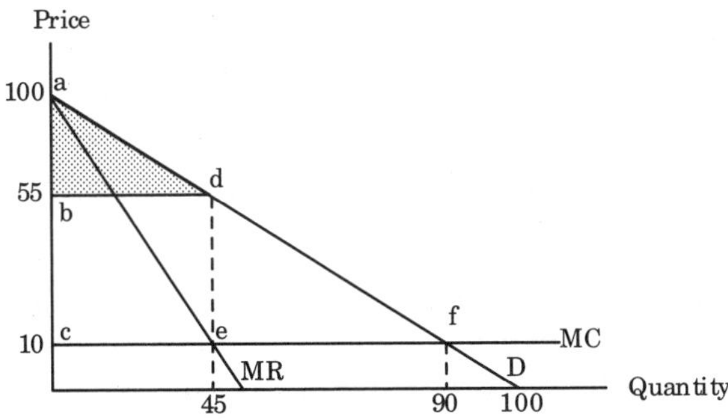

Figure 11.7

Even though the country club breaks even on the usage price when they set P = MC, they are generating a substantial revenue through the annual membership fee.

Exercise: ▶ ▶ ▶ ▶ ▶ ▶ ▶

7. In the above example, where $Q = 100 - P$ and $MC = 10$, would the country club make even more money by setting $P = 0$ and charging an annual membership fee equal to all consumer surplus at that price?

To summarize, when consumers are identical the firm should set P* = MC per unit consumed and charge an entry fee equal to the total consumer surplus for each consumer. With identical consumers, a firm can extract all consumer surplus using this pricing strategy.

If consumers are not identical, the problem becomes much more complicated. Too high a fixed fee drives some consumers away from purchasing the good. Too low a fixed fee leaves consumers with too much consumer surplus. It turns out that the optimal per unit price to set is now above marginal cost. The next exercise provides a numerical example to give you an idea of the tradeoffs involved when consumers differ.

Exercise: ▶ ▶ ▶ ▶ ▶ ▶ ▶

8. Suppose there are two types of consumers (in equal numbers) but the firm must charge the same price to everyone. Each "high demand" consumer has the demand curve $Q_H = 130 - P$, and each "low demand" consumer has the demand curve $Q_L = 100 - P$. Marginal cost is constant at $10. Calculate profit for the firm if it sets a two-part tariff with P = $10 and T = consumer surplus for the "low demand" consumers. Then calculate profits if P = $15 and T = consumer surplus for "low demand" consumers. Which pricing strategy is more profitable?

*BUNDLING (Section 11.5)

A firm practices *bundling* when it sells two goods together as a package. Restaurants frequently run specials offering a main course, along with an appetizer and dessert, for a single price. Some restaurants sell only complete dinner packages *(pure bundling)*; others offer both complete dinners and individual courses a la carte *(mixed bundling)*.

Bundling enables a monopolist to exploit the fact that consumers differ in their reservation prices for separate items. Bundling may be profitable if demands are negatively correlated, i.e., if consumers with higher reservation prices for one good tend to have lower reservation prices for the other good.

Exercise: ▶ ▶ ▶ ▶ ▶ ▶ ▶

***9.** A cosmetics firm is introducing a new skin moisturizer. It has decided to sell the new item by offering consumers a package of the moisturizer along with a designer scarf. The moisturizer costs $3 per unit to produce and the scarf costs $7 per unit to produce. Reservation prices of five consumers are given below.

a) What are the profit-maximizing prices to charge if the firm prices each product separately?

b) What is the profit-maximizing price to charge if the products are priced as a bundle?

c) Which pricing strategy delivers a higher profit?

Customer	Moisturizer	Scarf
1	$20	$ 5
2	$18	$12
3	$12	$18
4	$ 9	$21
5	$ 4	$24

Mixed bundling can be analyzed similarly. Suppose the monopolist offers both options to consumers—buy the bundle *or* buy either good separately. The bundle is only a worthwhile option if the bundle or package price is set below the sum of the two individual prices. To buy the bundle, the consumer must prefer that option to buying only one of the goods separately. If the single good prices are P_1 and P_2, and P_B is the price of the bundle, a consumer with reservation prices r_1 and r_2 would buy only good 1 if her surplus from buying good 1 alone is higher than that from buying the bundle, i.e., if $r_1 - P_1 > r_1 + r_2 - P_B$, or $P_B - P_1 > r_2$. Figure 11.8 (on the next page) shows the choices different consumers will make when a firm uses mixed bundling. Note that some consumers for whom the sum of the reservation prices exceeds the price of the bundle choose to buy only one of the goods. For these consumers, the additional cost of the bundle versus buying only one good is higher than their reservation price for the other good.

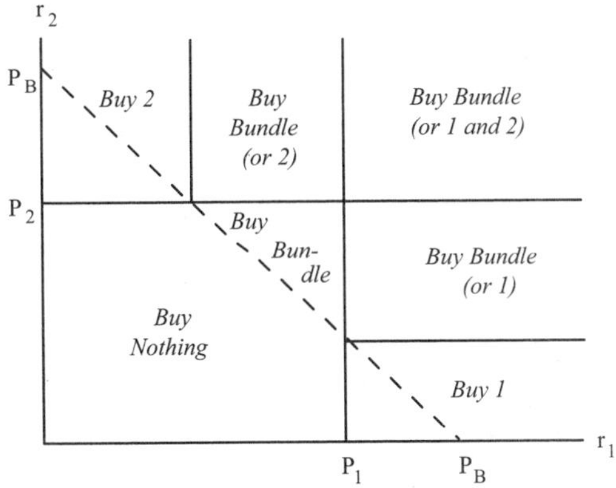

Figure 11.8

Exercise:

***10.** After the moisturizer has been successfully launched as a new product, the firm decides to consider another strategy—to offer the product for sale alone or with the scarf. The firm also decides to sell the scarf alone as well. Marginal cost for the moisturizer is $3 per unit and it is $7 per unit for the scarf. Which policy (separate pricing, pure bundling, or mixed bundling) is best, given the following consumer reservation prices?

Consumer	Moisturizer	Scarf
1	$22	$ 4
2	$17	$12
3	$13	$18
4	$12	$21
5	$ 5	$24
6	$ 8	$30
7	$12	$12

Tying occurs when a firm *requires* customers who buy one of their goods (the tying good) to buy another of their goods (the tied good). Xerox, for example, used to require companies leasing their Xerox machines to use only Xerox copying paper. Tying differs from bundling because the quantities purchased of the tied good vary across consumers. In the Xerox example, each consumer demands a different amount of copying paper. Tying can therefore be used as a way to meter demand, that is, customers who use the machine more intensively will demand more of the secondary good. Tying can also be used to protect customer goodwill connected with a brand name. Firms producing a specialized product, for example, may require customers to purchase a service contract through the same firm so that the firm can guarantee that repairs will be done properly and the customer will be satisfied with the product.

Tying also differs from bundling in that the first good (the Xerox machine) is useless without access to the secondary product (the paper). The firm has monopoly power only in the market for the machine; to sell the secondary good at a price above marginal cost it must tie the two goods together. If the tied good is sold above marginal cost, different consumers effectively pay different prices for the monopolized good (heavier users of supplies are probably willing to pay more for the machine).

*ADVERTISING (Section 11.6)

A successful advertising campaign will cause demand to shift to the right. Advertising raises fixed costs but leaves marginal costs unaffected. Since marginal cost is less than price for a firm with monopoly power, profit is increased if the firm can sell one more unit at the same price.

Exercise: ▶ ▶ ▶ ▶ ▶ ▶ ▶

***11.** a) Why will a Kansas wheat farmer not run advertisements encouraging consumers to buy more wheat or reminding consumers how good homemade bread can be? Who gains if the advertisements shift the market demand curve for wheat?

b) Despite the issues raised in part a), some goods sold in competitive markets are advertised. Examples are the "Got Milk?" and "Real Beef" campaigns. How do you think these advertisements are funded?

Explain how producers as a whole might benefit even if individual producers cannot profitably advertise.

To analyze advertising formally, let the firm's demand curve be a function of both price and advertising. For simplicity, measure advertising (A) in dollars, so its unit cost equals one. We can then write profit as:

$$\pi(P, A) = PQ(P, A) - C(Q) - A.$$

Using calculus, and setting $\partial\pi/\partial A = 0$, the profit-maximizing choice of advertising satisfies:

$$P(\partial Q/\partial A) - (dC/dQ)(\partial Q/\partial A) - 1 = 0, \text{ or}$$

$$MR_{Ads} = MC(\partial Q/\partial A) + 1.$$

The term on the left is the marginal revenue of advertising. The term on the right is the *full marginal cost of advertising* (MC of production times additional production required to meet demand on the margin plus the direct cost of advertising). Therefore, a firm should increase its advertising until the marginal revenue from an additional dollar of advertising equals the full marginal cost of the advertising (including marginal production cost for the additional sales that result from increased advertising).

Manipulating the equation describing the optimal choice of advertising yields

$$A/PQ = -E_A/E_P.$$

Therefore, the rule of thumb for setting the profit-maximizing advertising level is that the firm's advertising-to-sales ratio should be equal to minus the ratio of the advertising and price elasticities of demand.

Exercise: ◗ ◗ ◗ ◗ ◗ ◗ ◗

***12.** If a monopolist sells two products that have the same elasticity of demand with respect to advertising ($E^1_A = E^2_A$), but one of the products has a higher price-cost margin ($[P_1 - MC_1]/P_1 > [P_2 - MC_2]/P_2$), for which product should the firm spend a higher fraction of sales revenue on advertising?

PROBLEM SET

13. A monopolist sells Frisbees for use in two different markets: "Ultimate Frisbee" competitions (market 1) and play at the beach (market 2). The demand curves in the two markets are:

$$P_1 = 200 - Q_1 \quad \text{and} \quad P_2 = 190 - 3Q_2.$$

The cost function for producing Frisbees of either type is:

$$C(Q) = 500 + 40Q, \text{ where } Q = Q_1 + Q_2.$$

a) What are the profit-maximizing prices and quantities for the monopolist when it can sell at different prices in the two markets?

b) Suppose all consumers learn from a *Consumer Reports* study that the Frisbees sold in each market are identical. What is the total demand curve now? What are the monopolist's price and quantity now? (Hint: Write the demand curves with price on the right-hand side before adding them together to get the total demand curve.)

14. *[Bundling] A firm sells two different products to a market with three different types of consumers each of whom has different reservation prices. Consumers in group X have a reservation price of $15 for good 1 and $85 for good 2. Consumers in group Y have a reservation price of $60 for good 1 and $55 for good 2. Consumers in group Z have a reservation price of $75 for good 1 and $25 for good 2. Goods 1 and 2 each cost $20 per unit to produce.

a) If the firm sells both goods separately, what prices should it charge for goods 1 and 2? What profit will the firm earn with this policy?

b) Suppose the firm hires an economics student who suggests bundling the two goods and selling them as a package. What price should it charge under pure bundling (only selling the goods as a package)? What profit does the firm now earn?

c) Can the firm do even better with mixed bundling?

15. Matt Campbell has set up a for-profit tutoring service offering review sessions before economics tests. It costs him $5 per student for materials and $200 for the room and the tutor's wages to run a review session.

There are two different universities where Matt offers this service. Because of the distance between the campuses and the differences in course content, students only go to review sessions near their own campuses.

a) At Enormous University, the demand curve of students is $p_1 = 41 - 0.15q_1$. What is the profit-maximizing price and quantity?

b) At Middle University, the demand curve of students is $p_2 = 47 - 0.3q_2$. What is the profit-maximizing price and quantity?

c) Compare these solutions. Explain why price is higher in one market.

16. Suppose consumers are identical. Will an optimal two-part tariff be less efficient (create more deadweight loss) than perfect competition? Illustrate your answer.

***17.** Figure 11.9 displays the demand curves for low-demand (type 1) and high-demand (type 2) consumers. N_1 consumers have the D_1 demand curve and N_2 consumers have the D_2 demand curve. These demand curves can be written as:

(D_1) $p_1 = a_1 - bq_1$

(D_2) $p_2 = a_2 - bq_2$

We will refer to type 1 as low demanders and type 2 as high demanders. These demand curves have the same slope, but $a_2 > a_1$. Marginal cost and average total cost both equal k. The monopolist offers two different combinations of per-unit prices and fees. Consumers will have the choice of paying a fee F_1 to buy as many units as they wish at a per-unit price p_1 or paying a fee F_2 to buy as many units as they wish at a per-unit price p_2. In other words, a consumer who buys x units pays either $F_1 + p_1x$ or $F_2 + p_2x$. Assume that $F_1 < F_2$ and $p_2 < p_1$.

a) For an arbitrary p_1, what is the largest fee that type 1 consumers would pay? Show this in a diagram.

b) For $p_2 < p_1$ and F_1 equal to the largest fee that type 1 consumers will pay, what is the maximum fee that type 2 consumers are willing to pay in order to pay a per-unit price equal to p_2?

c) What is the profit-maximizing value of p_2? Explain why.

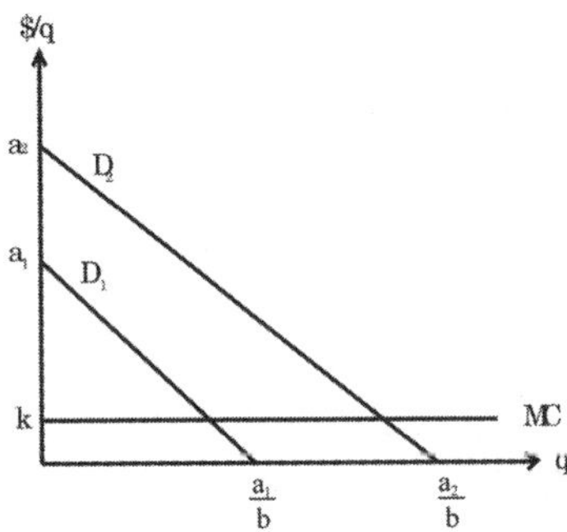

Figure 11.9

18. A monopoly seller of widgets in Amos, Iowa, has a constant marginal cost curve. Amos is a college town and the monopolist has two types of customers, college students and local residents. The demand curve for residents and the marginal cost curve are given in Figure 11.10.

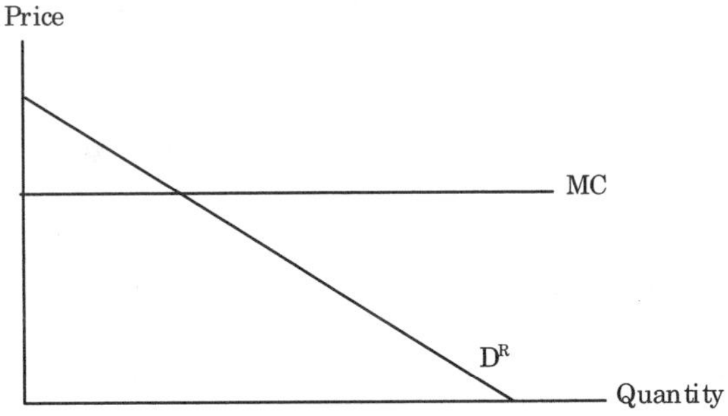

Figure 11.10

a) Draw a linear demand curve for college students such that the monopolist does not sell any of the product to college students when the monopolist must charge both groups the same price.

b) Now suppose that the monopolist can identify whether or not a purchaser is a student. Draw a linear demand curve for college students such that the monopolist does not sell any of the product to college students when the monopolist can charge different prices to the two groups.

SELF-TEST

19. A jewelry store does not set fixed prices for its products. Instead, the manager decides how much to charge each customer for each item. In this case, the store is practicing:
- a) first-degree price discrimination.
- b) second-degree price discrimination.
- c) third-degree price discrimination.
- d) tying.
- e) None of the above is correct.

20. During their annual sale, a liquor store gives a discount of 10 percent per bottle of wine if you buy one to five cases, and 20 percent if you buy more than five cases. The liquor store is practicing:
- a) first-degree price discrimination.
- b) second-degree price discrimination.
- c) third-degree price discrimination.
- d) bundling.
- e) None of the above is correct.

21. A pesticide manufacturer sells his product in two versions—a low-strength formula for retail sale in garden stores and a high-strength formula for sale to professional gardeners. The price per single application of pesticide is lower for professional gardeners. This firm is practicing:
- a) intertemporal price discrimination.
- b) second-degree price discrimination.
- c) third-degree price discrimination.
- d) peak-load pricing.
- e) None of the above is correct.

22. If the pesticide manufacturer in the above question is maximizing profit, then
- a) professional gardeners must have more elastic demand than homeowners.
- b) professional gardeners must have less elastic demand than homeowners.
- c) professional gardeners must buy smaller quantities of pesticide than homeowners.
- d) professional gardeners are more responsive to advertising.
- e) None of the above is correct.

23. Ski passes for weekend days are more expensive than on weekdays. An explanation for this is:
- a) peak-load pricing.
- b) less elastic demand on weekends than weekdays.
- c) more elastic demand on weekends than weekdays.
- d) a) and b)
- e) b) and c)

24. Two-part tariffs are:
a) a form of bundling.
b) profit-enhancing if consumers have different demand curves.
c) inefficient if all consumers are identical.
d) an uncommon price strategy.
e) None of the above is correct.

25. A monopolist practicing third-degree price discrimination will maximize profits by:
a) charging a higher price to the market segment with the more elastic demand.
b) equating the price-cost margin across market segments.
c) charging prices that equate marginal revenue in different markets.
d) setting an entry fee to extract all consumer surplus.
e) charging a price equal to marginal cost.

The next two questions use the following data: Forty thousand potential customers of a cable TV franchise are each willing to pay $11/month for HBO and $11/month for Cinemax. Twenty thousand potential customers are each willing to pay $20/month for HBO and only $5/month for Cinemax. Assume costs are zero.

26. If the two services are sold separately, the franchise should charge _____ for HBO and ______ for Cinemax.
a) $20 and $11
b) $11 and $11
c) $11 and $20
d) $11 and $5
e) $20 and $5

27. *[Bundling] If the franchise sells the two services in a bundle, it should charge:
a) $31.
b) $25.
c) $22.
d) $20.
e) $18.

28. *[Advertising] The Best Bakery sells a popular type of sandwich roll in Podunk. It spends 5 percent of sales revenue on advertising. It sells its rolls for $0.35 when each roll has a marginal cost of $0.25. If the firm is maximizing profits, its advertising elasticity of demand equals:
a) 0.2.
b) 0.175.
c) 0.143.
d) 0.125.
e) More information is needed.

29. Comparing first-degree price discrimination to perfect competition one can conclude that:
  a) total surplus is higher under competition.
  b) total surplus is lower under competition.
  c) producer surplus is lower and consumer surplus is higher under competition.
  d) marginal revenue is equal to price under competition, but not under first-degree price discrimination.
  e) deadweight loss is lower under competition.

30. Firms with market power attempt to capture consumer surplus through a variety of price discrimination practices. However, there can also be cost-based explanations for the price differences. Which of the following practices are likely to have cost justifications?
  a) A manufacturer sells brand-name cigarettes at a higher price than its identical generic cigarettes.
  b) A company passes along cost savings for large orders in the form of volume discounts.
  c) A company customizes its product or service for a particular buyer and charges more.
  d) All of the above are correct.
  e) Both a) and c) are correct.

ANSWERS TO CHAPTER 11

EXERCISE ANSWERS

1. Perfect first-degree price discrimination hurts consumers (like *a*) with reservation prices above P_m (the pure monopoly price) because they now pay more. Consumers with reservation prices below P_m but above MC (like *b*) are now offered the good at their reservation prices, so they are neither better nor worse off (i.e., they weren't buying before, and now they are buying but have no consumer surplus). Consumers with reservation prices below MC (like *c*) do not buy the good with or without discrimination.

2. Consumers 1, 2, and 4 each purchase the quantity where the demand curve intersects the price schedule. Consumer 3 is a more difficult case because her demand curve intersects the price schedule multiple times. In Figure 11A.1 (on the next page) we illustrate consumer 3's demand curve. Which intersection is best depends on the additional *net surplus* gained by purchasing the largest quantity (q_C) instead of the smallest quantity (q_A). (The consumer would never stop at q_B since $CS_A + CS_B < CS_A$.) Since CS_B is negative, the consumer will choose q_A if $CS_B + CS_C < 0$ (if the CS lost from moving from q_A to q_C is greater than the CS gained). She will choose q_C if $CS_B + CS_C > 0$ (if the CS gained by moving from q_A to q_C is greater than the CS lost). In this case, given the way the figure is drawn, $CS_B + CS_C < 0$, and she does better to buy q_A.

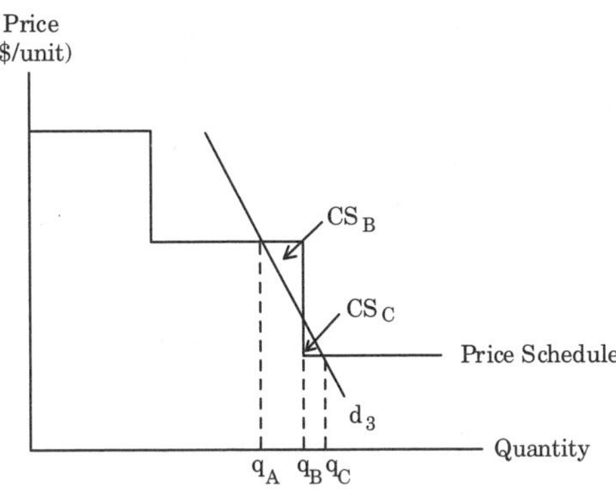

Figure 11A.1

3. a) The restaurants are choosing their pricing strategy to segment the market primarily on working versus non-working individuals. Although students and children and those who work out of the home could take advantage of these early bird specials, the primary market segment is retired senior citizens. They have the flexibility to eat earlier or later, which makes their demand more elastic. If they are offered a 50% discount for eating at 4 PM or 4:30 PM, many of them will take advantage of the deal.

b) Many other types of stores would be unable to prevent the elderly from buying and then reselling to younger people if discounts were offered. Even with the restaurants, if they applied the same pricing strategy to take-out food purchased between 4–6 PM, arbitrage might be too easy and too few people would purchase take-out after 6 PM. (Clearly there are arbitrage costs involved in doing this, which would also have to be taken into account.)

4. Recall the pricing rule of thumb from Chapter 10. Eliminating marginal cost from the equation gives us the price ratio as a function of the demand elasticities. Since $(P_i - MC)/P_i = -1/E_i$ where E_i is the demand elasticity in market i, we find $(3 - MC)/3 = -1/E_R$ and $(27 - MC)/27 = -1/E_D$, so "Lassie" perfume has a more elastic demand.

If $MC = 1$, then $(3-1)/3 = -1/E_R$ or $E_R = -3/2$ and $(27 - 1)/27 = -1/E_D$ or $E_D = -27/26$. Remember that a monopolist always chooses a price in the elastic portion of a linear market demand curve.

5. a) Set MR = MC in each market segment. (Recall that MR has the same intercept and twice the slope of a linear demand curve.)

First-class: $1{,}000 - 10Q = 100 \Rightarrow Q = 90$ and $P = \$550$, using the demand equation to determine the price.

Coach: $500 - 2Q = 100 \Rightarrow Q = 200$ and $P = \$300$.

b) $E_{first\text{-}class} = -bP/Q = -(1/5)(550/90) = -1.2$ (where –b is the slope of the demand equation
$Q = a-bP$).

$E_{coach} = -bP/Q = -1(300/200) = -1.5$.

Yes, these values for the demand elasticities in each market segment make sense, since the market segment with the less elastic demand is being charged the higher price.

6. a) Figure 11A.2 shows the off-peak price, P_1, is set where the AC curve crosses D_1. The utility will break even in off-peak periods. However, during peak periods, when demand increases to D_2, quantity rises to Q_2 and the firm will lose money since AC is above P_1 at Q_2.

b) In order for the utility to break even during peak periods, the peak price must be raised to P_2, where D_2 crosses the AC curve.

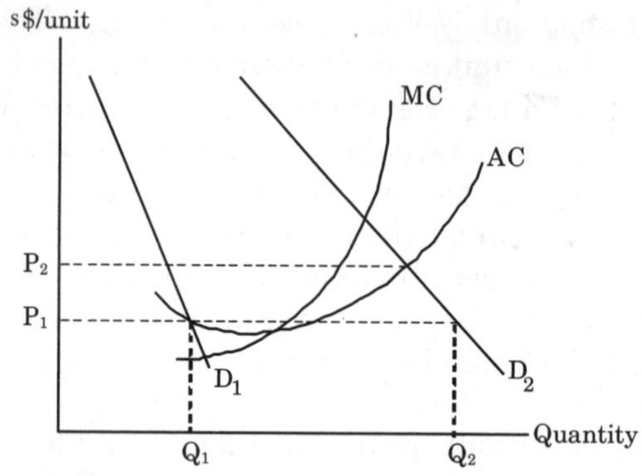

Figure 11A.2

7. If the country club set $P^* = 0$, consumers would demand $Q^* = 100$. Consumer surplus would be 0.5(100)(100) = \$5,000, which would be the entry fee or annual membership fee. Profits would therefore be: 0(100) – 10(100) + 5,000 = \$4,000. This is less than the \$4,050 profit earned by setting $P^* = 10$ and $T^* = \$4,050$.

8. At P = 10 and T = CS for the "low demand" consumers, as illustrated in Figure 11A.3, we have: $Q_H = 120$, $Q_L = 90$, and $CS_L = 0.5(90)(90) = \$4{,}050$. Since the firm is charging a unit price equal to marginal cost, its profit will come solely from the entry fee: $\pi = 2T = 2(4{,}050) = \$8{,}100$.

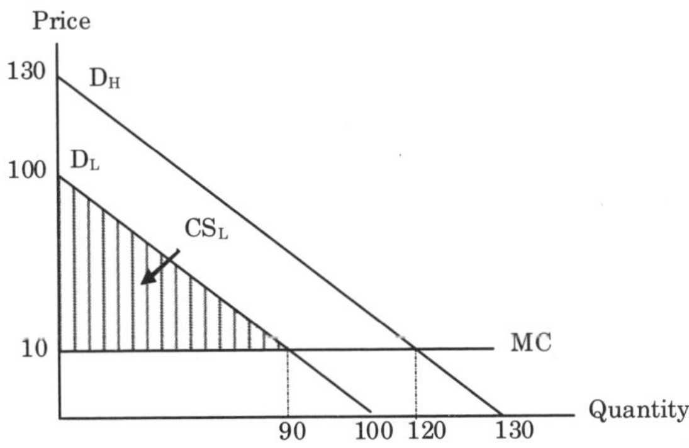

Figure 11A.3

If P = 15, then $Q_H = 115$, $Q_L = 85$, and $CS_L = 0.5(85)(85) = \$3{,}612.50$. Profits are $\pi = (P - MC)Q + 2T = (15 - 10)(115 + 85) + 2(3{,}612.5) = \$8{,}225$. Therefore, when consumers differ, the firm maximizes profit by charging a price above MC and a slightly lower entry fee.

9. a) To solve a bundling problem requires checking each possible price. This is simplified because the firm only benefits by cutting price if that attracts additional customers. Assume that a consumer buys as long as the price is *less than or equal to* his reservation price (if the price must be strictly less than the reservation price, we need to specify the smallest allowable price change).

For the moisturizer, check the following prices: \$20, \$18, \$12, \$9, and \$4. If P = \$20 profit is \$20 – \$3 = \$17 because only the first consumer buys. Profit if P = \$18 equals 2(\$18 – \$3) = \$30 because two customers buy. For P = \$12, \$9, and \$4, the logic is similar: $\pi(12) = 3(\$12 - \$3) = \$27$; $\pi(9) = 4(\$9 - \$3) = \$24$ and $\pi(4) = 5(\$4 - \$3) = \$5$. So the best price to charge for the moisturizer alone is \$18.

For the scarf we have: $\pi(24) = \$24 - \$7$ because only the fifth customer buys. Similarly, $\pi(21) = 2(\$21 - \$7) = \$28$; $\pi(18) = 3(\$18 - \$7) = \$33$; $\pi(12) = 4(\$12 - \$7) = \$20$; and $\pi(5) = 5(\$5 - \$7) = -\$10$. So the best price to charge for the scarf alone is \$18.

The total profit from selling separately equals \$30 + \$33, or \$63.

b) For pure bundling, add the two reservation prices for each consumer, and then check the profit at each relevant bundle price. The marginal cost of the bundle is \$10, the sum of the marginal costs of the separate items. Let P_B be the price of the bundle. Profit if $P_B = \$30$ is $\pi_B(30) = 3(\$30 - \$10) = \$60$ because the 2nd, 3rd, and 4th consumers buy the bundle at this price. If $P_B = \$28$, then $\pi_B(28) = 4(\$28 - \$10) = \$72$; and $\pi_B(25) = 5(\$25 - \$10) = \$75$. The best price for the bundle is therefore \$25 and profit is \$75.

c) Profit is higher with bundling (\$75 > \$63).

10. For separate pricing and pure bundling, we do the same analysis as above. First, find profit at each relevant price for the goods separately and for the bundle.

For selling the moisturizer alone, $\pi(12) = 5(\$12 - \$3) = \$45$ is the maximum profit available. For selling the scarf alone, $\pi(18) = 4(\$18 - \$7) = \$44$ is the maximum profit available. So, total profit from selling the goods separately is \$45 + \$44 = \$89.

For pure bundling, the relevant prices to consider are: \$38, \$33, \$31, \$29, \$26, and \$24. Profit from pure bundling is highest with $P_B = \$24$ because then all 7 customers buy the bundle for a profit of $\pi_B(24) = 7(\$24 - \$10) = \$98$.

Mixed bundling is more complex to analyze. For each price for the bundle, the number of consumers who will buy the bundle depends on the prices charged for each good alone. Let 1 = moisturizer and 2 = scarf, for simplicity:

If $P_B = \$38$, only the sixth consumer would be willing to buy the bundle and then only if $P_1 \geq \$8$ and $P_2 \geq \$30$. The best prices to charge separately in this case are $P_1 = \$12$ and $P_2 > \$30$. The sixth consumer will buy the bundle, and consumers 1, 2, 3, 4, and 7 will buy good 1. Let us write profit from mixed bundling as $\pi_M(P_B, P_1, P_2)$. So $\pi_M(38, 12, 31) = (\$38 - \$10) + 5(\$12 - \$3) = \$73$.

$\pi_M(33, 12, 31) = 2(\$33 - \$10) + 4(\$12 - \$3) = \$82$ because consumers 4 and 6 will buy the bundle and consumers 1, 2, 3, and 7 will buy good 1. No one buys only good 2.

$\pi_M(31, 17, 24) = 3(\$31 - \$10) + 2(\$17 - \$3) + (\$24 - \$7) = \$108$ because consumers 3, 4, and 6 buy the bundle, consumers 1 and 2 buy good 1, and consumer 5 buys good 2. Note that dropping the price of good 1 to \$12 would cause consumer 3 to switch from buying the bundle to buying only good 1, so that is not as profitable an alternative.

$\pi_M(29, 22, 31) = 5(\$29 - \$10) + (\$22 - \$3) = \$114$ because consumers 2, 3, 4, 5, and 6 buy the bundle, and consumer 1 buys only good 1.

$\pi_M(24, 19, 31) = 6(\$24 - \$10) + (\$19 - \$3) = \$100$ because everyone buys the bundle except consumer 1 who buys only good 1. Consumer 1 cannot be charged his reservation price for good 1, or else he would buy the bundle. Given the cost of good 2, the firm does better to sell him only good 1.

Mixed bundling is the best alternative (\$114 > \$98 > \$89).

11. a) The competitive wheat farmer produces up to the point where P = MC. The farmer is already selling the profit-maximizing quantity and does not wish to sell any more wheat at the going price. If advertising raised the price of wheat, all wheat farmers would benefit.

b) Trade associations fund these ad campaigns. That is, a group of producers collectively raises funds to advertise. If the group includes all producers, they benefit from shifting the demand curve to the right, since profits increase (as long as the supply curve is upward sloping). Note that, if the supply curve is horizontal, shifting the demand curve to the right leaves profits unchanged.

12. The firm should spend more on advertising as a fraction of sales revenue in the market with the higher price-cost margin. This is the market with less elastic demand (E_P is smaller in absolute value). Since $A/PQ = -E_A/E_P$ is the rule of thumb, the firm should spend more in market 1.

PROBLEM SET ANSWERS

13. a) First, find marginal revenue in each market: $MR_1 = 200 - 2Q_1$ and $MR_2 = 190 - 6Q_2$. Since marginal cost is constant at \$40, we can solve for output and price in each market separately.

In market 1, $MR_1 = MC$ means $200 - 2Q_1 = 40$, or $Q_1^* = 80$ and $P_1^* = \$120$. In market 2, $MR_2 = MC$, so $190 - 6Q_2 = 40$ or $Q_2^* = 25$ and $P_2^* = \$115$.

b) When the firm cannot price discriminate, $P_1 = P_2$. We need to rewrite the demand curves with Q on the left-hand side and then sum the two curves to get market demand. $Q_1 = 200 - P_1$, and $Q_2 = 63.33 - P_2/3$. With equal prices, $Q = Q_1 + Q_2 = 263.33 - 4P/3$. The inverse demand curve is therefore $P = 197.5 - 0.75Q$. The marginal revenue curve without discrimination is $MR = 197.5 - 1.5Q$. Setting MR = MC, we obtain $197.5 - 1.5Q = 40$, or $Q^* = 105$ and $P^* = 118.75$.

14. a) Selling the goods separately, the best prices are $P_1 = 60$ and $P_2 = 55$. The firm sells each good to two consumers. Total profits are $\pi_1 + \pi_2 = 2(60 - 20) + 2(55 - 20) = 150$.

b) For pure bundling, only two bundle prices need be considered: 115 and 100. At $P_B = 115$, only one bundle is sold. At $P_B = 100$, three bundles are sold: $\pi_B(100) = 3(100 - 40) = 180$.

c) With mixed bundling, one possibility is to sell the bundle for \$115, good 1 at \$75, and good 2 at \$85. $\pi_M(115, 75, 85) = (115 - 40) + (75 - 20) + (85 - 20) = 195$. If the bundle price is dropped to 100, all consumers buy the bundle, so profit would equal 180. The best outcome for the firm is mixed bundling.

15. a) $MR_1 = 41 - 0.3q_1$. Setting $MR_1 = MC$, we obtain $41 - 0.3q_1 = 5$, or $q_1 = 36/0.3 = 120$. Substituting back into the demand curve, we obtain $p_1 = 41 - 0.15(120) = \$23$.

b) $MR_2 = 47 - 0.6q_2$. Setting $MR_2 = MC$, we obtain $47 - 0.6q_1 = 5$, or $q_2 = 42/0.6 = 70$. Substituting back into the demand curve, we obtain $p_2 = 47 - 0.3(70) = \$26$.

c) Market 2 has the higher price and a smaller quantity sold. What matters is comparing the elasticities in the two markets to see which one would have the higher price. $E_d^1 = -\frac{1}{.15}\frac{23}{120} = -1.28$ and $E_d^2 = -\frac{1}{.3}\frac{26}{70} = -1.24$. Thus, we see that the market with less elastic demand faces the higher price.

16. An optimal two-part tariff with only one consumer type consists of P* = MC and an entry fee, T, equal to all consumer surplus at that price, as shown in Figure 11A.4. There is no deadweight loss because Q* is the same as it would be under perfect competition.

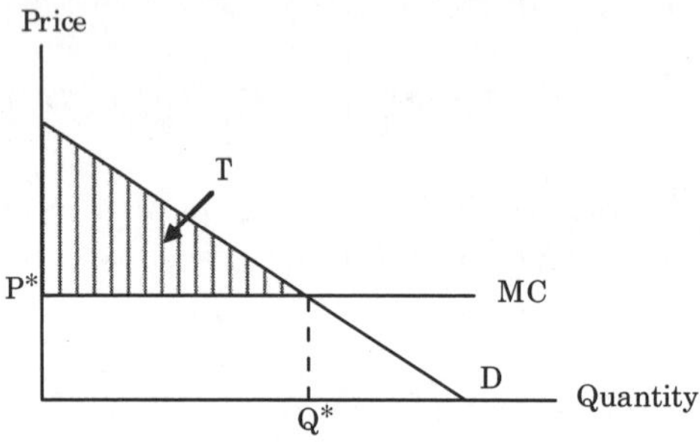

Figure 11A.4

17. a) See Figure 11A.5a. For any per-unit charge p_1, low-demand consumers will pay their entire consumer surplus as a fee.

b) The monopolist cannot extract all surplus from a high-demand consumer because these individuals could choose the (F_1, p_1) combination, which would give them positive consumer surplus. Thus, the shaded region in Figure 11.A.5b (on the next page) equals the maximum fee that high-demand consumers would be willing to pay to pay p_2 per unit.

c) The profit-maximizing value of p_2 is k. Just as with identical consumers, lowering p_2 toward k increases the amount of surplus that can then be extracted as a fee by more than the cost of providing the additional output.

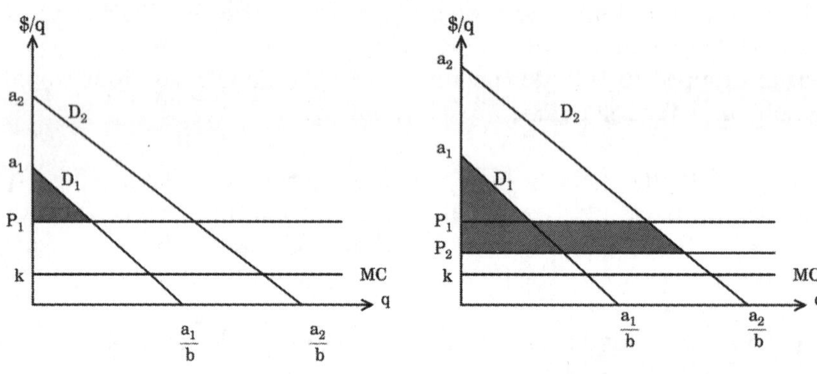

Figure 11A.5a Figure 11A.5b

18. a) Start with Figure 11A.6a, where D^R is resident demand, D^S is student demand and D^T is total demand (the slightly heavier line that follows D^R until P_0 and then is the horizontal sum of D^R and D^S below P_0). Marginal revenue from the D^T demand curve comes in two pieces. The first piece follows the MR^R curve up to Q_0, since only the D^R curve is relevant for quantities between zero and Q_0. The second piece (for quantities greater than Q_0) follows what MR^T would be if D^T were the only relevant demand curve. In other words, imagine extending D^T to the vertical axis and then drawing MR^T with the same intercept as D^T and twice the slope. Putting the two pieces together, Figure 11A.6a shows the final MR^T curve (the much heavier line).

Now that you have MR^T you can find the desired D^S that leads to zero sales to college students when the monopolist must charge both groups the same price. Intuitively, there will be zero sales to students if the price, P*, falls on the D^R demand curve and not the D^T demand curve. Figure 11A.6b illustrates this case. P* is the monopoly price (from the intersection of MR^T and MC at Q*) that satisfies this condition. Without price discrimination, there are no sales to students if the only intersection of MR^T (the marginal revenue curve for the two groups together) and MC is the same as the intersection of MR^R and MC.

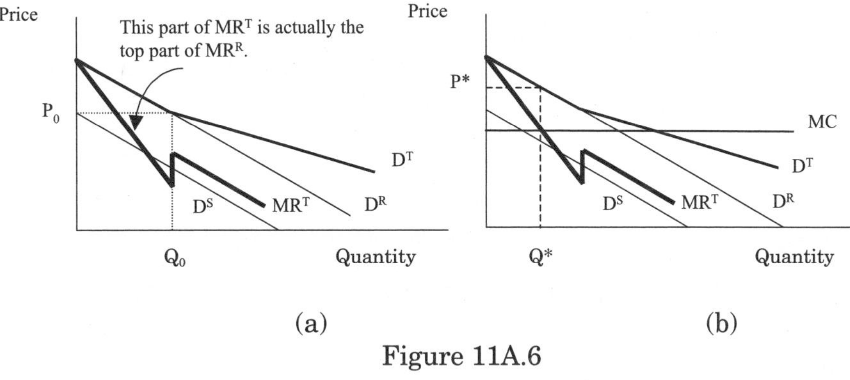

(a) (b)

Figure 11A.6

b) See Figure 11A.6c. With third-degree price discrimination, the question is simply whether MR^S is less than MC when $Q^S = 0$.

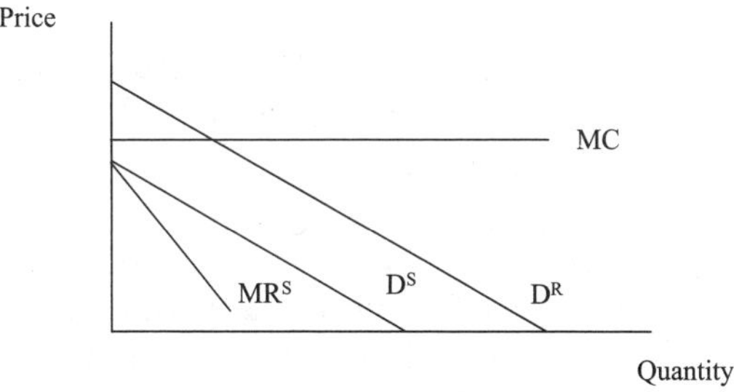

(c)

Figure 11A.6

SELF-TEST ANSWERS

19. a) Each customer pays the manager's estimate of their reservation price.

20. b) This is declining-block pricing, which is a form of second-degree price discrimination.

21. c) The firm has segmented the two markets according to the strength of the pesticide.

22. a) The lower price is charged in the market with more elastic demand.

23. d) Both peak-load pricing and third-degree price discrimination may be at work. We cannot say for sure without knowing if costs vary between peak and off-peak times.

24. b) Although not all surplus can be extracted when consumers' demand differs, two-part tariffs may still be profitable. Two-part tariffs can be just as efficient as perfect competition if consumers are identical and price is set at marginal cost (therefore, choice c) is wrong). Choice d) is certainly not true—separating prices into two components, an entry fee and a usage fee, is quite common. Examples are country club pricing or fitness club pricing (an initial membership fee and monthly fees as well) and utility bills (a charge for being connected and a separate charge for usage).

25. c) Under third-degree price discrimination the firm should set price such that $MR_1 = MR_2 = MC$. This will lead to a higher price in the market segment with the less elastic demand curve.

26. b) The cable franchise would earn revenues of \$11(40,000) + 11(20,000) = \$660,000 if it set P_{HBO} = \$11. It would earn revenues of 20(20,000) = \$400,000 if P_{HBO} = \$20. Therefore, the cable franchise should set P_{HBO} = \$11.

The franchise would earn revenues of \$11(40,000) = \$440,000 if it set $P_{Cinemax}$ = \$11. It would earn revenues of \$5(40,000 + 20,000) = \$300,000 if $P_{Cinemax}$ = \$5. Therefore, the cable franchise should set $P_{Cinemax}$ = \$11.

27. c) If the cable company charges a bundle price of \$22 then revenue is (40,000 + 20,000)22 = \$1,320,000. If the bundle price were \$25, revenues would be 25(20,000) = \$500,000. Note that bundling induces all customers to buy both services. Even though the total price (\$22) is the same as in Question 26, bundling is more profitable.

28. b) Use the pricing rule of thumb from Chapter 10: $-1/E_D = (P - MC)/P = (0.35 - 0.25)/0.35 = 0.2857$. Thus, $E_D = -3.5$. Since $-E_A/E_D = A/PQ = 0.05$, then $-E_A/-3.5 = 0.05$ or $E_A = 0.175$.

29. c) First-degree price discrimination extracts all consumer surplus, but it leads to the same output level as competition.

30. d) If the cigarette manufacturer uses different packaging or distribution methods for its generic cigarettes, the price difference may partially reflect a cost difference. Volume discounts are often cost-justified, if there are economies of scale, as well as savings in planning and shipping. There could clearly be additional costs of customizing a product that would need to be passed on to the consumer.

CHAPTER 12
MONOPOLISTIC COMPETITION AND OLIGOPOLY

IMPORTANT CONCEPTS

- Features of Monopolistic Competition
- Features of Oligopoly
- Models of Oligopoly
    - Cournot
    - Stackelberg
    - Bertrand
    - Prisoners' Dilemma
    - Dominant Firm
    - Cartel
- Nash Equilibrium
- Reaction Curve
- Elements of Game Theory
    - Payoff Matrix

CHAPTER HIGHLIGHTS

A monopoly market structure is an extreme form of imperfect competition. Two other, more common, forms, are considered in this chapter. One is *monopolistic competition*, which exists when many sellers compete to sell a differentiated product, and entry by new firms is not restricted. Due to the large number of firms in the market, no individual firm considers its rival's reaction when setting its price or quantity. This is a characteristic shared with perfect competition. However, because each firm sells a differentiated product, each firm faces a downward-sloping demand curve (sales decline if price is raised, but not to zero). This is a characteristic shared with monopoly. In the short-run, firms maximize profits by setting marginal revenue equal to marginal cost. Above-normal profits are earned if price exceeds average cost. In the long run, this profit will induce entry by other firms. Entry will continue in a monopolistically competitive market until each firm is earning zero economic profit in long-run equilibrium. That is, in the long-run equilibrium we have MR = MC and P = AC, which means that the demand curve will be just tangent to the firm's average cost curve.

Two sources of inefficiency arise in monopolistic competition: (1) price exceeds marginal cost, and (2) each firm has *excess capacity* that it is not utilizing (i.e., each firm sets output below the output level corresponding to minimum long-run average cost).

The second form of imperfect competition, *oligopoly,* focuses on the behavior of large firms in markets where there are only a few firms that account for most of the market. The other important characteristic of oligopoly is the "mutual interdependence" of the firms. Each firm is aware that price or output choices made by any one firm affects every other firm's profits. This mutual interdependence implies that oligopolistic firms must consider rivals' short-term and long-term reactions to any change in strategy.

Oligopoly theory has two principal branches, called cooperative and noncooperative. The *Cournot*, *Stackelberg*, and *Bertrand* models considered in this chapter are models of noncooperative behavior. In noncooperative models, each firm does the best it can given what its competitors are doing. This is the basis of *Nash equilibrium*. Each of these three models starts with a different assumption about what the firm assumes its competitors will do, but they all apply the Nash equilibrium concept.

In the Cournot model, firms compete by choosing quantities, and all firms make their decisions at the same time. The *reaction curve* for each firm shows how much it will produce as a function of how much it thinks its rival will produce. The Cournot equilibrium occurs at the intersection of the two reaction curves. In equilibrium, this leads to a total output level that is less than that of perfect competition but more than that of pure monopoly.

In the Stackelberg model, the firms again compete by choosing quantity, but one firm is able to choose first. The "leader" in the Stackelberg model sets its output first, and then the "follower" observes the leader's output and makes its own output decision. Going first gives the leader a first-mover advantage: the leader will produce more than the follower and earn a higher profit.

The Bertrand model is a model of price competition. Each firm must decide what price to set, treating the price of its competitor as fixed. With homogeneous products, the Nash equilibrium is the competitive outcome; i.e., both firms set price equal to marginal cost. With differentiated products, the equilibrium Bertrand price will be greater than under perfect competition but less than under pure monopoly.

Game theory can be used to illustrate the basic features of a noncooperative game. The *payoff matrix* of a game shows the profit to each firm, given its decision and the decision of its rival. The classic noncooperative game is called the *Prisoners' Dilemma*, in which each firm independently does the best it can, taking its competitors into account. Each firm, trying to maximize profits, will compete aggressively, but both firms would be better off if they cooperated. Each firm will have an incentive to "cheat" and undercut its rivals. In a one-period game, the competitive outcome will always be the equilibrium of the game because there is no chance of future punishment.

In a dynamic setting, *price leadership* may be one way to communicate (through market signals) to competitors that a higher price or more passive form of competition would make all players better off.

The firm with a reputation as the price leader does not necessarily have to be the largest firm in the market. In the *dominant firm model*, we explicitly look at markets with one large firm and a group of smaller (*fringe*) firms. The dominant firm finds the profit-maximizing price by setting marginal revenue from its demand curve (which is found by subtracting the supply of the fringe firms from the market demand) equal to marginal cost. Once the dominant firm sets the price, the fringe firms take that price as given and determine output from their supply curve.

A *cartel* is an explicit agreement between firms to coordinate their activities with the goal of raising price above the competitive level. Profits will be maximized when output is set where cartel marginal revenue equals marginal cost. The cartel output must then be divided into individual production quotas for each firm. Each member will be tempted to cheat on the agreement by selling more than its quota at a slightly lower price. This incentive to cheat creates chronic instability problems for the cartel.

CONCEPT REVIEW AND EXERCISES

MONOPOLISTIC COMPETITION (Section 12.1)

In *monopolistic competition*, there are many firms and no barriers to entry, but each firm's product differs to some extent from its competitors' products. In perfect competition firms sell the identical product, but in monopolistic competition products are differentiated. Each firm has some market power and faces a downward-sloping demand curve. For example, due to copyright protection, no rival publisher can sell this textbook, so Pearson has a monopoly on this particular book. However, two factors limit its market power: competition from publishers selling similar books, and free entry into textbook publication.

Product differentiation is crucial for monopolistic competition. It can take many forms, including differences in quality, ingredients, features, and durability. Location is another form of product differentiation. The convenience store nearest you would not lose all its customers if it raised its prices by a small amount—some consumers are willing to pay the higher price for convenience; if not, they would go to lower-priced supermarkets. As long as there is some product differentiation and entry is free, it is more appropriate to model the market as monopolistic competition than perfect competition.

Exercise: ▶ ▶ ▶ ▶ ▶ ▶ ▶

1. Would you describe your local restaurant market as monopolistically competitive? Why or why not?

In the short run, a firm in a monopolistically competitive market behaves just like a monopolist. It chooses to produce the output at which marginal revenue equals marginal cost. The firm's short-run demand curve slopes downward (because of the market power that product differentiation creates), so marginal revenue is less than price. In the long run, industry equilibrium requires that no firms wish to enter or exit. In the symmetric case when all firms are identical, all firms earn zero profits. Analogous to the case of perfect competition in the long run, each firm is trying to earn as much profit as possible, but above normal profits will attract new firms with competing products, driving profits to zero. Because each firm maximizes profit, marginal revenue equals marginal cost; and because there is free entry, price equals average total cost in long-run equilibrium. Together, these two conditions mean that the firm's demand curve is tangent to its average total cost curve at its profit-maximizing output, as shown in Figure 12.1. Although MR = MC, P > MC due to downward-sloping demand.

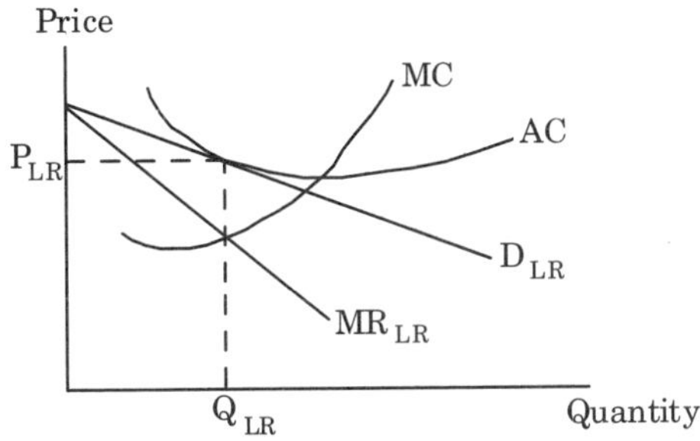

Figure 12.1

Exercise: ▶ ▶ ▶ ▶ ▶ ▶ ▶

2. At its current output level of 10, a monopolistically competitive firm has MR = 4, MC = 4, ATC = 6, and P = 8. Is this market in long-run equilibrium? If not, describe the adjustment process necessary to achieve long-run equilibrium.

Since price exceeds marginal cost in a monopolistically competitive market, too little output is being produced. There is a deadweight loss created by both the markup of price over marginal cost and by the fact that less output is produced than would be under perfect competition. A second inefficiency arises because each monopolistically competitive firm operates with *excess capacity*. In other words, the output level Q_{LR} in Figure 12.1 is to the left of minimum average cost. Society would be better off in terms of minimizing production costs if there were fewer firms, each producing at minimum average cost. However, this measure of loss ignores any gains to society from product differentiation. Each firm's customers place some value on being able to buy that particular variety. As a result, there is no general conclusion we can draw regarding the gains from additional variety versus the losses from underproduction by each firm.

OLIGOPOLY (Section 12.2)

In an *oligopoly* there are only a few firms. Products may be differentiated or homogeneous. Oligopoly can arise if *barriers to entry* (such as scale economies, patents, access to a specialized technology) prevent new firms from entering. In making strategic decisions, each firm must consider its rivals' reactions to those decisions. The basic concept for analyzing strategic behavior is the *Nash equilibrium*, which is discussed in more detail in Chapter 13. In a Nash equilibrium, each firm is doing the best it can, *given* what its rivals are doing. As a result, in a Nash equilibrium no firm has an incentive to change its action.

THE COURNOT MODEL

In the *Cournot model* of oligopoly, each firm must decide how much to produce and the firms make their decisions at the same time. Consider a market where two firms produce a homogeneous output and sell the output at the market-clearing price. The market price depends on the output choices of *both* firms. Each individual firm chooses its output, treating the output of its rival as fixed. Let P(Q) be the demand curve for the product where $Q = Q_1 + Q_2$. Firm 1's total cost is $C_1(Q_1)$, and Firm 2's total cost is $C_2(Q_2)$. The Nash equilibrium is a pair of outputs, Q_1^* and Q_2^*, that satisfies:

$$Q_1^* \text{ maximizes } \pi_1 \text{ given } Q_2^*,$$
and
$$Q_2^* \text{ maximizes } \pi_2 \text{ given } Q_1^*.$$

In equilibrium, neither firm can gain by producing a different quantity, given the rival's choice. To find the Nash equilibrium, we must solve simultaneously to find the pair of outputs satisfying these conditions.

Let's work through an example with a linear demand curve and constant marginal cost. The demand curve is $P = 400 - 2Q = 400 - 2(Q_1 + Q_2) = 400 - 2Q_1 - 2Q_2$. Marginal cost is constant (and equals average total cost) for both firms at \$10 per unit. The profits of the two firms are:

$$\pi_1 = PQ_1 - C_1 = (400 - 2Q_1 - 2Q_2)Q_1 - 10Q_1$$

$$\pi_2 = (400 - 2Q_1 - 2Q_2)Q_2 - 10Q_2.$$

Suppose Firm 1 expects Firm 2 to produce 65 units. The demand curve facing Firm 1 is then $P = 400 - 2Q_1 - 2Q_2 = 400 - 2Q_1 - 2(65) = 270 - 2Q_1$. This is the *residual demand curve* facing Firm 1, *given* that Firm 2 sells 65 units. Marginal revenue for this residual demand curve is $MR = 270 - 4Q_1$. Firm 1 acts as a monopolist over its residual demand curve—that part of the market that it believes it has access to, given that it expects Firm 2 to produce 65 units. Therefore, Firm 1 chooses output such that $MR(Q_1) = MC(Q_1)$ or $270 - 4Q_1 = 10$, which yields the solution $Q_1 = 65$.

Exercise: ▶ ▶ ▶ ▶ ▶ ▶ ▶

3. If Firm 2 produces 45 units, how many units will Firm 1 choose to produce? If Firm 2 produces 85 units, how many units will Firm 1 choose to produce?

For this example, $Q_1^* = 65$ and $Q_2^* = 65$ is the Nash equilibrium (we will solve this problem formally below). That is, if Firm 1 produces 65 units, Firm 2 will produce 65 units and vice versa. To verify this, we need to derive Firm 2's residual demand curve, and find its marginal revenue. Since the firms are identical, we can immediately write Firm 2's residual demand as $Q_1 = 65$ as $P = 270 - 2Q_2$ and therefore $MR(Q_2) = 270 - 4Q_2$. Setting $MR(Q_2) = 10$ yields $Q_2^* = 65$. Firm 2's best output choice is 65 when it expects Firm 1 to produce 65. The same is true for Firm 1. This is a Nash equilibrium: neither firm has an incentive to deviate from selling 65 units, given that the other firm is selling 65 units. Finally, we can solve for the market price: at $Q_1 + Q_2 = 130$, $P^* = 400 - 2(130) = 140$.

In general, the residual demand curve for Firm 1 is $\overline{P}(Q_1) = 400 - 2\overline{Q}_2 - 2Q_1$, where $\overline{Q}_2$ is the fixed output of Firm 2. Thus, $\overline{MR}(Q_1) = 400 - 2\overline{Q}_2 - 4Q_1$ (just think of $\overline{Q}_2$ as part of the intercept term). Equating $\overline{MR}$ and MC, Firm 1 produces $400 - 2\overline{Q}_2 - 4Q_1 = 10$, or $Q_1 = 97.5 - \overline{Q}_2/2$. Similarly, $Q_2 = 97.5 - \overline{Q}_1/2$. These two equations are called the *reaction curves*: they show how the profit maximizing output choice of one firm changes depending on how much it thinks its rival will produce. The simultaneous solution to these two equations is $Q_1^* = Q_2^* = 65$; this is the *Cournot equilibrium,* shown in Figure 12.2. Profit for Firm 1 is $\pi_1 = 140(65) - 10(65) = \$8{,}450$. Since Firm 2 has the same costs and output, $\pi_2 = \$8{,}450$ as well. Neither firm can do better given its rival's output.

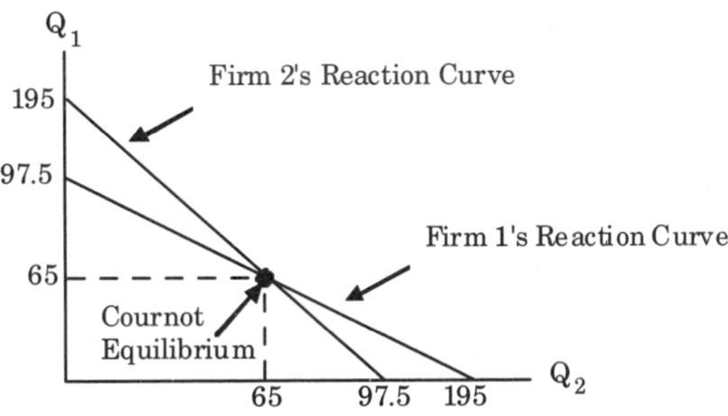

Figure 12.2

Total output in the Cournot equilibrium lies between the competitive output and the monopoly output. The competitive equilibrium is found by setting P = MC or $400 - 2Q = 10$, to find $Q_C = 195$. The monopoly outcome occurs where MR for the market demand curve equals MC or $400 - 4Q = 10$, which yields $Q_m = 97.5$. Therefore, the Cournot output of the two firms, which is $Q_1 + Q_2 = 130$, is greater than the monopoly output, but less than the competitive output.

*For those of you who prefer to approach this problem using calculus, you can solve for the Cournot equilibrium by differentiating profit with respect to Q_1 and Q_2. Since each firm chooses its output given its rival's output, the first order conditions for profit maximization for Firm 1 and Firm 2 are $\partial\pi_1/\partial Q_1 = 0$ and $\partial\pi_2/\partial Q_2 = 0$, or:

$$\partial\pi_1/\partial Q_1 = 400 - 4Q_1 - 2\overline{Q}_2 - 10 = 0, \text{ and}$$

$$\partial\pi_2/\partial Q_2 = 400 - 2\overline{Q}_1 - 4Q_2 - 10 = 0.$$

The first equation can be written as $Q_1 = 97.5 - \overline{Q}_2/2$, which is Firm 1's reaction curve. Firm 2's reaction curve is $Q_2 = 97.5 - \overline{Q}_1/2$. The simultaneous solution to these two equations is the Cournot equilibrium. As above, we find $Q_1^* = 65$ and $Q_2^* = 65$.

Exercise: ▶ ▶ ▶ ▶ ▶ ▶ ▶

4. Let market demand be given by $P = 1{,}000 - 0.1Q$. Marginal cost for Firm 1 is $MC_1 = 100$, while marginal cost for Firm 2 is $MC_2 = 190$.
   a) Find the residual demand curve for Firm 1 when $Q_2 = \overline{Q}_2$. Use this to find Firm 1's marginal revenue curve and its reaction curve.
   b) Find the residual demand curve for Firm 2 when $Q_1 = \overline{Q}_1$. Use this to find Firm 2's marginal revenue curve and its reaction curve.
   c) Calculate the Cournot equilibrium quantities by finding the intersection of the reaction curves.

FIRST MOVER ADVANTAGE—THE STACKELBERG MODEL

The Cournot model assumes simultaneous output choice. In contrast, the *Stackelberg model* assumes that firms move sequentially—one firm chooses its output first before the other. After the industry leader chooses its production, the follower observes the leader's output and then chooses how much to produce. Because the leader can look ahead and plan for the follower's reaction, the leader has a strategic advantage. It can commit to its output in advance of its rival, thereby forcing the rival to respond accordingly.

Suppose Firm 1 moves first. Profit for Firm 1 is:

$$\pi_1 = P(Q_1 + Q_2)Q_1 - C_1(Q_1),$$

where we've written $P(Q_1 + Q_2)$ to remind you that the market price is a function of *both* Q_1 and Q_2. After Firm 1 has chosen its output, Firm 2 can do no better than to maximize π_2, given Q_1.

We can solve for the Stackelberg equilibrium by finding Firm 1's marginal revenue (taking into account the change in Firm 2's output that will result), and then solving for the level of Firm 1's output at which $MR_1(Q_1) = MC_1(Q_1)$. Using the demand and cost curves from the Cournot example above, Firm 1's total revenue is:

$$R_1 = PQ_1 = (400 - 2\overline{Q}_2 - 2Q_1)Q_1.$$

Substituting in Firm 2's reaction curve:

$$R_1 = 400Q_1 - 2(97.5 - Q_1/2)Q_1 - 2Q_1^2$$
$$= 205Q_1 - Q_1^2.$$

Recall that $MR_1 = \partial R_1/\partial Q_1$. Setting $MR_1 = MC_1$ implies:

$$205 - 2Q_1 = 10,$$
$$\text{or } Q_1^* = 97.5.$$

When $Q_1^* = 97.5$, Firm 2 will do best to produce $Q_2^* = 97.5 - 97.5/2 = 48.75$.

Therefore, $\pi_1 = (400 - 2Q_1 - 2Q_2)Q_1 - 10Q_1 = (107.5)97.5 - 10(97.5) = \$9{,}506.25$, and $\pi_2 = (400 - 2Q_1 - 2Q_2)Q_2 - 10Q_2 = (107.5)48.75 - 10(48.75) = \$4{,}753.13$. Moving first gives Firm 1 a clear advantage.

Exercise:

5. Two firms have the same constant average and marginal cost, AC = MC = 20, and face the market demand curve $P = 500 - Q = 500 - (Q_1 + Q_2)$. Suppose Firm 1 is the Stackelberg leader.
   a) Find Firm 2's Cournot reaction curve.
   b) Write out the expression for Firm 1's total revenue and substitute in Firm 2's reaction curve.
   c) Derive MR_1 from your answer to part b) and set it equal to MC to find the profit maximizing output for Firm 1. Find the profit-maximizing output level for Firm 2 (the follower) from its reaction curve.
   d) What are profits for each firm?

PRICE COMPETITION (Section 12.3)

In the Cournot model firms choose output levels and let the market determine the price. In many markets it is more reasonable to use the *Bertrand* model, which assumes that firms are competing by choosing price rather than quantity. Consider what will happen in this market if two firms start out charging the same markup over marginal cost. If their products are identical, one firm will surely realize that they could capture *all* sales in the market by charging slightly less than their rival. The rival will also figure this out and undercut the first firm, as long as price is still greater than marginal cost. The only price that no one will want to undercut is the competitive price. Stated another way, when two identical firms compete on price, the equilibrium price is the competitive price. (The assumption that each firm has enough capacity to serve all customers is crucial for this result.)

We can also consider price competition between oligopolists with differentiated products. As in monopolistic competition, each firm has a downward-sloping demand curve for its product, which depends on rivals' prices, as well as its own price. The profits for each firm are:

$$\pi_1 = P_1Q_1(P_1, P_2) - C(Q_1(P_1, P_2)) \text{ and}$$

$$\pi_2 = P_2Q_2(P_1, P_2) - C(Q_2(P_1, P_2)).$$

The necessary conditions for the Bertrand equilibrium (the Nash equilibrium when firms choose prices) are:

$$\partial\pi_1(P_1,P_2)/\partial P_1 = 0 \text{ and } \partial\pi_2(P_1,P_2)/\partial P_2 = 0.$$

These equations give us the reaction curves, which are set equal to each other to determine the Nash equilibrium.

To summarize, with homogeneous products, the Bertrand equilibrium is the competitive equilibrium, where price equals marginal cost. With differentiated products, prices exceed marginal costs, but are less than what a monopoly would charge.

Exercise: ◗ ◗ ◗ ◗ ◗ ◗ ◗

6. *[Calculus] If $C(Q_1) = 10Q_1$ and $C(Q_2) = 5Q_2$, find the differentiated-products Bertrand equilibrium, given the following demand curves:

$$Q_1(P_1,P_2) = 1{,}000 - 20P_1 + 15P_2 \text{ and}$$

$$Q_2(P_1,P_2) = 800 + 5P_1 - 15P_2.$$

(Hint: First, derive the reaction functions $P_1(P_2)$ and $P_2(P_1)$. Then find the intersection of these reaction functions.)

COMPETITION VERSUS COLLUSION: THE PRISONERS' DILEMMA (Section 12.4)

Game theory is concerned with the general analysis of strategic interaction. The basic elements of any game are the players, strategies, and the associated payoffs. A game can be depicted in the form of a *payoff matrix*. A simple, one-period, two-firm game is written below, where the payoffs refer to profits for each firm: the first number in each cell is the profit for Firm 1 and the second number (after the comma) is profit for Firm 2.

		Firm 2	
		Low Output	High Output
Firm 1	Low Output	\$100, \$100	\$20, \$130
	High Output	\$130, \$20	\$50, \$50

In the above game there are two identical firms in the industry. Each firm has two possible strategies: produce at a low output level or produce at a high output level. The two firms must make their decisions simultaneously and independently. For example, if Firm 1 chooses "low" and Firm 2 chooses "high" then Firm 1 receives a payoff of \$20 and Firm 2 receives a payoff of \$130.

What should Firm 1 do? Firm 1 has no control over which strategy Firm 2 will select, so Firm 1 must analyze all of the possibilities. If Firm 2 produces "low," Firm 1 should produce "high" (since \$130 > \$100). If Firm 2 produces "high," Firm 1 should produce "high" (since \$50 > \$20). In this game, Firm 1 should choose "high" *no matter what Firm 2 does.* Firm 2 will reason exactly the same way. Thus, the equilibrium outcome is for both firms to produce "high."

This famous game is known as the *Prisoners' Dilemma.* Each firm, trying to maximize its own profits, will produce "high," but both firms would be better off if they both produced "low."

Exercise: ◗ ◗ ◗ ◗ ◗ ◗ ◗

7. Consider the following one-period game between an established monopoly, Yellow Pages Phone Directory, and a new competitor, Spartan Information Phone Directory. Each directory earns revenue by charging businesses for their listings and advertisements. Suppose each firm has only two possible strategies: charge a high price, P_H, or a low price, P_L, for advertising space. The payoffs from these strategies are given in pairs (Spartan, Yellow) for each firm for next year.

		Yellow Pages	
		P_H	P_L
Spartan Info.	P_H	\$20, \$60	\$5, \$70
	P_L	\$40, \$25	\$10, \$45

Is this an example of a Prisoners' Dilemma? Why or why not?

IMPLICATIONS OF THE PRISONERS' DILEMMA FOR OLIGOPOLISTIC PRICING (Section 12.5)

PRICE RIGIDITY

Dynamic models allow competitors to react to each other's moves in future periods, establish reputations, threaten punishments, and so on. This broadening of strategic responses makes it possible for collusive outcomes to be sustained. The *kinked demand curve model* does not explain collusion, but it does illustrate why prices can be inflexible. In this model, firms suppose that rivals will match price cuts but not respond to price increases. Marginal revenue jumps downward at the current price, and firms have no incentive to change price even when the cost curves shift. *Price leadership* is another way for firms to collude without formally communicating: each firm simply sets price at the level established by the leader.

THE DOMINANT FIRM MODEL

The *dominant firm* model captures the behavior of an industry with a single large firm and many smaller firms (the *fringe*). It is assumed that the fringe behaves competitively and that the large producer chooses output to maximize profit, given the market demand curve and the fringe's supply curve. The dominant firm acts like a monopolist over that part of the market that it controls, after accounting for supply from the fringe. It realizes that the fringe will supply more, the higher the price set by the dominant firm. The dominant firm derives its *residual demand curve* by subtracting fringe supply from the market demand curve. The dominant firm then chooses its output to equate marginal revenue from the residual demand curve to marginal cost. Once the dominant firm chooses output and price, the fringe sets P = MC to determine supply.

Exercise:

8. Assume that many years ago Brunswick had a monopoly in the market for home billiard tables. The market demand curve was $P = 1{,}000 - 10Q_B$. There were no fixed costs of production in those days, and marginal costs for Brunswick were $MC = Q_B$.
   a) What was Brunswick's profit-maximizing price and output?
   b) Eventually, many furniture manufacturers realized that home billiard tables were easy to make. Without the benefit of Brunswick's long experience, however, they have higher costs. The competitive supply curve for the fringe manufacturers is $Q_F(P) = P/4$. If Brunswick acts as a dominant firm, what price will it charge? What are the quantities that will be produced by Brunswick and by the fringe?

CARTELS (Section 12.6)

In a cooperative oligopoly, a small number of firms can tacitly or explicitly coordinate their actions to maximize joint profits. A *cartel* is an explicit association of producers who agree to coordinate their actions in order to increase profits above the competitive level. To achieve this goal, output must be restricted below the competitive level. Figure 12.3 uses basic microeconomic theory to illustrate why cartels form. Panel (a) of Figure 12.3 shows a typical firm's marginal cost and average cost curve. Panel (b) shows the industry supply curve, which is the sum of the firm's individual marginal cost curves if the industry is perfectly competitive. The competitive output, Q_c, is determined by the intersection of this supply curve and the industry demand curve. The market price is P_c and each firm produces q_c. Long-run economic profits under perfect competition are driven down to zero by free entry and exit. The long-run equilibrium is point *e* in Figure 12.3a.

Acting collectively, the firms in this industry can improve their condition. The marginal revenue for the cartel (or a monopolist) is given by MR in panel (b). Profits will be maximized when output is set at Q_m, where marginal revenue equals marginal cost. When output is restricted, price rises to P_m. This total output target must then be divided into individual production quotas for each firm. Setting a price target without restricting production levels will cause the cartel to fail. If the cartel is made up of n identical firms which reduce output equally, each firm must reduce its output to $q_m = Q_m/n$. As a consequence, each firm receives a total economic profit equal to the shaded area in Figure 12.3a.

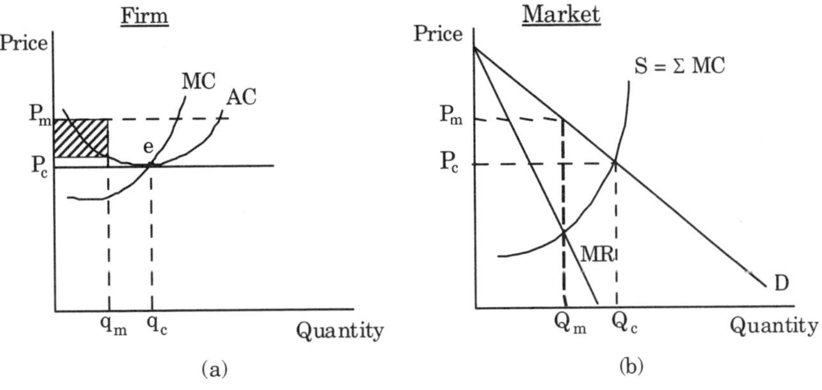

Figure 12.3

A cartel will not be successful if the firms within the cartel do not have sufficient market power to control the price. Even if the cartel has a large market share and raises the price in the short run, the increase in profits will only be temporary if consumers can easily switch to cheaper substitutes and/or if other firms, attracted by the profit opportunities, can easily enter the market. The speed with which non-cartel members can undermine the efforts of the cartel depends on the elasticity of supply of nonmembers. If nonmember supply is very elastic, entry into the cartelized market or into the production of close substitutes will be easy and the cartel will find it difficult to maintain its high price. In other words, if the long-run elasticity of demand or supply facing the cartel is high, the increase in profits from forming the cartel will be short-lived.

Even if the potential for long-run profits is high, a cartel may not form if organizing some or all of the firms in the industry is too costly. When firms are identical, reaching an agreement is relatively easy. The more asymmetries that exist across cartel members, the more complex the negotiations, and the greater the cost of creating the cartel. For example, agreeing on output and price levels will be harder if firms produce differentiated products (differentiated according to quality, location, distribution channels, etc.) and have different costs of production.

An individual cartel member always has an incentive to cheat on a cartel agreement that does not punish defectors. Figure 12.3a shows this incentive to cheat from an individual firm's perspective. When producing at their assigned quota, q_m, each cartel member is at a point where marginal revenue (which can be thought of as a horizontal line slightly below P_m if the firm has to discount price slightly to increase sales) is greater than marginal cost. Because of this gap between individual marginal revenue and marginal cost, each individual cartel member sees a profit opportunity from producing in excess of the assigned quota. In a static setting, there is nothing to deter a firm from cheating. In a dynamic setting, threats of future punishment may deter a firm from cheating.

Exercise: ▶▶▶▶▶▶▶

9. Suppose there are ten identical textile producers. Each firm produces at a constant marginal cost of \$2. The market demand curve is given by $P = 12 - 0.1Q$, where price is measured in dollars and quantity in pounds. The ten firms are currently behaving as competitive (price-taking) firms. They are thinking of forming a cartel with the purpose of restricting quantity and raising the price to the monopoly level.
   a) What is the current market price, market output, and output per firm?
   b) What would be the cartel price, cartel output, and output (individual quota) per firm?
   c) If profits from the cartel were divided equally, what would be each firm's share of the cartel profits?
   d) Suppose one firm decides to "cheat" by charging a price 25 cents below the cartel price. This firm will sell all of their output (their cartel quota from part b) plus the additional output demanded) at this discounted price. Will cheating be profitable, compared to your answer from part c)? (Assume that the other nine firms stay loyal to the cartel.)

PROBLEM SET

10. The Able Manufacturing Company and Better Bettors, Inc. are rival firms in the production of a calculator used by horse racing fans for handicapping (determining betting strategies). Each firm has a fixed cost of \$100 and a marginal cost of \$10 in producing calculators. The demand for the industry's product is:

$$Q = 900 - 5P, \text{ where P is the market price and } Q = Q_1 + Q_2.$$

If each firm must choose how many calculators to produce and sell without knowing of its rival's production decision, what will be the Cournot equilibrium price and quantities produced? Calculate profits for the two firms.

11. The frozen yogurt market in a small town has two firms. All frozen yogurt is the same, and the demand curve is $Q = 200 - 2P$. Firm 1 has constant average total cost of \$1 per unit, and Firm 2 has constant average total cost of \$2 per unit. If the two firms simultaneously choose prices, what is the Bertrand equilibrium? How much will each firm sell, and what will each firm's profit be?

12. Consider a market composed of four firms, each with a constant marginal cost of production of \$20, and facing a total market demand curve given by $P = 40 - 0.01Q$. Each firm is currently charging the competitive price. The four firms are thinking of forming a cartel, but they realize that they will each have to contribute funds to keep the cartel intact. How much would *each* potential cartel member be willing to pay to help enforce the cartel agreement?

13. In one year, three firms in a global steel oligopoly sold 10 million units. Total dollar sales for the three companies were \$100 billion. Estimated economic profits that year were approximately \$200 million. Under competitive conditions, roughly 10.5 million units of

steel would have been sold. Estimated average costs (including opportunity costs) in that same year were approximately \$8,000 per unit. Assume a constant average cost equal to marginal cost.

Suppose the three steel producers acted together as a cartel in that year. Calculate the resulting deadweight loss to society and illustrate.

14. Jerry owns a gas station at one end of a small town. His only competitor, Bill, is on the other end of town. The two compete in prices. Residents hate to drive across town due to traffic problems. The city council had recently considered a project to alleviate the traffic problems. Afterward, it was learned that Jerry bribed several members of the city council not to approve the project. Why did Jerry want to prevent approval of the project? Draw the reaction curves for Jerry and Bill. Show the shifts in the reaction curves that the improvements in traffic flow would have caused and relate them to your explanation.

15. Use Figure 12.4 of the text to answer this question. If Firm 1's marginal cost increases, its reaction curve will shift to the left (or inward). How far must it shift in so that the Cournot equilibrium is $Q_1 = 0$ and $Q_2 = 75$ (only Firm 2 produces in equilibrium)? Explain how Firm 1's MC compares with the price Firm 2 would charge if it were a monopolist in this case.

SELF-TEST

16. In a large metropolitan area, the furniture retailing business is best described as:
- a) perfectly competitive.
- b) an oligopoly.
- c) monopolistically competitive.
- d) a cartel.
- e) None of the above is correct.

17. In a small town, the furniture retailing business is best described as:
- a) perfectly competitive.
- b) an oligopoly.
- c) monopolistically competitive.
- d) a cartel.
- e) None of the above is correct.

18. In a monopolistically competitive industry, firms earn zero profit in long-run equilibrium because:
- a) each firm produces at minimum average total cost.
- b) the demand curve is tangent to the ATC curve for each firm.
- c) each firm has capacity less than desired output.
- d) a) and b)
- e) b) and c)

19. With homogeneous products, total output in Cournot equilibrium is:
  a) equal to the monopoly output.
  b) less than the monopoly output.
  c) greater than the competitive output.
  d) between the monopoly output and competitive output.
  e) None of the above is correct.

20. With homogenous products, total output in Bertrand equilibrium is:
  a) equal to the monopoly output.
  b) equal to the competitive output.
  c) greater than the competitive output.
  d) between the monopoly output and competitive output.
  e) None of the above is correct.

21. The distinguishing characteristics of oligopoly include:
  a) many small firms.
  b) ease of entry and exit.
  c) the necessity of assessing the response of competitors before making decisions.
  d) All of these.
  e) None of these.

22. In the kinked demand curve model, each firm believes:
  a) competitors will match all price changes.
  b) competitors will only match price cuts.
  c) competitors will hold output constant.
  d) competitors will hold price constant.
  e) None of the above is correct.

23. A cartel is likely to be more successful if:
  a) demand is less elastic.
  b) the members have similar production costs.
  c) each member produces roughly the same quantity as the others.
  d) b) and c)
  e) All of the above are correct.

24. In the Bertrand model with differentiated products:
  a) each firm chooses a price equal to its marginal cost.
  b) each firm chooses a price equal to its average cost.
  c) each firm earns positive profits (in the absence of fixed costs).
  d) only one firm serves the entire market.
  e) None of the above is true.

25. Whether a market is perfectly competitive or monopolistically competitive depends on:
  a) barriers to entry.
  b) the degree of product differentiation.
  c) the ability of firms to collude.
  d) a) and b)
  e) a), b), and c)

ANSWERS TO CHAPTER 12

EXERCISE ANSWERS

1. Each restaurant is distinct in menu and/or location from every other restaurant. But entry into the industry is relatively free. Unless a town is so small that it has only a few restaurants, the market is best described as monopolistically competitive.

2. The situation described is shown in Figure 12A.1. The market is *not* in long-run equilibrium because price is greater than average cost. These above-normal profits will attract entry, which will shift each firm's demand curve down as it loses market share. The market will reach equilibrium when MR = MC and P = AC (when the demand curve is tangent to the AC curve).

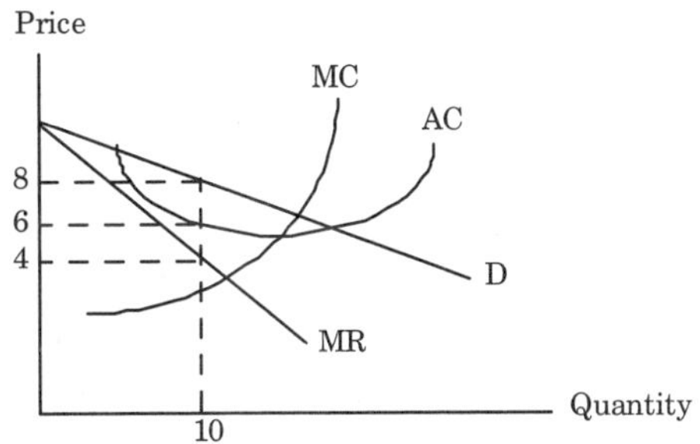

Figure 12A.1

3. If $Q_2 = 45$, $P = 400 - 2Q_1 - (45) = 310 - 2Q_1$. Then, $\overline{MR}_1 = 310 - 4Q_1$. Equating $\overline{MR}_1$ and MC_1 means that $310 - 4Q_1 = 10$, or $Q_1^* = 75$.

If $Q_2 = 85$, $P = 400 - 2Q_1 - 2(85) = 230 - 2Q_1$. $\overline{MR}_1 = 230 - 4Q_1$. Equating $\overline{MR}_1$ and MC_1 implies $230 - 4Q_1 = 10$, or $Q_1^* = 55$.

4. a) The residual demand curve for Firm 1 is $P = 1{,}000 - 0.1(Q_1 + Q_2) = 1{,}000 - 0.1\overline{Q}_2 - 0.1Q_1$. Therefore, $\overline{MR}_1 = 1{,}000 - 0.1\overline{Q}_2 - 0.2Q_1$. Setting $MR_1 = MC_1$ yields:

$$1{,}000 - 0.1\overline{Q}_2 - 0.2Q_1 = 100,$$

$$\text{or } Q_1 = 4{,}500 - 0.5\overline{Q}_2.$$

b) Similarly, $\overline{MR}_2 = MC_2$ yields:

$$1{,}000 - 0.1\overline{Q}_1 - 0.2Q_2 = 190,$$

$$\text{or } Q_2 = 4{,}050 - 0.5\overline{Q}_1.$$

c) Substituting in for Q_1 from (a) into the formula in (b) implies

$$Q_2 = 4{,}050 - 0.5(4{,}500 - 0.5Q_2), \text{ or } Q_2^* = 2{,}400.$$

Therefore, $Q_1^* = 4{,}500 - 0.5(2{,}400) = 3{,}300$.

5. a) $\overline{MR}_2 = 500 - \overline{Q}_1 - 2Q_2$. To find Firm 2's reaction curve set $MR_2 = MC$.

$$500 - \overline{Q}_1 - 2Q_2 = 20, \text{ or}$$

$$Q_2 = 240 - \overline{Q}_1/2.$$

b) Total revenue for Firm 1 is:

$$\begin{aligned} R_1 = PQ_1 &= (500 - Q_2 - Q_1)Q_1 \\ &= 500Q_1 - Q_2Q_1 - Q_1^2 \\ &= 500Q_1 - (240 - Q_1/2)Q_1 - Q_1^2 \\ &= 260Q_1 - Q_1^2/2. \end{aligned}$$

c) Given $R_1 = 260Q_1 - Q_1^2/2$ we get $MR_1 = \partial R/\partial Q_1 = 260 - Q_1$. Setting $MR_1 = MC_1$:

$$260 - Q_1 = 20, \text{ or}$$
$$Q_1^* = 240.$$

This means that $Q_2^* = 240 - (240/2) = 120$.

d) The market price is $P = 500 - Q = 500 - (240 + 120) = \$140$. Therefore,

$$\pi_1 = PQ_1 - 20Q_1 = 140(240) - 20(240) = \$28{,}800 \text{ and}$$

$$\pi_2 = 140(120) - 20(120) = \$14{,}400.$$

As we would expect, profits for the leader are higher than they are for the follower.

6. Firm 1's profit function is:

$$\pi_1 = P_1Q_1 - C_1 = P_1(1{,}000 - 20P_1 + 15P_2) - 10Q_1$$

$$= 1{,}000P_1 - 20P_1^2 + 15P_1P_2 - 10[1{,}000 - 20P_1 + 15P_2]$$

$$= 1{,}200P_1 - 20P_1^2 + 15P_1P_2 - 10{,}000 - 150P_2.$$

Similarly,

$$\begin{aligned} \pi_2 &= P_2Q_2 - C_2 \\ &= 800P_2 + 5P_1P_2 - 15P_2^2 - 5[800 + 5P_1 - 15P_2] \\ &= 875P_2 + 5P_1P_2 - 15P_2^2 - 4{,}000 = 25P_1 \end{aligned}$$

To derive the reaction functions, differentiate each firm's profit with respect to its own price to find the profit-maximizing price as a function of the other firm's price. For Firm 1, $\partial\pi_1/\partial P_1 = 1{,}200 - 40P_1 + 15P_2 = 0$. For Firm 2, we obtain $\partial\pi_2/\partial P_2 = 875 + 5P_1 - 30P_2 = 0$.

Firm 1's reaction function is then: $P_1 = 1{,}200/40 + 15P_2/40 = 30 + 0.375P_2$. Firm 2's reaction function is: $P_2 = 875/30 + 5P_1/30 = 29.17 + 0.17P_1$ (rounding).

The Bertrand equilibrium is found at the intersection of these two reaction functions. Solving for P_1, we get $P_1 = 30 + (0.375)[29.17 + 0.17P_1]$ or $0.936P_1 = 40.94$, or $P_1^* = \$43.74$ (rounding). Therefore, $P_2^* = 29.17 + 0.17(43.74) = \$36.61$.

7. Yes, this is a Prisoners' Dilemma. If Yellow Pages chooses P_H, Spartan should choose P_L (\$40 > \$20). If Yellow Pages chooses P_L, Spartan should again choose P_L (\$10 > \$5). Similarly, Yellow Pages should choose P_L no matter what it thinks Spartan might do. But if they both compete aggressively by setting P_L, they will earn (\$10, \$45).) If they could somehow agree to charge P_H, they could have earned (\$20, \$60).

8. a) As a monopolist, Brunswick's marginal revenue curve is MR = 1,000 – 20QB. Equating MR and MC, we find 1,000 – 20QB = QB or QB = 1,000/21 = 47.62 and P = \$523.80.

b) With a fringe supply curve $Q_F = P/4$ and market demand equal to $Q_D = 100 - P/10$, the residual demand facing Brunswick is $Q_B' = 100 - P/10 - P/4 = 100 - 0.35P$. Rewriting the residual demand curve yields $P' = 100/0.35 - Q_B/0.35 = 285.71 - 2.86Q_B$. The marginal revenue curve is therefore $MR' = 285.71 - 5.72Q_B$. Equating MR′ and MC, $285.71 - 5.72Q_B = Q_B$, or = 42.52. The price is $P' = 285.71 - 2.86(42.52) = \$164.10$. Fringe supply at this price is P/4 = 164.10/4 = 41.03.

9. a) P = MC implies 12 – 0.1Q = 2 or Q = 100. Therefore, the market price is P = \$2 and each firm produces q = 100/10 = 10.

b) MR = MC implies 12 – 0.2Q = 2, or Q = 50. The market price is P = 12 – 0.1(50) = 7 and each firm's share of the cartel output is q = 50/10 = 5.

c) Profit for each firm is $\pi = 7(5) - 2(5) = \$25$.

d) Market demand at P = \$6.75 (25 cents less than the cartel price) is Q = 52.5. The "cheater" can, therefore, sell an extra 2.5 units at P = \$6.75. Profits for the cheater are $\pi = (6.75)(7.5) - 2(7.5) = \$35.63$. This is more than the firm was earning by staying loyal to the cartel (\$25). If this cheating goes undetected, it will definitely be profitable.

PROBLEM SET ANSWERS

10. We can rewrite the demand curve as $P = 180 - (Q_1 + Q_2)/5$. Firm 1's residual demand curve is: $(Q_1) = 180 - Q_2/5 - Q_1/5$, so its marginal revenue from this demand curve is $(Q_1) = 180 - Q_2/5 - 2Q_1/5$. Since marginal cost is 10, Firm 1 will choose Q_1 such that $180 - Q_2/5 - 2Q_1/5 = 10$. This gives us Firm 1's reaction curve $Q_1 = 425 - 0.5Q_2$.

Similarly, we can find Firm 2's reaction curve. Since the firms are identical, $Q_2 = 425 - 0.5Q_1$.

The Cournot equilibrium is the intersection of these two functions:

$Q_1^* = Q_2^*$ or $Q_1^* = 425 - 0.5(425 - 0.5)$, which yields $Q_1^* = 283.33$. Similarly, $Q_2^* = 283.33$. The equilibrium price is $P = 180 - (283.33 + 283.33)/5 = \$66.67$. Profits for the two firms are equal, with $\pi_1 = \pi_2 = 66.67(283.33) - 10(283.33) - 100 = \$15{,}956.31$.

11. Firm 2 can never charge a price less than \$2 and make a profit greater than or equal to zero. Firm 1 will always want to charge just under Firm 2's price. The Bertrand equilibrium in this case is $P_1 = \$1.99$ and $P_2 = \$2$. Firm 1 captures all the sales in this case. Firm 1 will earn $(1.99 - 1)(200 - 2(1.99)) = \$194.06$. Firm 2 earns zero. Firm 1 would only wish to charge less than \$1.99 if Firm 1's profit-maximizing monopoly price were less than \$1.99.

12. Currently each firm is earning zero economic profit. If they form a cartel, each firm will receive one-quarter of the cartel profits (assuming the four firms divide the market equally). Since the four firms are the only firms in the industry, the cartel price and output are the monopoly price and output. Set MR = MC or $40 - 0.02Q = 20$, which implies = 1,000 and = $40 - 0.01(1{,}000) = 30$. Industry (cartel) profits will be $\pi = 30(1{,}000) - 20(1{,}000) = 10{,}000$. Therefore cartel profits per firm will be 10,000/4 = \$2,500, which is the maximum amount each firm would be willing to pay (i.e., the increase in profits they can expect if they move from competition to a cartel).

13. From the information in the problem, we have:

$$P_mQ_m = \$100 \text{ billion},$$
$$\pi = \$200 \text{ million},$$
$$P_m = \$100 \text{ bil}/10 \text{ mil} = \$10{,}000, \text{ and}$$
$$MC = \$8{,}000.$$

This is drawn in Figure 12A.2

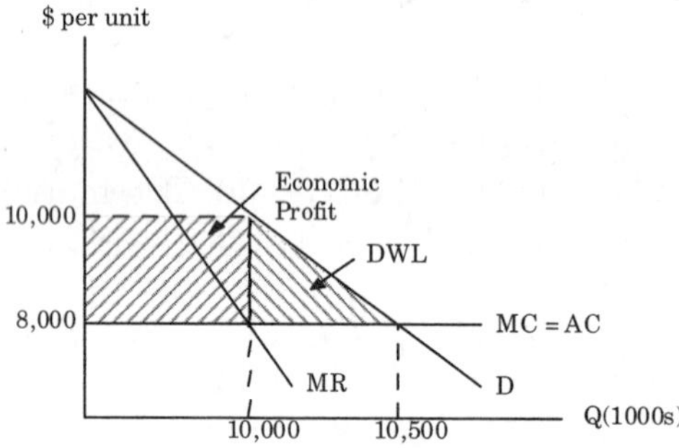

Figure 12A.2

Therefore, DWL = $0.5(10{,}500{,}000 - 10{,}000{,}000)(10{,}000 - 8{,}000) = \$50{,}000{,}000$.

14. The improvement in traffic flow would make it easier for consumers to go to Bill if Jerry's price were high. In effect, it would make the products better substitutes and lead to fiercer price competition. This would shift both firms' price reaction functions, leading to lower prices and lower profits. See Figure 12A.3.

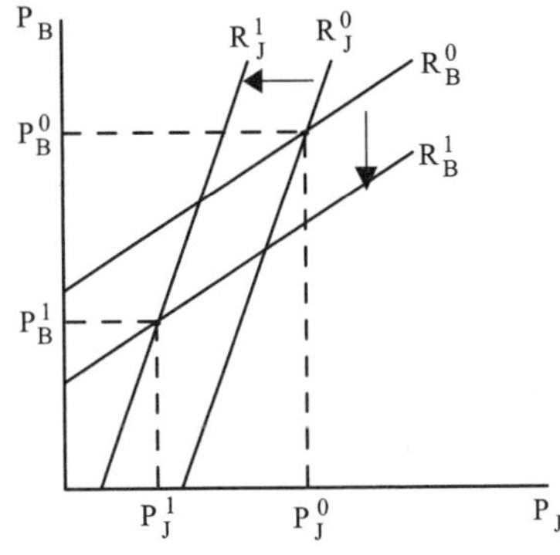

Figure 12A.3

15. Firm 1's reaction curve must shift far enough so that it intersects Firm 2's reaction curve along the $Q_1 = 0$ axis (the horizontal axis). Figure 12A.4 shows Firm 1's new reaction curve as a dotted line. In this case, Firm 2 produces 75 units. This is the same quantity that Firm 2 would choose if it were a monopolist (its residual demand when $Q_1 = 0$ is the same as the demand curve when it is a monopolist). For Firm 1, $P = a - b(Q_1 + Q_2) = a - b(75) - bQ_1$. Therefore, $\overline{MR}_1 = a - b(75) - 2bQ_1$. If Firm 1 produces zero, $MC_1 > a - b(75)$, which is firm 2's monopoly price.

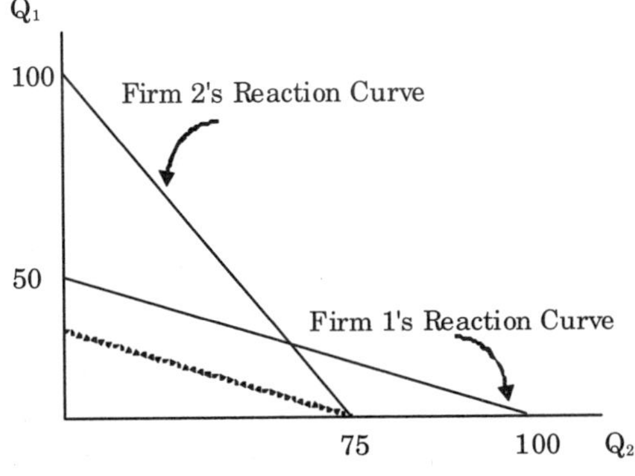

Figure 12A.4

SELF-TEST ANSWERS

16. c) Each store carries different products, but there are many stores.

17. b) The market only has a few stores.

18. b) Choice a) is false because there is excess capacity at the monopolistic competition equilibrium (firms are to the left of minimum average cost). Therefore, c) is also false.

19. d) The solution to a general Cournot problem will always yield this answer. Intuitively, the equilibrium resulting from Cournot competition is more competitive than monopoly, but less competitive than perfect competition.

20. b) The Bertrand equilibrium price equals the competitive price, and therefore total output is equal to the competitive output.

21. c) Oligopoly is characterized by an interdependence of decisions across firms in the industry. That is, profits of any given firm are affected by the actions of its rivals. Choices a) and b) are false because oligopoly is defined by the concentration of firms in the industry, and to have a limited number of firms there must be barriers to entry.

22. b) This is an assumption of the model.

23. e) If demand is less elastic there must be fewer substitutes, which is good for the cartel. If production costs are similar and cartel members produce similar output levels, then negotiation over quota shares should be easier initially and also easier to police.

24. c) In the case of differentiated products, price competition will not bid the price down all the way to marginal cost.

25. b) Free entry exists and collusion is difficult in both types of markets.

CHAPTER 13
GAME THEORY AND COMPETITIVE STRATEGY

IMPORTANT CONCEPTS

- Elements of Games
    - Players
    - Strategies
    - Payoff Matrix
- Noncooperative and Cooperative Games
- Dominant Strategy
- Nash Equilibrium
    - Maximin Strategies
    - Pure Strategies
    - Mixed Strategies
- Repeated Game
- Sequential Game
- Extensive Form of a Game
- Strategic Moves
- Credible Threat
- Entry Deterrence
- Auctions

CHAPTER HIGHLIGHTS

Game theory is the study of the behavior of the interactions of rational decision-makers. In an oligopoly, a firm's strategic decision about any important variable (output, price, capacity, or advertising expenditure, for example) depends on its prediction of rivals' choices over these same variables. These strategic choices are complex because other firms are also making choices based on their predictions about rivals' behavior. In order to choose its best action, a firm must simultaneously determine what the best choices of other firms will be, assuming rational behavior by all other firms.

The Cournot model studied in Chapter 12 is an example of a *noncooperative game*, in which each firm independently makes its output choice with no possibility of entering into binding commitments with other firms. Most games studied in economics are noncooperative games. In a *cooperative game*, firms can make binding commitments. Contract negotiations are an important example of cooperative games.

The simplest prescription for players in a game is to play a dominant strategy if one is available. A *dominant strategy* is an action that is best for a player no matter what strategies its opponents play. A player does not have a dominant strategy when its best action depends on what its opponents do. When no solution to the game exists in dominant strategies, players should play their Nash equilibrium strategies. A *Nash equilibrium* is a set of strategies such that each player is doing as well as possible given the actions of the other players. This condition must hold for every player for a set of actions to be a Nash equilibrium.

The Nash equilibrium suggests a sensible course of action for each player as long as each player can assume that others act rationally. If players doubt this, they may choose to play *maximin strategies*, which maximize the minimum payoff to a player. For some games, there is no Nash equilibrium using *pure strategies* (ones which are played with certainty). In such cases, the Nash equilibrium uses *mixed strategies* in which players randomly choose among several different alternatives.

In real markets, firms play a *repeated game* period after period. Repeated games often have equilibria that are different from games that are played only once. In the Prisoners' Dilemma game, two players each choose between confessing and not confessing. Both players do best if neither one confesses, but confessing is a dominant strategy for each player. Therefore, if the game is played only once, both players will confess. In the infinitely repeated version of the Prisoners' Dilemma game, cooperative behavior (not confessing) can be an equilibrium.

In a *sequential game*, players move in turn. The *extensive form* (decision tree form) of a game is a useful tool to analyze sequential games. To use the extensive form, find the best move for the player choosing in the last stage of the game. Then, work backwards to see what a player who moves earlier will do, looking ahead to see how that choice affects players moving later.

The player to move first in a sequential game can often benefit by taking a strategic move. A *strategic move* constrains one's own actions, but is beneficial because it affects the rival's response. A firm may want to engage in an entry deterrence strategy; for example, taking actions that convince firms outside the industry that entry would be unprofitable. Irreversible actions which reduce a firm's own payoffs, such as expanding plant capacity, can make it a *credible threat* not to accommodate entry if it occurs.

In auction markets, goods are bought or sold through a bidding process. In an English auction, the seller asks for bids from a group of potential buyers and the good is sold when only one bidder is left. The item is sold to the highest bidder at the price they bid.

In a Dutch auction, the seller initially sets a high price and then reduces the price if no bidder comes forward. The item is sold to the first buyer that accepts a price called out by the seller. In a sealed-bid auction, the bids are made privately and the item is sold to the bidder who submitted the highest bid. The price paid by the winning bidder will be the bid price if it is a first-price sealed-bid auction, and it will be the second highest bid if the auction was run as a second-price sealed-bid auction. The rules that govern the bidding process have a significant effect on the price at which the good is sold.

CONCEPT REVIEW AND EXERCISES

GAMING AND STRATEGIC DECISIONS (Section 13.1)

A game is a general concept; it includes almost any situation in which each decision maker's profits depend on actions of other decision-makers or *players*. To describe a game, we need to know the rules of the game, the possible *strategies* of each player, and the *payoffs* from each possible combination of actions. Players are assumed to want to maximize their payoffs. The rules include the order of moves by the players and whether binding agreements about actions are possible.

Consider a game with two players described in the *payoff matrix* of Table 13.1. We denote A's possible actions as Row 1 and Row 2, and B's possible actions as Column 1, Column 2, and Column 3. In this discussion the players are firms, and a firm's payoff is the profit it earns. For each of A's possible actions and for each of B's possible actions, the payoff matrix gives the payoffs for each player. The first entry in each cell of the payoff matrix is A's payoff, and the second entry is B's payoff. For example, if A plays Row 1 and B plays Column 1, A's payoff is $400, and B's payoff is $100.

		B 1	B 2	B 3
A	1	$400, $100	$500, $0	$200, $400
A	2	$200, $200	$600, $300	$500, $100

Table 13.1

Each player's influence on the outcome is limited: A selects the row, while B selects the column. A cannot control B's choice, and B cannot control A's choice. For example, if A chooses Row 1 it could earn $500. But if B chooses Column 3, A's payoff will only be $200. The remainder of the chapter explores how to find the equilibrium of a game.

DOMINANT STRATEGIES (Section 13.2)

To describe players' behavior, we must know precisely what information they have. To simplify the game, assume that players have complete information about all aspects of the game, including knowledge of the entries in the payoff matrix for all the other players. Each player needs this information to figure out what actions are rational for other players.

The simplest guide to players' actions is to see if any player has a best action regardless of what other players do. Consider the following example with two firms, A and B, and two possible actions for each firm.

		B	
		1	2
A	1	100, 40	70, 50
	2	80, 90	60, 100

Table 13.2

In Table 13.2, no matter what B chooses, A always does better to play Row 1. A must check its payoffs column by column. In this case A's payoff from playing Row 1 is better than its payoff from playing Row 2 *if* B plays Column 1 (100 versus 80) and its payoff from playing Row 1 is better than its payoff from Row 2 *if* B plays Column 2 (70 versus 60). (A must consider both possible columns, since A cannot control B's action.) Thus, Row 1 is a *dominant strategy* for A, and that is the strategy that A should play. A dominant strategy is an action that is best for a player no matter what strategies its opponent plays. Regardless of B's choice, A will do best to play its dominant strategy.

Now we know what A should do, but to solve this game completely, we must specify B's behavior. By inspecting the payoff matrix you can see that B also has a dominant strategy. Firm B should play column 2 no matter what A does (50 > 40 if A plays Row 1 and 100 > 90 if A plays Row 2). Therefore, assuming that both firms are rational, the outcome of the game will be that A plays Row 1 and B plays column 2.

Now alter the game slightly, as shown in Table 13.3, so that B's payoff in the lower right-hand corner changes from 100 to 80. What will be the outcome of the game?

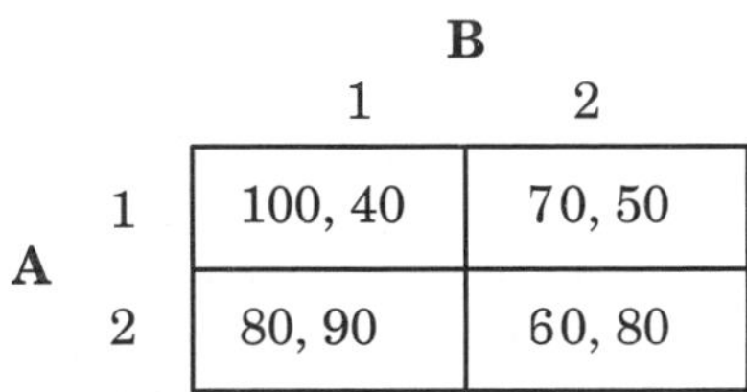

		B	
		1	2
A	1	100, 40	70, 50
	2	80, 90	60, 80

Table 13.3

Firm B now has no dominant strategy, since playing Column 2 is best if A plays Row 1, while playing Column 1 is best if A plays Row 2. However, B knows that Row 1 is A's dominant strategy. Hence, B should choose its best action given that knowledge and play Column 2. The outcome of the game is that A plays Row 1 and B plays Column 2 with payoffs of 70 for A and 50 for B.

The conflicting interests of the two players prevent them from choosing Row 2 and Column 1, which would give each player a higher payoff. The problem is that A will do even better to play Row 1 in that case, to the detriment of B. Clearly, the solution of a noncooperative game is not necessarily the most desirable outcome for all of the players.

Exercise: ◗ ◗ ◗ ◗ ◗ ◗ ◗

1. Revlon and L'Oreal cosmetics companies must choose between a high price and a low price for their makeup. Revlon's annual profit (in millions of dollars) is listed in the payoff matrix of Table 13.4 along with L'Oreal's profits for each combination of strategies. What will be the outcome of this game? Does each player have a dominant strategy?

		L'Oreal	
		Low Price	High Price
Revlon	Low Price	10, 10	20, 6
	High Price	6, 20	15, 15

Table 13.4

In other games, such as Table 13.5, no player has a dominant strategy.

		B 1	B 2	B 3
A	1	2, 3	3, 2	1, 2
A	2	1, 5	2, 9	5, 8
A	3	1, 4	4, 2	3, 5

Table 13.5

Here, A's best actions are: Row 1 if B plays Column 1,
Row 3 if B plays Column 2,
Row 2 if B plays Column 3.

B's best actions are: Column 1 if A plays Row 1,
Column 2 if A plays Row 2,
Column 3 if A plays Row 3.

Neither player has a dominant strategy. For this game, we need a more general solution concept.

A *Nash equilibrium* is a pair of strategies such that each player is doing the best it can, given what the other players are doing. Since neither player controls the other's choice, a rational player tries to establish what its opponents will do and act accordingly. In the game in Table 13.5, the strategies to play Row 1 and Column 1 are a Nash equilibrium. If A plays Row 1, B's best action is Column 1; if B plays Column 1, A's best action is Row 1. No firm has an incentive to change its decision.

Exercise: ◗ ◗ ◗ ◗ ◗ ◗ ◗

2. In the game of Table 13.6, does either player have a dominant strategy? What is the Nash equilibrium?

		B 1	B 2	B 3
A	1	3, 2	7, 7	5, 6
A	2	2, 8	1, 4	2, 9

Table 13.6

3. In the game of Table 13.7, does either player have a dominant strategy? What is the Nash equilibrium?

		B		
		1	2	3
A	1	3, 2	7, 7	9, 5
	2	4, 8	1, 4	6, 9

Table 13.7

THE NASH EQUILIBRIUM REVISITED (Section 13.3)

To help clarify the difference between an equilibrium in dominant strategies and a Nash equilibrium we repeat the comparison given in Section 13.3 of the text:

Dominant Strategies: I'm doing the best I can *no matter what you do.* You're doing the best you can *no matter what I do.*

Nash Equilibrium: I'm doing the best I can *given what you are doing.* You're doing the best you can *given what I am doing.*

Two difficulties can arise when one is looking for the Nash equilibrium solution to a game. The first difficulty is that there might be more than one Nash equilibrium. If a game has several Nash equilibria, it is obviously more difficult to predict what the players will do, especially if communication is not allowed.

Exercise: ▶ ▶ ▶ ▶ ▶ ▶ ▶

4. In the game of Table 13.8, does either player have a dominant strategy? Is there one Nash equilibrium or two?

		Firm 2	
		Sell Online	Don't Sell Online
Firm 1	Sell Online	50, 60	20, 30
	Don't Sell Online	40, 20	60, 40

Table 13.8

The second difficulty is that, for some games, there is no Nash equilibrium using pure strategies (ones which are played with certainty). As we discuss in a later section, this difficulty disappears if we allow for mixed strategies for some games, in which players randomly choose among several different alternatives.

MAXIMIN STRATEGIES

In the game depicted in Table 13.9 (a variation of the game in Table 13.3), player A has a dominant strategy of Row 1. Player B has no dominant strategy. When we solved the game in Table 13.3, we argued that since B knew that A would play its dominant strategy, then *B should play Column 2*. The game in Table 13.3 has a Nash equilibrium of (70, 50). The same is true of this game. Choosing Column 2 maximizes B's payoff, given that it assumes A will rationally play its dominant strategy.

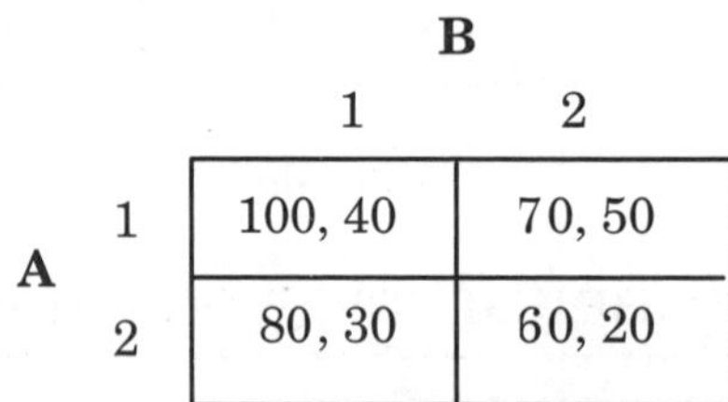

		B: 1	B: 2
A	1	100, 40	70, 50
	2	80, 30	60, 20

Table 13.9

But what if B is not sure about A's behavior? If A were to play Row 2, then B would be better off playing Column 1 (30 is greater than 20). A risk averse player might prefer to play a *maximin strategy*, which maximizes the minimum payoff. If B were to play Column 1, its worst outcome would be 30. If B were to play Column 2, its worst outcome would be 20. Therefore, choosing the best of the worst outcomes, *B should play Column 1.* If B is conservative and unsure of A's choice, the maximin strategy maximizes the game's minimum payoff for B.

The above maximin strategy might be used by a cautious firm that cannot estimate the probabilities of A's actions. Suppose instead that B thinks there is an 80 percent probability of A playing Row 1 and a 20 percent chance of A playing Row 2. Then the expected payoff to B from playing Column 1 is (0.80)(40) + (0.20)(30) = 38. B's expected payoff from playing Column 2 is (0.80)(50) + (0.20)(20) = 44. B should therefore play Column 2. This strategy maximizes B's expected payoff, but does not separately take into account how low the payoff might go. If B is risk neutral, this might be an appealing strategy.

Exercise: ▶ ▶ ▶ ▶ ▶ ▶ ▶

5. The payoff matrix shown in Table 13.10 (on the next page) is a Prisoners' Dilemma game. Each firm is choosing between a strategy of maintaining price at its current level or cutting price and starting a price war in order to gain market share. When we analyzed the Prisoners' Dilemma before, we looked for dominant strategies and concluded that Cut Price was a dominant strategy for both players. If both firms instead use a maximin strategy, will they still end up cutting price? (continued)

		Firm 2	
		Maintain Price	Cut Price
Firm 1	Maintain Price	200, 150	130, 180
	Cut Price	220, 125	135, 130

Table 13.10

*MIXED STRATEGIES

In the game of penny-matching, two players each place a coin on the table and simultaneously reveal whether they played heads or tails. Player A wins $1 from B if both coins are heads or if both coins are tails. Player B wins $1 from A if one coin shows heads and the other shows tails. Each player has two possible actions: H (heads) or T (tails). Table 13.11 gives the payoff matrix:

		B	
		H	T
A	H	1, –1	–1, 1
	T	–1, 1	1, –1

Table 13.11

In this game, no pair of actions is a Nash equilibrium. This is not surprising because player B always wants to choose the same action as player A, but player A wants to choose an action different from player B.

If you play this game, you soon realize that flipping the coin to decide whether to play heads or tails is as good as any other choice. In game theory, randomizing your choice of action is called a *mixed strategy*. Suppose A plays H fifty percent of the time and T fifty percent of the time. B's expected payoff from playing H equals 0.5(1) + 0.5(–1) = 0, since B wins when A plays H and loses when A plays T. Similarly, B's expected payoff from playing T equals 0.5(–1) + 0.5(1) = 0. A's mixed strategy makes B indifferent between its two actions. Playing either H or T is an optimal strategy for B given A's mixed strategy. Similarly, if B plays H fifty percent of the time and T fifty percent of the time, A is indifferent between any of its possible actions.

A player who is indifferent between actions is willing to choose randomly between them. This is the first requirement for playing a mixed strategy—a player only uses actions that give it equal expected payoffs. The second requirement is that the player chooses the probabilities of its actions such that its opponent is indifferent between its alternative possible actions. A pair of mixed strategies is a Nash equilibrium if neither player can do better with another pure or mixed strategy. An important result of game theory shows that every game with a fixed number of possible actions for each player has a Nash equilibrium involving either pure or mixed strategies.

Penny-matching is special in that all actions are played with equal probability. Not all games have this property, as the following exercise demonstrates.

Exercise: ◗ ◗ ◗ ◗ ◗ ◗ ◗

***6.** What is the Nash equilibrium of the game in Table 13.12? If there is no Nash equilibrium involving pure strategies, check that players are indifferent among the actions used in their mixed strategies in equilibrium. Calculate the expected payoffs.

		B: 1	B: 2
A	1	30, 40	70, 50
A	2	20, 100	80, 80

Table 13.12

REPEATED GAMES (Section 13.4)

The Prisoners' Dilemma presented in Chapter 12 is an example of a static or one-shot game. In most markets, however, there is a relatively stable set of firms competing with each other over a long period of time. If firms compete repeatedly over time, they can adjust their beliefs about rivals' behavior and react to it. "Bad" behavior in one period can be "punished" in a later period. Or, a firm has the opportunity to establish a reputation for cooperation, and thereby encourage other firms to do the same.

Repeated games often have equilibria that are different from games that are played only once. In the one-shot Prisoners' Dilemma game, for example, acting opportunistically is a dominant strategy for each player. In the infinitely repeated version of the game, cooperative behavior can be an equilibrium.

Exercise: ◗ ◗ ◗ ◗ ◗ ◗ ◗

7. What problem does tacit collusion raise for enforcement of the antitrust laws against price fixing?

Table 13.13 presents a simple Prisoner's Dilemma game for the two players "You" and "Your Rival": each player has two strategies "Cooperative" and "Aggressive." Suppose this game is going to be repeated 100 times. In the 100th play of the game, there is every reason to play aggressively. Your rival cannot retaliate, because next period the game will be over. You will do better by playing aggressively because your profits will be higher no matter what your rival does. Therefore, both you and your rival will choose to be aggressive in the last stage of the game. Now consider your choices in the 99th period. You now know that regardless of the choices made in period 99, both players will play aggressively in the next period. Therefore, you will both play aggressively in the second-to-last period. Extending this logic all the way to the beginning of the game, you can see that the equilibrium in this repeated game is aggressive behavior from the start. This conclusion rests on the assumption that players are rational, and that nothing that happens in the course of the game will make one player change his or her mind about the other player's rationality.

		Your Rival	
		Cooperative	Aggressive
You	Cooperative	5, 5	0, 10
	Aggressive	10, 0	1, 1

Table 13.13

Cooperation is not necessarily irrational when the Prisoner's Dilemma game is repeated an infinite number of times. A *tit-for-tat* strategy involves playing cooperatively as long as your opponent also cooperates. If your opponent ever chooses to play aggressively, you respond by playing aggressively for the remainder of the game. This means that any deviation from cooperative behavior will be severely punished. In this case, the expected payoff from cooperative behavior will outweigh the expected payoff from aggressive behavior (e.g., cheating on a cartel agreement) because the aggressive behavior will earn the player one period of high profits and a lifetime of competitive (zero) profits. Therefore, with a long time horizon, if you think that there is a *possibility* that your rival will play cooperatively, you may find it profitable to play cooperatively as well.

Exercise: ◗ ◗ ◗ ◗ ◗ ◗ ◗

8. Table 13.14 (on the next page) shows a Prisoner's Dilemma game in which the players are the two television networks, ABC and NBC. Their strategies are to advertise or not advertise their new fall lineup of shows. If they don't advertise, they will split the market and they will have saved on advertising expenditure. If they both advertise, ratings are high, but so are costs, so profits fall. If one advertises and the other doesn't, there is a clear gain to be made. Profits are indicated in the payoff matrix in millions of dollars per year.

		NBC Advertise	NBC Don't Advertise
ABC	Advertise	100, 100	300, 0
	Don't Advertise	0, 300	200, 200

Table 13.14

a) What is the Nash equilibrium if this game is played only once?

b) Now consider a repeated game based on Table 13.14. Suppose ABC refuses to advertise in the first period and continues not to advertise as long as NBC doesn't advertise. But if NBC fails even once to cooperate, ABC will revert forever to the safe policy of advertising. Although this is supposed to be an infinitely repeated game, consider a ten-period game to make the algebra easier. Calculate the sum of NBC's profits over time if it adopts a parallel strategy. Then calculate the sum of NBC's profits over time if it takes advantage of ABC's willingness to cooperate by choosing to advertise in the first period. Comparing these two income streams, what will NBC do?

SEQUENTIAL GAMES (Section 13.5)

A *sequential game* is a multiperiod game in which players move one at a time rather than simultaneously. Usually, players collect payoffs only at the end of the game. The simplest example of a sequential game occurs when player A moves, and then player B moves after observing A's move, as in the Stackelberg model. We can describe such a game by its *extensive form*. Figure 13.1 presents the extensive form of the game described by Table 13.3 with player A moving first. A's options are the same as the rows in the matrix game, and B's options are the same as the columns in the matrix game. The payoff for A is written before the comma, while B's payoff is written after the comma.

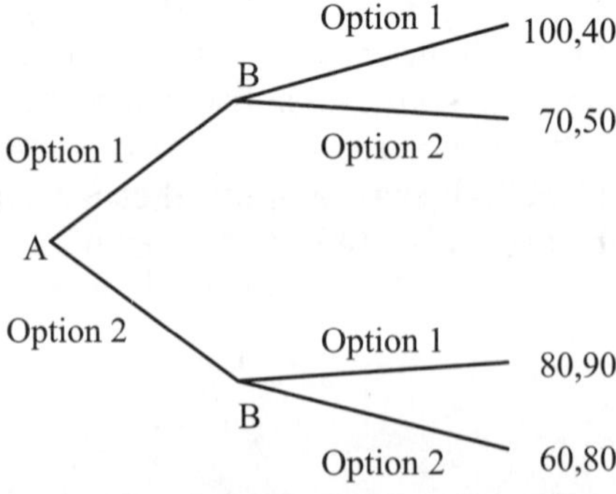

Figure 13.1

To solve a sequential game, work backwards from the end. If A has chosen Option 1, B's best choice is Option 2 (50 is greater than 40). If A has chosen Option 2, B's best choice is Option 1 (90 is greater than 80). If B has no ability to commit to a choice before A makes its choice, then B is maximizing its payoff over two alternatives at this point. This is why working backwards is the right approach. Thus, at A's turn, A can compute that choosing Option 1 will result in a payoff of 70, while choosing Option 2 will result in a payoff of 80. A thus chooses to play Option 2. The payoffs will be 80 for A and 90 for B.

Exercise: ◗ ◗ ◗ ◗ ◗ ◗ ◗

9. For the game given in Table 13.3, what is the extensive form of the sequential game in which B moves first? What is the Nash equilibrium of the sequential game?

THREATS, COMMITMENTS, AND CREDIBILITY (Section 13.6)

Often, the player moving first has an advantage because it can commit to an action. The first player to act can also benefit by taking a *strategic move*. A strategic move constrains one's own actions, but is beneficial because it affects the rival's response. For instance, one OPEC country could announce that if cheating on the cartel agreement is detected it will cut price below marginal cost until the cheater is driven out of the market. But this threat may not be *credible*. If called upon to carry out the punishment, it might not be in the firm's best interest to do so. Rivals will ignore an empty threat. If a firm has no choice but to carry through with its threatened action, the threat will be believable.

Exercise: ◗ ◗ ◗ ◗ ◗ ◗ ◗

10. Two office supply stores, Office Emporium and Office Station compete in a local market. Office Emporium is planning to cut prices storewide in order to gain market share. Office Station has stated in a press release that it will cut prices by even more in order to maintain its position in the market. The payoff matrix in Table 13.15 shows profits (in millions of dollars) for the two office supply stores. Assume that the profits are in present discounted value terms.

		Office Emporium	
		Maintain Price	Lower Price
Office Station	Maintain Price	20, 14	16, 20
	Lower Price	4, 1	2, 4

Table 13.15

Is the threat of a potential low price campaign by Office Station credible? Explain.

ENTRY DETERRENCE (Section 13.7)

Table 13.16 (on the next page) presents a payoff matrix for an established firm and a potential entrant. The entrant has two choices—either enter the industry or stay out. The established firm can respond by being "tough" (fighting the entry through lower prices and an advertising campaign), or by choosing to "accommodate" and share the market.

One possible Nash equilibrium is where the entrant comes in and the incumbent accommodates. The other Nash equilibrium entails a tough stance on the part of the incumbent and no entry. (Note that the incumbent is indifferent between its two choices if the entrant does not come into the market, but the potential entrant will have no incentive to switch strategies if it believes the incumbent will be tough.) Which outcome is most likely to occur? If the incumbent has no way of committing to a "tough" strategy, then the entrant should call its bluff and enter. Once the new firm is in the market, it will be in the incumbent's best interest to accommodate (since 2 > –2). The threat of acting tough is not credible.

		Established Firm	
		Tough	Accommodate
Potential Entrant	Enter	–1, –2	1, 2
	Don't Enter	0, 10	0, 10

Table 13.16

One way to make threats credible is to precommit to the threatened action (i.e., take an irreversible action). For example, the incumbent might do this by signing long-term contracts to engage in an all-out advertising campaign, or it might begin to expand capacity prior to entry. These actions will change the incumbent's payoffs. An example of how this might work is shown in Table 13.17.

		Established Firm	
		Tough	Accommodate
Potential Entrant	Enter	–1, 1	1, 0.5
	Don't Enter	0, 10	0, 10

Table 13.17

By arranging ahead of time to fight the entrant certain costs are incurred prior to entry, but the strategy can be carried out with more planning and thought, which might lower the costs of acting tough. Now if the firm enters the incumbent has a payoff of 1 from continuing with its tough strategy, versus a payoff of 0.5 from not using the capacity it has built or the advertising campaign for which it has paid. In this case, the threat of acting tough is credible. The entrant will be deterred from coming into this industry.

*AUCTIONS (Section 13.8)

There are several common auction formats:

- *English auction*: This is an ascending open-outcry auction, where bidders call out their bids in public. The seller asks for bids from a group of potential buyers and the good is sold when only one bidder is left. The item is sold to the highest bidder at the price they bid. A bidder's strategy entails deciding on a price at which to stop bidding. If, for example, your reservation price is R, you should drop out of the bidding if the bid, B, rises above R. If the last bid is below R, you can bid the price up (in small increments). You will get the item for your last bid and your profit will be $R - B$.

- *Dutch auction*: The seller initially sets a high price and then reduces the price if no bidder comes forward. The item is sold to the first buyer that accepts a price called out by the seller. A bidder's strategy requires choosing the single price to bid. The interesting question is whether you should bid R or something less. The answer is something less. There is a tradeoff between the risk of losing the item by bidding too low, and making a zero profit if you bid exactly R. Due to this tradeoff, it is optimal to bid a price slightly below your valuation. How much less you should bid falls as the number of bidders increases.

- *Sealed-bid auction*: The bids are made privately and the item is sold to the bidder who submitted the highest bid. The price paid by the winning bidder will be the bid price if it is a *first-price sealed-bid auction*, and it will be the second highest bid if the auction is a *second-price sealed-bid auction*. The strategic choice here is choosing which single price to enter as your bid. Just as with Dutch auctions, the optimal bid for a first-price sealed-bid auction should be a bit below your valuation.

If bidders have different reservation prices (valuations) for the item being auctioned, then the auction is a *private-value auction*. For example, bidders would be likely to place different values on the ruby slippers worn by Judy Garland in the movie The Wizard of Oz. If everyone bidding has roughly the same valuation for the item, then we have a *common-value auction*. Although the valuation of the item is the same for all bidders in a common-value auction, any single bidder only has a rough estimate of the true value. For example, oil companies bidding for a drilling tract may know generally how much oil lies beneath the ground, but each bidder will have a different point estimate.

Different auction rules can influence the optimal bid. In a private-value second-price sealed-bid auction the dominant strategy is to bid truthfully. In a common-value auction, on the other hand, you must reduce your maximum bid to account for the expected error of the winning bidder (assuming there is uncertainty surrounding the value of the item). A *winner's curse* often arises in common value auctions, where the winner is in fact worse off for having won the bid because the winner overestimated the value of the item.

Exercise:

11. There are five potential buyers in a second-price sealed-bid auction for a single object. Each buyer has a private value and there is no possibility of later resale. The bidders and their valuations are:

Bidder	Value
A	$420
B	$760
C	$550
D	$430
E	$600

a) How much should each person bid? If they all bid optimally, who will win the auction and how much will that buyer pay? (continued)

b) Now suppose that the bidders' values are the following:

Bidder	Value
A	$380
B	$760
C	$500
D	$490
E	$540

How much should each person bid? If they all bid optimally, who will win the auction and how much will that buyer pay?

c) Suppose instead that the seller had used a first-price sealed-bid auction in both cases. Would there be a difference between the winner's payment given the valuations in part a) and part b) if all buyers believed that the private values were drawn from the same underlying distribution in both cases?

PROBLEM SET

12. In the game displayed in Table 13.1, does either player have a dominant strategy? What is the Nash equilibrium of the game?

13. Suppose that Intel and PowerHouse Systems Inc. are the only two firms that can produce a particular type of microprocessor. The payoffs from entering this product market are as follows:

		PowerHouse	
		Enter	Stay Out
Intel	Enter	10, –40	250, 0
	Stay Out	0, 200	0, 0

The entries in the payoff matrix are profits, in millions of dollars. Intel has a head start over PowerHouse, and can make the first move.

a) What will be the outcome?

b) Suppose the government commits to paying PowerHouse a subsidy of $50 million if it produces the microprocessors. What will be the outcome now?

c) How would the payoffs have to change so that the subsidy would discourage Intel from entering the market?

14. Cartels face two obstacles to their success: cheating by current members and erosion of their market power by entry of new firms into the market. The following payoff matrix illustrates the situation faced by the cartel and an entrant:

		New Firm	
		Enter	Stay Out
Cartel	Price War	50, 5	–40, 0
	No Price War	90, 10	100, 0

a) The cartel threatens a price war if the new firm enters. Should the new firm take this as a credible threat?

b) Suggest one method that the cartel can use to alter the situation in its favor.

15. Assume that two firms sharing the market have formed a cartel, and that there is no possibility of entry. If both firms behave cooperatively they will earn profits of $50 per period. If Firm A cheats on the agreement while Firm B cooperates, then firm A will earn $75 in that period and firm B will earn $0. If B cheats while A cooperates, B earns $75 and A earns $0. If both firms cheat they will each earn $20 that period.

a) Write the payoff matrix for this game.

b) Suppose this game is repeated twice. Player B commits to a strategy of cooperating in round 1, and in round 2 will play whatever Player A did in round 1. Will this strategy deter cheating by Player A?

16. In the following game, what are the maximin strategies of each player? Are these also Nash equilibrium strategies?

		Player 2		
		1	2	3
Player 1	1	18, 5	–20, 45	40, 70
	2	30, 20	10, 35	20, 40
	3	25, 40	30, 30	30, 50

17. The payoff matrix below presents the *payoffs to Player 2* from three different strategies against Player 1's two possible strategies.

		Player 2		
		1	2	3
Player 1	1	10	0	4
	2	0	10	3

Is strategy 3 dominated by either strategy 1 or 2? Would Player 2 ever use strategy 3?

SELF-TEST

18. A noncooperative game is one in which:
a) one player's gain equals the other player's loss.
b) no binding agreements are possible.
c) players' interests are diametrically opposed.
d) no player has a dominant strategy.
e) None of the above is correct.

19. A dominant strategy for a player:
a) has all payoffs greater than all payoffs from every other strategy.
b) is best for a player, whatever the opponent's choice.
c) is best for a player, given the opponent's equilibrium choice.
d) a) and c)
e) None of the above is correct.

20. In the infinitely repeated Prisoners' Dilemma:
a) each player has a dominant strategy always to confess.
b) each player has a dominant strategy never to confess.
c) cooperation may be sustained by the threat of future punishment.
d) cooperation requires communication between players.
e) None of the above is correct.

21. In a sequential game, a threat is credible:
a) if rivals cannot make the same threat themselves.
b) if it will be in a player's interest to carry out the threat.
c) if carrying out the threat punishes everyone.
d) a) and c)
e) None of the above is correct.

The next two questions refer to the following game.

		B: 1	B: 2
A	1	−30, −5	40, 0
	2	0, 80	0, 0

22. If A moves first, the Nash equilibrium strategies are:
a) Row 1 and Column 1.
b) Row 2 and Column 1.
c) Row 1 and Column 2.
d) Row 2 and Column 2.
e) This game does not have an equilibrium in pure strategies.

23. If A and B move simultaneously, the Nash equilibrium strategies are:
a) Row 1 and Column 2.
b) Row 2 and Column 1.
c) Row 1 and Column 1.
d) a) and b)
e) a) and c)

24. Consider the following payoff matrix.

		Firm B: Advertise	Firm B: Don't Advertise
Firm A	Advertise	20, 10	32, 0
	Don't Advertise	15, 12	20, 5

If each firm follows their dominant strategy, what will be the resulting outcome?
a) 20, 10
b) 20, 5
c) 32, 0
d) 15, 12
e) There is no equilibrium to this game.

25. A Nash equilibrium occurs when:
a) each firm has selected its maximum possible payoff out of all the feasible options.
b) each firm is doing the best it can given what its rival is doing.
c) one firm has a strategy, which is best regardless of its rivals' actions.
d) firms choose quantities rather than prices.
e) each firm can commit to a strategy before the game starts.

26. Two rational rival firms that manufacture cassette tapes must choose between an "aggressive" low price strategy, and a "cooperative" high price strategy. They realize that cassette tapes will soon become obsolete (with the invention of compact discs), and therefore they both know that they will be competing against each other for a finite period of time. If the firms have adopted a "tit-for-tat" strategy, they will each:
a) set a high price.
b) set a low price.
c) set a high price in all periods but the last, and set a low price in the last period.
d) set a low price in all periods but the last, and set a high price in the last period.
e) None of the above.

27. An example of a sequential game is:
a) the Stackelberg model.
b) a chess game.
c) a preemptive investment game.
d) an entry deterrence game.
e) All of the above.

28. In the following game the players' interests coincide: whatever is good for one player is also good for others.

		Player 2: Left	Player 2: Right
Player 1	Left	2, 2	0, 0
	Right	1, 1/2	1, 1

In this game:
a) Player 1 has a dominant strategy of "Left" and the outcome will be (2,2).
b) both players have a dominant strategy of "Left" and the outcome will be (2,2).
c) both players have a dominant strategy of "Right" and the outcome will be (1,1).
d) neither player has a dominant strategy, but a Nash equilibrium of this game is (2,2).
e) Player 1's credible threat of playing "Right" will force the outcome to (1,1).

29. Consider the following game in extensive form, which describes Player 1, an incumbent monopolist in an industry, and Player 2, a firm that could enter the industry.

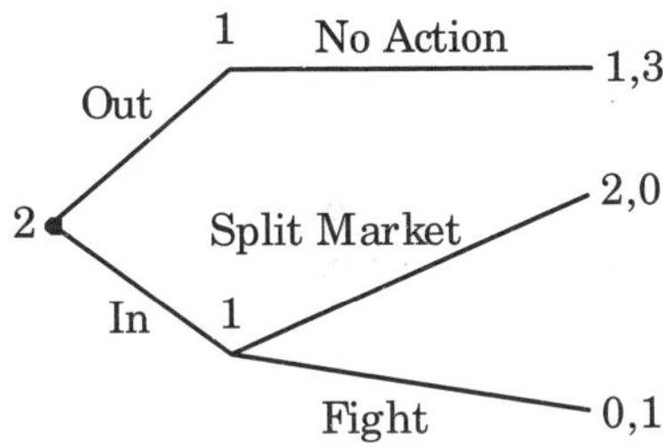

Player 2's payoff is given before the comma, and Player 1's payoff is listed after the comma. Player 1 has made an irreversible investment in extra capacity, which will only be used if it decides to fight the entrant. The outcome of this game will be:

a) entry by Player 2 will be deterred.
b) Player 2 will enter and Player 1 will split the market.
c) Player 2 will enter and Player 1 will fight.
d) Player 2 will not enter because the payoff of 3 is greater than 0.
e) Player 1 will not deter entry because its threat to fight is not credible.

ANSWERS TO CHAPTER 13

EXERCISE ANSWERS

1. Revlon's dominant strategy is to charge a low price, regardless of what it thinks L'Oreal might do. (If L'Oreal prices low, then Revlon should price low since 10 > 6, and if L'Oreal prices high, then Revlon should again price low since 20 > 15.) L'Oreal also has a dominant strategy of pricing low. The outcome of the game will be that both will choose to price low and both will earn $10 million in profits.

2. A's dominant strategy is to play Row 1 against each of B's possible strategies, i.e., A's payoff is greater if it plays Row 1 than if it plays Row 2. B does not have a dominant strategy because Column 2 is its best strategy against Row 1, while Column 3 is its best strategy against Row 2. The Nash equilibrium of this game is for A to play its dominant strategy, Row 1, while B plays Column 2. The equilibrium payoffs are 7 for A and 7 for B. Once these strategies are chosen, no player will have an incentive to deviate from them.

3. Here, neither player has a dominant strategy. Row 2 is best for A against Column 1, while Row 1 is best against Column 2 or Column 3. Similarly, Column 2 is best for B against Row 1, while Column 3 is best against Row 2. In the Nash equilibrium, A plays Row 1, and B plays Column 2. The equilibrium payoffs are 7 for A and 7 for B.

4. Neither player has a dominant strategy and there are two possible Nash equilibria. One Nash equilibrium is "sell-sell" (50, 60), where both firms develop an on-line retail presence. This qualifies as a Nash equilibrium because neither firm has an incentive to change strategies, given the strategy chosen by the other firm. The second Nash equilibrium is "don't sell-don't sell" (60, 40) and is the exact opposite. In this case neither firm sells online. Either outcome is a potential "stable" point, given the payoffs. Without additional information about the product or the firms, it is difficult to tell which of these two equilibria will prevail in the market.

5. Yes, if the firms adopt a maximin strategy, they will find themselves in an equilibrium where both cut price. If Firm 1 maintains price, its lowest profit is 130. If Firm 1 cuts price, its lowest possible profit is 135. Therefore, using the conservative maximin decision rule, Firm 1 will maximize its lowest payoff by cutting price. Firm 2 also realizes that by maintaining price its worst payoff would be 125, but by cutting price it raises its worst possible payoff slightly to 130. Therefore, Firm 2 will also cut price. The maximin equilibrium in this case is exactly the same as the dominant strategy (Nash) equilibrium.

6. Neither player has a dominant strategy. An equilibrium mixed strategy will have A indifferent between playing Row 1 and Row 2, and B will be indifferent between playing Column 1 and Column 2. Let p be the probability A plays Row 1, and 1 – p the probability that A plays Row 2. Let q be the probability that B plays Column 1, and 1 – q the probability that B plays Column 2.

For A to mix over Row 1 and Row 2, its expected payoff from each of these strategies must be equal. A's expected payoff from Row 1 is $30q + 70(1 - q)$, while its expected payoff from Row 2 is $20q + 80(1 - q)$. Therefore, q^* is the solution to $30q + 70(1 - q) = 20q + 80(1 - q)$. Collecting terms, $20q = 10$, so $q^* = 1/2$. For B to mix over Column 1 and Column 2, its expected payoff from each of these must be equal. So p^* is the solution to $40p + 100(1 - p) = 50p + 80(1 - p)$. Collecting terms, $30p = 20$, or $p^* = 2/3$. A's expected payoff from Row 1 is therefore $(1/2)30 + (1/2)70 = 50$; its expected payoff from Row 2 is $(1/2)20 + (1/2)80 = 50$. Checking that the expected payoffs from each of the strategies are equal verifies that q^* is correct. B's expected payoff from Column 1 is $(2/3)40 + (1/3)100 = 60$; its expected payoff from Column 2 is $(2/3)50 + (1/3)80 = 60$.

7. Tacit collusion is collusion that occurs without an explicit agreement between the parties. Thus, there may not be any illegal behavior to observe (such as communication about prices among managers of different firms). Each firm can claim that its behavior was individually rational, given its expectations about rivals' behavior.

8. a) If this game is played only once, both ABC and NBC will choose to advertise and each will earn 100. (Advertising is a dominant strategy for each player.)

b) If NBC adopts a parallel strategy, calculating profits over only the first ten periods, we get:

$$\pi_{NBC} = 10(200) = 2{,}000.$$

If NBC tries to take advantage of ABC it will advertise in the first period and earn 300, but ABC will retaliate by advertising in each period after that. Profits are:

$$\pi_{NBC} = 300 + 9(100) = 1{,}200.$$

Clearly, it is not in NBC's interest to follow the latter strategy.

9. See Figure 13A.1. At A's turn, A will play Option 1, whether B has played Option 1 or Option 2. Thus, B prefers to play Option 2 because that yields a payoff of 50 instead of the payoff of 40 from playing Option 1. So, the Nash equilibrium is that B plays Option 2, and then A plays Option 1. The equilibrium payoffs are 70 for A and 50 for B.

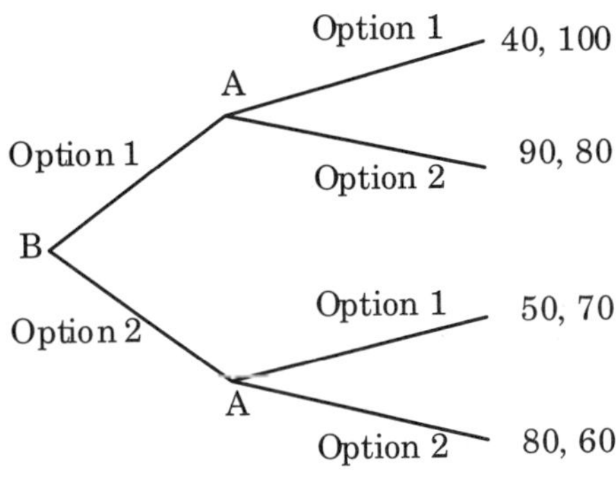

Figure 13A.1

10. According to the payoff matrix, Office Station will be better off maintaining prices if Office Emporium lowers its prices. The threat by Office Station is not credible.

11. a) Everyone should bid his or her true private value in this case. Person B will bid $760 and win the object, but only pay $600, the second-highest bid,

b) Person B will bid $760 and win the object, but only pay $540, the second-highest bid.

c) In a first-price sealed-bid auction, the optimal strategy is to bid an amount less than one's own private value. These two auction formats have the same expected revenue for the seller. Therefore, person B should bid an amount equal to her expectation of the second-highest value (conditional on her value being the highest). This will be the same in both auctions, since the information about the distribution of values used by other bidders and the highest private value are the same in both cases.

PROBLEM SET ANSWERS

12. Neither player has a dominant strategy. A does best to play Row 1 against Column 1, while it does best to play Row 2 against Column 2. B does best to play Column 3 against Row 1, while it does best to play Column 2 against Row 2. The Nash equilibrium is Row 2 and Column 2, with payoffs of 600 for A and 300 for B.

13. a) Intel will enter, because that is its dominant strategy, and PowerHouse recognizing this, will decide to stay out of the market. The payoff for Intel is 250 and the payoff for PowerHouse is 0.

b) The payoff matrix would change to:

		PowerHouse	
		Enter	Stay Out
Intel	Enter	10, 10	250, 0
	Stay Out	0, 250	0, 0

Intel will still enter, but PowerHouse will enter too. The payoff to Intel and PowerHouse will be 10 each.

c) In order for Intel to decide to stay out, its payoff from staying out would have to be higher than its payoff from entering when PowerHouse enters. This could happen if, for example, there were large economies of scale in microprocessor production and the subsidy allowed PowerHouse to build a large enough plant to lower its costs below that of Intel's.

14. a) The cartel will not succeed in deterring entry with this threat. If the new firm chooses to enter, it can anticipate (if the cartel is rational) that the cartel will not start a price war (since 90 is greater than –50). If entry occurs the cartel will find it in its best interest to accommodate the entrant into the market. The threat of a price war is not credible.

b) The cartel could: (i) commit to guaranteeing customers a low price if a new firm enters the industry, (ii) commit their reputations to fighting new entrants, thus raising the cost of giving in, or (iii) occasionally act irrationally and fight new entrants in order to send a signal to other potential entrants.

15. a) The payoff matrix is:

		B	
		Cooperate	Cheat
A	Cooperate	50, 50	0, 75
	Cheat	75, 0	20, 20

b) If A cooperates both periods: $\pi_A = 50 + 50 = 100$.

If A cheats both periods: $\pi_A = 75 + 20 = 95$.
(Recall that B will cheat in period 2 if A cheats in period 1.)

If A cooperates, then cheats: $\pi_A = 50 + 75 = 125$.

If A cheats, then cooperates: $\pi_A = 75 + 0 = 75$.

This strategy does not deter cheating by A in round 2. The most profitable strategy for A is to cooperate in period 1 and then cheat in the last period of the game, knowing that B can't retaliate.

16. Player 1's worst payoffs from her three strategies are –20, 10, and 25, respectively, so Player 1's maximin strategy is strategy 3. Player 2's worst payoffs from his three strategies are 5, 30, and 40, respectively, so Player 2's maximin strategy is strategy 3.

However, the unique Nash equilibrium is strategy 1 by Player 1 and strategy 3 by Player 2 with payoffs of 40 and 70.

17. If Player 1 plays her strategy 1, strategy 2 is worse for Player 2 than strategy 3, and if Player 1 plays her strategy 2, strategy 1 is worse for Player 2 than strategy 3. So no other pure strategy dominates strategy 3 for Player 2.

Player 2 would never use strategy 3, since no matter what 2 predicts 1 will do, strategy 1 or 2 will yield a higher payoff. In fact, a 50–50 mix over strategy 1 and 2 guarantees Player 2 an expected payoff of 5, which is better than the best payoff from strategy 3.

SELF-TEST ANSWERS

18. b) The definition of noncooperative behavior does not rest on particular payoffs (so choices a), c), and d) are false), but rather on firm behavior. If firms act independently, then the game is noncooperative. If they can make binding agreements, then it is cooperative.

19. b) Choice a) is stronger than necessary, while c) is true for any equilibrium strategy.

20. c) When the game is repeated infinitely, the expected gains from cooperation will outweigh those from undercutting.

21. b) If carrying out the threat punishes *everyone* as in choice c), the player who made the threat will choose not to carry it out.

22. c) If A plays Row 1, then B will play Column 2. If A plays Row 2, then B will play Column 1. A's payoff is 40 in the former case and 0 in the latter case, so A will choose to play Row 1 and then B will play Column 2. Once they make these choices, neither player will have an incentive to deviate.

23. d) Both (Row 1, Column 2) and (Row 2, Column 1) are Nash equilibria. If players simultaneously choose either pair of strategies, no player wants to deviate, given the rival's choice.

24. a) "Advertise" is the dominant strategy for both firms.

25. b) This is the definition of Nash equilibrium. It has nothing to do with individual payoffs, quantities versus prices, or commitment (choices a), d) and e)). Choice c) is the definition of dominant strategy.

26. b) In a *finitely* repeated game, the strategy of cooperating as long as your rival cooperates and lowering price if your rival lowers price (a tit-for-tat strategy) will lead to a low price equilibrium. The game is solved from the last period backwards.

27. e) In each case one player makes the first move, rather than two or more players making simultaneous moves.

28. d) The outcome (2, 2) is a Nash equilibrium (neither player will have an incentive to deviate once they reach this outcome), but there are no dominant strategies in this game. The other Nash equilibrium is the outcome (1,1).

29. a) If Player 2 enters, Player 1 will fight (1 > 0) and Player 2 will get a payoff of 0. It would be better for Player 2 to stay out and get a payoff of 1. In this case, Player 1's threat to fight is credible.

CHAPTER 14
MARKETS FOR FACTOR INPUTS

IMPORTANT CONCEPTS

- Marginal Revenue Product of Labor
- Individual Firm Demand Curve for Labor
- Industry Demand Curve for Labor
- Input Supply Curve
- Backward-Bending Labor Supply Curve
- Monopsony Power
- Marginal Expenditure
- Bilateral Monopoly

CHAPTER HIGHLIGHTS

Factor markets are markets for labor, raw materials, and other inputs to production. The important element in understanding the demand for a factor of production is that it is a derived demand, depending on production costs and the firm's level of output. Adding another unit of input is profitable only if the additional revenue from the output generated by this extra input is greater than the cost of the input. The additional revenue from one more unit of labor input is the *marginal revenue product of labor* (MRP_L). In general, this equals the marginal product of labor times the firm's marginal revenue. If a firm buys inputs in a competitive market, the MRP_L curve is its *labor demand curve.*

In the long run, when there are several variable inputs, the firm responds to a lower wage by increasing output and hiring more capital. This shifts the MRP_L curve to the right, so the labor demand curve is flatter than when capital is held constant. In addition, the *industry demand curve for labor* is steeper than the sum of the firms' demand curves. This occurs because a fall in the wage rate causes each firm to expand output, which lowers the price of output. With a lower price of output, each firm's MRP_L curve shifts to the right.

The market supply curve for an input usually slopes upward. However, the labor supply curve may be *backward bending*. Since consumers sell their own labor, an increase in the price of labor makes them better off. If leisure is a normal good, the income effect of a wage increase encourages workers to supply less labor.

The substitution effect works in the opposite direction: as the wage rises leisure becomes more expensive, relative to other goods, which encourages workers to supply more labor. If the income effect is large enough, it will outweigh the substitution effect. In that case, the quantity of labor supplied will fall as the wage rises.

Equilibrium in a factor market is found at the intersection of the marginal revenue product curve and the supply curve for that factor. This holds for both competitive and monopolistic output markets, although MRP curves differ in these two cases. As long as the labor supply curve is upward sloping, the total payments to labor in equilibrium exceed the minimum payment that workers must receive to supply that quantity of labor. The difference between these payments is *economic rent*, which is analogous to producer surplus in product markets. If the supply of an input is perfectly inelastic, all payments to that factor of production are economic rents (since the factor will be supplied no matter what price is paid).

Monopsony power exists whenever the buyers of a factor face an upward-sloping supply curve. The *marginal expenditure curve* for the monopsonist describes the additional amount paid to buy one more unit, and it lies above the average expenditure curve because the firm must pay all units a higher price in order to hire more units. The monopsonist hires labor up to the point where the marginal expenditure curve intersects the MRP_L curve and pays the wage on the supply curve for that quantity.

Monopoly power arises frequently in factor markets in the form of labor unions. These unions can set different wages depending on their goals—maximizing employment, maximizing rents, or maximizing total wage payments. When labor unions succeed in raising wages in the unionized sector, some workers will lose their jobs. When these workers move into the nonunion sector, the effect will be to lower nonunion wages.

CONCEPT REVIEW AND EXERCISES

COMPETITIVE FACTOR MARKETS (Section 14.1)

A competitive input market consists of many buyers and sellers. Consider the market for unskilled labor in a single city. In such a market, each worker chooses how many hours to work given the market wage. Conversely, each firm decides how many workers (or labor-hours) it wishes to hire at the market wage.

The cost of an additional hour of labor input is simply the hourly wage, w. The benefit to the firm from an additional hour of labor is the additional output generated from one more hour of labor input times the additional revenue earned by selling another unit of output, or $MP_L \cdot MR$. The product of the marginal product of labor and marginal revenue is called the *marginal revenue product of labor* (MRP_L). For a perfectly competitive firm, marginal revenue equals price, so that $MRP_L = P \cdot MP_L$.

Whether or not the *product* market is competitive, if a firm buys its *inputs* in a competitive market, the MRP_L curve is its labor demand curve. This is due to the fact that a cost-minimizing (profit-maximizing) firm hires labor up to the point where the marginal revenue product of labor equals its marginal cost, or $MRP_L = w$. The demand for labor curve is downward sloping, so that the quantity of labor demanded increases as the wage rate falls, as Figure 14.1 (on the next page) shows. Note that labor demand curve depends on the quantity of other factors employed by the firm, e.g., a change in the firm's capital input shifts its MP_L curve, causing a shift in the MRP_L curve. Demand for inputs is a derived demand, depending on production and output market conditions.

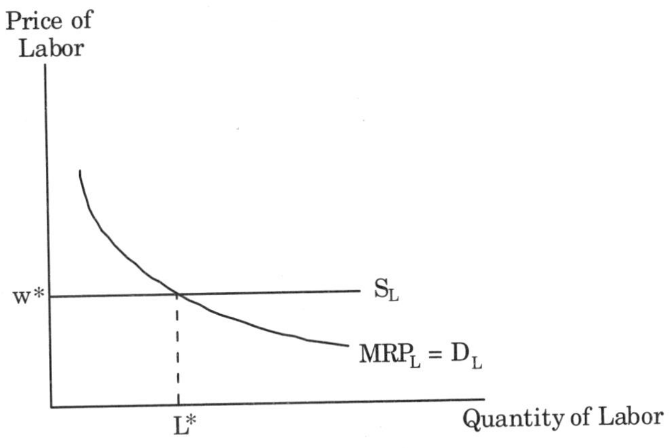

Figure 14.1

Exercise: ◗ ◗ ◗ ◗ ◗ ◗ ◗

1. Anderson Industries produces anvils and sells them in a perfectly competitive market. In the short run, its capital inputs are fixed, and its marginal product of labor curve is $MP_L = 3.10 - 0.02L$ where L is the number of persons employed per week.

a) If Anderson Industries sells anvils for \$200 per unit, find its MRP_L curve.

b) If the weekly wage is \$300, how many workers will it employ?

c) If the weekly wage falls to \$240, how many workers will it employ?

2. *[Calculus] Baxter Industries produces air drills, and it has a patent on its output. Its marginal product of labor curve is $MP_L = 60 - L$, where L is the number of persons employed per week. Its total product of labor curve is $Q = 60L - 0.5L^2$, where Q is output per week. The demand curve for the firm's output is $P = 100 - Q$. What is its marginal revenue product of labor curve?

In the long run, when all inputs are variable, the individual firm's demand for labor curve is not equal to the MRP_L curve. For example, consider a home-building firm that uses carpenters and capital. In response to a drop in the wage of carpenters, the firm's marginal cost curve shifts down. As a consequence, the firm expands its output, hiring more carpenters and more capital. Hiring additional capital shifts the MP_L curve (and the MRP_L curve) to the right. Consequently, the long-run demand for labor curve for carpenters is flatter than the short-run MRP_L curves, as shown in Figure 14.2.

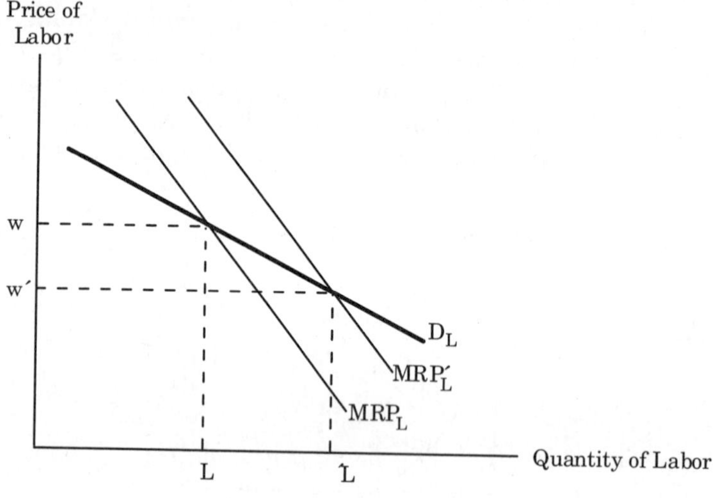

Figure 14.2

Similarly, the industry demand curve for labor is not simply the sum of the firms' demand curves for labor. As the wage drops, each firm produces more, which lowers the equilibrium output price. Since a firm's demand curve for labor was derived holding constant the output price, simply adding the curves together is not correct. The lower output price causes the MRP_L curve for each firm to shift to the left. Adding up the quantity of labor demanded at each wage, we find that the industry demand curve for labor is steeper than the horizontal sum of individual firm demand curves. This is shown in Figure 14.5(b) of the text, which is reproduced below.

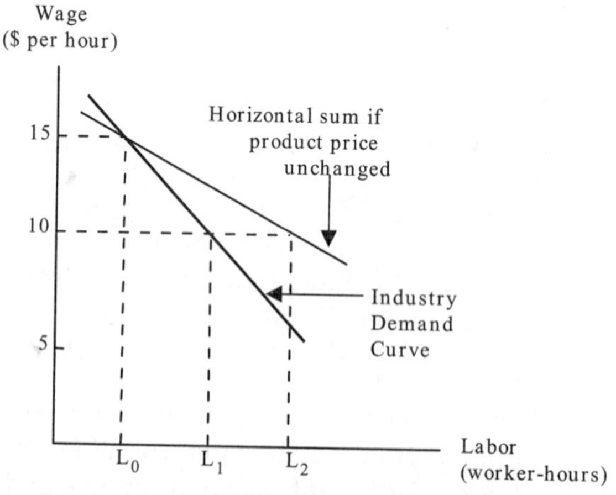

Text Figure 14.5(b)

INPUT SUPPLY CURVES

The input supply curve for an industry is usually upward sloping. However, the supply curve facing an *individual firm* is horizontal at the market price for the input. A firm takes the input price as given and demands as much of the input as it wants. This parallels the assumption that a competitive firm takes the price of its output as given, even though there is a downward-sloping demand for industry output.

If a firm is the only buyer of the input (a *monopsony*), then the firm's optimal choice is to hire the amount of the input such that its *marginal expenditure* on the input (ME) equals the marginal revenue product (which is the marginal valuation (MV) of Chapter 10). For example, suppose the homebuilder is the only employer of carpenters in a small city. If 100 person-hours per day are supplied at a wage of $14 per hour, and 101 person-hours are supplied at a wage of $14.50 per hour, the firm would spend $1,400 for 100 person-hours per day, and it would spend $1,464.50 for 101 person-hours per day. Thus, its marginal expenditure on the 101st person-hour per day is $64.50.

In contrast, if the firm hires carpenters in a competitive market, its marginal expenditure equals the wage. If the firm faces a horizontal supply curve at a wage of $14/hour, the marginal expenditure for the 101st person-hour will simply be $14/hour. The firm would then hire carpenters until the MRP_L equals $14/hour. Since ME = w in this case, the two rules (MRP_L = ME and MRP_L = w) are the same.

Although the market supply curve for an input normally slopes upwards, the labor supply curve may be *backward bending*. At low wages a wage increase will increase labor supply, but at higher wages a wage increase may decrease the quantity of labor supplied. Whether this happens depends on the relative magnitude of the substitution and income effects of a wage change. Since consumers sell their own labor, an increase in the price of labor makes them better off.

If leisure is a normal good, the income effect of a wage increase will lead to more consumption of leisure, and therefore less labor supplied. Conversely, the substitution effect of a wage increase causes *more* labor to be supplied (as the price of leisure increases less leisure is consumed). If leisure is a normal good, the income and substitution effects have opposite signs. If the income effect is large enough, it will outweigh the substitution effect. If this happens, the quantity of labor supplied falls as the wage rises. At low wage levels, the tendency is for the substitution effect to be greater, while at high wage levels, the income effect tends to dominate. This causes the backward bend in the labor supply curve, as shown in Figure 14.3 (on the next page).

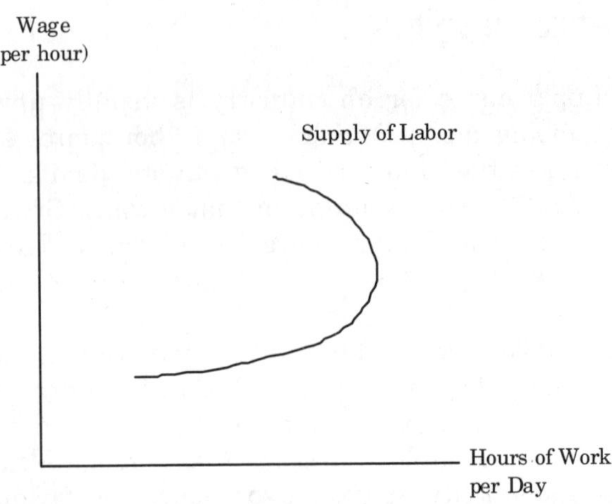

Figure 14.3

This discussion may sound similar to our earlier discussion of Giffen goods, but there is an important difference. An individual sacrifices leisure when she supplies labor in the market. A wage increase raises the value of the total amount of time available to her and also raises the effective price of an hour of leisure. If leisure is a normal good, the increase in the value of her time has the effect of raising her total income. As a result, we would expect her to demand more leisure at any given wage rate. This positive income effect can be substantial. However, the higher price of leisure decreases the quantity of leisure demanded, holding utility constant, so there is a substitution effect as well. Thus, to have income and substitution effects go in opposite directions does not require that any goods be inferior, as was required with Giffen goods. Backward-bending labor supply curves are more common than Giffen goods because labor income is by far the largest income source for workers.

Exercise: ▶ ▶ ▶ ▶ ▶ ▶ ▶

3. A local moving company is currently paying a constant wage of w and the typical worker is working 8 hours per day. The company wants to induce its employees to work overtime (more than 8 hours per day). To accomplish this, it is thinking of adopting one of the following plans:

a) Offer each employee a wage $\hat{w} > w$.
b) Offer each employee an overtime rate of wage $\hat{w} > w$, which will be paid for each hour worked beyond 8.

Which plan should the company use if it wants to *guarantee* that workers will work more than 8 hours per day? Justify your answer using indifference curves and budget constraints where the two goods are "Income" (on the vertical axis) and "Hours of Leisure" (on the horizontal axis), both measured per day.

EQUILIBRIUM IN A COMPETITIVE FACTOR MARKET (Section 14.2)

The intersection of the labor supply curve and the labor demand curve determines the wage rate (w) and the quantity of labor (L) supplied in a competitive equilibrium. With a perfectly competitive output market efficiency requires that $w = MRP_L = (P)(MP_L)$; with a monopolistic output market, the equilibrium condition is $w = MRP_L = (MR)(MP_L)$. Less labor is demanded with monopolistic output markets simply because less output is produced.

When the labor supply curve is upward sloping, the total payment to workers in equilibrium exceeds the minimum amount necessary to encourage the workers to supply that quantity of labor. The difference is the *economic rent* earned by labor, shown in Figure 14.4 (recall that the supply of labor is also the average expenditure curve), which is analogous to producer surplus in output markets. Since all workers are paid the same wage in equilibrium, workers who would supply labor at a lower wage receive a payment in excess of their opportunity cost. In the special case of a perfectly inelastic factor supply curve, such as for unimproved land, all factor payments are economic rent. However, with a horizontal factor supply curve, there is no economic rent in a competitive equilibrium.

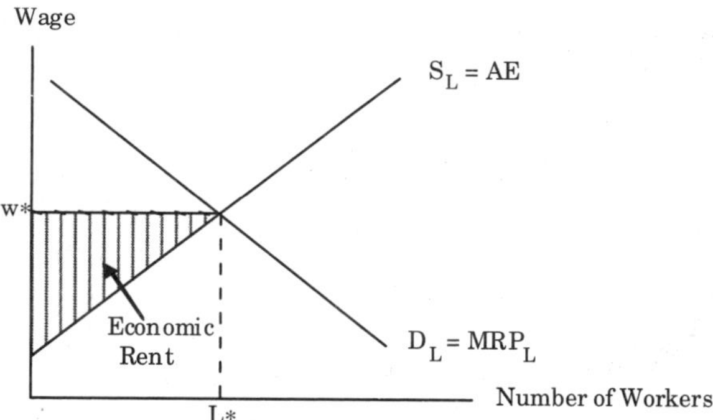

Figure 14.4

Exercise:

4. a) Given the information in Figure 14.5, identify the competitive equilibrium wage and amount of labor hired. Then, assuming a monopoly in the output market, identify the monopoly wage and amount of labor hired.

b) To maximize economic rent, would workers prefer a wage of w_0, w_1, or w_2?

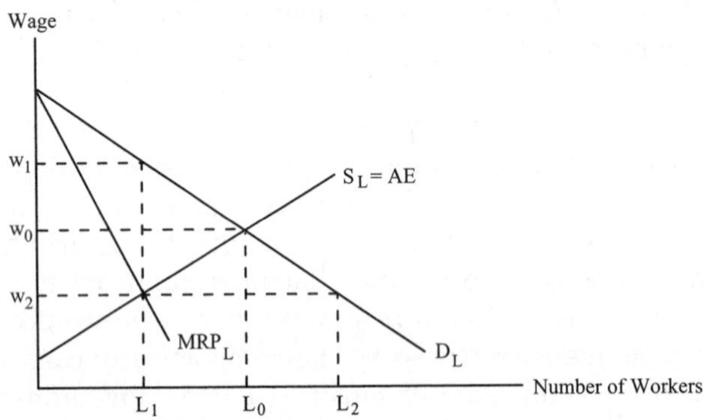

Figure 14.5

FACTOR MARKETS WITH MONOPSONY POWER (Section 14.3)

In Chapter 10, we saw that a monopsonist would equate its marginal valuation of the good with its marginal expenditure, which is the additional amount paid to buy one more unit. The marginal valuation (MV) curve described in Chapter 10 is identical to the MRP_L curve described earlier in this chapter. The condition that MV = ME in Chapter 10 tells us that the monopsonist should hire labor up to the point where MRP_L equals marginal expenditure, ME. Note that the ME curve lies above the supply curve whenever the labor supply curve is upward sloping. The monopsonist hires labor up to the point where the marginal expenditure curve intersects the MRP_L curve and pays the wage on the supply curve for that quantity. This means that a monopsonist will hire less labor than a firm hiring in a perfectly competitive market will, even with an identical MRP_L. Figure 14.6 summarizes the monopsony outcome.

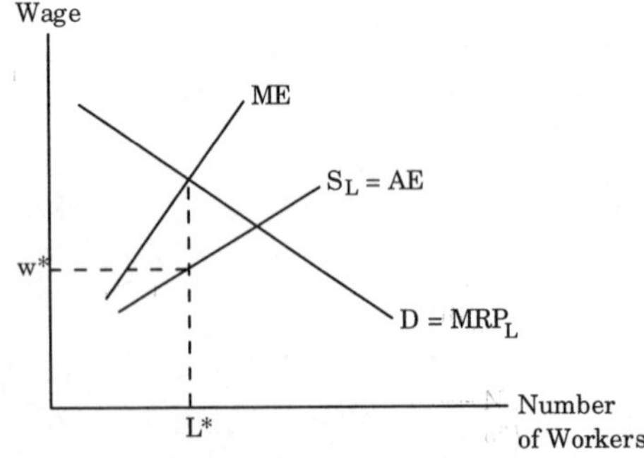

Figure 14.6

Monopsony power exists whenever a firm faces an upward-sloping supply curve for an input. Monopsony power is more common in factor markets than in product markets. Just as a seller can have monopoly power even though it is not the only seller in the market, a firm can have monopsony power even though it competes with other buyers. What matters is that the firm can affect the market price of the input by changing the amount of the input that it purchases. A large employer in a small town will often have some monopsony power. If the local residents have few other job opportunities, the firm will have considerable monopsony power.

Exercise: ▶ ▶ ▶ ▶ ▶ ▶ ▶

5. The only employer in the town of Dustbowl is the local textile mill. The mill faces the supply curve for labor shown in Table 14.1:

Wage Rate Per Hour ($)	Units of Labor Supplied Per Hour	Total Expenditure	Marginal Expenditure
4	10	40	n.a.
5	11	_____	_____
6	12	_____	_____
7	13	_____	_____
8	14	_____	_____

Table 14.1

a) Fill in the blanks in Table 14.1.

b) The mill's demand curve for labor is a horizontal line at a wage of $17 per hour. How much labor will the mill demand? What will be the equilibrium wage rate?

FACTOR MARKETS WITH MONOPOLY POWER (Section 14.4)

Although it is rare, input markets, like output markets, can be monopolized. For example, if union workers must unload cargo from a ship, then the union is the only "seller" of labor for that particular job. A union may have several objectives—maximizing employment, maximizing economic rent (the difference between the wages a union member earns and his or her opportunity cost), or maximizing total wage payments. We can see the effects of different union policies by using an analysis similar to the one we used for monopoly in an output market.

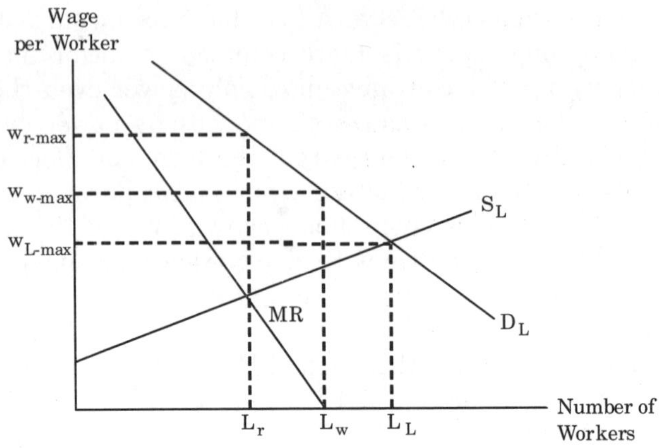

Figure 14.7

Consider Figure 14.7. If the union wishes to maximize employment, it should agree to a wage of $w_{L\text{-max}}$. If it wants to maximize *total* wages paid to its members it should agree to a wage of $w_{w\text{-max}}$ and allow only L_w workers to work. (Note that this is exactly the same as a monopolist in an output market who chooses price where elasticity is –1 in order to maximize total revenue.) If the union wants to maximize rent (the same as a monopolist wanting to maximize producer surplus), it should restrict the quantity of labor supplied to L_r, which is the point where the marginal revenue curve intersects the supply of labor curve. There are winners and losers with each of these plans. Union leaders must therefore choose their bargaining strategy carefully if they want to maintain a loyal membership.

Exercise: ▶ ▶ ▶ ▶ ▶ ▶ ▶

6. a) Figure 14.8 (on the next page) displays a labor supply curve, an industry labor demand curve, and the corresponding marginal revenue curve. A union chooses the wage. How much labor is hired and what is the wage if the union wishes to maximize the economic rent obtained by the members of the union?

   b) What is economic rent at this wage?

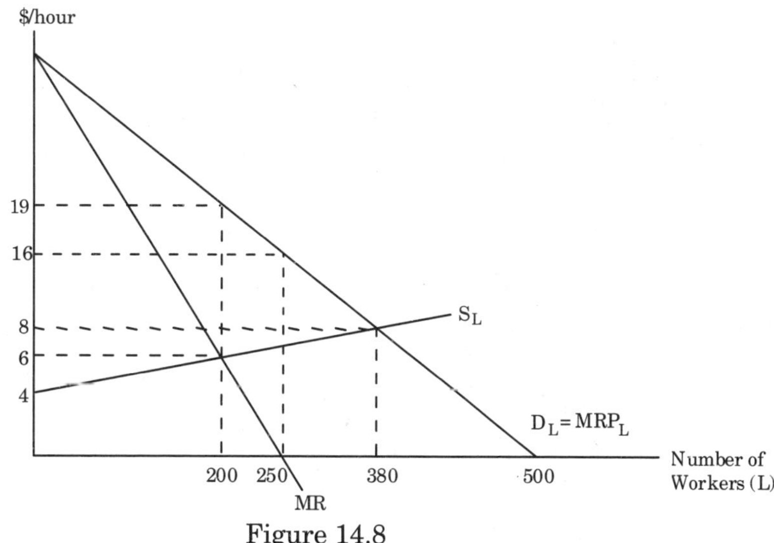

Figure 14.8

At the rent-maximizing wage, fewer workers are employed than at the competitive wage. This creates inequality between the employed union members and those who cannot find employment at the union wage. The union may pursue goals other than rent maximization to reduce the inequality among its members. The next exercise looks at two possible outcomes.

Exercise:

7. Consider the union discussed in Exercise 6.

a) Suppose the union wishes to maximize total employment. At any wage set by the union, the amount of labor hired will be the lesser of the quantity demanded and the quantity supplied at that wage. What wage does the union choose, and how much labor is hired?

b) Suppose instead that the union wishes to maximize total wage payments. What wage does it choose, and how much labor is hired?

PROBLEM SET

8. For the firm in Exercise 1 what wage would a union demand if its goal were to maximize the total payments to labor?

9. *[Calculus] A firm has the production function $Q = 12L - L^2$, where L is labor input per day and Q is output per day. The marginal product of labor equals $12 - 2L$. If the firm is a monopolist with a demand curve $P(Q) = 100 - Q$, what is the MRP_L curve?

10. The demand for labor by an industry is given by the curve L = 72 – 5w, where L is the labor demanded per day, and w is the wage rate. The supply curve is given by L = 3w.
   a) What is the equilibrium wage rate and quantity of labor hired?
   b) What is the economic rent earned by workers?
   c) If the workers wanted to maximize economic rent, is the wage from part a) the one that they would choose? Explain using the concepts you learned in this chapter or calculate economic rent for a different wage rate (e.g., a wage $1 more than your answer to a)) and show how it differs from your answer to b).

11. Some unions limit the number of union members and require employers to hire union members only. This type of arrangement is called a "closed shop." Suppose a closed shop union limits union membership to L_u and lets the firm determine the wage.
   a) Illustrate the equilibrium wage and quantity of labor hired using a diagram with the demand and supply curve for labor. (Hint: Remember that the supply of labor of union workers is completely fixed at L_u.)
   b) Does your graph explain why there is often a waiting list for union membership when a union establishes a closed shop?

12. Consider the market for nursing services in a town with only one large hospital.
   a) What would happen to the number of nurses employed and the deadweight loss if the government instituted a minimum salary for nurses that was above the prevailing market wage? Why? Illustrate your answer in a graph, assuming a linear factor supply and marginal revenue product.
   b) Suppose a geriatric facility opens up in a neighboring town, so that local nurses have more employment options. What would you expect to happen to the number of nurses employed and the wages paid by the hospital? Illustrate your answer assuming that the supply curve shifts up in a parallel fashion.

SELF-TEST

13. The marginal revenue product of labor equals:
   a) MP_L/MR.
   b) MR/MP_L.
   c) $P \cdot MP_L$.
   d) $MR \cdot MP_L$.
   e) None of the above is correct.

14. A firm is hiring the optimal amount of labor when:
   a) $w = P \cdot MP_L$.
   b) $w = MRP_L$.
   c) $MC = MRP_L$.
   d) $MR = MP_L$.
   e) None of the above is correct.

15. A firm should hire less labor when the marginal revenue product of labor is:
a) equal to the output price.
b) equal to the wage rate.
c) less than the wage rate.
d) downward sloping.
e) backward bending.

16. A firm's long run demand curve for labor is:
a) flatter than the short-run demand curve for labor.
b) steeper than the short-run demand curve for labor.
c) to the left of the short-run demand curve for labor.
d) to the right of the short-run demand curve for labor.
e) None of the above is correct.

17. With identical firms, the industry demand curve for labor is:
a) more elastic than a firm's demand curve for labor.
b) less elastic than a firm's demand curve for labor.
c) horizontal.
d) vertical.
e) None of the above is correct.

Use the following information to answer the next two questions: A competitive firm has a marginal product of labor curve given by $MP_L = 100 - 0.4L$. The price of its product is P = \$2.50 per unit. The wage rate is \$15 per hour.

18. Given this information, what is the marginal revenue product of labor?
a) $40 - 0.16L$
b) $1500 - 6L$
c) $100 - 0.4L$
d) $100 - 0.8L$
e) $250 - L$

19. Given this information, how many hours of labor will be hired to maximize profit?
a) 235
b) 106.25
c) 212.50
d) 250
e) 156

20. In the range in which labor supply is backward bending:
a) the substitution effect dominates the income effect.
b) the income effect dominates the substitution effect.
c) leisure is a Giffen good.
d) consumption is a Giffen good.
e) None of the above is correct.

21. A monopsonist is hiring the optimal amount of labor if:
a) $w = MRP_L$.
b) $w = ME$.
c) $MRP_L = ME$.
d) $ME = MP_L$.
e) None of the above is correct.

22. The marginal expenditure for an input will always be:
a) downward sloping.
b) identical to the average expenditure.
c) higher than the input's price if its supply curve is upward sloping.
d) lower than the input's price if its demand curve is downward sloping.
e) None of the above.

23. In Figure 14.11, when *g* workers are hired, economic rent is equal to the area:
a) abc.
b) bcgf.
c) bcd.
d) ced.
e) dcgf.

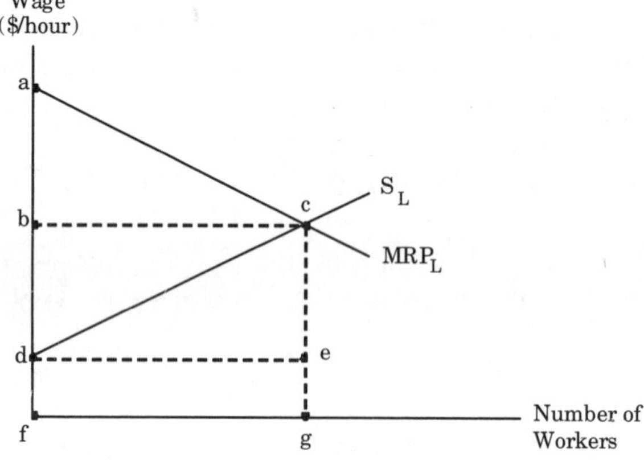

Figure 14.11

24. Before free agency was put into practice in the 1970s in professional baseball, players had a choice of either playing for the team that "owned" them or leaving baseball. Until the 1970s, baseball players' salaries were substantially lower than they are now because:
a) attendance was lower.
b) the players' union was only interested in increasing employment.
c) the owners behaved as a monopsony.
d) the MRP_L was lower.
e) None of the above is correct.

ANSWERS TO CHAPTER 14

EXERCISE ANSWERS

1. a) The MRP_L equals price times the MP_L. Here, $MRP_L = 200(3.10 - 0.02L) = 620 - 4L$.
   b) If the wage is \$300, then labor is hired up to the point where $620 - 4L = 300$, or $L = 80$.
   c) If the wage is \$240, labor is hired such that $620 - 4L = 240$, or $L = 95$.

2. For a monopoly, the MRP_L equals marginal revenue times the MP_L. However, since the MRP_L also depends on L, we must rewrite MR in terms of L instead of Q. Since $P = 100 - Q$, then $MR = 100 - 2Q$. Since $Q = 60L - 0.5L^2$, $MR = 100 - 2(60L - 0.5L^2) = 100 - 120L + L^2$. The MRP_L then equals $[100 - 120L + L^2][60 - L] = 6{,}000 - 7{,}200L + 60L^2 - 100L + 120L^2 - L^3 = 6{,}000 - 7{,}300L + 180L^2 - L^3$.

3. Figures 14A.1a and 14A.1b show the effects of Plan 1 and 2, respectively. In each figure, L_0 has a slope of w and L_1 has a slope equal to $\hat{w}$.

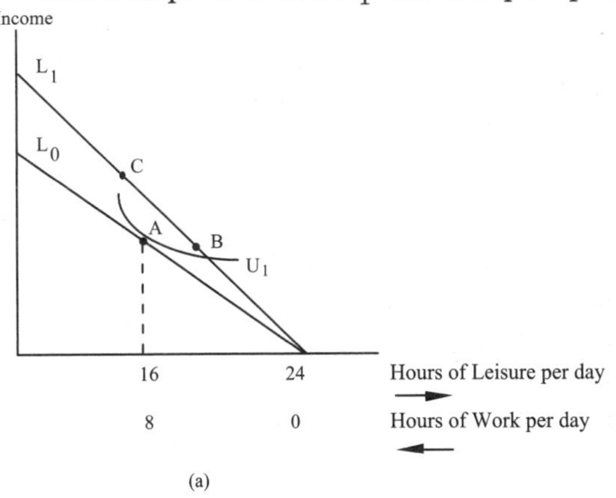

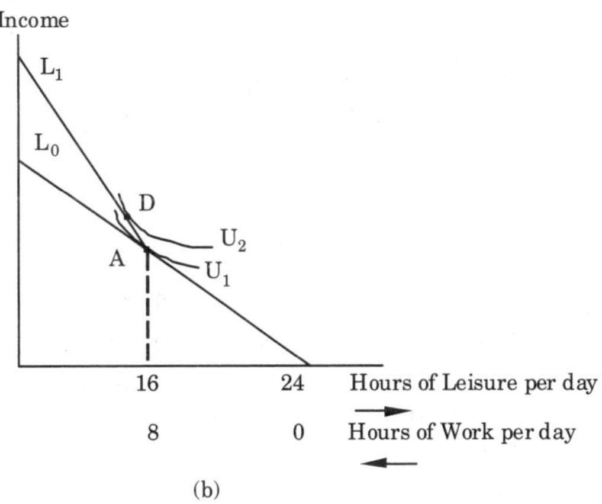

Figure 14A.1

Only Plan 2 will guarantee that the worker will work overtime. In Plan 1, shown in Figure 14A.1a, the worker could move from A to a point such as B or C, depending on the strength of the substitution and income effects (at point B the income effect of the wage increase outweighs the substitution effect). Plan 2, shown in Figure 14A.1b, elicits an unambiguous response to decrease leisure hours. This is due to the fact that the response to the overtime wage is basically a pure substitution effect. (Only if the indifference curve U_1 were L–shaped would the worker choose not to work overtime.)

4. a) The competitive equilibrium is w_0 and L_0. The monopoly equilibrium is w_2 and L_1.
   b) Economic rent is the area below the wage and above the S_L curve up to the quantity of labor hired. A wage of w_1 will maximize economic rent.

5. a)

Wage Rate Per Hour ($)	Units of Labor Supplied Per Hour	Total Expenditure	Marginal Expenditure
4	10	40	n.a.
5	11	55	15
6	12	72	17
7	13	91	19
8	14	112	21

b) The textile mill is a monopsonist, and will set ME = D_L to find the optimal amount of labor to hire and pay the wage given by the supply of labor curve. Therefore, if D_L = 17 = ME, the corresponding value of L = 12 and w = \$6.

6. a) In Figure 14.8, the MR curve intersects the S_L curve at L = 200. The firm is willing to pay a wage of \$19 for this number of workers, so L = 200, and w = \$19.

b) Economic rent is equal to the area above S_L, below w = 19, out to L = 200. Thus, economic rent is 200(19 – 6) + 0.5(200)(6 – 4) = \$2,800.

7. a) To maximize total employment, the union will set a wage equal to the competitive wage. (Note that setting any other wage causes less labor to be demanded or supplied.) The union chooses a wage of \$8, and L = 380 in Figure 14.8.

b) To maximize the total payments to labor, the union will set the wage at the level where the MR curve intersects the horizontal axis. At this wage of \$16, the firm will hire 250 workers.

PROBLEM SET ANSWERS

8. Given $MP_L = 3.10 - 0.02L$ and P = \$200, we have $MRP_L = (3.10 - 0.02L)200 = 620 - 4L$. Since w = MRP_L tells us how many workers are hired, total wage payments equal $wL = (620 - 4L)L = 620L - 4L^2$. This is total revenue. Since the labor demand curve is linear, marginal revenue on the labor demand curve is twice as steep: MR = 620 – 8L. Setting MR = 0 maximizes total wage payments, so $L^* = 77.5$ with a wage equal to \$310.

9. $MR = 100 - 2Q$, or $MR = 100 - 2(12L - L^2) = 100 - 24L + 2L^2$. $MRP_L = MR \cdot MP_L = (100 - 24L + 2L^2)(12 - 2L) = 1{,}200 - 288L + 24L^2 - 200L + 48L^2 - 4L^3 = 1{,}200 - 488L + 72L^2 - 4L^3$.

10. a) Set supply equal to demand, or 72 – 5w = 3w, which yields w^* = \$9 and $L^* = 27$.

b) Economic rent is equal to 0.5(27)(9) = \$121.50.

c) The intersection of the marginal revenue curve and the labor supply curve determines the wage that maximizes economic rent. Or, if you worked out the example with w = \$10 (\$1 higher than your answer to a)), you would find that economic rent would be \$139.70, showing that the competitive equilibrium wage is not the wage that maximizes economic rent.

11. a) The supply curve of union labor is vertical at L_u, as Figure 14A.2 shows. Because the firm can only hire union members, there is no supply of labor from any other source. The equilibrium wage that the firm is willing to pay is w_u.

b) As indicated in Figure 14A.2, L′ workers are willing to supply labor at a wage of w_u. This excess supply of labor will reveal itself as a waiting list for union membership.

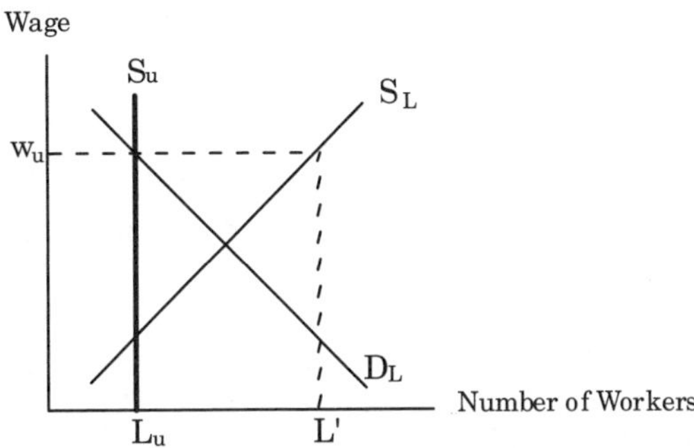

Figure 14A.2

12. a) The initial wage is w_0 and N_0 are initially hired. The minimum wage flattens out the ME (marginal expenditure) curve to the left of the supply of nurses at that wage. In Figure 14A.3 the new ME curve is equal to the minimum wage, w_m, to the left of N_m. Below N_m, hiring another nurse does not increase the wage. Therefore, if the minimum wage is not too high relative to the initial wage, w_0, more nurses are employed. Deadweight loss at the initial wage is the shaded triangle, A. The minimum wage law actually eliminates the DWL in this case.

b) The supply curve shifts to S^1 and ME^0 becomes ME^1. Since the nurses have more opportunities, wages will increase. This will decrease the number of nurses the hospital wants to hire. In Figure 14A.3 w_1 and N_1 are the new wage and number of nurses employed.

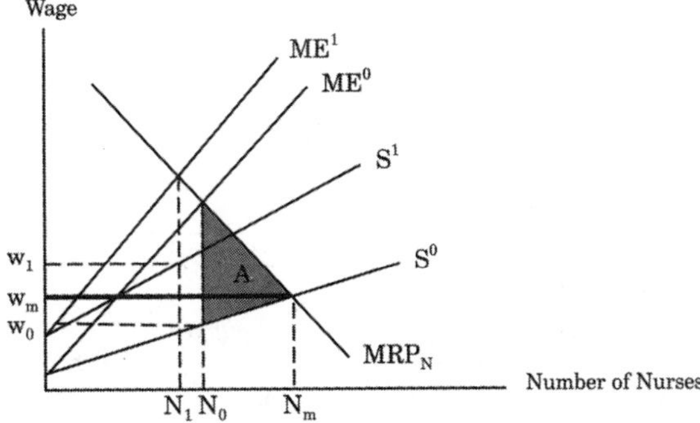

Figure 14A.3

SELF-TEST ANSWERS

13. d) Choice c) is only correct for perfectly competitive sellers, while choice d) is always true.

14. b) Again, choice a) is only correct for perfectly competitive sellers.

15. c) When $MRP_L < w$ then the value of the last worker hired is less than the cost to the firm.

16. a) As the wage falls, the firm increases its output and hires more capital. This shifts the MP_L curve, and therefore the MRP_L curve, to the right. See Figure 14.2.

17. b) Since the industry demand curve is steeper than a firm's demand curve, it is less elastic.

18. e) $MRP_L = P \cdot MP_L = 2.5(100 - 0.4L) = 250 - L$.

19. a) Set $w = MRP_L$: $15 = 250 - L$, or $L = 235$.

20. b) The income effect causes labor supply to fall as the wage rises, while the substitution effect causes labor supply to increase as the wage rises.

21. c) The monopsonist should hire up until the point where the revenue brought in by the last unit of labor hired (MRP_L) is equal to the expenditure on the last unit hired (ME).

22. c) If the supply curve is upward sloping, then as the firm increases the price of the input to hire more units, the firm must pay all units that higher price.

23. c) Payments to labor equal area **bcgf**, while area **dcgf** is the opportunity cost of supplying **fg** units of labor, leaving **bcd** as economic rent.

24. c) Before free agency, the owners did not compete by bidding players away from each other.

CHAPTER 15
INVESTMENT, TIME, AND CAPITAL MARKETS

IMPORTANT CONCEPTS

- Stocks vs. Flows
- Present Discounted Value
- Bonds
- Perpetuities
- Effective Yield
- Net Present Value
- Discount Rate
- Risk Premium
- Risk (Diversifiable and Nondiversifiable)
- Capital Asset Pricing Model
- Price Path for Depletable Resources
- Interest Rate

CHAPTER HIGHLIGHTS

The essential difference between capital and other productive factors, such as labor, is time. Labor input provides immediate benefit to the firm; machines built today, however, will deliver services for many years. In general, labor and raw materials inputs are measured as *flows*, while capital equipment is measured as a *stock*. Capital stock is durable and allows the firm to earn a flow of profits over many years.

The basic concept for comparing flows of rentals of capital with its cost of production is *present discounted value* (PDV). Since funds used to build machinery today could be loaned to others and earn interest, a dollar earned from a machine rental one year from now is currently worth only $1/(1 + R), where R is the interest rate. In other words, lending $1/(1 + R) now will return $1 one year from now. From this basic relationship, we can find the PDV of any amount received any number of years from now.

With the concept of PDV, we can find the present value of a variety of streams of receipts and expenditures, such as bonds and perpetuities. A *bond* is a contract in which a borrower agrees to pay the bondholder a stream of money. A *perpetuity* is a bond that pays out a fixed amount of money each year, forever. From the price of a bond, we can use the PDV formula to find the *effective yield* on a bond, which is the interest rate that equates the present value of the bond's payment stream with the bond's market price.

To decide whether a capital investment is worthwhile, a firm should compare the cost of the investment to the present value of the future cash flows from the investment. The *net present value* (NPV) equals the PDV of future cash flows minus the initial cost of the investment. If NPV > 0, the investment is worthwhile. A risk-neutral firm should undertake all projects available with positive NPVs.

In deriving NPVs, it is necessary to distinguish between real and nominal *discount rates*. The discount rate is the interest rate used to discount the future stream of profits; it is defined as the opportunity cost of the investment. Future inflation will often increase the future yearly cash flows, but it will affect the opportunity cost of funds as well. We can eliminate future inflation from NPV calculations by using real cash flows and using the real interest rate as the discount rate.

When future cash flows are certain, the appropriate discount rate is a risk-free rate. Most of the time, however, future cash flows are uncertain. How should a firm considering an investment adjust future cash flows when these cash flows are subject to risk? One simple technique is to use a risk-adjusted discount rate. The difference between the risk-adjusted rate and the risk-free rate is the *risk premium,* and the appropriate adjustment depends on whether the risk is *diversifiable* or *nondiversifiable*. The risk premium should only reflect the nondiversifiable risk on an investment. Investors who do not wish to bear diversifiable risk can avoid it by holding a well-diversified portfolio. The *Capital Asset Pricing Model* (CAPM) finds the risk premium by comparing the expected return on an investment to the expected return on the stock market.

Petroleum and mineral resources are capital assets. Owners of these resources constantly face a choice between selling the resource or keeping it in the ground for future sale. In order for producers to be willing to sell the resource now and in the future in a competitive market, the owners must expect the difference between price and extraction cost to increase at the rate of interest. From this implicit rule for extraction, we can derive the expected future *price path* of a depletable resource. In a monopoly market, the owner of a resource would require the difference between marginal revenue and extraction cost to grow at the interest rate.

Interest rates are determined like other prices, according to the equilibrium between supply and demand. The quantity demanded of loanable funds falls as the interest rate increases, while the quantity supplied grows as the interest rate rises. There are many interest rates set in a variety of markets, e.g., the Treasury Bill rate, the prime rate, and the corporate bond rate. These rates differ because of differences in the risk of holding the assets and in the length of the time horizon for the investment.

CONCEPT REVIEW AND EXERCISES

STOCKS VERSUS FLOWS (Section 15.1)

In Chapter 7, we analyzed the demand for capital inputs by a single firm using the rental rate as the price of capital (for the use of one machine for a given period of time). To the owner of the machines, this is a *flow* (an amount of money per period). In other cases, the firm itself will buy the machine and use the flow of its capital services in combination with other inputs to produce its product. It is not the number of machines that is relevant for production, but the number of machine-hours. However, we assume that the flow of capital services is proportional to the *stock* of machines. This lets us make the connection between a firm's demand for capital services and its demand for capital. The cost of capital services is given by the rental rate for capital. If the firm rents the machine, this rental rate will be an explicit cost. If the firm owns the machine, the rental rate is an implicit cost (since the firm could be renting it to someone else).

Exercise: ◗ ◗ ◗ ◗ ◗ ◗ ◗

1. A firm owns a $20 million paper mill which uses labor and lumber to produce paper products. Which of the following are stocks and which are flows?

a) Labor
b) Lumber
c) Plant and equipment
d) Paper products

PRESENT DISCOUNTED VALUE (Section 15.2)

To compare the cost of the stock with the value of the flows received, we need to determine *present discounted values*. The same analysis applies whether the firm rents or owns machines. Thus, if the firm using the inputs to produce final goods owned the machines itself, it would still use the concept of present discounted value to derive the rental rate per machine to use in its cost minimization calculations.

Impatience means that you value consumption now more than the same consumption in the future. Therefore, a dollar today is worth more than a dollar to be paid next year. We can derive the value of a dollar in the future using the *interest rate* (the amount paid by a borrower for the use of a dollar for one year). If the interest rate equals R and you lend $1 today, you will receive $1(1 + R) dollars one year from now. We call the 1 + R dollars the *future value* of $1 today. The value today of $1 paid one year from now is called the present discounted value (PDV). The PDV of $1 paid one year from now is $1/(1 + R).

For longer periods, the process is similar. Assume that the interest rate will not change in the future. Then, lending one dollar for one year and re-lending the proceeds (the dollar plus the interest received) for another year will give you $1(1 + R)(1 + R) at the end of the second year. Consequently, the PDV of $1 two years from now is $\$1/(1 + R)^2$. Extending this concept, the general formula for the PDV of \$1 paid n years from now is $\$1/(1 + R)^n$.

Exercise: ▶▶▶▶▶▶

2. a) Suppose the interest rate is constant at 8 percent. What is the PDV of \$1 two years from now?

   b) Suppose the interest rate is constant at 10 percent. What is the PDV of \$1 two years from now?

   c) Now suppose the interest rate is not constant. This year's interest rate is 10 percent, and next year's interest rate is 8 percent. What is the PDV of one dollar two years from now?

To calculate the PDV of a stream of payments, just add the PDV of the payments to be received in each year. Similarly, we can obtain the PDV of a sequence of negative and positive cash flows in different years by adding together the PDV of amounts received and subtracting the PDV of amounts paid.

THE VALUE OF A BOND (Section 15.3)

Many different patterns of payment streams are used in the capital market. A *bond* is one of the most common; a bond has constant payments for a number of periods (the "coupon" payments) and a final larger payment (the "principal"). The value of a bond is simply the PDV of this payment stream. If a bond pays a coupon of \$100 each year for 8 years and has a principal of \$1,000 to be returned in 8 years, and the interest rate is R, the value of this bond is:

$$PDV = \frac{100}{(1+R)^1} + \frac{100}{(1+R)^2} + \cdots + \frac{100}{(1+R)^8} + \frac{1{,}000}{(1+R)^8}.$$

Note that in the last year the owner of the bond receives both a coupon payment and the principal payment.

Exercise: ▶▶▶▶▶▶

3. The current interest rate is 7 percent, and it will remain at that level for five years. What is the present discounted value of a bond that pays a coupon of \$70 per year with a principal payment of \$1,000 at the end of 5 years?

Perpetuities are a special type of bond with coupon payments that continue forever with no principal payment. The value of such a stream is:

$$PDV = \frac{c}{(1+R)^1} + \frac{c}{(1+R)^2} + \frac{c}{(1+R)^3} + \cdots = \frac{c}{R}.$$

The result that the PDV = c/R can be derived by arithmetically summing this series. It is easier, however, simply to observe that the relationship must hold because

\$(c/R) invested at the interest rate R would pay \$c per year, just as the perpetuity does.

While perpetuities are a rarity in the investment world, the formula for perpetuities can be used to value other financial instruments, including bonds. Thus, the PDV of a three-year bond paying \$70 per year on a \$1,000 principal equals the PDV of a \$70 perpetuity with the first payment in one year, minus the PDV of a \$70 perpetuity with the first payment 4 years from now, plus the PDV of the \$1,000 principal payment. To see this, write the PDV of this bond as:

$$PDV = \frac{70}{(1+R)^1} + \frac{70}{(1+R)^2} + \frac{70}{(1+R)^3} + \frac{70}{(1+R)^4} + \ldots - \left[\frac{70}{(1+R)^4} + \frac{70}{(1+R)^5} + \ldots\right] + \frac{1000}{(1+R)^3}$$

where the term in brackets is the \$70 perpetuity with payments starting 4 years from now.

Exercise: ▶ ▶ ▶ ▶ ▶ ▶ ▶

4. What is the PDV of a perpetuity with payments starting 6 years from now? Use the relationship above to value the bond in Exercise 3.

A mortgage is similar to a bond, except that generally there is no single principal payment. In most mortgages, each payment is partly interest and partly return of the principal borrowed. Thus, a mortgage is a bond with a coupon that continues for a fixed period with no final larger payment (if one exists, the larger final payment is called a "balloon" payment).

Exercise: ▶ ▶ ▶ ▶ ▶ ▶ ▶

5. Calculate the PDV of a mortgage that has an annual payment of \$8,000 for 24 years if the interest rate is 12 percent. What is your answer if the interest rate is 6 percent? (Hint: Use the perpetuity formula.)

The price of the bond is determined in the bond market. Interest rate changes will cause the bond's price to differ from its price at the time of issue. The *effective yield* on a bond is found by solving to find the interest rate that discounts the flows of interest and principal payments such that the PDV equals the price of the bond. Alternatively, given the market interest rate, we can also solve for the price of the bond by discounting the flows of interest and principal payments.

Exercise: ▶ ▶ ▶ ▶ ▶ ▶ ▶

6. A zero-coupon bond is one that only has a single payment at maturity. Such bonds obviously sell for less than the principal payment. If the interest rate is 7 percent, what is the value of a three-year zero coupon bond with a principal of \$1,000?

THE NET PRESENT VALUE CRITERION FOR CAPITAL INVESTMENT DECISIONS (Section 15.4)

The *net present value (NPV) criterion* states that one should invest in a project if the PDV of future cash flows exceeds the cost of the investment. The cost of the investment (C) is paid immediately: therefore, the PDV of the cost equals the cost itself. Suppose the cash flows in succeeding years are given by F_1, F_2, F_3,..., F_n, where the project will yield returns for n years. Then,

$$NPV = -C + \frac{F_1}{(1+R)} + \frac{F_2}{(1+R)^2} + \cdots + \frac{F_n}{(1+R)^n}.$$

If NPV > 0, make the investment. We can use the NPV criterion even if the flow is negative in some years—as when an investment project takes several years of continued outlays before the return begins.

The value of R to use in discounting the future cash flows is the opportunity cost of funds for the firm. Usually, this *discount rate* will be the rate at which the firm can borrow money. When calculating NPV, it is important to treat inflation correctly. If the cash flows of the project are given in real terms, the discount rate must be the real interest rate (the interest rate minus the inflation rate). If the cash flows are in nominal terms (thus building in future inflation), the discount rate should be the nominal interest rate (uncorrected for inflation).

Exercise:

7. A $200,000 investment this year will increase your firm's profits by $75,000 in each of the next four years. What is the net present value of this investment if your firm's opportunity cost of capital is 10 percent?

ADJUSTMENTS FOR RISK (Section 15.5)

Investment projects are rarely sure things. Firms face uncertainty about the future cash flows from almost any investment. What effect does the risk associated with future returns have on the choice of the discount rate to use in NPV calculations?

It is important to understand that risk associated with the returns to a project is not necessarily undesirable. What matters is the effect that this variability has on the overall return to the project's investors.

Since investors can diversify their portfolios over many different investments, what matters is the contribution of each project to the overall risk of an optimal portfolio of investments. If one project had returns that were perfectly negatively correlated with a second project, undertaking both projects would involve no risk at all. For example, suppose two firms each file for a patent on an identical discovery. Investors in the firm awarded the patent will gain, while investors in the other firm will lose money. But someone who invests in both firms will neither gain nor lose from the outcome of the competing claims for the patent.

We can break risk up into two general categories—*diversifiable* and *nondiversifiable risk*. Diversifiable risk is that portion of the risk of an investment that is not correlated with the risk associated with other investments. By investing in many projects, one can insure that the diversifiable risk in any one project does not affect the overall risk of one's portfolio. Nondiversifiable risk is that portion of risk that is correlated with the risk in the optimal portfolio—it cannot be eliminated by pooling the risk with the risks of other investments. For an investment to be attractive, a higher expected return must compensate for the nondiversifiable risk.

With the *capital asset pricing model* (CAPM), we can determine the *risk premium* for different stocks. First, consider the rate of interest of investments subject to no risk, called the *risk-free rate*, r_f. This risk-free rate might be the interest rate on short-term Federal debt, for example. If r_m is the expected rate of return on a portfolio of all stocks (the market portfolio), then $r_m - r_f$ is the risk premium of the market as a whole. Now for each stock, we can split its risk into the diversifiable and nondiversifiable components. One measure of the nondiversifiable risk is the correlation of the return on a stock with the return on the market portfolio. From the correlation, we can derive a number, β, for each stock. This constant, β, called the *asset beta,* measures how sensitive the asset's return is to movements in the stock market as a whole. (Note that β is equal to the covariance of the stock return and market return, divided by the variance of the market return.) If $\beta = 2$, when the overall stock market has a return of 15 percent above its average return, the stock has an expected return of 30 percent above its average return. The CAPM tells us that the expected return on stock *i* is:

$$r_i = r_f + \beta(r_m - r_f).$$

This is an equilibrium relationship between each stock's characteristics and the market as a whole. From β, we can determine the discount rate implicitly used by investors in that stock. The discount rate is: $r_f + \beta(r_m - r_f)$. For the firm's managers, β tells the firm what discount rate to use to determine the present discounted value of the expected cash flows from a project.

One important implication of the CAPM is that firms do not gain simply by reducing the variance of the firm's cash flows—in the CAPM, it is the correlation with the market as a whole that matters. Since investors have already diversified and eliminated the diversifiable risk from their portfolios, they will not be willing to pay a higher price for the stock if the managers perform the same function of diversification within the firm. Thus, when two corporations with unrelated business activities merge, the combined value of the new corporation should equal the sum of the values of the two corporations.

Exercise: ▶ ▶ ▶ ▶ ▶ ▶ ▶

8. Use the CAPM to calculate the discount rate for a stock given the following information: (1) the stock market on average has provided 8 percent returns; (2) the risk-free rate is 5 percent; and (3) a one percent rise in the stock market leads to a two percent rise in the price of this stock.

*INTERTEMPORAL PRODUCTION DECISIONS—DEPLETABLE RESOURCES (Section 15.8)

Oil in the ground is an exhaustible or depletable resource. If a firm pumps oil out of a well today, less oil will be available to be pumped out in the future. This additional opportunity cost of producing and selling a unit today is called the *user cost of production*. Since a firm can choose when to pump its oil, and the amount of oil is fixed, a firm that gradually pumps its oil should expect the real price of oil to rise over time. If not, the firm would wish to pump all its oil now and invest the profit to earn a positive return. Profits from pumping oil in the future are worth less than profits today because of discounting.

Let P_t be the expected price of oil at time t, and let c_t be the cost per unit of pumping the oil at time t. The path for the expected price is given by $P_{t+1} - c_{t+1} = (1 + R)(P_t - c_t)$. Thus, if R is 8 percent and costs are constant, the profit per barrel of oil should rise at 8 percent per year. If the price rises at a slower rate, the owners of oil should pump oil now, sell it, and invest the profits at the rate of interest; since less oil will be available in the future, the price will then be higher in the future. In contrast, if the price rises at a faster rate, the owners should delay pumping oil; since less oil is pumped now, the current price will be higher. Note that this formula is sufficiently general to allow for costs to change over time.

Exercise: ▶ ▶ ▶ ▶ ▶ ▶ ▶

***9.** Suppose an oil producer anticipates that extraction costs will remain constant at $15 per barrel. Assume that oil today sells for $20 per barrel, and that the firm plans to pump oil out each year for the next three years. What is the firm's prediction of the price over that time horizon if the interest rate is 4 percent? (All prices are in real terms, as is the interest rate.)

***10.** The interest rate affects the path over time of an exhaustible resource. This question examines some of the short-run and long-run effects.

a) Suppose that the long-term interest rate declines. What effect will that have on the anticipated price of oil ten years from now, assuming no change in the current price of oil? What effect will that have on the anticpated quantity demanded ten years from now

b) If producers anticipate selling more oil in the future than when interest rates were high, what effect will that have on the current price?

c) What can we say about the effect of a fall in the interest rate on the slope of the price path for oil?

Note that this production rule should not be taken too literally. For a number of reasons, the price of oil minus the extraction costs will not *always* rise at the rate of interest. Uncertainty and unexpected events also play a role as do technological improvements that lower extraction costs.

PROBLEM SET

11. What is the present discounted value of a mortgage with 12 annual payments of $4,500 each if the interest rate is 9 percent? (Hint: After writing down the basic formula for this mortgage, see if you can simplify it into fewer terms.)

12. An entrepreneur is faced with the following investment opportunity: For an investment of $100 today and a further investment of $150 next year, he can earn a return of $300 two years from now. Should he undertake this investment if the interest rate is 5 percent? If the interest rate is 15 percent? Explain.

13. The risk-free rate of interest on short-term government bonds is 7 percent. The expected average yield on all common stocks is 14 percent. The managers of a pension portfolio have calculated that the stock of Gamma Faucets has a β of 1.5. What is the appropriate discount rate to use for the expected cash flows from owning Gamma Faucets stock?

14. You are deciding whether to purchase a used car. The price of the car is $1,200 and you expect the car to last for four years. You have determined that the value of the flow of services you will receive from the car in each of the four years is $500 and that in years 2, 3, and 4 you will incur upkeep costs of $100 per year. The interest rate is 20 percent. (Assume that all figures are in real terms.)

a) Without discounting future cash flows and benefit streams, is the benefit of buying this car greater than the cost?

b) When costs and benefits are appropriately valued, what is the net present value of this investment? Should you buy the car?

15. Suppose Sarah's Sandals is undertaking an investment project designed to improve the efficiency of their production process. The project involves an up-front, non-recoverable cost of $C. There is some uncertainty about the gross value of the project, which will not be realized until next year. The gross return may be either π_1 or π_2. The probability that the return will be π_1 is x, and (1–x) is the probability the return will be π_2. R is the discount rate. While the present value of the expected return exceeds the project's cost, π_2 is less than the cost ($\pi_1 > C > \pi_2 > 0$), so the firm will take a loss on the project if the return turns out to be low.

a) Write down the expression for the expected net present value of the project. (Let ENPV stand for this expression.)

b) Write down the expected net present value if instead the firm learns the gross return before spending C. (Let ENPV′ stand for this expression.)

c) Now suppose that the firm does not automatically know what the return will be before making the investment, but can discover it for a significant additional cost. The firm will decide to obtain the information about the gross return if its value exceeds its cost. (The value of the information is simply ENPV′ – ENPV.) Let VI stand for the value of the information. Write out an expression for VI.

d) Indicate whether an increase in π_2 would increase VI, decrease VI, or leave it unchanged and explain why.

e) Repeat d) for changes in π_1, x, and R.

SELF-TEST

16. Which of the following is a stock as opposed to a flow for a manufacturing company?
    a) The cost of purchasing new packaging machines
    b) Interest payments each year on its debt
    c) Monthly health insurance premiums
    d) a) and b)
    e) a) and c)

17. What is the present discounted value of $20 to be received 4 years from now if the interest rate is 11 percent?
    a) $18.02
    b) $4.50
    c) $13.17
    d) $13.89
    e) None of the above is correct.

18. What is the present discounted value of a perpetuity paying $300 per year if the interest rate is 6 percent?
    a) $300
    b) $283.01
    c) $319.15
    d) $5,000
    e) None of the above is correct.

19. The current interest rate is 8 percent. What is the equilibrium price of a bond that will pay $140 in interest and $1,000 in principal at the end of this year?
    a) $1,000
    b) $925.93
    c) $1,140
    d) $1,055.56
    e) None of the above is correct.

20. For an investor buying stock in a company building beachfront housing, which of the following sources of uncertainty represents nondiversifiable risk?
    a) A rainy sales season
    b) A hurricane wiping out the development
    c) A sudden price increase for building materials
    d) A recession
    e) None of the above.

21. A decrease in the supply of loanable funds in the economy will (other things being equal):
    a) decrease the market rate of interest.
    b) increase the market rate of interest.
    c) decrease the quantity of funds demanded for investment.
    d) increase the quantity of funds demanded for investment.
    e) both b) and c)

22. Consider a perpetuity that pays \$210 per year. By how much would its price rise if the interest rate fell from 6 percent to 4 percent?
a) \$5,250
b) \$3,500
c) \$1,750
d) \$198
e) \$3.81

23. A firm is considering purchasing the rights to a project. They think that, in their hands, the project will cost \$10,000 next year and return \$5,000 per year in two years and every year thereafter. If the interest rate is 10 percent, what is the most the firm would be willing to pay for the rights to the project?
a) Nothing, since the PDV is negative.
b) \$36,363.64
c) \$40,000
d) \$32,231.41
e) \$32,231.41

24. Suppose the real interest rate is 6 percent. If the expected rate of inflation is 8 percent, the present discounted value of \$2000 to be received one year from now is:
a) \$1886.79
b) \$1754.39
c) \$1851.85
d) \$2037.74
e) \$1962.96

25. After carefully reading *Consumer Reports*, you decide that it is worthwhile to purchase an energy-efficient refrigerator as part of remodeling your kitchen. Before you make the purchase, the Federal Reserve Board raises interest rates. Which of the following actions should you take?
a) Go ahead and buy the energy-efficient refrigerator since its NPV has increased.
b) Go ahead and buy the energy-efficient refrigerator since its NPV has decreased.
c) You need to re-evaluate your decisions because the NPV of the energy-efficient refrigerator has fallen relative to a conventional refrigerator.
d) You need to re-evaluate your decisions because the NPV of the energy-efficient refrigerator has risen relative to a conventional refrigerator.
e) If you are paying cash for the refrigerator, the interest rate change is irrelevant.

26. *[Depletable Resources] The real price of minerals is expected to rise over time because:
a) of inflation.
b) mining has a slow rate of technological improvement.
c) higher prices are necessary to reward mine owners for waiting to sell their ore.
d) wages are rising faster in that industry than in others.
e) None of the above is correct.

27. *[Depletable Resources] Suppose that a technological advance that will drastically lower the future price of oil extraction is announced. Which of the following reactions to the announcement make the most sense?

I. Oil producers will lower price today in anticipation of lower costs.
II. Oil producers will raise price today in order to save their oil for the future when extraction costs are lower.
III. The expected future price will rise because oil producers will want to make their supplies last longer since future sales will be more profitable.
IV. Expected future prices will fall, as oil producers will attempt to sell more in future periods in response to lower unit costs.

a) I and IV
b) I and III
c) II and III
d) II and IV
e) None of the above represents a reasonable combination of effects.

ANSWERS TO CHAPTER 15

EXERCISE ANSWERS

1. a) Flow
b) Flow
c) Stock
d) Flow

2. a) One dollar invested today would be worth \$1.08 one year from now, and this can be reinvested for a second year. After 2 years, an investor would have \$(1.08)(1.08) = \$1.1664. So, the PDV of one dollar 2 years from now is \$1/1.1664 = \$0.8573.
b) The PDV here is $\$1/(1.10)^2 = \$0.8264$.
c) The investor would have \$1.10 one year from now. Reinvesting this at 8 percent for the second year, she would have \$(1.10)(1.08) = \$1.188. So, the PDV of one dollar 2 years from now is \$1/1.188 = \$0.8418.

3. We can write this payment stream as:

$$\frac{70}{(1.07)}+\frac{70}{(1.07)^2}+\frac{70}{(1.07)^3}+\frac{70}{(1.07)^4}+\frac{1{,}070}{(1.07)^5}=\$1{,}000$$

When the coupon equals the discount rate times the principal, the PDV of the bond will equal the principal.

4. A perpetuity has the value c/R. A perpetuity with payments starting six years from now is worth $[c/R]/(1 + R)^5$ (remember that a perpetuity's first payment comes after 1 year). We can split the bond up into two pieces—the coupon payments and the return of the principal. The principal payment is worth $\$1{,}000/(1.07)^5 = \$712.99$. The stream of coupon payments is like a perpetuity beginning today *minus* a perpetuity with payments starting 6 years from now. Thus, the stream of coupon payments is worth $70/0.07 – (70/0.07)[1/(1.07)^5] = $1,000 – $712.99 = $287.01. Adding these pieces together, we get $1,000 for the value of the bond.

5. Using the perpetuity value formula, the PDV of the mortgage is $8,000/0.12 – (8,000/0.12)/(1.12)^24 = $62,274.52.
At an interest rate of 6 percent, the PDV is $8,000/0.06 – (8,000/0.06)/ (1.06)^24 = $100,402.86.

6. The PDV is $1,000/(1.07)^3 = $816.30.

7.

$$NPV = -200,000 + \frac{75,000}{(1+0.1)} + \frac{75,000}{(1.1)^2} + \frac{75,000}{(1.1)^3} + \frac{75,000}{(1.1)^4}$$

$$= \$37,739.89$$

8. Discount rate $= r_f + \beta(r_m - r_f)$
$= 0.05 + 2(0.08 - 0.05)$
$= 0.11$, or 11%.

9. The expected price is given by $P_{t+1} = c_{t+1} + (1 + R)(P_t - c_t)$. Net earnings per barrel are currently $20 – $15 = $5. At an interest rate of 4 percent, the producer must be anticipating a price next year of (15 + 5(1.04)) = $20.20. Two years from now, the anticipated price is (15 + 5(1.04)^2) = $20.41. Three years from now, the anticipated price is (15 + 5(1.04)^3) = $20.62.

10. a) At a lower interest rate, the price ten years from now will be a smaller multiple of the current price ($P_0(1+r')^{10} < P_0(1+r)^{10}$ if $r' < r$). With a lower price ten yars from now, consumption should increase.

b) Producing more oil every year in the future requires producing less today, so the current price should rise.

c) Whether the current price rises or falls when the interest rate falls, the slope of the price path over time becomes flatter.

PROBLEM SET ANSWERS

11. The PDV can be found by summing up 12 terms:
$4,500/(1.09), $4,500/(1.09)^2, ..., $4,500/(1.09)^12.

The simpler way is to write it as the difference between two perpetuities: one starting immediately and one with payments starting in 13 years. The first is worth $4,500/.09 = $50,000. The second is worth (4,500/.09)/(1.09)^12 = $17,776.74. So the mortgage's PDV is $32,223.26.

12. At 5 percent, the NPV is –$100 – $150/1.05 + $300/(1.05)^2 = $29.25. The investment is worthwhile.

At 15 percent, the NPV is –$100 – $150/1.15 + $300/(1.15)^2 = –$3.59, so the investment is not worthwhile.

Since the benefits are only received in the future, a higher discount rate lowers the present value of these benefits. Hence, the investment becomes less profitable.

13. The expected rate of return on a stock is the risk-adjusted discount rate that the managers should use. In the CAPM for stock i, $r_i = r_f + \beta_i(r_m - r_f) = 0.07 + 1.5(0.14 - 0.07) = 0.175$ or 17.5 percent.

14. a) The stream of benefits for the four years is \$500 + \$500 + \$500 + \$500 = \$2,000. The stream of costs over the four years is \$1,200 + \$100 + \$100 + \$100 = \$1,500. Therefore, the benefits outweigh the costs.

b) The PDV of the benefit stream is:
$\$500/(1.2) + \$500/(1.2)^2 + \$500/(1.2)^3 + \$500/(1.2)^4 = 416.67 + 347.22 + 289.35 + 241.13 =$ \$1294.37.
The PDV of the costs is:
$\$1{,}200 + \$100/(1.2)^2 + \$100(1.2)^3 + \$100/(1.2)^4 = 1{,}200 + 69.44 + 57.87 + 48.23 =$ \$1375.54.
The net present value is negative (1,294.37 – 1,375.54 = –\$81.17), and therefore you should not buy the car.

15. a) $ENPV = x\left(\frac{\pi_1}{1+R}\right) + (1-x)\frac{\pi_2}{1+R} - C$

b) $ENPV' = x\left(\frac{\pi_1}{1+R} - C\right)$ (Sarah's will not do the project if the return is low.)

c) $VI = (1-x)\left(C - \frac{\pi_2}{1+R}\right)$ (Sarah's uses the information to save the loss when the return is low.)

d) If π_2 goes up, VI goes down because the potential loss is smaller.

e) If the return is high, Sarah's always wants to do the project, so π_1 does not affect VI. If x goes up, the loss is less likely, so VI goes down. If R increases, the loss increases, so avoiding it is more important and VI goes up.

SELF-TEST ANSWERS

16. a) The amounts in b) and c) are recurring expenditures, so they are flows. The amount in a) is a one-time expenditure, so it is a stock.

17. c) The PDV equals $\$20/(1.11)^4$.

18. d) The PDV equals \$300/0.06.

19. d) The price will equal the PDV, and the PDV equals \$1,140/1.08.

20. d) The risks in a), b), and c) are specific to this project, so the investor can eliminate this risk by investing in other projects as well. The recession will affect all industries, so it is not a diversifiable risk.

21. e) A leftward (or upward) shift of the supply curve for loanable funds will increase the market interest rate and decrease the equilibrium quantity of loanable funds demanded and supplied in the market.

22. c) The price of the perpetuity at 6 percent is \$210/0.06 = \$3,500. The price at 4 percent will be \$210/0.04 = \$5,250. Therefore, the price increase is \$1,750.

23. b) Next year, the project will cost \$10,000 and will have the same yield as a perpetuity with a \$5,000 payment. Thus, next year the NPV of the project will be (5,000/0.1) – 10,000 = \$40,000. This must be discounted as it is one period in the future, so the most the firm would pay today is 40,000/1.1 = \$36,363.636.

24. b) The nominal interest rate equals the real interest rate plus the rate of inflation, so \$2000/(1 + 0.06 + 0.08) = \$1754.39.

25. c) The benefits of the energy saving come in the future, so the NPV has fallen as a consequence of the increase in the interest rate.

26. c) Inflation does not affect real prices directly. Choices b) and d) may or may not be true, while c) will always be true.

27. d) On the original price path, future production is more profitable than current production. With even lower costs of extraction in the future, oil producers' price-cost margins rise at an even faster rate unless the time path of production changes. Firms would seek to produce more of their output in the future and less in the present. Thus, the present price rises and the future price falls.

CHAPTER 16
GENERAL EQUILIBRIUM AND ECONOMIC EFFICIENCY

IMPORTANT CONCEPTS

- General Equilibrium Analysis
  - Feedback Effect
- Pareto Efficient Allocation
- Social Welfare Functions
- Edgeworth Box
- Contract Curve
- Equity and Efficiency
- Utility Possibilities Frontier
- Production Possibilities Frontier
- Marginal Rate of Transformation
- Comparative Advantage
- Market Failure

CHAPTER HIGHLIGHTS

This chapter moves us from partial equilibrium analysis—looking at markets one at a time—to general equilibrium analysis—looking at all markets simultaneously. For example, a reduction in beef supply due to disease or floods will affect the demand for hamburger buns, at least to some degree. Such *feedback effects* are additional changes in price or quantity in one market in response to changes in price or quantity in a related market.

Using a general equilibrium analysis, we can examine the efficiency of market transactions. An allocation of goods is *Pareto efficient* if no one can be made better off without making someone worse off. With fixed total quantities of goods, as in an exchange economy, the *Edgeworth box* can be used to describe all possible efficient allocations between two individuals. The *contract curve* connects *all* the efficient allocations. In a competitive equilibrium with price-taking consumers the marginal rates of substitution between consumers are equal to each other and equal to the ratio of market prices. This provides the rationale for the first theorem of welfare economics: if everyone trades in the marketplace, and all mutually beneficial trades are completed, the resulting equilibrium allocation will be Pareto efficient.

The *utility possibilities frontier* for two consumers describes how much satisfaction each consumer can obtain given the total resources available in the economy. A point on the frontier represents an allocation on the contract curve. An economically inefficient allocation (a point inside the utility possibilities frontier) may be more *equitable* than the allocation achieved by a competitive equilibrium, and therefore it will have a higher level of social welfare. A *social welfare function* attaches weights to each individual's utility, and is used to make interpersonal comparisons of utility. Examples of social welfare functions are the utilitarian (social welfare is the sum of individuals' utilities) and the Rawlsian (social welfare equals the satisfaction of the worst-off individual).

Edgeworth boxes can also be used to study the production of two goods. With fixed total supplies of factors, an allocation is defined to be technically efficient if it maximizes output of one good for a given level of output of another good. In an Edgeworth box with factor supplies on the axes, we can derive the *production contract curve* that connects all factor combinations where the marginal rate of technical substitution is the same in both industries. Since cost-minimizing firms set their MRTS's equal to the wage-rental ratio, technical efficiency occurs in a competitive equilibrium.

The *production possibilities frontier* (PPF) displays the maximum level of output of one good, given every level of output of other goods, as well as any resource or technological constraints. A point on the PPF represents an allocation of factors on the production contract curve. The slope of the PPF is called the *marginal rate of transformation* (MRT), which equals the ratio of the marginal costs of the two goods. For efficiency in output choice, the MRT should equal each consumer's MRS. In a competitive equilibrium, firms operate where marginal cost equals price, and individuals consume where their MRSs are equal to the price ratio. Thus, a competitive equilibrium has the efficient output combination.

We can use the PPF to study the gains from international trade. The existence of *comparative advantage* (where the cost of making a good, compared with the cost of making other goods, is lower in one nation than in another nation) makes trade between nations mutually beneficial. With trade, both countries will specialize in producing those goods for which they have a comparative advantage. While consumers in general will be better off, certain firms and their workers will be worse off if their domestic industry declines as demand is satisfied through imports.

The last section of this chapter discusses *market failure*—the inefficiency in market outcomes. Important causes of market failure include market power, incomplete information, externalities, and public goods.

CONCEPT REVIEW AND EXERCISES

GENERAL EQUILIBRIUM ANALYSIS (Section 16.1)

Chapters 3 and 4 analyzed effects of individual price changes on the demand for different goods. Chapters 8 and 14 worked out supply responses to individual input price changes. Yet a single price change may shift many demand curves, causing further price changes in related markets. Some of these "second-round" price changes can shift the demand curve in the market where the price initially changed. General equilibrium analysis studies these *feedback effects*. General equilibrium analysis also accounts for the fact that consumers' incomes depend on prices at which consumers can rent out factors (labor and capital) in the market.

If the feedback effects are small in magnitude, partial equilibrium analysis is a useful approximation to general equilibrium analysis. Often, we are only interested in qualitative changes (does a price rise or fall?). For such questions, partial equilibrium analysis is frequently a useful guide. However, if two markets are closely linked either on the supply or demand side, we should take account of feedback effects.

Suppose a decrease in the supply of coffee increases the price of coffee from P_0 to P_1 in Figure 16.1a. The quantity of coffee demanded will decline from Q_0 to Q_1. However, the increase in the price of coffee, a complement for doughnuts, will decrease the demand for doughnuts from D_0 to D_1, as shown in Figure 16.1b. As the price of doughnuts falls (from P_0 to P_1) the demand for coffee will increase slightly, to D′ in Figure 16.1a. In addition, there will be other feedback effects from other markets (e.g., the demand for tea will increase causing the price of tea to rise and feeding back to an increase in demand for coffee). These feedback effects will continue until a general equilibrium exists, where there will be no further shifts in demand or supply in any market.

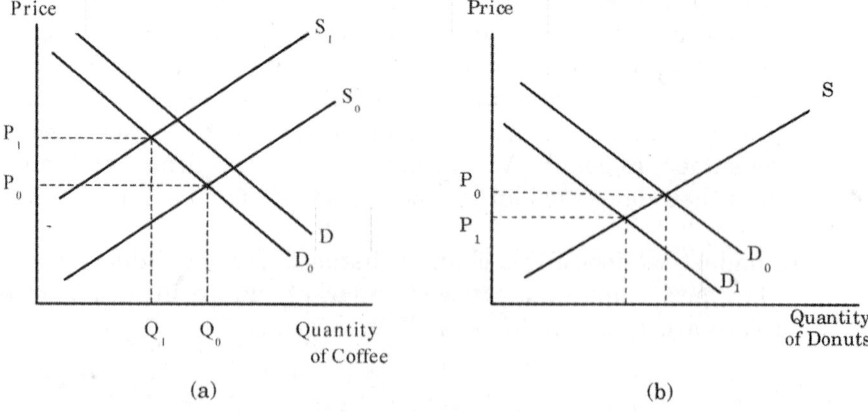

Figure 16.1

Exercise: ▶ ▶ ▶ ▶ ▶ ▶ ▶

1. Tortilla chips and tomato salsa are a popular snack food combination. Suppose a genetically altered bacteria helps protect tomatoes from frost damage, and the tomato harvest increases. Analyze qualitatively the resulting changes in the prices of tortilla chips and salsa. How does your analysis differ from a partial equilibrium analysis?

EFFICIENCY IN EXCHANGE (Section 16.2)

Consider a model of exchange in which individuals meet to trade goods before consuming them. The goods each trader brings to the market are called *endowments*. The total quantity of each good is simply the sum of each trader's endowment of that good. Trades are voluntary—no one is coerced into giving up goods they do not wish to trade. Thus, a trade only takes place if it is *mutually beneficial* (if both traders become better off or each obtains a market basket that is preferred to the initial endowment).

With two traders and two goods, we can use an analytical device called the *Edgeworth box* to learn how to allocate goods across consumers efficiently, and whether more than one efficient allocation exists. Suppose that the traders are Alfred and Betty, and the two goods are food and clothing. Draw a rectangle with a length equal to the sum of the two endowments of food and a height equal to the sum of the two endowments of clothing. Alfred's endowments are F_A and C_A, and Betty's endowments are F_B and C_B. The dimensions of the box are F (= $F_A + F_B$) by C (= $C_A + C_B$), as shown in Figure 16.2.

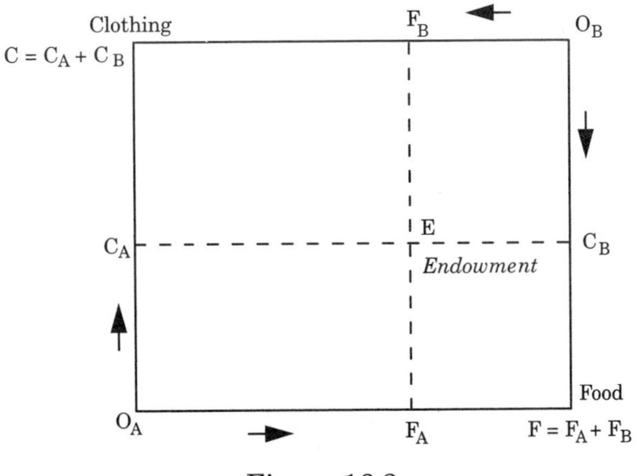

Figure 16.2

We can describe both traders' consumption by a single point in the box. The origin for Alfred is labeled O_A, and that for Betty is O_B. In Figure 16.2, the distance between point E and the bottom border of the box is Alfred's clothing consumption, and the distance between point E and the left-hand border is his food consumption. Since Betty consumes everything else, Betty's consumption of clothing is the distance from point E to the top border of the box, and her food consumption is the distance between point E and the right-hand border.

Alfred's indifference curves can be drawn as usual. Betty's indifference curves must be drawn upside down, because they are seen from the perspective of O_B rather than O_A.

Exercise: ▶ ▶ ▶ ▶ ▶ ▶ ▶

2. Mark and Jackie are packing their suitcases to go to a movie festival. The only two goods they are packing are popcorn and candy. Mark has 10 bags of popcorn and 5 pounds of candy. Jackie has 10 bags of popcorn and 12 pounds of candy.

a) Draw an Edgeworth box showing Mark and Jackie's endowment of popcorn and candy.

b) Sketch an indifference curve for Mark through his endowment point. Do the same for Jackie.

Assume there are no transactions costs associated with bargaining. If the indifference curves at the initial endowments intersect, as in Exercise 2, mutually beneficial trades are possible. Pinning down what particular trade takes place is a difficult question, but we can identify the area in which trades will take place. In Figure 16.3 two consumers, A and B, with an initial allocation of resources that puts them at point X, will trade to an allocation within the bounds of the two darker indifference curves. In other words, starting from point X, both consumers can be better off if they trade to a point inside the boundaries of U_{B1} and U_{A1}. For example, trading from X to Y moves both consumer A and consumer B to a higher indifference curve. At point Y there are still possibilities for mutually beneficial trade (since the consumers' MRS's are not the same). When the consumers reach a point where their indifference curves are tangent (point Z in Figure 16.3), then the MRS's are the same, and no further mutually beneficial trades will exist.

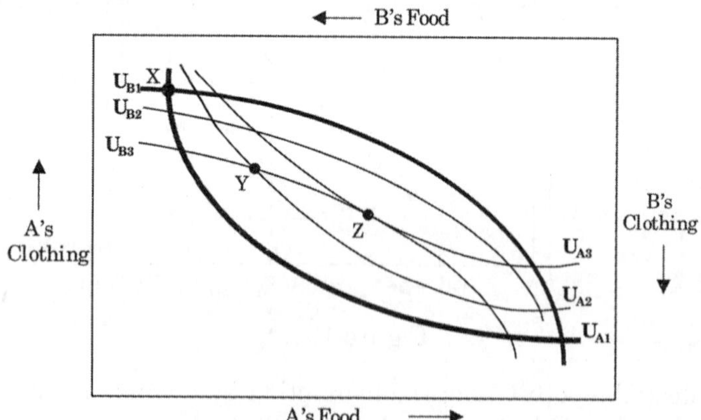

Figure 16.3

When there are no mutually beneficial trades, the economy is at a *Pareto efficient allocation*. A Pareto efficient allocation is one in which no one can be made better off without making someone else worse off. There are many such allocations that can be reached through mutually beneficial trades. Figure 16.4 displays the locus of all tangencies between the indifference curves in the Edgeworth box. This is called the *contract curve*. The contract curve between the indifference curves that pass through an initial endowment tells us which efficient allocations might be reached from that endowment. For example, point Z in Figure 16.3 would be a point on the contract curve that consumers A and B might reach starting from the endowment point X.

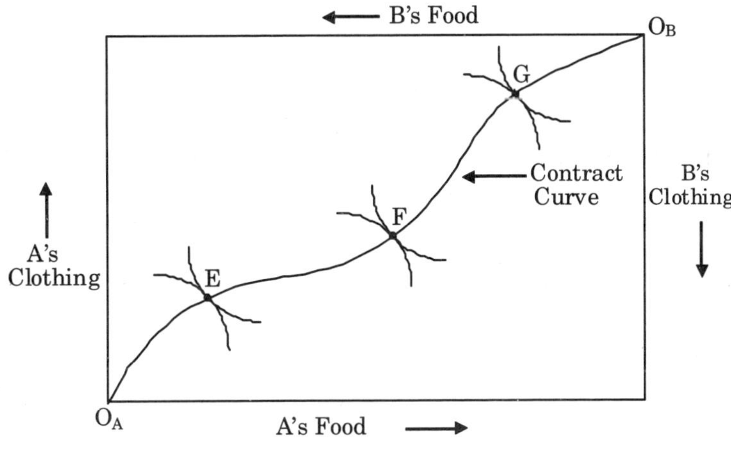

Figure 16.4

An allocation is not Pareto efficient if reallocating goods can make both individuals better off. Thus, an allocation is not Pareto efficient if the individuals can agree on a mutually beneficial trade between themselves.

In a bargaining game between two people, the outcome (final allocation) can depend on the relative bargaining strength of each person. In a competitive market, where there are many buyers and sellers behaving as price takers, this cannot happen. In a competitive equilibrium each buyer will trade to the point where his or her MRS equals the market price. Since the market price is the same for everyone, it will also be true that the MRSs are equal across all consumers. Therefore, a competitive equilibrium is a set of prices and associated quantities at which the quantity demanded equals the quantity supplied in every market; and at a competitive equilibrium, each consumer's indifference curve is tangent to the budget line and tangent to each other. The competitive equilibrium is Pareto efficient.

Exercise:

3. State the result that a competitive equilibrium is Pareto efficient in terms of MRS's and price ratios.

4. Jim has 40 gallons of gas and $100 to spend on other goods; for that market basket his MRS is $1/1 gallon. Linda has 10 gallons of gas and $300 to spend on other goods; her MRS is $1/4 gallons.
   a) Is this a Pareto efficient distribution of gas and dollars between Jim and Linda?
   b) Should they trade? If so, in what direction?

EQUITY AND EFFICIENCY (Section 16.3)

The contract curve is the locus of points where one person's utility has been maximized, given the other person's utility. This description of Pareto efficiency can be shown another way. For each point on the contract curve, we can draw a diagram with axes that measure Alfred's and Betty's utility. Each point on the contract curve is a point on the *utility possibilities frontier*. This frontier tells us the maximum utility Alfred can obtain, given the resources available, for each possible utility level of Betty. Figure 16.5 (on the next page) takes the points E, F, and G on the contract curve from Figure 16.4 and plots them to show that Alfred's utility is higher at G than at E, although both are efficient allocations. Which particular point on the frontier turns out to be the competitive equilibrium depends on the initial endowments.

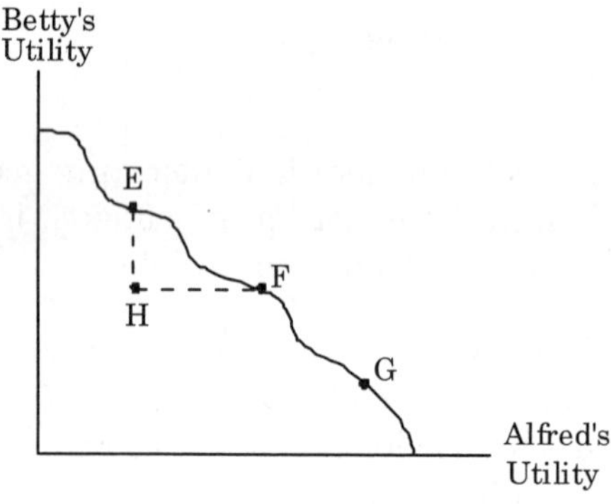

Figure 16.5

Exercise:

5. Consider points F, G, and H in Figure 16.5. F and G are on the utility possibilities frontier, while H lies inside the frontier. Is a move from H to F a Pareto improvement? Is a move from H to G a Pareto improvement? Why or why not?

You should have found in Exercise 5 that point H in Figure 16.5 is an inefficient allocation. That does not necessarily mean that it is less *equitable* than points E, F, or G. In fact, who is to say which of the efficient allocations is the most equitable? Answering that question involves choosing whose well being is more important,

Alfred's or Betty's. There is no objective basis for such a decision because it involves interpersonal comparisons of utility (e.g., is it "better" if Alfred is happier?). Economists who analyze these issues use what is called a *social welfare function* that assigns weights to different individual's preferences. The utilitarian social welfare function weights everyone's utility equally and leads to an allocation that maximizes the total utility of all members of society. Under the egalitarian view, everyone receives an equal amount of goods. Under the Rawlsian view, the equitable allocation is the one that maximizes the utility of the least-well-off person in society. Under the market-oriented view, the market outcome is the most equitable.

EFFICIENCY IN PRODUCTION (Section 16.4)

Suppose that capital and labor are fixed in supply and are the only inputs into food and clothing production. In order to determine how to allocate these inputs to the two industries, we can draw an Edgeworth box for production analogous to that for consumption. The length of the box is the total amount of labor available, L, and the height is the total amount of capital available, K. A point in the box describes labor and capital inputs into both production activities. Production is efficient if we cannot increase the output of clothing without reducing food output. Geometrically, production efficiency occurs when the isoquants are tangent for a particular allocation of inputs.

Exercise: ▶ ▶ ▶ ▶ ▶ ▶ ▶

6. Recall from Chapter 6 that minus the slope of an isoquant is the marginal rate of technical substitution (MRTS). Restate the condition for production efficiency in terms of the MRTS in the production of food and clothing.

7. What is the necessary condition for cost minimization for a firm that buys inputs in competitive factor markets? Explain why a competitive equilibrium in factor markets is an efficient allocation in the production Edgeworth box.

Just as we derived the utility possibilities frontier from the contract curve in the consumption Edgeworth box, we can also derive the *production possibilities frontier* (PPF) from the contract curve in the production Edgeworth box. For each possible level of food output, we find the maximum possible output of clothing, given the inputs, K and L. In Figure 16.6, we graph this information with food output on the horizontal axis and clothing output on the vertical axis.

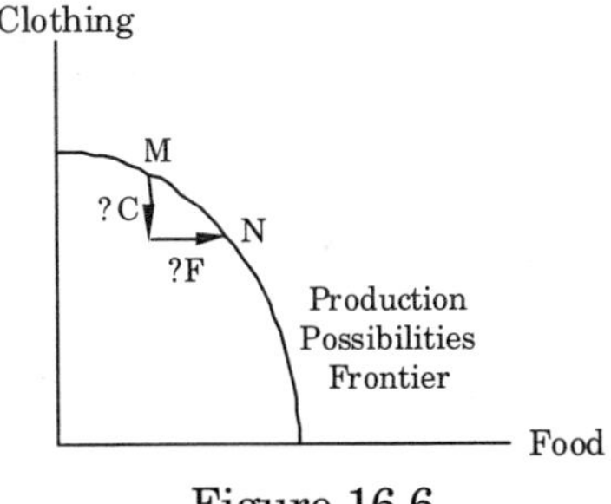

Figure 16.6

Exercise: ▶ ▶ ▶ ▶ ▶ ▶ ▶

8. Explain why an allocation of capital and labor that does not lie on the contract curve yields outputs that lie inside the PPF.

9. If the amount of productive resources available for use in an economy were to increase, what would happen to the production possibilities frontier?

The slope of the PPF at a point represents the tradeoff in production between output of food and clothing. If we reduced food output by one unit, we could increase clothing output by the number of units given by the magnitude of the slope of the PPF (which equals $\Delta C/\Delta F$, as shown in Figure 16.6 as we move from point M to point N). The slope of the PPF equals $-MC_F/MC_C$ (since $1/MC_F$ represents the resources freed up by reducing food output by one unit). The absolute value of the slope of the PPF is called the *marginal rate of transformation* (MRT) between food and clothing. Along the production possibilities frontier, $MRT = MC_F/MC_C$.

EFFICIENCY IN OUTPUT MARKETS

Maximizing the output of one good given output of the second good is a necessary, but not a sufficient, condition for efficiency. It is not sufficient because all points on the PPF are not equally desirable. The outputs produced may not be the combination most preferred by consumers.

To illustrate the condition for the efficient output mix, suppose one individual consumes the entire output of food and clothing that is produced from K and L. From the production Edgeworth box, we can derive the PPF for this two-good economy. Output efficiency is achieved if $MRT = MRS^j$ for each consumer j. Since $MRT = MC_F/MC_C$, and $P_F/P_C = MRS^j$, profit maximization by producers and utility maximization by consumers guarantees that $MRS^j = MRT$.

THE GAINS FROM FREE TRADE (Section 16.5)

Country A has a *comparative advantage* over Country B in producing a good if the cost of producing that good in Country A, relative to the cost of producing other goods in A, is lower than the cost of producing that good in Country B, relative to the cost of producing other goods in B. Country A has an *absolute advantage* in producing a good if its cost is lower than the cost in Country B. Trade between these two countries will be mutually beneficial when the two countries each have a comparative advantage. In other words, if a country is relatively more efficient at producing a particular good, it should specialize in that good and then trade with the rest of the world to obtain the other goods that it needs. By trading, the country with a comparative advantage is able to consume outside its production possibilities frontier. If we move from a world where markets are closed to one where free trade is allowed, consumers will be better off, but it is likely that certain firms and their workers will be worse off as selected domestic industries decline due to increases in imports.

AN OVERVIEW—THE EFFICIENCY OF COMPETITIVE MARKETS (Section 16.6)

To summarize, we have seen that there are three different conditions for efficiency that are satisfied in perfectly competitive markets (assuming two goods, food and clothing):

Efficiency in Consumption: $MRS^A = MRS^B$ ($= P_F/P_C$), for the two consumers, A and B;

Efficiency in Production: $MRTS_F = MRTS_C$ (= w/r), for the two inputs, labor and capital;

Efficient Output Mix: MRT ($= MC_F/MC_C$) = MRS^A ($= P_F/P_C$) = MRS^B, for the two goods.

WHY MARKETS FAIL (Section 16.7)

Up until now we have assumed that a competitive market can exist so that an efficient allocation will be possible. There are certain occasions, however, when the competitive market fails. The sources of market failure dealt with in this chapter are as follows:

1) *Market Power*: A monopolist will set marginal revenue equal to marginal cost to determine the profit-maximizing output level. This output level will be less than the competitive output and the price will be higher than the competitive price. At a lower output level the monopolist will have a lower marginal cost, i.e., the firm will use fewer resources to produce that good. These resources will be able to move into the production of other goods. The output mix will be different from the competitive and therefore inefficient.

2) *Incomplete Information*: A lack of information can lead producers and consumers to make the wrong decisions (that is, decisions that leave them worse off because they were not fully informed). Informational inefficiencies are discussed further in Chapter 17.

3) *Externalities*: An externality exists when a consumption or production activity has an indirect effect on another consumption or production activity. The market "fails" because market prices do not reflect these indirect effects. Externalities, and how to address them, are discussed in Chapter 18.

4) *Public Goods:* Once a public good is provided to some consumers, it is very difficult to prevent others from consuming it (e.g., public parks or national defense). If private firms cannot charge each consumer a price for consuming their product, the market will under-supply public goods. Chapter 18 discusses public goods in detail.

Exercise: ▶▶▶▶▶▶▶

10. For each of the following sources of inefficiency, state which efficiency condition is violated and why. If a second condition is only violated occasionally, explain why. (Hint: Think about th efficiency conditions in relation to the various contract curves and frontiers.)
    a) Agricultural price supports
    b) A monopolist selling at a single price
    c) Third-degree price discrimination
    d) A dominant firm as the price leader

PROBLEM SET

11. Demonstrate that the utility possibilities frontier can never be upward sloping. (This is a direct consequence of its definition.)

12. If a point lies inside the utility possibilities frontier, is a Pareto improvement always possible?

13. A medium-sized city has two major industries, financial services and manufacturing of electronic equipment. Suppose that restrictions on interstate competition in the market for financial services lead to a large expansion of the financial services sector in the city.
    a) What effect do you predict that this increase in jobs would have on wages and housing prices in the city?
    b) What effect do you think there would be on the manufacturing sector in the city? Would you expect that manufacturing employment would rise or fall?

14. Sally and John are the only two citizens in a small country. The only thing they care about is their aggregate consumption this year, X_1, and aggregate consumption next year X_2 (both in dollars). Sally's endowment of X_1 and X_2 is $E^S = (80,40)$. John's is $E^J = (40,80)$. There is no way for the two to arrange loans. For instance, John cannot arrange to borrow a few dollars from Sally in year one in exchange for repayment plus interest in the second year. Now, suppose the government must raise \$20 in year one to provide national defense and that both consumers are taxed equally.
    a) Draw an Edgeworth box using the after-tax endowments of $E^{ST} = (70,40)$ and $E^{JT} = (30,80)$. Plot the endowment point and label it E.
    b) Now suppose that the government instead borrows the \$20 from Sally. In return, the government taxes both Sally and John \$15 in the second year and pays Sally the \$30. Plot this new point, labeled B, in the Edgeworth box. Draw indifference curves through the endowment point E from part a) in such a way that point B is a Pareto improvement over the endowment. Explain why both citizens are better off, in this example, when the government borrows than when they tax everyone up-front.

SELF-TEST

15. General equilibrium analysis:
- a) determines all prices simultaneously.
- b) allows for feedback effects.
- c) is useful for studying closely related markets.
- d) can consider goods and factor markets simultaneously.
- e) All of the above are correct.

16. In an exchange economy with two consumers A and B:
- a) $MRS^A = 1/MRS^B$ everywhere.
- b) $MRS^A = MRS^B$ everywhere.
- c) $MRS^A = 1/MRS^B$ on the contract curve.
- d) $MRS^A = MRS^B$ on the contract curve.
- e) None of the above is correct.

17. If an allocation is Pareto efficient:
- a) no trade can make both individuals better off.
- b) it lies on the contract curve.
- c) both individuals are better off than with their initial endowments.
- d) a) and b)
- e) a), b) and c)

18. The utility possibilities frontier:
- a) may have an upward-sloping portion.
- b) describes the utilities for allocations on the contract curve.
- c) depends on the distribution of the initial endowments.
- d) a) and b)
- e) a), b), and c)

19. At a Pareto efficient allocation with production:
- a) $MRS^A = MRS^B$.
- b) $MRS^A = MRT$.
- c) MRTS is equal in all industries.
- d) a) and b)
- e) a), b), and c)

20. A small country will gain from free trade:
- a) if the pre-trade price ratio differs from the world price ratio.
- b) if it produces a good at lower absolute cost than the rest of the world.
- c) if its consumers have certain preferences.
- d) a) and b)
- e) None of the above is correct.

21. An exchange that results in a move from a point off the contract curve to a point on the contract curve:
a) makes someone better off but others worse off.
b) can make someone better off without making anyone worse off.
c) makes no one better off.
d) is possible only if the initial endowments are changed.
e) corresponds to a movement along the utility possibilities frontier.

22. Suppose that Alfred's marginal rate of substitution of food for clothing is 3, while Betty's marginal rate of substitution of food for clothing is 2. We can conclude that in a market, Alfred and Betty:
a) voluntarily choose not to trade.
b) trade, but Alfred will be worse off.
c) trade, but Betty will be worse off.
d) trade from their current allocation to a point on the contract curve.
e) won't know what to do, without more information.

23. In comparing two points, Q and R, on a contract curve, we can say that:
a) they are efficient.
b) consumers will voluntarily move from Q to R.
c) the distribution of goods is the same across Q and R.
d) an egalitarian would view either allocation as equitable.
e) Both a) and b)

24. General equilibrium analysis is more appropriate than partial equilibrium analysis when:
a) more than one answer is possible.
b) both consumers and producers are being considered.
c) there are significant feedback effects between markets.
d) markets operate independently.
e) interpersonal comparisons of utility cannot be made.

The next two questions concern a hypothetical economy in which two goods, food (F) and clothing (C), are produced using two inputs, labor (L) and capital (K).

25. If the $MRTS_{LK}$ in the food industry is greater than the $MRTS_{LK}$ in the clothing industry:
a) production of food could only be increased by decreasing clothing production because resources are scarce.
b) production of clothing could only be increased by decreasing production of food because the MRTS is lower in the clothing industry.
c) production of food could be increased without decreasing clothing production by transferring capital from the clothes industry to the food industry and labor from the food industry to the clothing industry.
d) production of food could be increased without decreasing clothing production by transferring labor from the clothing industry to the food industry and capital from the food industry to the clothing industry.
e) None of the above is correct.

26. If the marginal rate of substitution of food for clothing is 4 for all consumers and the marginal rate of transformation of clothing into food is 2, then:

a) more clothing should be produced since consumers are willing to give up a greater amount of food for more clothing than the opportunity cost of clothing.

b) more clothing and less food should be produced to equate the MRS to the MRT.

c) more food should be produced since consumers are willing to give up a greater amount of clothing for more food than the opportunity cost of food.

d) a) and b).

e) None of the above is correct.

27. If there is a monopoly in the clothing industry and perfect competition in the food industry, MC_F/MC_C will be _________ than P_F/P_C. This means resources will be _________ -allocated to the clothing industry.

a) greater; over

b) less; over

c) greater; under

d) less; under

e) None of the above is correct.

ANSWERS TO CHAPTER 16

EXERCISE ANSWERS

1. The frost inhibitor will shift the tomato supply curve to the right and decrease the price of salsa. This decrease, in turn, causes demand for tortilla chips to shift to the right and raises their price. But a higher price of tortilla chips will shift the demand for salsa to the left, which decreases the price of salsa even more. So the price of salsa falls more than it would in partial equilibrium analysis.

2. See the Edgeworth box in Figure 16A.1 for the answer to both a) and b).

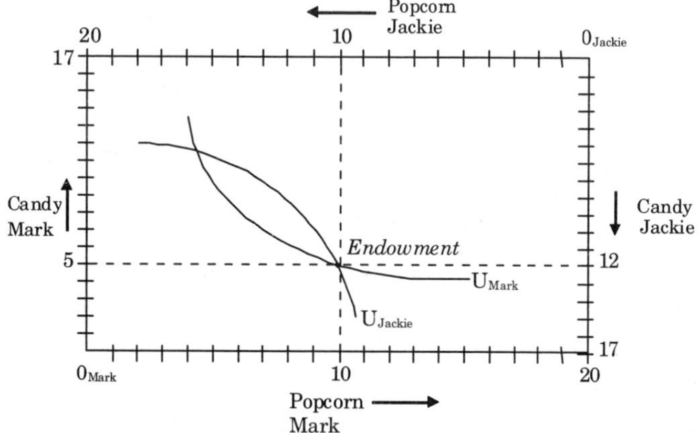

Figure 16A.1

3. For example, a tangency of the budget line between food and clothing to Alfred's indifference curve implies $MRS^A = P_F / P_C$. Similarly, for Betty, $MRS^B = P_F / P_C$, so $MRS^A = P_F / P_C = MRS^B$.

4. a) This is not a Pareto efficient distribution of the goods since $MRS_{Jim} \neq MRS_{Linda}$.

b) They can both be made better off if Jim gives Linda some of his income and Linda gives Jim some of her gas. (Jim is willing to give up as much as $1 to get an additional gallon of gas; Linda is willing to accept as little as $0.25 to sell him the gallon of gas. Thus, they can both be made better off if a gallon of gas is exchanged at a price between $0.25 and $1.)

5. It is possible to move from H to F and make Alfred better off without making Betty worse off. Therefore, H is inefficient. Or, one can say that to move from H to F is a Pareto improvement. At H, Betty is better off than at G, while Alfred is better off at G than at H. A move from H to G is not a Pareto improvement because it makes one consumer worse off. Since H is not a Pareto optimal allocation, there are allocations inside the utility possibilities frontier that would make both consumers better off than at H. But not all Pareto efficient allocations (on the frontier) are Pareto improvements over a particular allocation inside the frontier.

6. At an efficient allocation, $MRTS_F = MRTS_C$. Since $MRTS = MP_L/MP_K$ for both food and clothing, we can describe this tangency of the isoquants as having equal *ratios* of marginal products. Note that MP_L and MP_K in the two industries will not generally be the same, since marginal products will change as output of one good increases and output of the other good decreases.

7. A cost-minimizing firm operates where MRTS = w/r (the wage/rental rate ratio). If firms take factor prices as given, $MRTS_F = w/r$ and $MRTS_C = w/r$, so $MRTS_F = MRTS_C$, which is the condition for efficiency in the production Edgeworth box.

8. If an allocation lies off the production contract curve, then more of both goods can be obtained by reallocating factors in the two industries. If more of both goods can be obtained, the original allocation must lie southwest of some points on the PPF.

9. This will shift the production possibilities frontier outward.

10. a) An output price distortion means that $MRS^j \neq MRT$ for each consumer j. If the agricultural output is an input into production of other goods, then $MRTS_F \neq MRTS_C$ if it is used in only one of the industries.

b) The only distortion a monopoly creates is that $MRS^j \neq MRT$.

c) Price discrimination by a monopolist has two distortions: as with any monopoly, $MRS^j \neq MRT$, *and* $MRS^A \neq MRS^B$ for consumers A and B who face different prices.

d) Here, $MRS^j \neq MRT$ and marginal cost is not equal across all firms in that industry, so the economy is producing inside the PPF as well.

PROBLEM SET ANSWERS

11. If the utility possibilities frontier is upward sloping, then by moving from one point to another on the utility possibilities frontier, the utilities of both consumers can be increased. If so, the first point cannot have been Pareto efficient, and thus, it cannot lie on the utility possibilities frontier.

12. Consider Figure 16.5: beginning at point H, any movement within the area EHF will be a Pareto improvement since it raises both consumers' utilities. However, a move from H to G would make one consumer worse off. Therefore, only a move to the northeast would be a Pareto improvement. Only if a point lies on the utility possibilities frontier is no Pareto improvement possible.

13. a) An increase in the demand for labor should increase wages in equilibrium. Higher wages will attract new workers to the city, as well as raise the incomes of all workers in the city. This, in turn, should increase the demand for housing, and thus raise the price of housing.

b) Wages in the manufacturing sector would presumably rise due to competition for workers from other sectors. Increased housing prices would also raise the wages needed to attract new workers from other cities. Thus, this city's manufacturing sector faces higher costs than manufacturing in other cities. If the electronics industry is mobile, firms are likely to transfer production to other cities. Hence, manufacturing employment will likely fall when employment in other sectors rises.

14. a) See Figure 16A.2. The point E shows the after-tax endowments.

b) When the government borrows, it allows those who are less patient to benefit by deferring their tax liability and those that are more patient to benefit by earning interest. (If the impatient person had access to unlimited credit and could be held to his agreements, it would not matter. It is the fact that the impatient person lacks the ability to borrow that causes the improvement.)

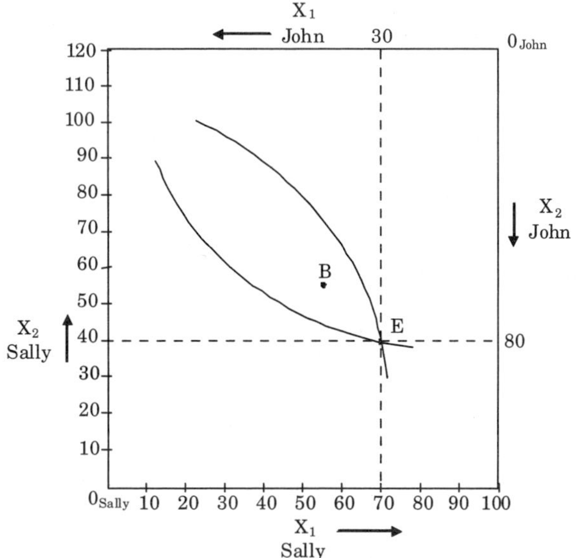

Figure 16A.2

SELF-TEST ANSWERS

15. e) General equilibrium analysis satisfies all of these statements.

16. d) MRSs are only equal at indifference curve tangencies in the Edgeworth box (along the contract curve).

17. d) The initial endowments might lie on the contract curve, making c) false.

18. b) The utility possibilities frontier depends on the total endowments, but not on their distribution because a move along the utility possibilities frontier is a redistribution of goods along the contract curve.

19. e) These are the three marginal conditions for efficiency.

20. a) Only this condition is necessary to gain from free trade. If a) is true, then trade will benefit a country no matter what its consumers' preferences are.

21. b) Any point off the contract curve is inefficient and therefore it is possible to reallocate the goods to make at least one person better off without making others worse off.

22. d) Since their MRSs are unequal they must be at a point off of the contract curve. They will engage in mutually beneficial exchange until they reach a point on the contract curve, i.e., until $MRS^A = MRS^B$.

23. a) We can only say that they are both efficient allocations. Once a point on the contract curve is chosen, there is no way to move to another point on the contract curve without making one person worse off, and therefore b) is false. Also, the distribution of goods clearly cannot be the same across both allocations. The egalitarian would only consider an equal distribution of goods equitable, and we do not know how the goods are distributed at points Q and R.

24. c) If feedback effects between markets are likely to be significant, then partial equilibrium analysis will give a poor approximation to the correct answer and general equilibrium analysis is called for.

25. d) If one worker was transferred from the clothing industry to the food industry, the amount of capital which could be taken out of food production without lowering output below the original level would exceed the amount needed to make up for the loss of the worker in the clothing sector. The extra capital could be used to increase output of either good.

26. c) Consumers would give up 4 units of clothing for one more unit of food, but a unit of food costs society only 2 units of clothing. Thus, more food and less clothing should be produced.

27. c) Since a monopoly charges a price greater than marginal cost while price equals marginal cost in a competitive industry, $MC_F/MC_C > P_F/P_C$. Since the monopoly's price exceeds marginal cost, clothing output is too low.

CHAPTER 17
MARKETS WITH ASYMMETRIC INFORMATON

IMPORTANT CONCEPTS

- Adverse Selection
- Lemons Problem
- Signals
- Moral Hazard
- Principal-Agent Problem
- Efficiency Wages

CHAPTER HIGHLIGHTS

In Chapters 5 and 15, we studied some of the effects of uncertainty on consumer and firm behavior. However, all parties in those transactions were equally well informed. For example, in the Capital Asset Pricing Model, all investors have identical expectations about the riskiness of each firm. Now we consider another possibility—that buyers and sellers have different information about the quality of the good or service being traded.

Insurance and credit markets are two examples of markets that suffer from asymmetric information problems. In these cases, the consumers know what type of risk they represent better than the sellers do. Low-risk individuals may choose not to buy insurance because the price of insurance coverage is based on the *average* risks in the population. This *adverse selection* (the fact that only high-risk individuals buy insurance) means that insurance companies must base prices on loss rates that are greater than the average for the target population. Information about previous losses and credit histories are often used by insurers and lenders to reduce the adverse selection problem.

In a product market, asymmetric information about product quality can drive the market price low enough to force high-quality goods out of the market. This is known as the *lemons problem*. When the buyer knows only the overall distribution of the qualities of the good, each buyer's willingness to pay depends on the average quality expected. However, the price a seller will accept depends on the actual quality of that seller's product.

This information asymmetry results in market failure: sellers of high-quality products prefer not to sell their goods, even though buyers, if they knew the quality, would be willing to pay more than the value to the sellers. The goods that are offered for sale on the market will generally be of below-average quality. Sellers may attempt to resolve this problem by developing a reputation for quality. Thus, chain store operations reduce uncertainty for buyers by standardization in circumstances where individual stores would find it difficult to build reputations.

Information asymmetries are also present in the labor market. Education may be a way that highly skilled workers can demonstrate their skills to potential employers. Education may thus act as a *signal* and eliminate the information asymmetry between a worker and an employer. If it is less costly for high-ability workers than low-ability workers to provide a signal, then high-ability workers can credibly reveal their ability to employers. It does not matter if the signal has no direct productive value. To work as a signal, the cost of acquiring education must be less for high-ability workers than for low-ability workers. Another kind of signal is a product warranty. Warranties can signal product quality because manufacturers of higher quality products find it less costly to offer warranties.

Moral hazard creates another type of information problem that arises when the insured individual changes her behavior after obtaining insurance against a risk. For example, after buying insurance, an insured individual may be less careful about avoiding a loss. If the insurer cannot directly observe the insured's level of care, the cost of insurance must be higher to compensate for the greater risk faced by the insurer.

Unobservable behavior is the root of the *principal-agent problem*. A principal hires an agent to perform a task, but the principal cannot perfectly observe the agent's behavior. If the agent's output depends on both effort and a random event (which the principal does not observe), an incentive scheme based on output may be necessary to get the agent to supply the desired level of effort.

Efficiency wage theory predicts that wages paid to employees will affect their productivity. Shirking models give one explanation of this. If monitoring employees' work effort is expensive, firms can pursue an alternative of monitoring workers randomly and firing employees who are caught not working hard. In a competitive labor market equilibrium, fired employees could find new jobs at the same wage, so the threat is not very severe. If, however, workers were paid above the equilibrium wage, they would suffer when they lose their jobs because their next job is unlikely to pay as well. Thus, a high wage can induce workers not to shirk and risk being fired even when there is a small probability of actually being fired.

CONCEPT REVIEW AND EXERCISES

QUALITY UNCERTAINTY AND THE MARKET FOR LEMONS (Section 17.1)

On his way out the door each morning, a friend grabs the loose change on his bedside table and puts it in his pocket. He tells you that, on average, he starts the day with $2.50 in change, and the distribution of change ranges uniformly between $1 and $4. The friend then offers you all the change in his pocket for $2.00. Would you be willing to accept the offer? If he does not know how much change he has today, it seems like a reasonable gamble—pay $2 for an expected reward of $2.50. Now change the problem. Suppose your friend asks you to make a bid for the change in his pocket. After you make an offer, he will then count his change and decide whether to accept the offer. In this case, don't take the offer—you can never win because your offer will only be accepted if your friend comes out ahead. Since he will have information you don't have when bidding, he has an advantage due to *asymmetric information*.

Individuals face many important choices under similar circumstances. The seller of a used car has a better idea of the quality of the car than does the buyer. An individual buying automobile insurance knows whether he tends to drive cautiously or dangerously. A borrower knows whether he plans to pay off the loan or fraudulently avoid repayment. A *lemons problem* arises due to asymmetric information about product quality. For example, in the used car market buyers determine the prices they are willing to pay according to their belief regarding the average quality of the cars offered for sale. Sellers, in contrast, know the quality of their cars and base the asking prices on the quality of the individual cars to be sold. In this framework, the seller of the highest quality car will never be able to get a price that properly reflects that quality. As a result, this seller will not offer her car for sale in the market. But now, the seller of the second highest quality car will not be able to get a price that reflects the quality of the car she is offering, and will also withdraw it from the market. This process may continue until only the lowest quality cars are offered in the market. (Only if buyers place much higher values on low-quality cars than sellers do is it possible for high-quality cars to be sold in equilibrium.)

At any time, some people are selling used cars for reasons unrelated to the quality of the car (new parents may need a larger car; salespeople need an attractive up-to-date car to make a good impression, and so must occasionally trade in an old, yet reliable car). Even when many trades take place in a market with asymmetric information, the quantity traded will be less than the efficient level. The information asymmetry causes some individuals not to sell their cars, even though they would sell their cars if quality could be truthfully revealed, and even though some consumer would be willing to pay a higher price for a car known to be high quality. The labor market also exhibits information asymmetries, as the following exercise illustrates.

Exercise: ▶▶▶▶▶▶▶

1. Burt currently holds a job, and he decides to interview for a different job. If a new employer, Sam, makes Burt an offer, one of Burt's options is to ask Harry, his current employer, for a raise.
   a) If Burt receives a counteroffer, what does that indicate to Sam? If Burt does not receive a counteroffer, what does that indicate?
   b) Should Sam base his wage offer on the expected quality of the worker (determined from the interview process), or should a lower wage offer be made? Why?

2. Consider the market for compact stereos, which are units that typically include a radio, compact-disc player, and a set of relatively small speakers. Both high and low quality stereo systems are sold on the market.
   a) Assuming that sellers have more information regarding quality than buyers (although buyers do have some information), would the fraction of high quality systems on the market be higher, lower, or the same as in the case of full information for the buyer and seller?
   b) What practices have arisen in the market to help alleviate the asymmetric information problem that consumers face?

MARKET SIGNALING (Section 17.2)

Many firms sell replacement auto parts, such as shock absorbers. Some offer warranties against the part failing for as long as you own your car. Others offer shorter warranties, and still others offer no warranty at all. Although you would be willing to pay more for new shock absorbers with a warranty, how much more depends on your estimate of the probability that each type of shock absorber will break down while you still own the car. The firm with a high-quality product will find it less expensive to offer a warranty than firms with lower-quality products because the high-quality manufacturer has a low expected cost of servicing the warranties. Even with full warranties, you would prefer to buy the brand with the smallest probability of breakdown because you suffer some inconvenience in exercising your warranty rights (taking your car into the shop, at the least). Thus, you are willing to pay a premium for the higher quality product.

Sellers of low-quality products are kept from offering warranties because their cost of servicing the warranties will be higher than for sellers of high-quality products. This cost differential means that a warranty can serve as a strong *signal* of quality. If consumers are willing to pay a premium for the brand with a warranty that is greater than the cost of servicing a warranty on high-quality goods, but less than the cost of servicing a warranty on low-quality goods, then warranties will be offered only with high-quality brands.

In general, a signal will be effective if it is less difficult (less costly) for sellers of high quality to offer it than for sellers of low quality. The cost of the signal must be high enough to prevent low-quality sellers from signaling, but low enough so that high-quality sellers prefer to signal. For example, if it is easier for good workers to get more education, education can serve as a signal of worker quality.

Exercise: ▶▶▶▶▶▶▶

3. If financial aid were expanded and more students attended college as a result, would you expect that more students would get Masters of Business Administration degrees? Why?

MORAL HAZARD (Section 17.3)

If insurance companies cannot monitor the behavior of their policyholders, the individuals may change their behavior after purchasing the insurance. For example, a firm with fire insurance will spend less effort in fire prevention than will a firm without fire insurance. In many such circumstances, the level of effort chosen depends on the risks one faces. Since fire insurance reduces the risk, it also discourages effort to avoid fires. A *moral hazard* problem occurs when the insured party can affect the degree of risk involved in an uncertain situation. Despite the terminology, there is no immoral behavior or fraud when one reduces prevention activities after buying insurance. It is the profit-maximizing response whenever the insurer cannot observe prevention activities. For the insurer, it means that the uninsured population's behavior will not be an accurate guide to the probabilities of fires (or other accidents) among the insured.

Exercise: ▶▶▶▶▶▶▶

4. Even though Joe has an excellent comprehensive health insurance policy, he has no wish to risk a heart attack. He continues to watch his diet and exercise regularly to reduce the risk of heart disease even though he is insured. Is there any element of moral hazard about which his health insurance company would still need to be concerned?

THE PRINCIPAL-AGENT PROBLEM (Section 17.4)

Moral hazard is a problem for insurers because they are often unable to identify whether an accident occurred because of carelessness or bad luck. In fact, this problem applies to almost all firms. For example, the owner of a firm cannot perfectly observe the effort expended by its sales representatives who visit potential customers. Designing the best compensation system for the owner is an example of a *principal-agent problem*. An agency relationship exists when one person's welfare depends on what another person does. The owner of the firm is the principal (the beneficiary of the effort) and the salesperson (who undertakes the effort) is the agent.

If a salesperson brings in little business, the owner cannot distinguish between two possibilities: the salesperson shirked and made few calls; or, in that person's territory, potential customers had low demands that period. Given this inability to observe effort, how can the owner design a compensation system to encourage effort? One possible solution is to pay each salesperson based on assigned territory sales (a commission system). But a pure commission system may impose a lot of risk on the individual salesperson (which the owner may be in a better position to bear). A compromise solution is to pay each salesperson a small fixed salary and a bonus based on sales in each salesperson's territory. There is still an incentive to supply effort, but not as much as with a pure commission system. With a mixed system the owner is absorbing some of the risk.

Exercise: ◗ ◗ ◗ ◗ ◗ ◗ ◗

5. The demand for automobiles is highly cyclical, going up when the economy is doing well, and going down when the economy is in a recession. The owners of the automobile companies realize this, and have to consider different payment schemes knowing that the profits each year for the firm will depend on the strength of the economy *and* the performance of their managers. Which of the following payment schemes would you recommend to the owners and why?

a) Pay the managers a flat salary that is not tied to the firm's performance.

b) Pay the managers a share of the profits.

c) Pay the managers a flat salary plus a bonus that is tied to the firm's performance.

ASYMMETRIC INFORMATION IN LABOR MARKETS: EFFICIENCY WAGE THEORY (Section 17.6)

The *efficiency wage* is the wage that will induce employees to be productive, rather than shirk on the job. The efficiency wage is higher than the competitive wage. In other words, suppose an employee is caught shirking and then fired. The cost of being fired is higher if the wage at the original company is higher than the going market wage.

The extent of the difference between the efficiency wage and the market wage depends on a number of factors. For example, the higher the level of unemployment, the smaller the difference. When unemployment levels are high, the cost of shirking and losing one's job is high (there is a significant risk of being unemployed for a long period of time). Therefore, the firm does not have to raise the wage by as much to induce employees to be productive. Or consider the effect of the frequency of monitoring by the employer. If the employer can monitor workers constantly, the wage need not be adjusted. But if the employer can only monitor infrequently, then there must be a greater wage differential to lessen the extent of shirking.

Exercise: ◗ ◗ ◗ ◗ ◗ ◗ ◗

6. Presumably, all firms are interested in eliminating shirking. If all firms raise their wages, will there be any effect on shirking?

PROBLEM SET

7. In the used car market, would there be a market failure if neither buyers nor sellers knew the quality of the cars being traded at the time of sale? How would the market equilibrium differ from the market equilibrium under asymmetric information?

8. Adverse selection and moral hazard are problems that occur in insurance markets. Are these concepts two names for the same problem, two distinct but mutually exclusive problems, or two distinct problems that may both be present at the same time? Explain.

9. Suppose that 40 percent of the population is highly skilled even with no education, and each person has a marginal product with a present discounted value of $200,000. These highly skilled people can acquire a college education at a cost in present value terms of $40,000. The remaining 60 percent of the population is less skilled with a present discounted value of their marginal product equal to $120,000, regardless of educational attainment. These less-skilled people can obtain a college education at a cost of $90,000 in present value terms. Potential employers are unable to identify who is highly skilled, but individuals know their skill levels.
   a) In equilibrium, what is the PDV of wages paid to college graduates and to those without college degrees? Explain.
   b) Suppose that the cost of college rises dramatically to $100,000 for the highly skilled and $140,000 for the less skilled. What is the PDV of wages paid to workers with and without college degrees? Explain your answer.

10. Employee group health insurance is usually considerably less expensive than insurance purchased by individuals. Group auto insurance policies are not much less expensive than individual auto policies. State laws require individuals to buy at least some auto insurance. Can you explain the relative prices of group versus individual insurance policies in light of this fact?

11. Explain why we would expect moral hazard to have a more significant effect on the market for auto insurance than on the market for airplane flight insurance (that insures a passenger's life in case the flight crashes).

12. Suppose that users of rental cars each have a demand curve for miles driven per day as given in Figure 17.1 (on the next page). It costs a rental car firm $30 per day to supply the car to a customer plus $0.25 per mile driven. Assume the rental car market is perfectly competitive.

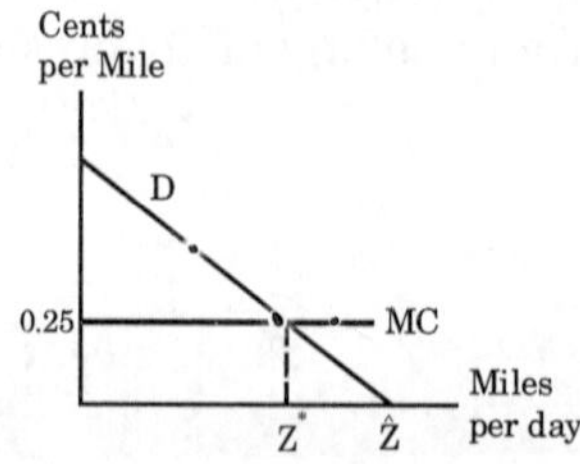

Figure 17.1

a) What would be the equilibrium rental car contract price when the renting firm can measure miles driven (price per day and price per mile)?
b) In one community, unscrupulous car rental firms had been caught in the past tampering with odometers on rental cars. As a result, the local government passed a consumer protection regulation stating that car rental firms could not charge per mile driven. What would be the equilibrium daily rate for car rentals in this case?
c) What is the deadweight loss from the inability to charge per mile driven?

SELF-TEST

13. When renting a car, the rental firm will sell you a waiver that releases you from any monetary liability for damage to the car from collisions. Compared to other types of car insurance, these waivers seem quite expensive. A possible explanation is:
a) the moral hazard problem is more severe.
b) the adverse selection problem is more severe.
c) it is more expensive to repair rental cars.
d) a) and b)
e) b) and c)

14. A manufacturer is *less* likely to offer warranties for its products if:
a) consumer misuse is a likely source of failure and difficult to detect.
b) its products are of higher quality than those of its competitors.
c) its products are of lower quality than those of its competitors.
d) a) and b)
e) a) and c)

15. From whom would you prefer to buy a used car (everything else being equal)?
a) Someone trading it in for a new car.
b) An amateur car mechanic.
c) A graduating Ph.D. student returning home to his native country.
d) A family planning to buy another used car.
e) a) or d)

16. The signaling model of education would break down if:
a) skills learned in school were useful in employment.
b) the costs of acquiring education were equal for individuals of different abilities.
c) individuals could not identify their own abilities.
d) b) and c)
e) a), b) and c)

17. The efficiency wage theory states that:
a) it is more efficient to pay workers the minimum wage.
b) higher pay can deter workers from shirking.
c) more highly paid workers are less fearful of unemployment.
d) workers should never be paid their marginal products.
e) None of the above is correct.

18. Laundry detergent is a frequent purchase for most households. That high-quality detergents are advertised more heavily can be seen as an example of:
a) adverse selection.
b) moral hazard.
c) market signaling.
d) the principal-agent problem.
e) None of the above is correct.

19. Which of the following is the best example of adverse selection?
a) A consumer buys a lawnmower that does not perform as advertised.
b) A restaurant owner who has a fire insurance policy sets fire to the restaurant.
c) Risk-averse individuals always buy more insurance than they need.
d) Less healthy people are more likely to purchase health insurance.
e) Only manufacturers of high-quality products choose to offer warranties.

20. There are 100 used cars potentially available for sale in the town of Manchester. The owners of the low-quality used cars value their cars at $4,000, while the high quality car owners value their cars at $8,000. Buyers believe that 50 percent of cars are lemons (low quality). There are 100 potential buyers who value low-quality cars at $5,000 and high-quality cars at $10,000. The price a buyer is willing to pay is a function of the average car quality they expect to be offered on the market. We can conclude that in the long run:
a) buyers are willing to pay $7,500, and only low-quality cars will be offered for sale.
b) buyers are willing to pay $7,500, and both types of cars will be offered for sale.
c) buyers are willing to pay $5,000, and only low-quality cars will be offered for sale.
d) buyers are willing to pay $10,000, and both types of cars will be offered for sale.
e) buyers are willing to pay $10,000, and only high-quality cars will be offered for sale.

21. In which of the following industries would you predict that nationally advertised brands have the largest market share?
a) Plumbing contractors
b) Bottled milk
c) Hotels and motels
d) Tuxedo rentals
e) None of the above.

22. Long-term stock options to top management in publicly-traded corporations:
a) provide a way for managers with little personal wealth to have a larger stake in the firm.
b) align the interests of managers and stockholders.
c) give managers incentives not to focus on the short-term.
d) b) and c)
e) a), b), and c)

23. An unlimited return policy for a mail-order clothing company may:
a) function as a signal to customers.
b) reduce customer uncertainty about product quality.
c) be less effective for a new entrant.
d) a) and b)
e) a), b), and c

24. Most states require owners of automobiles to buy liability insurance. For the sellers of insurance policies, this may alleviate:
a) the moral hazard problem.
b) the adverse selection problem.
c) the principal-agent problem.
d) All of the above are correct.
e) None of the above is correct.

ANSWERS TO CHAPTER 17

EXERCISE ANSWERS

1. a) The information asymmetry here is between Sam, the prospective employer, and Harry, the current employer. No matter what Sam offers Burt, Harry will make a counteroffer if Burt is worth at least Sam's wage offer. Burt will stay if he gets a counteroffer. Burt is hired away only when the prospective employer has overestimated the worker's ability.

b) If Burt never leaves when a counteroffer is made, and all firms would place the same value on the worker, no offers to workers currently holding jobs should ever be made. That result is obviously too strong—but employers need to be aware that the ability of a worker's current employer to make a counteroffer means they will be more successful in bidding away lower-ability workers.

2. a) The fraction of high quality stereo systems will be less than it would be with perfect information. This is a direct application of the lemons problem.

b) The problem with buying a stereo system is that the buyer needs to hear it to judge the quality (at least in part). Thus, most stores selling stereos have them plugged in so that shoppers can test them. Also, publications such as *Consumer Reports* provide ratings after extensive testing (not only for sound, but durability, and ease of use, etc.). Buyers can use these ratings to alleviate the asymmetric information problem.

3. If education is serving as a signal, having more education than the average worker indicates that one is of better than average ability. When average education levels rise, to signal the same relative ability, one needs to have even more schooling. So, if more people have college degrees, high-ability workers need even more schooling to signal their abilities, and we would expect more students to get MBA degrees.

4. Even in Joe's case moral hazard is still a problem for health insurers with respect to the cost of health care. Without insurance, if your physician tells you that a bypass operation will cure the problem, but that a change in diet and exercise might cure it too, you would certainly try the latter. If your insurance policy covers all the costs of the operation, you are more likely to try the operation.

   Being insured means that you are more willing to have expensive tests done for some medical problems, rather than waiting to see if any symptoms persist. Thus, the costs experienced for insured individuals will differ from those of the uninsured, even if both types are equally likely to become ill.

5. a) A flat salary will not provide the right incentives to the managers to pursue the owner's goal of profit maximization.
   b) This scheme will provide the right incentives, but will also greatly increase the risk that the manager has to bear. If the firm is risk-neutral and the manager is risk-averse, it would be better if the firm shared the risk.
   c) The bonus scheme has the potential to be effective. The manager is insured with the flat salary against a large downside risk, but will share in the gains if he or she puts in extra effort and helps to increase profits for the firm.

6. If all firms raise their wages and cannot raise their prices to make up for the increased cost, they will have to cut back somewhat on labor input. This means that the unemployment rate will rise. This in turn means that workers are less likely to shirk, since the risk of being unemployed for a lengthy period of time is high.

PROBLEM SET ANSWERS

7. If no one knew the quality of the cars for sale, then both buyers and sellers would base their decisions on the average quality of the product. All qualities of the good would be offered for sale, and there would be no market failure. (Risk aversion might reduce demand to some extent, but this would be efficient.) The market equilibrium under asymmetric information could differ drastically, depending on the degree of information asymmetry. If the asymmetry is severe and there are no "lemon laws" or warranty provisions in place to help protect the buyer, then the market could fail.

8. Moral hazard arises from the change in behavior of individuals when they obtain insurance. Adverse selection arises from individuals selecting insurance policies based on their knowledge of their own risk exposure. These are two distinct problems. In health insurance, both problems could certainly be present at the same time.

9. a) Since 40 percent of the population is highly skilled, the expected PDV of the marginal product of the average worker is 0.40($200,000) + 0.60($120,000) = $152,000. If no workers go to college, an employer would be willing to pay a PDV of $152,000 in lifetime earnings. Given that the highly skilled can get an education for $40,000, each of them would do so, since employers would pay them $200,000, resulting in a gain to each worker of 200,000 – 40,000 – 152,000 = $8,000. The unskilled workers would be paid

$120,000, but they are not willing to spend $90,000 for an additional $80,000 in earnings. Education works as a strong signal here.

b) Here, education is too expensive for either group to obtain, so no one goes to college, and all workers receive $152,000 as the PDV of wages.

10. Since all drivers must purchase auto insurance, the insurance companies do not have the concern over adverse selection of risks that they have with respect to health insurance. Group insurance bundles together individuals who are good and bad risks, so it reduces the adverse selection problem for an insurer. Since this is less of a problem with auto insurance, the group discounts are smaller. An alternative is that being employed is more highly correlated with good health than with good driving. Even if that is true, insurers might try to base rates for non-group health insurance on employment status.

11. A moral hazard problem arises when the insured party can affect the probability that the event they are insured against will occur. Individuals have much more control of whether they get into a car crash than a plane crash, and therefore we would expect auto insurance companies to worry much more about moral hazard problems.

12. a) Since all firms have identical costs, prices for each component of the car rental will equal cost, so renters will pay $30 per day plus $0.25 per mile.

b) Each renter will drive $\hat{Z}$ miles per day, since there is no charge for each mile driven. The daily rental charge must cover all costs, so renters will pay $(30 + 0.25$\hat{Z}$).

c) See Figure 17A.1. All miles in excess of Z* are valued by the consumer at less than the cost of providing those miles. The consumer earns less surplus than if miles driven were observable, but is still willing to rent the car (since surplus is positive).

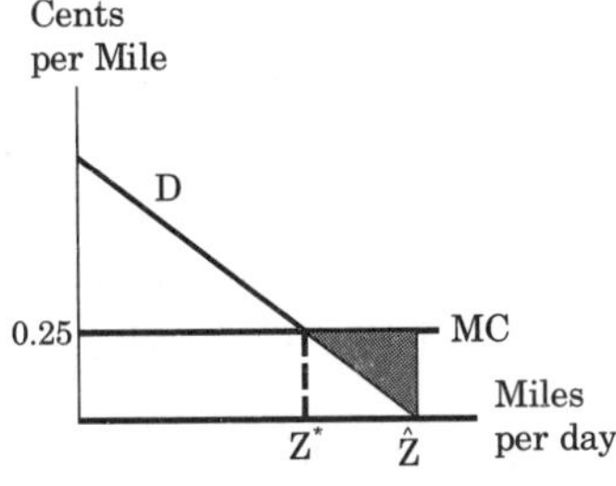

Figure 17A.1

SELF-TEST ANSWERS

13. d) If it is not your car, you might be less careful (moral hazard). Also, since each person is offered the option of this insurance when renting a car, it is possible that only unsafe drivers will choose to purchase the insurance (adverse selection).

14. e) Choice b) is the only factor that makes warranties a strong signal. If consumers can affect the probability of breakdowns, the manufacturer has a moral hazard problem with offering a warranty.

15. c) The Ph.D. student is the only potential seller who is not selling by choice, and because of this, there is a good chance that the car might be of high quality.

16. d) In order for signaling to work, the opposite of b) and c) must hold. If a) is true, education can still serve as a signal, but it is less costly than otherwise.

17. b) The theory of efficiency wages takes for granted that higher wages either attract better employees or that a given employee will work harder if he is paid more.

18. c) High-quality detergents can expect more repeat sales and thus advertising is relatively more profitable for them.

19. d) Note that b) is an example of moral hazard, and e) is an example of signaling.

20. c) If all used cars are offered for sale, the expected value of a car from the perspective of a buyer is 0.5(5,000) + 0.5(10,000) = \$7,500. Since the buyers' initial willingness to pay is less than \$8,000, only low-quality cars will be offered for sale. But if only low-quality cars are offered, buyers will only be willing to pay \$5,000 < \$8,000. Therefore, we conclude that in the long run, only low-quality cars will be offered for sale.

21. c) While firms in all these industries may have a need to establish a reputation for quality, only the hotel industry is selling predominately to consumers from out-of-town. The other industries can use word-of-mouth and local advertising, so they have less need for brand names to establish a reputation.

22. e) Stock options have all these effects.

23. e) A firm that is willing to offer a liberal return policy anticipates higher consumer satisfaction with its products. This firm is therefore signaling its confidence in its product to consumers, which also serves to reduce customer uncertainty. A similar return policy would be less effective for a new entrant because consumers will be less certain that the new firm will stay in business.

24. b) When the lowest risk car owners do not buy insurance, the insurers face an adverse selection problem. This problem disappears when the lowest risk drivers are prevented by law from opting out of the market. The moral hazard problem is still present with compulsory insurance. The principal-agent problem does not apply here —the car owner is not the agent of the insurance company.

CHAPTER 18
EXTERNALITIES AND PUBLIC GOODS

IMPORTANT CONCEPTS

- Positive and Negative Externality
- Marginal Social Cost
- Emissions Standard
- Emissions Fee
- Tradeable Emissions Permits
- Stock Externality
- Property Rights
- Coase Theorem
- Common Property Resources
- Public Goods
- Nonrivalry
- Nonexcludability
- Free-Rider Problem

CHAPTER HIGHLIGHTS

This chapter examines two causes of market failure in competitive markets—externalities and public goods. An *externality* is present when one individual's consumption or production activity affects others' satisfaction or production possibilities. An externality is *negative* if others are made worse off, as with air pollution, and it is *positive* if others are made better off, as with vaccinations. In either case, the equilibrium output is inefficient when externalities are present, because social and private costs and benefits differ. When negative externalities exist the *marginal social costs* (MSC) are higher than the marginal cost of production. In a competitive market, the equilibrium output will be at the intersection of supply (the sum of the firms' MC) and demand. However, the efficient output level is at the intersection of demand and MSC.

One of the most important negative externalities that society has to deal with is pollution. There are three basic ways of correcting the inefficiency of the market in the face of pollution: (1) An *emissions standard* is a legal limit on how much pollutant a firm can emit; (2) An *emissions fee* is like a tax on each unit of a firm's emissions; (3) Under a *transferable emissions permit* system firms must have a permit to generate emissions and these permits can be bought and sold.

Both emissions fees and emissions permits force the firm to internalize the external costs that its pollution imposes on society. With sufficient information, the pollution control authority can obtain the efficient level of pollution by following any of these methods.

The legal system can also be used to regulate externalities. *Property rights* are the legal rules that describe what people or firms may do with their property. If residents near an airport have property rights to a quiet neighborhood, then they can prevent noisy planes from disturbing them. Or they can offer to give up their property rights in return for compensation. The efficient outcome can be achieved no matter who holds the property right if all parties can bargain costlessly. This proposition is called the *Coase Theorem*.

Common property resources, such as fishing grounds, are resources that can be used with free access, i.e., without payment. Free access means that individuals "pay" only their private cost of using the resource. This is clearly inefficient—the private cost is less than the total social cost because one person's use means that less of the resource is available for others. One way to eliminate the inefficiency is private ownership of the resource. The owner has an incentive to restrict access and to charge users for the external costs they generate. If private ownership is not practical, then government ownership may be more appropriate.

Public goods have two characteristics: *nonrivalry* and *nonexcludability*. Nonrivalry means that the marginal cost of providing the good to another consumer is zero. Nonexcludability means that individuals cannot be prevented from consuming the good. Society's willingness to pay for a public good is the sum of individuals' willingness to pay because everyone has the opportunity to consume the total amount produced. In order to reflect the sum of consumers' willingness to pay, the demand curve for a public good is the vertical (rather than the horizontal) summation of individual demand curves. The efficient output for a public good is the output at which this aggregate demand curve intersects the marginal cost curve.

Public goods will generally be under provided in the market because *free riding* occurs when individuals know that they can benefit from consuming the good without contributing to the cost of providing it. In order to prevent free riding, governments often subsidize or provide public goods because the free-rider problem makes it difficult to provide these goods in the private sector. The government then faces the question of how much to provide. If public good levels are determined by majority rule voting, the preferred spending level of the median voter will be chosen over any other alternative. This outcome may be inefficient because it weights all voters equally, regardless of the strengths of their preferences.

CONCEPT REVIEW AND EXERCISES

EXTERNALITIES (Section 18.1)

External effects in consumption or production are present whenever one person's utility or a firm's production function depends directly on others' consumption or production activities. A *negative externality* is present when the action of one party imposes costs on another party. When the action of one party benefits another party, we say that a *positive externality* exists.

Exercise:

1. In each of the following situations, explain what type of externalities are present, if any: (Multiple answers are possible.)
   a) Smoking in an elevator
   b) Playing a loud radio on the beach
   c) Getting clothing dry-cleaned
   d) Planting an attractive garden

To analyze negative production externalities, we can use supply and demand diagrams. In Figure 18.1, a town has many producers of steel, each of which emits sulfur dioxide as a by-product of steel production. The firms are perfect competitors (even taken together as a group they have a negligible effect on the market price). The demand curve for the firms' output is therefore horizontal at the market price P′. The supply curve shows the marginal cost of a unit of steel to the producers. With no externalities, the equilibrium production of steel in the town is Q_0.

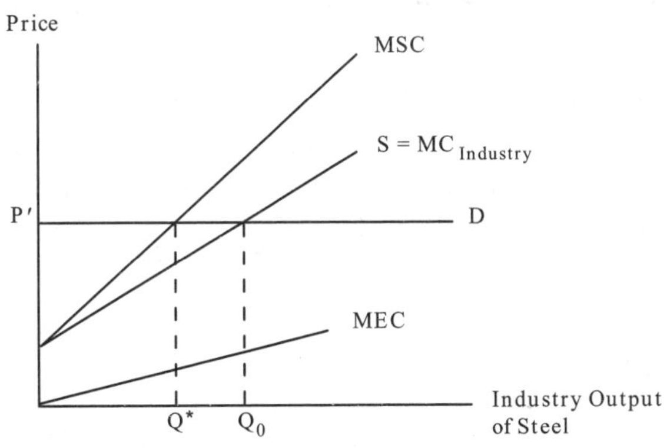

Figure 18.1

Unfortunately, the steel production creates an externality—the residents' health is damaged by the sulfur dioxide emissions. In fact, each unit of output causes an increasing amount of damage. Marginal external cost, the additional costs borne by the residents, are given by the MEC curve in Figure 18.1. The vertical sum of the MEC and MC curves is the marginal social cost of producing a unit of steel, MSC. The efficient output is Q^*, where P′ = MSC. You can see that in the presence of negative externalities too much steel is being produced, i.e., $Q^* < Q_0$.

Exercise: ◗◗◗◗◗◗◗

2. What is the efficiency loss when Q_0 is produced?

When there are positive externalities we get the opposite result: The efficient level of output is higher than the private market will supply. This happens because private individuals will choose output by setting marginal benefit (demand) equal to marginal cost, even though the marginal social benefits (MSB) are higher than the marginal private benefits. As shown in Figure 18.2 (on the next page), where we assume constant marginal cost, the market will supply Q_0, while the efficient level of output is Q^*.

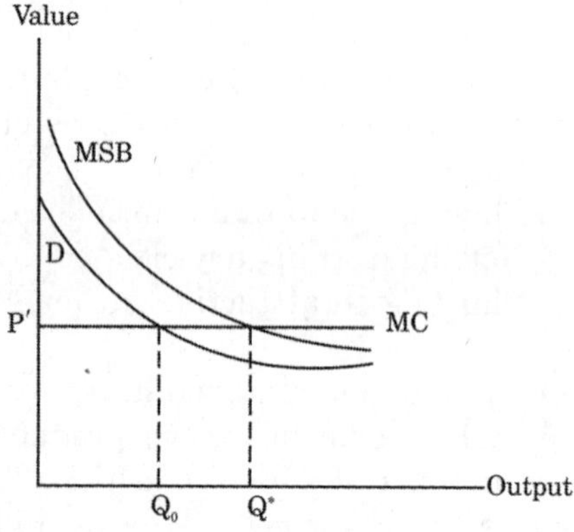

Figure 18.2

WAYS OF CORRECTING MARKET FAILURE (Section 18.2)

Several regulatory instruments are available to encourage steel producers to decrease their production to Q^*. Perhaps the easiest one is a tax on the *output* of the firms. In Figure 18.3, the firms pay a tax of t^* per unit of output, which causes the MC curve to shift up vertically to MC′. Now the firm will produce Q^*, where P = MC′. Since MC′ equals MSC at Q^*, price equals MSC and, hence, the outcome is efficient.

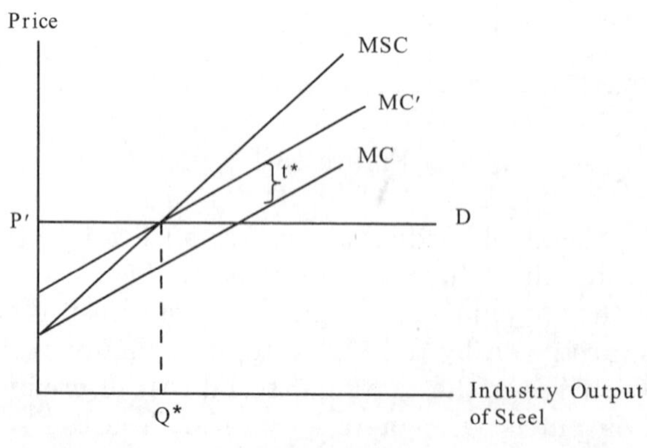

Figure 18.3

We can also analyze several methods of correcting externalities that focus on the basic source of the externality. For example, air pollution emissions are a by-product of the production of certain goods. Firms can reduce emissions in two ways: indirectly by reducing output, or directly by reducing pollution per unit of output. The latter method means finding a cleaner production process, which will often not be the lowest-cost method of production.

In general, the marginal cost of abating emissions, which is the additional cost to the firm of installing pollution control equipment, increases as emissions are decreased. The marginal social cost of emissions increases as emissions are increased, since the marginal cost of the externality is higher the more extensive it is. Figure 18.4 (on the next page) shows the marginal social cost of emissions (MSC) and the marginal cost of abatement (MCA). Total costs are minimized when these marginal costs are equal. Thus, the efficient level of emissions is attained by setting MSC = MCA, which occurs at E*.

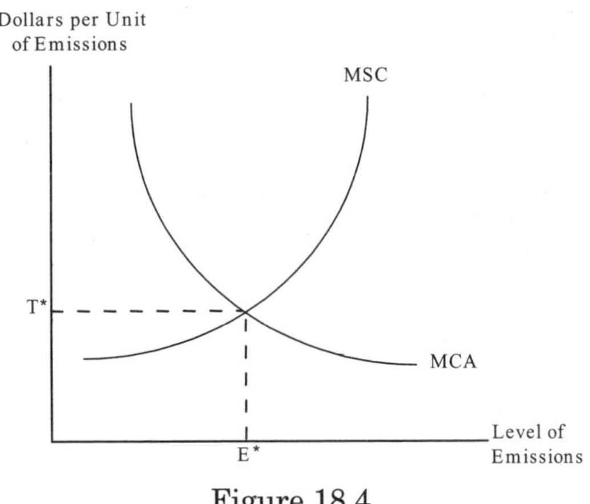

Figure 18.4

An *emissions standard* sets a maximum level of emissions for the firm. The firm meets the standard by installing pollution abatement equipment. If the standard requires that the firm release no more than $\hat{E}$ in emissions, it will release that amount unless $\hat{E} > \bar{E}$, where $\bar{E}$ is the level of emissions in the absence of any pollution regulation.

We have already described how a tax on the firm's output can be used to reduce external damage. Now we consider an *emissions fee*, which is a charge levied on each unit of a firm's emissions. Suppose the firm has the MCA curve given in Figure 18.4 and has to pay T^* per unit of emissions released. The firm will reduce emissions up to the point where MCA = T^*, which occurs at E^* units. If the marginal cost of abatement is less than the emissions tax, the firm gains by reducing emissions. If the marginal cost of abatement is greater than the tax, increasing emissions by one unit would cost the firm an amount equal to the tax, but it would save MCA, so the firm gains by increasing emissions. If the fee equals the marginal damage cost at E^*, the efficient level of pollution, then the firm reduces emissions to the efficient level.

In general, economists prefer emissions fees to emissions standards. In particular, fees achieve the same emissions reduction at a lower cost. However, the exact reduction in emissions as a result of a fee is uncertain. This has prompted some countries to set standards instead.

In a system of transferable emissions permits, each firm is issued a "permit to pollute" and is allowed to buy and sell permits. If there are enough firms and enough permits, a competitive market for the permits will develop. In equilibrium, the price of a permit equals the marginal cost of abatement for all firms.

STOCK EXTERNALITIES (Section 18.3)

The effects of some externalities, either positive or negative, depend on the *accumulated stock* rather than the flow. An example of a positive *stock externality* would be the stock of knowledge that accumulates from investments in R&D over time. Greenhouse gasses (GHGs), on the other hand, illustrate a negative stock externality since it is the concentration of GHGs built up over many years in the atmosphere which causes harm.

Given that the stock accumulates (as well as dissipates) over time, policy analysis must be undertaken in the same way that a firm calculates the net present value of an investment. For GHG, for example, society should compare the present value of the annual cost of reducing GHG emissions with the present value of the annual benefit resulting from a reduced stock of GHGs. As the text points out, this calculation is particularly sensitive to both the dissipation rate and the social discount rate assumed for the calculation. Thus, given the dynamic nature of the problem, the problem society faces in trying to choose the "efficient" level of pollution is vastly more complex once we consider the type of pollution that persists over time and potentially causes additional harm to future generations.

EXTERNALITIES AND PROPERTY RIGHTS (Section 18.4)

The tax and standard-setting approach to controlling externalities assumes that those damaged are unable to prevent the damage. However, in some cases, the damaged parties have legal rights that can be exercised to prevent the damage from occurring in the first place. When individuals have *property rights* to be free from pollution, the firm emitting pollution and those who suffer from it can negotiate over how much pollution should be allowed and how much should be paid to the individuals in compensation for the damage they suffer.

Economic efficiency can be achieved when the externality affects relatively few parties and when the property rights are well specified. A Pareto efficient outcome results from bargaining if there are no costs of negotiation. The *Coase Theorem* states that it does not matter for efficiency whether the polluter has a right to pollute or whether the victims have a right to prevent all pollution. If the efficient level of pollution involves some emissions, the parties will bargain to reach the efficient outcome. The owner of the property right receives compensation from the other party. (If the firm has the right to pollute, the firm is paid its lost profit when it reduces emissions.)

COMMON PROPERTY RESOURCES (Section 18.5)

Common property resources are those to which anyone has free access. Examples of common property resources are fishing grounds and grazing lands. Individuals have the right to use these resources, but cannot sell their access rights or exclude others. For example, consider a lake used by commercial fishermen. Each fisherman incurs costs in time and fishing equipment to take a fish from the lake. The more fish taken from the lake, the more costly it is to catch an additional fish. Thus, in Figure 18.5 (on the next page), the private cost curve tells us how the average cost of taking fish from the lake varies in relation to the number of fish taken. This average cost is the cost actually paid by each fisherman.

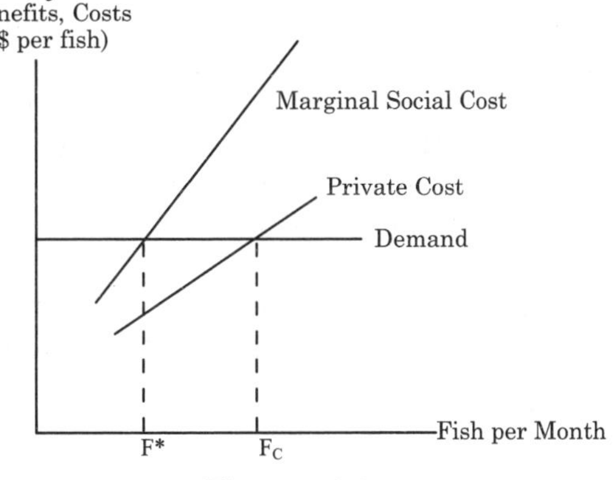

Figure 18.5

In this case, the private cost does not equal the social cost because each fish taken raises the cost of taking additional fish from the lake. The marginal social cost (MSC) curve lies above the private cost curve and is steeper. The MSC curve includes the increased cost of taking additional fish for all other fishermen. The efficient number of fish to take, F^*, is found at the intersection of the marginal social cost and demand curves. Without regulation, the competitive equilibrium, F_C, is the quantity given by the intersection of the private cost and demand curves—this is the zero profit, free entry equilibrium.

There are a variety of solutions to common property resource problems. Giving ownership rights to an individual, charging a fee per fish taken, and limiting the number of fish each person can take are all practical solutions.

Exercise: ▶▶▶▶▶▶▶

3. What is the efficiency loss from public access to the lake?

PUBLIC GOODS (Section 18.6)

In studying consumer behavior, we assumed that goods had two basic properties. These standard properties are "rivalry" and "exclusivity." Rivalry means that if I consume a certain quantity of a good, that amount is not available for your consumption. Each person's consumption reduces the amount available for others. Exclusivity means that I can be prevented from consuming the good. The producer of a good can charge me a price for the good's consumption and can take legal action to prevent my consumption if I do not pay for it. If a good is rival and exclusive, it is called a pure private good.

Some goods are *nonrival* and *nonexclusive*. Police protection is an example. If patrolling prevents burglaries within a neighborhood, all residents of the neighborhood benefit (this is the nonrival property). More importantly, each person's enjoyment of police protection does not interfere with that of others. The patrol discourages all criminal activity, not just crimes with particular victims. With police patrols, it is difficult, if not impossible, to protect only some of the residents in the neighborhood (this is nonexcludability). If the police patrol a given area, even if they only answered calls from those who paid for the service, criminals will be deterred from breaking into all houses, unless they know precisely which houses are protected. Since the police will pursue anyone they observe in a criminal act, no one can be prevented from enjoying at least some benefits of police patrols.

A good that is nonrival and nonexcludable is a pure *public good*. Some goods are nonrival, but excludable. Other goods are nonexcludable, but rival, as the following exercise illustrates.

Exercise: ◗ ◗ ◗ ◗ ◗ ◗ ◗

4. Explain whether the following goods are rival or nonrival and whether they are exclusive or nonexclusive:

a) Broadcast television
b) Cable television
c) Beaches
d) Fishing grounds

If a good is nonrival, each individual can benefit from the total amount of the good produced. In Figure 18.6, three individuals' demands for police protection are presented. The quantity is measured in person-hours of patrol time. For 5 hours of patrol time, Albert is willing to pay $6 per hour, Bernice is willing to pay $3 per hour, and Carol is willing to pay $7 per hour. Since each will benefit from 5 hours of patrol time, together they are willing to pay $16 per hour for 5 hours of patrol time. In other words, we add individual demand curves *vertically* to find the market demand curve for a public good.

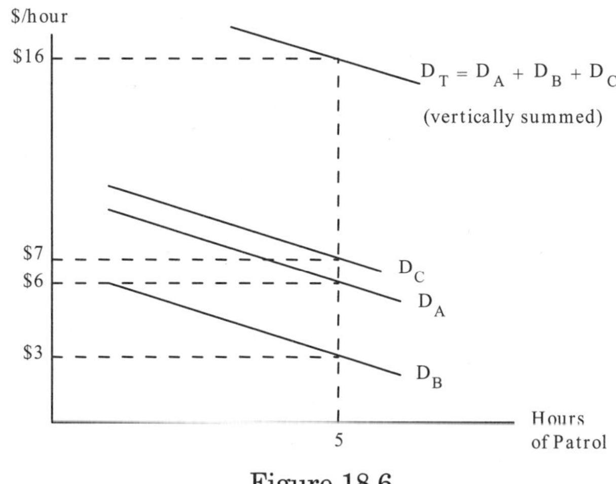

Figure 18.6

The efficient output of the public good is found at the intersection of the market demand curve and the marginal cost curve. At the efficient output, the sum of the willingness to pay of all consumers equals the cost of the last unit produced.

Exercise: ◗ ◗ ◗ ◗ ◗ ◗ ◗

5. In Figure 18.6, suppose Carol leaves the community. Now the only consumers are Albert and Bernice. What is the marginal willingness to pay for five hours of patrol now?

PROBLEM SET

6. Comment on the following: There is no need for government intervention when positive externalities are present because no one is being harmed.

7. Compare the effects of taxing output of a good whose production causes pollution and taxing the by-product emissions directly.

8. With transferable emissions permits, firms must have permits to generate emissions. If a firm emits less pollution than its permits allow, it can sell its leftover permits to another firm that wishes to emit more pollution than its permits allow.

Comment on the following: These permits have the advantages of both standards and fees, therefore, they may be the best technique of controlling pollution.

9. Why is the efficient level of pollution not equal to zero?

10. a) Initially, the styrofoam cup industry produces with a constant marginal cost of $4. The market demand for its product is given by P = 22 – Q. What output will the industry choose to produce? What is the sum of consumer surplus and producer surplus at this quantity?

b) This industry produces air pollution along with styrofoam cups. These pollution costs are represented by the marginal external cost function, MEC = 0.2Q. From an efficiency standpoint (i.e., society's standpoint), how many styrofoam cups should be produced?

c) The Environmental Protection Agency, concerned about the pollution problem, requires this industry to adopt a new, lower pollution production technology that raises the marginal cost of production to MC = \$10. Given this new technology, what output level will the industry choose? What is the sum of CS and PS at this point?

d) Illustrate your answers to parts a) through c).

e) A consulting firm estimates the total benefits of reducing pollution using this new technology at \$80. Is the reduction in pollution worth its costs to the producers and consumers of styrofoam cups?

11. The local environmental authority has levied an emissions fee of \$30 per ton of waste on a firm that has the marginal cost of abatement (MCA) curve displayed in Figure 18.7.

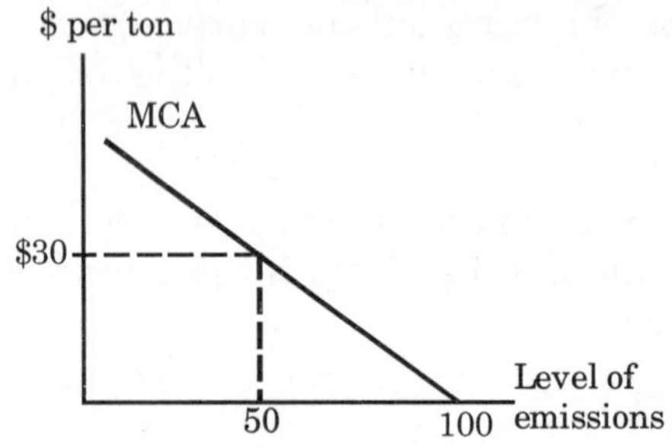

Figure 18.7

a) What level of emissions will the firm release? How much will it pay in emissions fees?

b) Suppose that the emissions fee is only charged for emissions in excess of 40 tons. What level of emissions will the firm release? How much will it pay in emissions fees? Explain the firm's decision.

SELF-TEST

12. Which of the following are examples of negative externalities?

a) An electronics manufacturer dumps solvents on the ground that end up in the water supply.

b) I plant an attractive flowerbed in the front yard.

c) A policy of peanut quotas in the U.S. causes the domestic price of peanut butter to rise.

d) a) and b)

e) a) and c)

13. In Figure 18.8, which area is the efficiency loss from a negative externality?
a) cgj
b) gdk
c) cag
d) efgjh
e) None of the above is correct.

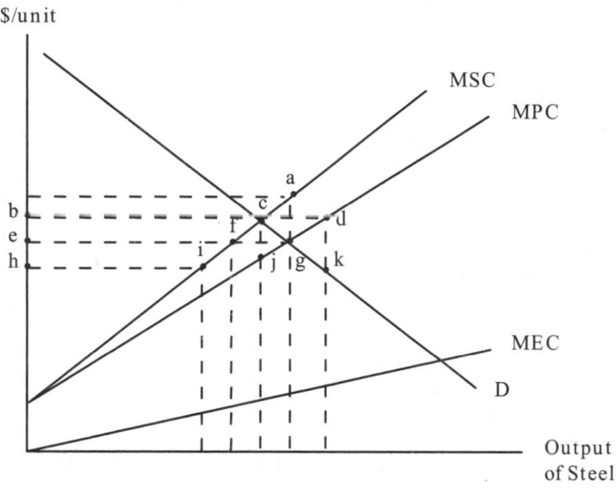

Figure 18.8

14. With an emissions fee, a firm will pollute up to the level where:
a) the fee equals MSC.
b) the fee equals the price of the product.
c) the fee equals MCA.
d) Zero because the firm must pay to pollute
e) None of the above is correct.

15. An emissions standard is better than an emissions fee if:
a) there is limited information about costs and benefits of pollution abatement.
b) the MSC curve is steeper than the MCA curve.
c) the MSC curve is flatter than the MCA curve.
d) a) and b)
e) a) and c)

16. If Podunk's airport allows night takeoffs and landings, the 40 houses nearby each have a market value $3,000 less than when no night takeoffs and landings are permitted. Suppose the residents have a property right to prevent nighttime noise. The outcome of bargaining between the residents and the airport authority will be:
a) night flights unless each resident pays as much as $3,000.
b) no night flights unless the airport pays $120,000 in compensation.
c) night flights if the present discounted value of these flights exceeds $120,000.
d) a) and c)
e) b) and c)

17. For a common resource, the efficient output is ___ and the free access equilibrium output is ___.
   a) the intersection of private cost and demand; the intersection of marginal social cost and demand
   b) the intersection of marginal social cost and demand; the intersection of private cost and demand
   c) the intersection of private cost and demand; the intersection of private cost and demand
   d) the intersection of marginal social cost and demand; the intersection of marginal social cost and demand
   e) None of the above is correct.

18. A pure public good is:
   a) rival and exclusive.
   b) nonrival and nonexclusive.
   c) nonrival.
   d) nonexclusive.
   e) provided by the government.

19. When negative externalities are present the private market output level will be:
   a) too low.
   b) too high.
   c) socially optimal.
   d) at the intersection of demand and marginal social cost.
   e) at the point that minimizes the marginal external cost.

20. Marginal cost at a plant making aerosol cans of hair spray is $MC = 2 + 0.01Q$, but because the use of aerosol spray destroys the earth's ozone layer, the marginal social cost is given by $MSC = 2 + 0.5Q$, where Q is measured in cans of hair spray per month. The competitive market price for hair spray is $4 per can. What is the efficient level of output?
   a) 0
   b) 2
   c) 4
   d) 20
   e) 200

21. The Coase Theorem states that:
   a) regardless of how property rights are assigned, the outcome will be efficient if transactions costs of bargaining are zero.
   b) if property rights are assigned to the party imposing a negative externality on society, an efficient outcome is achievable.
   c) efficiency can be achieved when a single owner manages the common property resource.
   d) with incomplete information, standards are more efficient than emissions fees.
   e) None of the above is correct.

22. A free-rider problem is likely to arise when:
a) the private costs exceed the social benefits.
b) the good is nonrival but excludable.
c) the good is nonexclusive.
d) the market level of production is greater than the socially optimal level.
e) the market sets a zero price.

23. Deposit-refund systems:
a) encourage recycling of materials.
b) should base the refund on the externality of improper disposal.
c) should use higher refunds if the cost of recycling by the consumer is higher.
d) All of the above are correct.
e) None of the above is correct.

24. Which of the following are true?
a) With negative stock externalities, current activity results in future exteranl costs.
b) Negative stock externalities are less severe if the dissipation rate for the pollutant is high.
c) With a higher social discount rate, it becomes more beneficial to reduce emissions which create a negative stock externality.
d) a) and b).
e) a), b), and c)

ANSWERS TO CHAPTER 18

EXERCISE ANSWERS

1. a) This is a negative externality. Nonsmokers suffer the negative effects of second-hand smoke without enjoying any benefits of the cigarette.
b) If the radio disturbs others, it is a negative externality. If others enjoy listening, it is a positive externality.
c) Dry cleaning releases volatile organic chemicals into the atmosphere, reducing air quality, so the externality is negative.
d) An attractive garden makes a neighborhood more pleasant for everyone (and might raise property values), so the externality is positive.

2. Efficiency losses from negative externalities result from *overproduction*. The deadweight loss is the triangle between MSC and D from Q^* to Q_0. In Figure 18A.1, this is area **abc**.

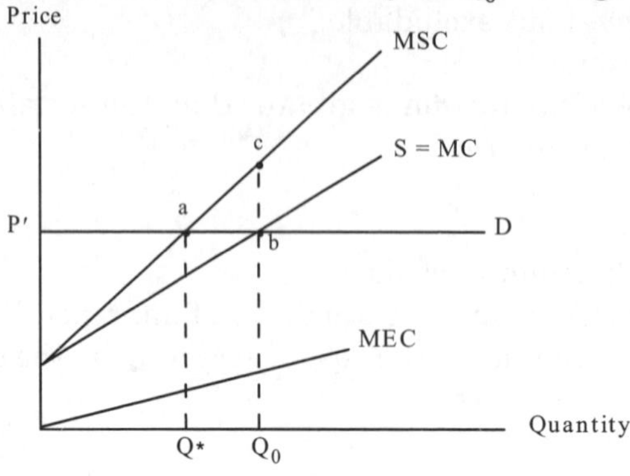

Figure 18A.1

3. In Figure 18.5, the efficiency loss is the area between marginal social cost and demand from F^* to F_C. Free access results in overproduction.

4. a) It is nonrival within a viewing area, and nonexclusive without signal scramblers.

b) Cable access is exclusive. The original hookup is rival because each installation uses some wire and digging. However, once hooked up, viewing an additional program is nonrival.

c) Beaches are subject to congestion, so they are rival. People could be excluded from a beach by charging admission, so they are also exclusive.

d) Fishing grounds are rival because each fisher's catch reduces the number of fish left for others. Exclusion is probably costly in practice.

5. Sum the D_A and D_B curves vertically to obtain $\hat{D}_T = 9$ at 5 hours of patrol.

PROBLEM SET ANSWERS

6. In Figure 18.2, the efficiency loss is the area between the MSB and D curves between Q_0 and Q^*. Too little of the good is produced. Since no one is harmed by consumption of the externality-creating good, it may seem that there is no cause for concern, but the net social benefits are lower than they could be. With positive externalities, agreements may be easier to reach because all parties benefit by moving to the efficient allocation. In contrast, polluters are usually made worse off by regulation.

7. In response to an output tax, a polluting firm's only response will be to decrease output. In response to an emissions fee (or tax), a polluting firm can reduce its tax liability by reducing output or by switching to a less polluting, but more expensive, production process (or by doing both).

8. With transferable permits, the pollution control authority can be certain of the resulting level of pollution, even if the costs and benefits are known only approximately. In Figure 18.6 in the text, it is shown that the standard may be superior in these circumstances. With many sources of pollution, each firm would need to have its maximum permissible level of pollution set by the regulator. It is a difficult task to set standards such that the pollution reduction is achieved at the least cost. With transferable permits, firms will trade among themselves so that, on the margin, each firm will have an equal marginal cost of abatement. Thus, the reduction in emissions is achieved at minimum cost.

9. If regulators mandated zero-level pollution, we would have to sacrifice consumption of many goods. Pollution occurs because individuals want to consume those goods. The desirable level of pollution balances damage to the environment with benefits to consumers. Think about a world with no transportation powered by gasoline, coal or electricity produced from fossil fuels or nuclear power.

10. a) Set P = MC, or 22 – Q = 4, which implies Q = 18. Then, CS + PS = 0.5(18)(18) + 0 = \$162. (PS = 0 in this special case, since MC is a horizontal line.)

b) Set MSC = MC + MEC = P, or 4 + 0.2Q = 22 – Q, which implies Q = 15.

c) The industry will choose to produce where P = MC′, or 22 – Q = 10, which implies Q = 12. Then CS + PS = 0.5(12)(12) + 0 = \$72.

d) See Figure 18A.2.

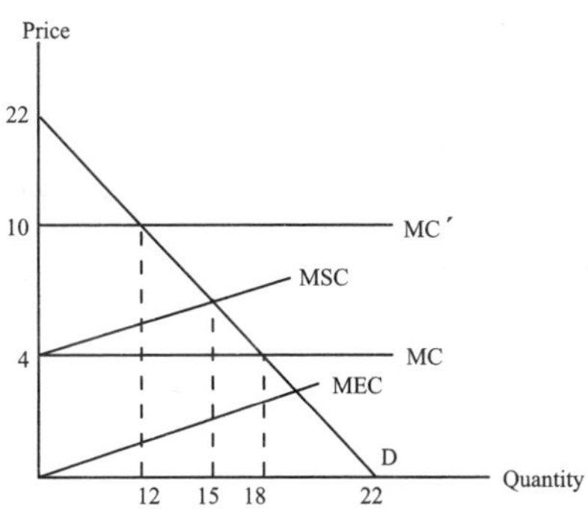

Figure 18A.2

e) Total benefits are \$80, while the loss in CS = 162 – 72 = \$90. Therefore, the reduction in pollution is not worth its costs to producers and consumers of styrofoam cups.

11. a) The firm would save \$30 per ton in fees by reducing emissions to 50 tons, and its marginal cost of abatement (MCA in Figure 18A.3 on the next page) is less than \$30 for each ton until it reduces its emissions to 50 tons. It would pay \$30 per ton in fees on the 50 tons it still releases (rectangles A and B in Figure 18A.3), or \$30(50) = \$1500.

b) In Figure 18A.3, the dashed line gives the firm's fee schedule. The firm should still reduce its emissions to 50 tons, but now it only pays $30 per ton for 10 tons of emissions, or $30(10) = $300 (rectangle B only). In both cases, the firm reduces emissions until its MCA equals the fee.

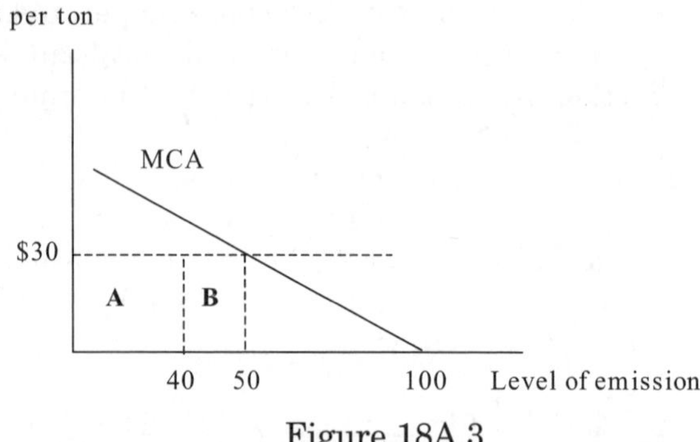

Figure 18A.3

SELF-TEST ANSWERS

12. a) Choice b) is an example of a positive externality, while c) merely illustrates the effect of an increase in the price of an input.

13. c) The socially efficient equilibrium is at point *c*, while the market equilibrium is at point *g*. The overproduction by the market creates an efficiency loss of **cag**.

14. c) The firm should reduce emissions as long as the marginal cost of abatement (MCA) is less than the emissions fee. If the MCA is greater than the fee, the firm should pay the fee rather than continue to reduce emissions.

15. d) When the marginal social cost (MSC) curve is much steeper than the MCA curve, the cost of not reducing emissions is high. (A steep MSC curve means that society finds it very costly to have a high level of emissions.) If there is less of a chance for error with standard setting than emissions fees, society will prefer standards. Note, however, that although there is more certainty about emissions levels with standards, there is less certainty about costs of abatement across firms.

16. e) The outcome will depend on the value of night flights to the airport.

17. b) Private cost determines the free access outcome, while social cost determines the efficient outcome.

18. b) Both these conditions are part of the definition of a public good.

19. b) The private level of output will be too high, since the parties generating the negative externality do not take into account the extra cost they are imposing on either consumers or producers.

20. c) Set MSC = P to find that Q = 4.

21. a) The Coase theorem is stated in the text: "When parties can bargain without cost and to their mutual advantage, the resulting outcome will be efficient, regardless of how the property rights are specified."

22. c) When the good is nonexclusive, there will be a tendency for people to free ride and try to enjoy the benefits of the good without paying for it.

23. d) The deposit should serve to align the marginal private cost of scrapping with the marginal social cost of scrapping. (b) relates to the MSC of scrapping, and (c) relates to the marginal (net) private cost.

24. d) Choice c) is false because a higher discount rate reduces the present discounted value of reducing emissions.